David Hutchinson
dhutch@uwindsor.ca

D1605214

The Parish
and Cathedral of
St James', Toronto
1797–1997

F.W. Cumberland's design for St James' Cathedral from the northwest; perspective drawing, c. 1858, attributed to William Storm.

The Parish
and Cathedral of
St James', Toronto

1797–1997

───────────────

A COLLABORATIVE HISTORY

Carl Benn

Giles Bryant

William Cooke

Paul H. Friesen

Alan Hayes

C. Thomas McIntire

Shirley Morriss

───────────────

General Editor: William Cooke

Printed for the Cathedral by
University of Toronto Press

Printed and bound by University of Toronto Press Incorporated
Printed in Canada

ISBN 0-8020-4714-9

Printed on acid-free paper

Canadian Cataloguing in Publication Data

Main entry under title:

The Parish and Cathedral of St. James', Toronto, 1797–1997 :
a collaborative history

Includes index.
ISBN 0-8020-4714-9

1. St James' Cathedral (Toronto, Ont.) – History. I. Benn, Carl, 1953–
II. Cooke, William, 1947–   III. St. James' Cathedral (Toronto, Ont.)

BX5617.T6S368 1998   283'.713541   C98-901462-2

Contents

Foreword

THE RT REVD TERENCE E. FINLAY
10TH BISHOP OF THE ANGLICAN DIOCESE
OF TORONTO

IN SPITE OF HARDSHIP, fire, and controversy, the Cathedral Church of St James has been a living symbol of Anglican faith and witness in this community for two hundred years. This book contains details of that adventure.

In the early days of Toronto, 'Muddy York' was a wilderness settlement in which people struggled to survive. Immigrants from England and Ireland placed emphasis on building a church for the community to gather in, for strength to persevere. They were sustained by the traditions of their faith and shared their hopes and values with others.

Through the years of Toronto's growth and development, generation after generation have placed a similar emphasis on the worship of God, proclaiming the good news of the gospel, and reaching out in love and compassion to others. It is this commitment and this sense of community that we celebrate with the publication of this volume.

I thank all the many contributors to this history for their efforts in providing us with a tangible record of this milestone. May it encourage us to go forward with a renewed sense and understanding of the glory of God.

Preface

THE VERY REVD DOUGLAS STOUTE, DEAN OF TORONTO

IT HAS BEEN SAID THAT the Christian faith came about as the result of the collision of two passions: God's passion for us and our passion for God. This book is about the collision of these passions as it has taken place over the course of two hundred years at St James'. It is a tale that begins in another age, when the colonists on the fringes of a sprawling empire gathered to build a church in the small town of York on the shores of Lake Ontario. Over the centuries the empire faded and disappeared, the town of York became the city of Toronto, and the small wooden church grew into a great cathedral. But in every age, both as parish and as cathedral, St James' has stood in the heart of Toronto as a powerful sign of God's love and compassion for all people.

This book is the work of many authors. The risk involved in this approach is that focus gets blurred and quality becomes uneven. This is not the case here. Each contributor has brought unique gifts and particular perspectives, but there is an evenness and a vitality throughout that are most engaging. Some of the conclusions that are drawn you will share; others you may want to challenge; but that is the nature of the historical enterprise. What we shall all agree upon, however, is that this is a fine piece of historical scholarship that will enrich our understanding not only of the cathedral but of Canadian history.

It is impossible to conclude without acknowledging the contribution of three people: Pamela Guy, who chaired the Bicentenary Committee and has provided judicious oversight; Dr William Cooke, a founding member of the Archives Committee, who has worked diligently on the project; and Canon Philip Hobson, vicar of the cathedral, whose work behind the scenes has been invaluable.

Introduction

THE GENERAL EDITOR

A CAMEL HAS BEEN DEFINED as a horse designed by a committee. While not the most elegant of God's creatures, it is perfectly adapted to its environment and much more useful than a horse for crossing a desert.

This bicentenary history of the church at York that became St James' Anglican Cathedral in Toronto is also the work of a committee. At the earliest planning stage, it became clear that a collaborative effort was needed if the many facets of the story were to receive adequate treatment. Several of the authors recruited had already made substantial contributions, but most of these either existed as unpublished theses or had appeared in specialized journals, while another's projected work remained in manuscript. A camel seemed clearly required, to bring members of the reading public through what was still, for them, a desert.

Our hope is that we have produced a not ungainly beast. The varied roles of a cathedral and parochial church and the individual contributors' expertise dictated the preparation of three parts: first, a continuous narrative of what might be called its public and social history; second, an account of the construction and later history of the four successive church buildings on the site and the adjunct structures there and in St James' Cemetery, which falls under the cathedral's jurisdiction; and lastly, a close look at the two activities that most distinguish an Anglican cathedral, its music and its worship. As might have been expected, though, rigid adherence to these divisions proved neither practicable nor desirable. Readers will find the same matters treated in two or more chapters but in different contexts and from differing perspectives. They will also encounter authors writing in different styles and from diverse points of view. Such is the nature of the beast.

Each part in turn seemed to fall into different logical divisions. For the public history of the church, its changing functions seemed better milestones than successive incumbencies, and hence the four chapters treat respectively St James' earliest days as a parish church in a small colonial town, its first period as the cathedral of a rapidly growing city, its time as (in canon law, at least) a purely parochial church, and its evolution since being formally restored to joint cathedral and parochial status. The architectural chapter naturally divided itself into sections dealing with the successive church buildings and a final one dealing with the outbuildings; here Carl Benn has treated the original church building, and Shirley Morriss the rest. The history of music and worship seemed to fall into four stages – the very modest beginnings; the years as a

Victorian pro-cathedral that nevertheless functioned essentially as a large parish church; the era beginning in the late 1890s, when a real attempt began to be made to approximate the English cathedral style; and the most recent decades, when that tradition was refined upon and consolidated. This chapter represents a close collaboration between Giles Bryant and me. The book's six chapters are necessarily of uneven length, but the aim was to achieve clarity and completeness, not symmetry. Nor are the chapters equally supplied with notes; the last two sections of 'Music and Worship' in particular are based almost wholly on service leaflets and music programs surviving in the St James' Cathedral Archives or on entries in the service registers, from which it seemed gratuitous to make constant citations, or else on living memory.

The work has been collaborative throughout. The authors met frequently during the research and writing, read each others' work in draft, and freely exchanged insights and tips about sources. We are all in each others' debt; and we all owe an immense debt to Canon Philip Hobson, who as secretary and convenor of the authors' committee arranged and chaired all the authors' meetings, circulated all the progressing drafts, and was also our chief liaison with the Publishing Committee. Without his support, tact, and unfailing good humour, seven authors, each with idiosyncrasies and heavy personal and professional responsibilities, could never have finished their task.

Several of us also owe a great debt to Stephen Otto, who has dipped into his unrivalled knowledge of early Toronto history to provide us with many valued sources and details. We received unstinting help and courtesy from chief archivists and their staffs at the National Archives of Canada in Ottawa, the Archives of Ontario, the City of Toronto, the University of Toronto, the General Synod of the Anglican Church of Canada, the Anglican Diocese of Toronto, Trinity College, Wycliffe College, and St James' Cathedral, and from the curators of the Thomas Fisher Rare Book Library at the University of Toronto, the Baldwin Room at the Toronto Reference Library, and the Rare Book Department of Trinity College Library, both with identifying and using their materials and in the form of their kind permission to reproduce illustrations and extracts from sources.

The Revd Douglas Graydon made the reconstruction drawings of the first church at York appearing in chapter 5 and agreed to their publication here. Joyce Sowby, chair of the Cathedral Archive Committee, and Sandra Fuller, the Cathedral Archivist, devoted much time and effort to identifying sources and procuring illustrations from outside institutions. Especially valuable reminiscences were contributed by the Rt Revd George B. Snell, retired bishop of Toronto; the Revd Keith Gleed, who served at St James' as a boy chorister, a server, and an assistant priest; Mr Thomas W. Hanlon, for many years vestry clerk; Mrs Ruth Veno, church secretary in Dean Riley's time; Dr Ian Storey, head server under Bishop Stiff and Dean Abraham; and Mr Harry Wright.

The Publishing Committee was ably chaired, first jointly by Graham and Elizabeth Lang, then by Wayne Wolfe, and lastly by Pamela Guy. They worked out the design concept for the book and doggedly pursued grants in aid of publication. St James' gratefully acknowledges the generosity of the St George's Society of Toronto, the Jackman Foundation, Dr Edward Turner, Marjorie Colloton, and Pamela Guy in helping to fund the production of this book.

Shirley Morriss wishes to pay particular tribute to Professor Douglas Richardson for first suggesting parishioner Frederic W. Cumberland's church architecture to her as a thesis topic, for his encouragement when she wrote her article on the same subject, and for his contribution to the preparation of this book; to Christine Bourolias, reference archivist for Special Collections at the Archives of Ontario, for her generous assistance with the use of that collection; and to Stephen Otto, for reading her chapter in draft and making many valuable suggestions. I wish particularly to thank Giles Bryant for his industry in bringing to light the musical history of St James' and for the close and easy collaboration that we enjoyed in writing our chapter. Nancy Benson, Brian Gilchrist, Elizabeth Lang, and Joyce Lewis all read parts of the book in proof and made valued corrections and suggestions.

For Shirley Morriss and me, this book represents the culmination of a quarter-century of research, writing, and accumulation of material on the history of St James'. But neither we nor our colleagues are so vain as to suppose that our camel has carried home every last treasure. In one sense the early history of St James' is that of the Anglican Church throughout what was then called the Home District of Upper Canada, and it is a matter for regret that space was not available to treat that subject more fully here. A lingering feeling remains that the immense and indispensable contribution of women to the life and work of the parish also rests under-represented, particularly during the first hundred years; but it is, as so often, poorly and obscurely documented, and justice will have to await the appearance of more specialized studies. Our hope is that this book will stimulate others to take up the unfinished task as St James' continues into its third century.

William Cooke
Honorary Archivist, St James' Cathedral
The Feast of St James, 1998

Coat of arms of St James' Cathedral, granted by
the Canadian Heraldic Authority, 25 July (the Feast of St James) 1996.

A NOTE ON THE CATHEDRAL COAT OF ARMS

ST JAMES' RECEIVED its official coat of arms from the Canadian Heraldic Authority on the Feast of St James (25 July) 1996. The shield, which is the main feature, is a slightly simplified and regularized version of a design in use for many years and can be seen in several places in the church. All its components can be explained in terms of the life or legend of the church's patron saint, James the Great, but several also carry other references to the life and history of the church.

A wavy line divides the shield into two portions, the smaller and upper one being blue and the larger and lower one green. These can be thought of as water and land. The golden ship placed in the upper portion can represent the boat in which St James was mending his fishing nets when Jesus called him to discipleship (Matthew 4:21, etc.) or the ship that according to legend, bore his body from the Holy Land to its resting place at Santiago de Compostela in northwestern Spain. The arms, however, depict this ship as a three-masted vessel of the eighteenth century, recalling the ships in which the Loyalist refugees and British settlers who founded the congregation of St James' came to York, now Toronto. Similarly the crossed golden sword and pilgrim's staff surmounting the whole design represent the sword with which St James was martyred at the order of King Herod Agrippa of Judea (Acts 12:2) and the staffs that pilgrims still carry when journeying to Compostela; but the sword as depicted on the Heraldic Authority's patent is modelled on the one shown in the Great Seal of Upper Canada, as a reminder that several members of the original congregation served as officials of the fledgeling colony. The scallop shells placed in the angles between the sword and staff are traditional emblems of the saint, worn by medieval pilgrims as proof that they had made the journey to his shrine.

In the full version of the arms this shield rests on a 'cathedra.' This term means a bishop's chair, but the one shown in the patent has deliberately been made to resemble the coronation chair in Westminster Abbey, in token of St James' status as a royal church, which received its site and its original endowments from the Crown and has been repeatedly honoured by the presence at its worship of members of the royal family. Above the main shield in the full version are the arms of the Anglican diocese of Toronto and two white York roses.

The motto, which may be used with the full version of the arms or with the shield alone, is *In fines orbis terrae*, meaning 'Unto the ends of the earth'. This verse from the Psalms (18:5 in the Latin Vulgate, 19:4 in the Book of Common Prayer) was the offertory chant for the Feast of St James in the Sarum rite. It can refer to the journey of the ship carrying the saint's body to Compostela, which is near Cape Finisterre at the edge of the then-known world, or to the voyages of the early settlers at York to what was in their time considered the furthest limit of civilization; but one can also read it as a commitment to spread the Gospel of Christ throughout the world, a task to which St James' remains committed now as in times past.

The Parish
and Cathedral of
St James', Toronto
1797–1997

I

A Georgian Parish, 1797–1839

CARL BENN

THE DOMINANT STORY in Upper Canadian Anglicanism was the Church of England's campaign to secure its place as the colony's established church, as anticipated in the province's constitution.[1] The Constitution or Canada Act of 1791 reserved one-seventh of the colony's land to support a 'Protestant Clergy' and authorized the creation of endowed Anglican rectories. The British politicians who drafted the legislation saw establishment as both a useful restraint on the popular will and a device to promote internal peace and stability. Other checks included the fostering of a landed aristocracy and the creation of an executive branch of government that could operate independently of the elected assembly.

Fundamentally, establishment was seen as a counter-revolutionary measure, made in fearful reaction to the disaster and chaos of the American and French revolutions. Not only was establishment seen as normal historically, but it also was regarded as attainable, since denominational loyalties in the province were still fluid. Yet the act was ambiguous. 'Protestant' easily could include the Church of Scotland, which also was established in Britain, and the provincial parliament received the right to change the act's religious clauses with imperial consent. Thus Anglican establishment was not assured in 1791, a situation which heralded the beginning of a long period of strife as the Church of England struggled to attain its dream of becoming Upper Canada's state church. Of all the Anglican parishes in the colony, St James' in Toronto, as the most prominent congregation in the provincial capital, was the most active participant in the campaign.[2]

Through establishment, church leaders hoped to fulfil a Christian mission as one of the two pillars – along with the British constitution – on which a moral society could be fashioned on the colonial frontier. According to Bishop Jacob Mountain of Quebec (Figure 1.1) whose diocese then included Toronto, establishment, aside from fulfilling Christ's work, would 'prove the best security to Government for the submission, fidelity, and loyalty of its subjects.'[3] The crusade ultimately failed. Upper Canada was too heterogeneous and the times were too liberal and democratic to accept a privileged place for a particular denomination.

By the eve of Archdeacon John Strachan's consecration as the first bishop of the new diocese of Toronto in 1839, local Anglicans had begun to acknowledge defeat, to recognize reluctantly the imprudence of investing in secular ideologies, and to seek a future in areas where the church had been both faithful and successful: celebrating the sacraments, preaching

1.1 Rt Revd Jacob Mountain, first bishop of Quebec 1793–1825. This portrait shows him as a younger man in the late 1770s. York (now Toronto) was in the diocese of Quebec throughout Mountain's episcopate.

the word, and ministering to the needy. The church's own internal reforms began to provide succour through an affirmation of Anglicanism's sacred roles and its special standing in the apostolic succession at the same time that the Erastian4 and rational Georgian version of the faith slowly gave way to a more mystical and transcendent Victorian Christianity. Historians have neglected the church's devotion to its fundamental purposes, treating them very much as secondary to the Erastian failure in Upper Canada. This chapter, however, tells both stories through the experience of St James' in the Georgian era.

FOUNDING A CHURCH, 1793–9

The first recorded Anglican service in what is now Toronto occurred on 11 August 1793, when the town of York (as it was then called) was about three weeks old. 'Lt. Smith of the 5th Regiment,' wrote Elizabeth Simcoe, 'read Prayers to the Queen's Rangers assembled under some Trees near the Parade.'5 That little service, held where Fort York now stands, was representative of the Anglican experience in Georgian Canada. Smith, standing in his officer's uniform and holding the Book of Common Prayer of 1662 in his hand, symbolized the church's acceptance of the hierarchical society of the old country and its belief that the well-being of the social order depended on its replication in the new world through a partnership between church and state.

Yet the fact that Smith was a soldier and not a priest represented Anglicanism's weakness on the frontier and its corresponding inability to fulfil the promise of establishment. Elizabeth Simcoe's husband, John, the lieutenant-governor of Upper Canada, had dreamed of sailing into

Toronto Bay with a bishop and a full cathedral chapter at his elbow. The fact that he did not do so was frustrating because he believed that 'the best security, that all just Government has for its existence is founded on the Morality of the People, and that such Morality has no true Basis but when placed upon religious Principles.' Therefore he wanted, 'both from political as well as more worthy motives,' to ensure that the Church of England 'should be essentially established' in his province.[6] Later, with considerable precision, York's third parson, Dr John Strachan, would devote his substantial skills to refining Simcoe's ideas in sermons, in pamphlets, and in letters, becoming in the process Upper Canada's most prolific thinker.

Smith's congregation – incorporating the governor's entourage, the families of the most humble soldiers, and everyone in between – was typical of the range of people that the church served in the colony and gave the lie to the claim that Anglicanism was merely the denomination of the élite. At the same time, the overrepresentation of soldiers and Crown officials was symbolic of Toronto's social composition and of the people who would dominate the congregation at St James' throughout the period.

The men of the Queen's Rangers arrayed in front of Lieutenant Smith sported little crescent moon devices on their caps, emblems of Diana, the Roman goddess of the hunt. This conceit to the glories of the ancients later found reflection in the Neoclassical architecture of the buildings that would serve Toronto Anglicans until the 1850s, when changing views of the church found form in the construction of the Gothic Revival gem that now stands at the corner of King and Church streets. The classical ideal inspired not only the architecture of the Georgian church but also the architecture of state, commerce, and home in York: it thus proclaimed the church's perception of itself as an institution integrated fully into society rather than as something set apart from the secular world. For example, John Strachan in 1817 was a leading figure in an attempt to obtain a bank charter in the capital that eventually led to the chartering of the Bank of Upper Canada in 1821, and he regularly lobbied to further the cause of his town and province over rival interests in Niagara, Kingston, and Lower Canada.[7]

Inscribed on the soldiers' crescent moons was the word 'Monmouth,' an honour to a battle won in a war lost – the American Revolution – whose legacy tormented the fearful loyalism of Upper Canadian Anglicans, as exemplified by the words above of Bishop Mountain and Governor Simcoe. The founding of York three weeks earlier was itself a hurried response to the march of an American army against Britain's Aboriginal allies south of Lake Erie. Simcoe suspected that the army was headed for Upper Canada and wanted to fortify Toronto harbour to serve as a provincial arsenal in preparation for hostilities.[8]

If Lieutenant Smith preached a sermon, it was not one that he had written himself. The church thought theologically untrained people were not competent to do so, being likely to 'proceed from error to error,' as Jacob Mountain claimed Methodists and other dissenters did through discussing questions of the 'deepest, and most difficult research' without proper qualifications.[9] Methodists, as recent Anglican schismatics, were a particular target for the Church of England; and dissenters as a whole were tarred by their anti-British roles in the American Revolution, their democratic principles, their enthusiasm for the separation of church and state, and their uncomfortably robust growth on the frontier. Thus if the troops heard a homily, it probably was something that Smith read out of an approved book of sermons. Years later, John Strachan would not trust even his divinity students to preach their own sermons, though in the 1820s he had to relent in the face of a shortage of clergy and commission catechists to serve outlying regions.[10] High standards, combined with a paucity of clergy, contributed to the failure of establishment, because the Church of England did not deploy adequate resources to win widespread acceptance among a largely unchurched or dissenting population.

Simcoe laid out a town site some distance to the east of Fort York, bounded by George, Front, Parliament, and Lot (now Queen) streets. (Toronto Bay extended to the foot of Front Street until much later, when lakefill operations moved the shoreline south.) The areas east and west of the town and south of Lot Street formed government and military reserves. Simcoe divided the land north of Lot into one-hundred-acre park lots, mainly to give to senior government officials to ease the pain of moving from the then-capital at Niagara to little York. Gradually, Simcoe's new settlement changed from a military camp to a backwoods government town.

However, there still were few civilians in the settlement in the autumn of 1796, when the first missionary arrived under the sponsorship of the Society for the Propagation of the Gospel. (Then, and in later years, the SPG spurred the church's growth in Canada by raising money in Britain to support missionaries, subsidize local divinity students, and supply communion plate, Bibles, prayer books, and other literature.)[11]

The priest was Thomas Raddish, an Oxford graduate with thirteen years' experience in holy orders. He came well recommended; the Duke of Portland described him as a principled cleric with an excellent character. Peter Russell, who administered the province after Simcoe returned to England in 1796, also was impressed, noting that Raddish's sermons had an 'Attracting Eloquence' and that he was 'just the sort of Clergyman most likely to impress upon the Inhabitants of this new Country a proper sense of their religious duties, being a Gentleman of an easy familiar manner yet properly measured and respectable in his Conduct.'[12] Shortly after arriving in York, however, Raddish decided that the grim little frontier town was not the place for him, being under threat of attack by the Mississaugas, cut off from other communities throughout the winter, and so short of food that army rations had to be distributed to prevent starvation. Perhaps he felt some small consolation that the threat of American invasion, so strong in 1793 and 1794, had passed because of diplomatic efforts. After speculating in land, including selling the park lot set aside as a glebe, he left when the shipping season opened in the spring of 1797. Although he never returned, he did not resign his post until 1799.[13]

The main effect of Raddish's short ministry was to delay the putting of the church on a solid foundation. In 1797, Peter Russell extended the town westward and reserved six acres for the church (which the Crown later granted to the church's trustees in 1820), but little could ensue from his decision until a new priest could be appointed, and that could not occur until Raddish stepped down. The people of York in the late 1790s had to content themselves with worshipping in public buildings under the ongoing leadership of laypeople, graced by occasional visits from the rectors of Kingston and Niagara, John Stuart and Robert Addison respectively. In 1799, Bishop Mountain made the first of several visits to the provincial capital.

Stuart and Addison came to York mainly as chaplains to parliament but used their time in the capital to further the church's work on a broader front. Stuart, for example, typically officiated at divine service two or three times a week in York to what he considered an indolent, quarrelling, and hard-drinking congregation. When there was no cleric, tavernkeeper William Cooper often led worship and preached out of a book of sermons. In 1799 a member of the provincial legislature conducted a special thanksgiving service to honour Britain's victory over Napoleon at the Battle of the Nile. Worship took place in various government and public

1.2 Part of the town of York in 1804, from a watercolour by Elizabeth Frances Hale.
The church had not yet been built; but Cooper's Tavern in the foreground was an early centre of
Anglicanism, and the houses along the waterfront include those of Duncan Cameron, William Warren
Baldwin, William Allan, and Peter Russell, all prominent early parishioners. In the background at
the far right, near the blockhouse, are the brick parliament buildings, where services
were held from 1797 until the opening of the first church in 1807.

buildings, including the town jail, where inmates and townspeople praised God together. Beginning in 1797 most services occurred in the new, brick parliament buildings (see Figure 1.2) at the foot of Berkeley Street.[14]

GEORGE OKILL STUART, 1800–11

York's second 'minister and missionary,' as he styled himself, was George Okill Stuart (Figure 1.3), the son of John Stuart and Jane Okill, United Empire Loyalist (UEL) refugees from the Mohawk mission at Fort Hunter in New York. The younger Stuart had received his education under his father's tutelage and at King's, Union, and Harvard colleges. He taught school before Mountain ordained him deacon in 1800. In that year Lieutenant-Governor Peter Hunter appointed him to York, and in 1801 he was priested in Quebec. The York that Stuart encountered had progressed out of the very first bleak stages of settlement: farmers had begun to produce surpluses of pork and flour in the surrounding region, roads to connect the settlement

1.3 Revd George Okill Stuart, minister and missionary at York 1800–12.
This portrait was painted when he was archdeacon of Kingston.

to the outside world were under construction, and seven hundred people lived in the village and the neighbouring townships.[15]

Stuart held meetings in 1803 to organize a subscription to build a church and seek out the professional assistance of William Berczy, the closest thing that York had to an architect. However, Stuart was not an effective fund-raiser, and his congregation was not dissatisfied enough with the parliament buildings to hurry along construction. It was not until 1807 that the parishioners had a useable church, located at King and Church streets – the present cathedral site – and then it took another two or three years to complete the structure. Rather than a fine stone edifice, as initially planned, the parish church at York was a simple frame building (Figure 1.4). Nor did it have a name, typically being called the 'Episcopal church in York' until about 1827, when the name St James' began to appear, a year before its consecration by Mountain's successor as bishop of Quebec, Charles James Stewart.[16]

Once the church opened in 1807, the congregation held a meeting at Gilbert's Tavern to choose a people's warden, under the provisions of a provincial statute providing for the election of parish officials. They selected William Allan, a militia officer, merchant, and government official. Stuart's nomination for rector's warden was the solicitor-general of Upper Canada, D'Arcy Boulton. Although the church's membership was broad, the appointment of these men was typical of the élite leadership of its affairs at a time when the Baldwin, Boulton, Jarvis, Macaulay, Robinson, and other prominent families dominated the lists of wardens, building-committee members, and subscribers to worthy causes. The Boultons and Macaulays also produced clergymen in the Georgian era.[17]

1.4 The original church at York, as engraved in 1848 from a drawing by William Allan. He based his sketch on the recollections of his father – one of the first wardens – and other older parishioners. While the larger features of the building are probably reliable, this romantic image has been severely criticized by historians. For a reconstruction based on other sources see Figures 5.1 to 5.3 (pp. 180–3).

The wardens auctioned off the pews and set ground rents to finance the church's operating costs. Sunday collections went to poor relief, and fees for baptisms, marriages, and burials went to the sexton and officiant. (The sexton, who also acted as clerk, was tavernkeeper George Hunt – 'a very decent and honest man.')[18] The SPG and the government paid the priest's salary, which Stuart supplemented through his property holdings (including the sale, for personal profit, of some land intended to support the church) and by teaching school, first privately and then, as of 1807, as headmaster of the new government District Grammar School.[19] The state provided other assistance, including subsidies for construction of the church (and later, contributions to a parsonage in the 1820s, and endowment of the rectory in the 1830s). Subscriptions and donations from individual people addressed special projects, such as installing a gallery to provide free seating.[20] Building the gallery in 1810 was a cause of some scandal; one worshipper noted that before its construction he had been 'reduced to the uncomfortable necessity' of either 'standing as a public spectacle' or seating himself among the garrison soldiers, who had benches set aside for their use. To make matters worse, some of the people who had donated money to the construction of the church in the first place could not afford pews and therefore needed the gallery seats to attend church services.[21]

Although itinerant missionaries of various denominations visited the provincial capital, Anglicans had a monopoly on regular worship during Stuart's incumbency. The Methodists were the second denomination to offer regular worship when they opened a chapel in 1818. Anglicans almost certainly formed the largest group, and non-Anglicans also attended Stuart's services. In his first report to the SPG he wrote that he had a large congregation but only ten communicants, a number that rose to fifteen in 1805 and twenty-five in 1812.[22] (A sense of personal unworthiness seems to have kept many people from the Eucharist, despite clergy efforts to encourage reception.)[23] However, it is unlikely that the bulk, or even a small majority, of the townspeople went to church. In 1802 there was an attempt either to increase the congregation or at least to prevent worship from being interrupted by drunken townsfolk, when the wardens visited tavernkeepers to 'represent to them the indecency and impropriety of allowing people to drink intoxicating liquors and be guilty of disorderly behavior during the hours of Divine Service.'[24]

Stuart's 1804 report to the SPG suggested that he had made some progress in increasing attendance and in reducing 'irreligion & licentiousness,' but the task was particularly difficult because 'the labouring class' consisted 'almost wholly of disbanded soldiers, whose manner of life has been ill calculated either to improve or preserve their morals.'[25] Privately, Stuart also acknowledged that the town's élite were not particularly upright either. By his reckoning, prominent parishioners included at least six men who kept mistresses. Furthermore, 'not a Gentleman' in the congregation 'except Mr Small' honestly 'professes our religion.'[26]

Stuart married Lucy Brooks of Massachusetts in 1803, and they had four children while in York, one of whom died in infancy. His family life seems to have been a source of happiness – he was 'miserable' when his wife went home for a short visit in 1806 – but his work caused him considerable despair. While his SPG reports were generally positive, his private letters spoke of his 'unthankful occupation,' and his father acknowledged that lack of success in York inclined his son 'to despond.'[27]

An example of his frustrations was his confrontation with Chief Justice Henry Allcock. In 1803 Stuart read marriage banns during the Good Friday service. At that point, a drunken Allcock stood up in front of everyone and denounced Stuart for breaking the law by reading banns on a day other than Sunday. After church the two men exchanged heated words in public. The chief justice was in a good position to make Stuart squirm: the lieutenant-governor was absent from York at the time, and Allcock had to sign a certificate declaring that Stuart had fulfilled his duties if the cleric were to receive his stipend. Not wishing to call on Allcock, Stuart sent his servant for the certificate; but the judge dismissed the man with the message that Stuart had to come himself. The priest refused and had to go without his money for a time. Allcock infuriated Stuart further by not allowing him to serve as chaplain to the legislative council, thus depriving him of the accompanying salary, and tried to magnify the insult by calling upon his father, John Stuart, to take his place. The elder man refused and protested to the bishop, claiming that his son was the victim of a gross injustice. Jacob Mountain, however, took Allcock's side and rebuked John Stuart for supporting his son's 'rebellious cause.' (In the end, Robert Addison served as parliamentary chaplain.)[28]

Another parishioner, joiner and shopkeeper George Duggan, did not like Stuart or his preaching. Every Sunday, as Stuart climbed into the pulpit to deliver his sermon, Duggan stood up and stormed out of church. This was such a dramatic and regular event that some of the younger parishioners assumed that Duggan's angry march was part of the liturgical flow of the service. That Stuart dealt with Allcock so poorly and let Duggan get away with his silly behaviour, and that other parishioners did not get either worshipper to behave himself, all suggest that Stuart was not particularly well regarded or popular.

Stuart's preaching style, which perhaps matched his general demeanour, did not command respect. In the pulpit, according to one source, he was given to 'unexpected elevations and depressions of the voice irrespective of the matter, accompanied by long closings of the eyes, and then a sudden re-opening of the same.' Furthermore, he was ineffective at collecting debts; his school and the church were owed substantial amounts in unpaid tuition and pew rents. One contemporary described him as 'haughty, sullen, and austere' – marks of an individual who was probably unhappy with himself. Yet he also was called 'benevolent' and 'amiable,' and there is anecdotal evidence to suggest that his failings may have derived from a kindly, but bumbling and inconsistent, disposition.[29]

In 1811, John Stuart died, which opened up the more desirable parish of Kingston for his son. In July 1812, George left York for greener pastures. His departure marked the end of one chapter in Anglicanism's history in York. By 1812 the church was on a firm, if not particularly strong foundation, with a modest house of worship, and had got used to having a resident cleric who also played a fundamental role in education. The church probably had come to be regarded as a relatively significant part of the town's life, and its dominance in worship and education made it the largest non-governmental institution in the capital.

JOHN STRACHAN AND HIS MILITANT CHURCH, 1812–15

Sadly, life would not be normal for either the church or the town over the next three years because the United States declared war on Great Britain and invaded Canada. Fortunately, the cleric who would minister to the townspeople during that dark time, John Strachan, was the strongest priest in the Canadian church.

He had been born in Aberdeen in 1778, the son of a quarry foreman who had died when John was a teenager. His father had taken him to Scottish Episcopalian services, but his mother had hoped that he would enter the Presbyterian ministry and had sent him to King's College, Aberdeen, where he earned an MA in preparation for divinity studies at the University of St Andrews. His limited financial resources and lack of patronage persuaded him that his future in Scotland was bleak, so he crossed the Atlantic in 1799 to accept a tutoring position in Upper Canada. Towards the end of his contract, Strachan sought ordination in the Presbyterian church, under the impression that the kirk in Montreal needed a minister. He was wrong; and influenced by Lieutenant-Governor Peter Hunter, the rector of Kingston, John Stuart, and his employer, Richard Cartwright, he then sought Anglican orders, being ordained deacon in 1803 and priest in 1804.

The change in denomination did not then seem odd to Strachan because of his youthful experiences in both churches and his perception that there were no significant theological differences between the two. Only later would a more mature Strachan realize just how far Canterbury was from Geneva. The lieutenant-governor appointed Strachan to the parish in Cornwall, where he constructed a church and parsonage and opened the best school in the province, for which he received an honorary doctorate in divinity in 1811 from the University of Aberdeen. As his school became famous, the colony's leading citizens sent their children to Strachan, who did his best to prepare his students to take command of the province's

1.5   Ann Wood McGill Strachan, wife of the Revd John Strachan, in 1807.

affairs in the next generation. In 1807 he married Ann Wood McGill, a beautiful and wealthy twenty-two-year-old widow (Figure 1.5).[30] One of his scholars recorded his impressions of the newlywed priest: 'Mr. Strachan ... lives in great style, and keeps three servants. He is a great friend of the poor, and spends his money as fast as he gets it. He is very passionate.'[31]

John, Ann, and their three young children moved to York in July 1812, just after the outbreak of war. As they sailed west from Kingston, another vessel appeared behind them. Thinking that they were being chased by an American ship, the captain panicked and prepared to strike his colours. John Strachan objected, seized command of the vessel, locked the captain below, had the schooner's gun loaded, and prepared to fight! The other vessel soon overtook Strachan, but fortunately it was British, and the Strachans proceeded to York peacefully.

Obviously John Strachan was a different type of person from his predecessor, as the parishioners soon learned when he ordered the wardens to collect outstanding pew rents and other money owing to the church, even if they had to take the debtors to court. Yet Strachan was not hard-hearted. His aggressiveness reflected his sense of duty, hierarchy, and charity. He confined collecting payments to the relatively affluent and prominent, and he insisted that he and the wardens pay the sexton's gravedigging fee out of their own pockets when poor people were buried in the graveyard beside the church.[32]

In October 1812 Strachan advertised that the York District Grammar School (Figure 1.6) was ready to take scholars under his tutelage. Subjects included English, elocution, mathematics, accounting, civil and natural history, geography, Latin, Greek, and religion as seen through Anglican eyes. He offered a reduced rate to poorer people who could not pay the full tuition, as long as the parents kept their children 'neat and clean' and supplied them with 'proper Books.' Strachan did not want to exclude the humble from secondary education and advocated the creation of provincial scholarships so that 'we might live to see the children of the farmer and

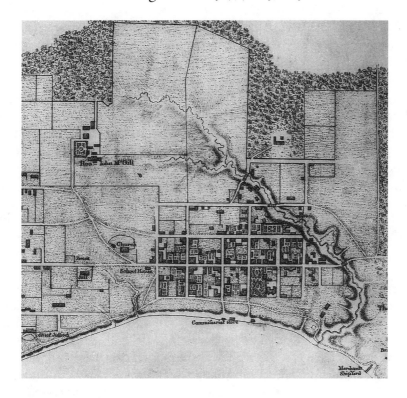

1.6 Part of a map of the town of York in 1813 by George Williams. Strachan's school appears
on the south side of King Street across from the church.

mechanic filling the highest offices in the Colony, to which they had risen by their superior talents, fostered by the benevolent institutions of their Country?' However, he did not offer free tuition, probably because he could not afford to, since the school barely broke even financially.[33]

One of Strachan's first efforts in York was the presentation of a long and impressive sermon to the provincial parliament in support of Canadian defence, in which he resolved the problems of being both a soldier and a Christian largely by affirming that the Christian was an honourable and restrained combatant when fighting for a just cause. He also entered political controversy by supporting the suspension of some civil liberties, because of the invasion crisis, at the very time when legislators were debating the controversial suspension of *habeas corpus*. The sermon's propaganda value led to its publication and distribution throughout the province.[34]

Strachan wrote regularly to the British commanders on the conduct of the war, often chiding them for not being sufficiently aggressive. Sometimes he was a bit too warlike for the generals; on one occasion the governor-in-chief in Quebec City had to ask him to refrain from publishing his views because they might hurt British interests.[35]

When Major-General Isaac Brock captured Detroit in August 1812, at a time when most Canadians had assumed that an American conquest was a foregone conclusion, Strachan wrote in triumph, 'The brilliant victory ... has been of infinite service in confirming the wavering &

adding spirit to the loyal.' Strachan also admitted his own frightened loyalism when he noted: 'Many of our Settlers are recently from the States and by no means acquainted with the obligation which they contract when they come to live under this government – a signal advantage gained over the enemy was therefore necessary to keep them to their duty.'[36]

Strachan encouraged the young women of York's leading families to embroider colours for the York Militia, using patterns made by twenty-year-old Mary Warren Baldwin. Upon their completion, the colours were presented to the men by Anne Powell, a daughter of one of the town's most prominent families. Strachan also began a subscription to provide shoes and clothing to the York militiamen serving on the Niagara Peninsula. To help alleviate the problems created by wartime shortages of coinage and small-denomination paper money, he organized the York Association so that merchants could deposit army bills and bullion in large sums in return for locally produced notes to facilitate commerce. The interest that the association earned went to Strachan, who used it for poor relief.[37]

The most important charitable effort of the war, in which York's Anglicans took a leading part, was the establishment of the Loyal and Patriotic Society of Upper Canada in December 1812. The idea came from Elizabeth Selby, a young woman in the congregation. The society ultimately raised £21,500 in British North America, the West Indies, and the United Kingdom. It made cash donations to distressed militiamen and their families, subsidized bread in the inflation-ravaged provincial capital, engaged in other charitable acts, and struck, but never issued, medals for conspicuous service. (In 1840 the medals were melted down for bullion, and the proceeds were donated to the Toronto General Hospital, which the society had founded in 1819 with the donation of a postwar surplus of £4,000.) However, the society's heroic efforts were hindered by the limitations inherent in charitable institutions: it could help only a tiny portion of the war's victims, and then only modestly. The £25 payment typically given to the widows or parents of militiamen who died on service, for example, was not much compensation for the loss of a family's principal breadwinner, even by the standards of 1812.[38]

The Loyal and Patriotic Society exemplified the marriage of the Church of England's Christianity to its allegiance to King George III. It attempted to integrate all levels of society throughout the empire, in an effort to unify disparate peoples in support of a charitable enterprise, as defined by the state church. It tried to include donors of many denominations and appointed clergy to its board of directors from the two other churches considered legitimate by Anglicans, Rome and Scotland; but it did so in Upper Canada in a way that asserted the primacy of the Church of England, while downgrading the status of its main competitors, the Methodists, Baptists, and other dissenting denominations, who were excluded from the board. It also represented the Church's perception of how the established order should work, through collecting money broadly but channelling aid from the top down. Recipients of the society's generosity were expected to be grateful for the recognition that they received for their fidelity and in return to serve as patterns of loyalty for others to emulate.[39]

To wean Strachan away from the comforts of Cornwall to York in 1812, the government had offered him the chaplaincies of the garrison and the legislative council to augment his income. Strachan took his military appointment very seriously, calling on the sick and wounded in hospital twice each week, as army regulations required. During weekday visits he usually spoke privately to the patients, asked how they were doing, 'dropped something concerning their spiritual welfare,' and gave out as many tracts, Bibles, and prayer books as he could, although he never had enough to meet the demand. On Sundays he repeated the process and also read prayers and gave a fifteen- or twenty-minute extempore homily in each ward. Because ambulatory patients followed him through the hospitals, he felt that he had to say something different in each ward, sometimes delivering as many as five separate homilies per visit. This he found fatiguing. During the summer of 1813, as casualties on the Niagara front rose at an alarming rate, and as many of the wounded were shipped to York for care, Strachan agreed to let his church be converted into a hospital if needed, which was done in 1814.[40]

Strachan's visits to the hospitals seem to have moderated his earlier militancy. Faced with ministering to hundreds of wounded men at a time, 'many of them sadly mangled,' and burying as many as eight a day, he lamented, 'I wish that those who are so ready stirring up wars would traverse the field of battle after an engagement or visit the hospitals next day and they would receive a lesson that might be very beneficial to them in future.'[41]

John Strachan's most dramatic contributions to the King's cause between 1812 and 1814 were his efforts to protect the capital during two enemy occupations. On 27 April 1813 a U.S. naval squadron took up a position west of the town and disgorged 1,750 soldiers to attack York. The defenders – 750 regulars, militiamen, and Natives – fought for six hours yet ultimately had to yield, but not before blowing up their gunpowder store at Fort York, killing and wounding 250 Americans in the process. The regulars retreated to Kingston, the warriors evaporated into the forest, and the militia remained behind to surrender the town.

During the battle, Strachan evacuated wounded from one of the British batteries until it was destroyed by an accidental explosion. He was away from the site at the time of the disaster and, once he realized that the battle was lost, went home to send Ann and the children to the security of a friend's house in the country. He then joined the two senior militia officers in York to arrange a capitulation. They surrendered the troops remaining in York as prisoners-of-war and turned over all government supplies to the Americans. In return the enemy pledged to respect private property, allow the civil government to function without hindrance, and let surgeons and others attend to the British wounded.[42]

Sadly, things began to go wrong almost from the moment the capitulation was signed. American troops, uncontrolled by their senior officers and angry at their losses from the explosion of the magazine, broke into homes, molested and robbed the townspeople, and pillaged the church. They also locked up the British and Canadian wounded in the garrison blockhouse, where they languished for two days without food, water, or medical attention. On 28 April, an outraged Strachan raged up to the enemy commanders to demand satisfaction. Undaunted by attempts to brush him aside, he raged on until he got the Americans to post sentries in the town, feed the prisoners, and release the wounded to his care. Significantly, Strachan acted alone when negotiating with the Americans, without any support from the town's militia and civil officials, who seem to have decided to lie low during the crisis.

Once satisfied, the rector of York rallied help to transfer the wounded to more comfortable quarters in private homes. The move took two days because the weather was bad and the enemy had commandeered most of the available vehicles to carry government supplies to their ships. Besides relocating the wounded, Strachan procured food, medicine, dressings, and clothing and deployed his own limited medical skills to care for the casualties. Looting, however, continued, and at one point Strachan rescued one parishioner, Angélique Givins, from a gang of Americans who nearly shot her while robbing her house.

On 30 April, a frustrated Strachan called a meeting of the magistrates to write a memorandum of grievances to give to the U.S. commander, Major-General Henry Dearborn. Once he received the document, Dearborn 'promised everything,' as Strachan wrote, and increased the town guard, although the enemy continued to violate the capitulation. The most famous incident was the torching late in the occupation of the governor's house and the parliament buildings; this was to lead to the retaliatory burning of the White House and the Congress in Washington, DC, in 1814. Just after the Americans left the capital in early May, Strachan conducted a funeral service over the mass grave at the garrison where the enemy had burned and buried the dead, presumably from both armies. Then, for the next six weeks, he looked after the wounded and procured supplies and medicines for them. He also travelled to the Niagara Peninsula to bring wounded men to York after the Battle of Fort George at the end of May, when casualties could not sail across Lake Ontario because American ships controlled water communications.[43]

In July 1813, the enemy squadron returned to a defenceless York for two days to destroy military buildings missed earlier and to gather up supplies. At the sight of their approach, most of the male population, consisting of militiamen on parole from the previous attack, fled in fear of being taken to prisons in the United States. Strachan once again assumed responsibility for protecting the town's interests against the enemy as best he could.[44]

The war years proved profoundly traumatic for the Strachans. In 1812 one of their children died, leaving them in deep grief. John confessed his sadness at 'how transitory even our most innocent and laudable enjoyments are,' while Ann found 'relief in tears' at the loss of one of their 'pillars of happiness.'[45] A few months later, John heard the sad news that his mother had died. Reflecting on these painful losses, he noted: 'My mind is strong to bear misfortune[,] it never gives away tho' it sometimes recoils upon itself and my heart would break before a mere Spectator knew that I was much affected[.] I always think that I can bear calamity better than others and have frequently administered to relief of persons who were less affected than myself because I thought that they were less able to bear up against it.'[46] After the Battle of York he sent Ann and the children to Cornwall, where he hoped that they would be safer. He was very wrong: two companies of American troops moved through the town. Ann, who was pregnant, was robbed, assaulted, and probably raped by a gang of enemy soldiers. She was left an emotional and physical wreck, and for a time her friends and family despaired of her life. While she recovered enough to give birth to a baby girl in early 1814, she was too frail to return home until June. John managed to visit her at the time of their daughter's birth, but the war mostly kept them apart, and he had to limit himself to sending her little poems in a forlorn attempt to console her.[47]

The war also caused the Strachan family considerable financial difficulty, and then, just after the end of hostilities, fire gutted their home. Two more children were born during this time, both boys, one in 1815 and another two years later. A second fire burned them out of their home again in 1817. They decided to build a new house, in brick, with good chimneys, near the corner of modern Bay and Front streets in what was the most desirable residential area in the town (Figure 1.7). Strachan thought his new house delightful, although it kept him in debt for many years. It was the finest home in York and became known as a place of frequent and elegant festivities. Ann presumably played a key role in advancing the interests of both her family and the church among the colonial élite through her hospitality and conversation.[48]

1.7 John and Ann Strachan's house on Front Street West, built in 1818. After Strachan was made bishop, it was popularly known as 'the Palace.' On his arrival for a visit from Scotland, the bishop's brother James is said to have remarked, 'I hope it's a' come by honestly.' This photo was taken shortly before the house was pulled down, about 1898.

Word of the war's end and confirmation of the successful defence of Canada reached York in February 1815. In early April the people of the town attended a special service of thanksgiving (see Figure 1.8). John Strachan preached the day's sermon. He and his family had experienced the war's privations severely but had served the king's cause honourably. He looked to the postwar period with qualified hope, noting that 'Since the return of Peace, a great change is observable among our inhabitants, many are desirous of religious instruction who used to be cold and indifferent.'[49] There were good reasons why people should have had a change in heart, according to the day's sermon.

His text for that day was Romans 8:28, 'And we know that all things work together for good to them that love God, to them who are the[sic] called according to his purpose.' He saw a divine purpose in the horrible, almost-continuous warfare that had engulfed the world since 1793, but which culminated in Britain's triumph over her enemies – a victory that had not seemed possible three years earlier, when the United Kingdom had been struggling against Napoleonic tyranny at the very time when the United States, 'with horrid joy,' used the European crisis to launch a war of expansion. Despite Britain's own failings, he argued that the King's subjects had 'abundant cause to give thanks to Almighty God for the successful issue of the contest; that we are a free and happy people; have never bowed to a foreign yoke; and have preserved in all its vigour our most excellent constitution.'

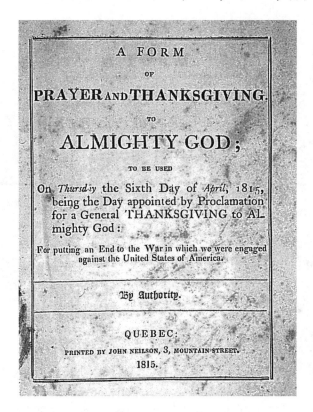

1.8 Form of service of thanksgiving for the end of the War of 1812, as used in the church at York.

The events of recent decades had proved that revolution did not work: 'Of the two experiments made in America and France to constitute governments productive of virtue and happiness only, both have completely failed. – In the former, the most base and wretched policy is pursued; and the latter ended in a military despotism.' Rather, he continued, 'It is by peaceable and gradual steps, and not by revolutions, that the most solid improvements in the Science of government can be obtained – It is the power of God only to extract good.' Upper Canadians ought therefore to recognize the 'superintending Providence of God' in human affairs, cherish their liberties as British subjects, take hold of the solid morality and true religion inherent in the British way, and rise to new levels of exertion in building a godly society on the Canadian frontier.⁵⁰

ERASTIAN DEFEAT, 1815–39

Girded with his supreme self-confidence and positioned to impose his Anglican views from his privileged post as rector of the province's most important parish, John Strachan (Figure 1.9) intended to take the lead in creating a devout and British society in Upper Canada, one that would be moral, deferential, and loyal. His objectives were to encourage the population to appreciate the twin glories of church establishment and the British constitution and to persuade most of them to decide to find shelter in the purity and excellence of Anglican doctrine and liturgy against the storms of dissent, irreligion, and republicanism. His error was that the

1.9 Ven. John Strachan, archdeacon and parson of York, c. 1827.

High Tory ideology that he embraced so vigorously – and which often had trouble distinguishing dissent from disloyalty – virtually guaranteed an anguished defeat, if for no other reason than that any fervent ideology is a poor basis for addressing the complexity of human need. His ideological vehemence was discredited further by the petty, ruthless, and selfish actions that his peers (including prominent St James' parishioners) undertook in advancing the Georgian Tory agenda, to say nothing of its outmoded values in postwar Upper Canada. Ultimately, Strachan's rout was made the more poignant by the immense hostility and backlash generated in reaction to the skill and energy that he had applied to propagating this antiquated ideology – a backlash that drowned out the more defensible spiritual underpinnings of his efforts to bring people to a relatively mature and sophisticated Christianity in comparison to what dissenting denominations then had to offer.[51]

Strachan's Waterloo, however, lay in the future. In 1815, his wartime contributions led to his appointment to the province's executive council, roughly equivalent to a cabinet, as an honorary member. Two years later he became a full member, and in 1820 he was appointed to the legislative council, the upper house of the provincial parliament. Political office allowed Strachan to play a particularly strong partisan role in colonial affairs, especially to encourage loyalty, pursue his plans to give the Church of England a secure footing, and promote education. Nevertheless, he frequently met with setbacks, as in 1817, when, to his surprise, he could not get the colony's legislature to provide an annual subsidy to help educate Anglican theological students. That fund was intended to be part of a broader plan to provide the church with enough money and authority to exercise fully its role as the established church, and which included efforts such as opening an Anglican university, creating a separate diocese in Upper Canada, and maximizing the financial potential and Anglican control of the clergy reserves through the Clergy Reserves Corporation, which he founded in 1819.[52]

A fundamental problem with education in Upper Canada at the end of the war was the limited number of state-supported schools. Strachan deployed his energies to rectifying the problem through establishing government-supported schools beginning in 1816. In 1823 he resigned as headmaster of the District Grammar School to become president of the newly formed provincial General Board of Education, which loosely oversaw the operations of some 450 common schools serving about twelve thousand children. Ultimately, however, education was secularized in 1841 because of the tremendous opposition to Anglican leadership in the field, which regularly was equated with Tory rule.

Strachan deserves recognition, however, for his role in laying the foundations for future growth and for addressing the immediate need for schooling in the province. He also helped convince his brother-in-law, James McGill, to provide money to establish McGill College in Montreal in 1821, although his efforts to open a university in Upper Canada bore no fruit until the chartering of Anglican-controlled King's College in 1827. King's, however, did not open until 1843 because Lieutenant-Governor Sir John Colborne diverted its original endowment to establish Upper Canada College in 1829. Colborne believed that a good grammar school was more urgently needed than a university and also seems to have thought that Strachan's university was too Anglican for his pluralistic province, especially because its exclusiveness produced sectarian strife – much of it generated by Strachan, whom Colborne did not like.[53]

Colborne's discomfort with King's College contrasted with his desire to help the Church of England on other fronts, as manifested by the personal support that he and his wife gave to St James'. Perhaps his most controversial act as governor came at the end of his administration in 1836, when he endowed forty-four Anglican rectories in the province with glebes carved out of the clergy and Crown reserves (and in the process forced the eviction of a number of rent-paying tenants with little or no compensation). St James' got eight hundred acres – four times the usual allotment. His action did not please imperial authorities in London and angered many people in Canada – church establishment clearly was a dying possibility, and most people resented the existence of the reserves, because these uncleared lands hindered local development and the majority wanted them to be either used to benefit all Christians equitably or secularized outright to finance education and public works. Eventually, in 1854, the reserves were secularized, although the Church of England received considerable financial benefits in the process.

Colborne's endowment sparked a new degree of political controversy, which contributed materially to his successor's decision to dissolve the legislative assembly, which in turn helped set in motion the machinery of rebellion. Yet Colborne's action made sense in Anglican minds, because the church faced a financial crisis. In 1832, the imperial government had cut grants to the colonial churches severely, both directly and through its subsidies to the Society for the Propagation of the Gospel. Bishop Stewart, Archdeacon Strachan, and others had done what they could to mitigate the loss by encouraging voluntary agencies, stimulating early efforts to resurrect synodical government, generating income, and winning the church some independence from increasingly hostile governments, but many clergy and their families in Upper Canada nevertheless faced destitution; hence Colborne acted.[54]

Controversy over establishment, as exemplified in debates over education, the clergy reserves, the endowment of rectories, and restrictions on religious liberty, created vicious tensions in Upper Canada and pitted the Anglican leadership against majority opinion. In the early 1820s, when the law still severely limited who could conduct marriage services, a Baptist minister illegally solemnized a marriage and was banished from the province for fourteen years. This event caused a furore in the provincial parliament, where Robert Nichol denounced the law, claiming that there was no established church in Upper Canada. John Beverley Robinson, the attorney-general and prominent St James' parishioner, proposed a compromise that would reduce the crime of conducting illegal marriages to a misdemeanour and extend the right to solemnize marriages to Methodist and Baptist clergy, but another decade would pass before the right was given to those and most other denominations. Nichol's vehemence seems to have inspired retaliation on the capital's Anglican church as an icon of the Church of England's pretensions.[55] On the night of his speech, some people broke into the building, 'tore the covering from the Communion table, *voided their excrement upon it*, ... reversed the Kings Arms over the Govs. Pew and committed other acts equally horrible.'[56]

Brutish behaviour characterized both sides in muddy York as people struggled either to shape society to their own vision or to free themselves from élite domination, while bitter debate reverberated through the town and province over such fundamental issues as religion, government, immigration, citizenship, education, and development. Angry vulgarity showed how mean and oppressive politics could be and how alienated and threatened people might feel. A good example involving Strachan's parish was the controversy surrounding the dismissal and reinstatement of its clerk, John Fenton, and the subsequent 'Types Riot.'

As clerk, Fenton helped lead worship, collected pew rents, and otherwise provided useful assistance around the church. He further supplemented his income as a teacher in the York Common School, as a police clerk, and as a messenger for the Bank of Upper Canada. In 1826 he attended an anti-government meeting and contributed money to buy a printing press for Charles Fothergill, the recently dismissed king's printer, who had lost his place because of his opposition to the province's leaders. As punishment, Fenton lost his jobs at both the church and the bank, although the churchwardens soon reinstated him at St James'.

In his *Colonial Advocate*, the radical reformer William Lyon Mackenzie (elected first mayor of Toronto in 1834) claimed that Fenton got his job back because he had threatened to publish a pamphlet that would have embarrassed the congregation. In contrast, one of the wardens, Tory lawyer James Buchanan Macaulay, claimed that the parish had rehired Fenton only out of regard for his poor health and poverty. Macaulay then published a pamphlet attacking both

Mackenzie's politics and person. Mackenzie retaliated with a stunningly vicious political satire in his newspaper, in which he defended himself by attacking Macaulay and the church's other leading parishioners. His theme was that the members of the York élite of the 1820s all came of humble origins, which undermined their pretentious claims to social leadership, the monopolization of public office, and domination over the rest of the population.[57] Of John Beverley Robinson's loyalist family, for example, he wrote: 'Is it a secret in these parts that many ... such Virginian nobles as the Robinsons assume themselves, were descended from mothers who came there to try their luck and were purchased by their sires with tobacco at prices according to the quality and soundness of the article? And is it from such a source that we are to expect the germ of liberty? Say rather is it not from such a source that we may look for the tyranny engendered, nursed and practised by those whose blood has been vitiated and syphilized by the accursed slavery of centuries.' Referring to the Strachans and prominent parishioner William Allan, Mackenzie wrote, 'The time was in Judge Cartwright's house where the widow of old McGill (Mrs. S.) was chamber-maid and house-maid – in the kitchen, the Rev. Doctor in the garret as the scholar's guide to arithmetic, and the Honourable William Allan as boot-polisher inhabited the lower regions of the scullery: – why are they not there yet? They were well enough there.' Although risen from such rude a background himself, John Strachan now was preaching 'political sermons,' in which he prescribed 'how far a whole people shall be or not represented and allowed to manage their own affairs.' Mackenzie found Strachan's elevation in provincial society shocking, because he considered him nothing more than a 'diminutive, paltry, insignificant, Scotch turn coat parish schoolmaster.'[58] Of course, Mackenzie chose to overlook the fact that Strachan was a hard-working and intelligent person, who had risen to prominence largely through his own talents.

Mackenzie's diatribe led another parishioner at St James', Samuel Peters Jarvis, to round up a gang of young men connected to the province's legal and administrative élite to destroy Mackenzie's printing shop and throw his types and other equipment into the bay. After the 'Types Riot,' Mackenzie successfully sued the unrepentant rioters and their well-heeled supporters for £625 and cited the incident in the press as an object lesson on the unworthy character of the colony's leadership.[59] Strachan and his church were implicated, since they had supported the cause of a hierarchical provincial society, in which they thought that legal and other professionals should form a natural ruling class. However, this group had shown its unworthiness and its contempt for both the law and the British constitution that it affected to champion through its treatment of Fenton and through its sons' behaviour in the riot.

It was a Reformer in the St James' congregation, Dr William Warren Baldwin, whose account of the events read as if he had listened to Strachan's sermons with more care than some of the Tory parishioners. He wrote, 'McKenzie's conduct was very bad; the libel alledged by the rioters as the excuse for their conduct had my cordial disapprobation and he should have suffered for his slander, but not by outrage,' especially at the hands of 'Gentlemen.' Referring to the oaths to uphold the constitution and the other statutory obligations that the rioters had to assume when entering their professions, he asked, 'Is this all idle form?' before answering, 'there is in the object of the statute and in the Barrister[']s oath not merely legal wisdom, but a religious obligation from morality and the true spirit of English liberty well worthy of the contemplation of the student[,] who if insensible to those impressions must be unworthy of the Calling.'[60]

The 1820s and 1830s were the decades that saw the dream of establishment die. Not only was the province as a whole opposed or indifferent, not only was the imperial government increasingly unsympathetic, not only was the established church in Britain losing its favoured place, but Anglicanism's resources in Canada simply were not adequate even to serve its own people, let alone evangelize others. Strachan acknowledged the problem from time to time, as in his 1825 sermon on the death of Bishop Jacob Mountain. Instead of focusing on the bishop's accomplishments, which were few, he spoke of the difficulties that Mountain had faced in attempting to achieve his goals and lamented that 'a Christian nation without a religious establishment is a contradiction.'[61]

The sermon caused considerable controversy because it questioned the loyalty of the non-Anglican clergy in the province. Egerton Ryerson, the great Methodist apologist and educator, used the pages of the *Colonial Advocate* to attack Strachan's assertions and publish a detailed critique of establishment. Strachan reacted badly to Ryerson, publishing his notoriously inaccurate *Ecclesiastical Chart* to advance the Anglican cause among colonial authorities in England. His outraged opponents reacted vociferously. Six thousand people signed a petition demanding an inquiry into Strachan's anti-Methodist charges. In 1828 both a select committee of the provincial legislative assembly and the Canada Committee of the British House of Commons criticized the concept of establishment as impractical in a pluralistic society and suggested that the clergy reserves be used to support Protestant denominations beyond the Church of England. However, neither local nor imperial authorities were yet ready to follow the suggestion.[62]

In 1837 Strachan preached a sermon to the clergy of the archdeaconry, in which he encouraged them to work hard to advance the cause of establishment but also seemed to admit that the campaign already had been lost – warning them that if the clergy reserves 'be taken from us by legal oppression, we must receive it as a trial of our faith, and, submitting in all patience, seek consolation in turning with redoubled ardour to our sacred duties.' For, he continued, 'From teaching the Gospel in the purest form to the inhabitants of Upper Canada we cannot be driven. We are a Missionary Church; – in this consists our true character; and as our organization is Missionary, let us cherish more and more a Missionary Spirit.' Success, he now believed, could be achieved 'amidst the wreck of our temporalities as well as amidst the slander and contumely of our enemies, without affording them a single just cause of irritation. By thus proceeding we shall exhibit the character and principles of the Church in all their attractive beauty, and win far more friends in the day of our adversity than in that of our prosperity.'[63]

As the state's support for establishment evaporated, the question arose for Anglicans: what was distinct about their church in comparison with the dissenters? The answer was clear to the theologically informed, but that clarity was sharpened during the reinvigorating 1830s as the leaders of the Oxford Movement in England and other Anglicans rethought their church's place in society, largely by searching backward past the Reformation for inspiration in the medieval and primitive churches. To them, solace could be found in the church's unbroken tradition reaching back to the apostles, which gave the Church of England, beyond its political legitimacy within the British Empire, a spiritual authority on a par with that of the Orthodox and Roman Catholic churches, and a standing higher than anything that the dissenting bodies could claim.

It was here that Archdeacon Strachan increasingly found comfort. Already moving in this direction from at least about 1820, he eagerly read the Oxford Movement's *Tracts for the Times* (which in part advanced an anti-Erastian ideology) and went on to commend them to his clergy and divinity students, who, along with a few organists, then began to develop a cautious enthusiasm for liturgical reform and a celebration of Anglicanism's catholic heritage. At the same time, these men came to see that their church might be able to achieve its spiritual mission of saving souls and building up a Christian society without significant state support. Yet enthusiasm for the high-church revival was by no means universal. Other clergy denounced the Oxford Movement as an evil return to popery, and in time Strachan himself grew sceptical about some of its more radical tendencies.[64]

Strachan also formed a friendship with John Henry Hobart, the Episcopalian bishop of New York, a man who provided inspiration for the archdeacon as he contemplated a place for his church outside the state's embrace. In 1832, Strachan published his thoughts on Hobart's work, in which he praised his successes without giving up on the idea of establishment. Hobart had waged war against denominations that he considered enemies of Episcopalianism by arguing, with force and effect, that his church's doctrinal purity, authoritative liturgy, and ecclesiastical government in the apostolic succession gave it a legitimacy that simply did not exist among other reformed churches. For Strachan, Hobart had roused people through 'his cogent reasons, apt illustrations, and powerful appeals to ecclesiastical history, which proved, beyond controversy, that the government of the Church, the orders of the ministry, and their regular succession from the Apostles, were not questions of slight moment, or to be treated safely either with silence or contempt.' This was an attractive model for Strachan, who stated, with some obvious satisfaction, and in marked contrast to his earlier comfort with Presbyterianism, that the obligation to retain the apostolic succession through a legitimate order of bishops, priests, and deacons 'was universally acknowledged and acted upon by the Church, from the days of St Paul, till the pride of Calvin, raising him in his own conceit above the Apostle, tempted him to question, and then overturn it,' and that it remained 'an obligation still felt and adhered to by the purest portion of the Christian church.'

Strachan also found solace in Hobart's achievement in increasing the number of his clergy in New York from twenty-three at the time of his consecration in 1811 to a respectable 111 by 1830. Hobart had also proved a jealous guardian and promoter of Christian orthodoxy and high clerical standards. Yet Strachan also detected weakness in Hobart's corps of clergy, in that they were still too few to reach all the people in the state. In contrast, because of establishment, the Church of England had enough priests to staff nearly all its parishes. English clergy, moreover, were financially independent of their congregations, unlike their American peers, who 'too frequently sink below the rank which they ought to hold in society; and whatever be their personal merit, they fail to command that respect from a vain, and thoughtless, and undiscerning people, which is necessary to secure attention to their instructions.'[65] Behind this statement lay Strachan's enduring conviction that an educated and independent clergy, preaching the word without fear or favour and administering the sacraments in the purity of the Anglican tradition, within the bosom of the state's approbation, was essential to creating a godly society. He continued to think this way in part because he rejected the idea that Christian conversion could come about suddenly and rapturously, as many Methodists claimed; he believed instead that true conversion normally required a long process of rational Christian education, presented by qualified clergy who taught their inherently sinful people how to control their passions, to lead virtuous and restrained lives, to perform good works as an outward mark of faith, and to obey the divinely sanctioned civil authorities.[66] As he noted in the Kingston *Gazette* as early as 1812, 'Enthusiasm,' as practised by Methodists and others, was 'the fruit of deplorable ignorance, of pride and presumption,' while true religion was anchored in reason, which 'must always be the guiding and ruling faculty – the affections must not lead but follow.'[67]

Strachan found his views validated by the Rebellions. In early December 1837, William Lyon Mackenzie attempted to overthrow the government in Toronto at the same time as an armed rebellion in Lower Canada confronted established authority with a much more serious challenge. Both revolts were crushed; but tensions remained high through 1838 and 1839 because of the government's heavy-handed oppression of its opponents and several serious raids into the Canadas by rebels and American sympathizers from south of the border. Yet the majority of Upper Canadians in general, and Anglicans in particular, supported the government with enthusiasm.[68]

A week after the Mackenzie uprising, John Strachan preached a sermon that addressed the immediate crisis. His text came from Hosea 6:5: 'And thy judgements are as the light that goeth forth.' He saw the rebellion as a judgement upon the Canadian and imperial governments for failing to fulfil their 'first duty' of creating a Christian government. Had they done so, then Upper Canada would have become 'a Christian Society built up in righteousness' instead of 'being exposed to traitorous conspiracies.' After decades of fighting for his Erastian dream, and even while he began to accept a new model for his church, the Venerable Dr Strachan could not pass up the opportunity to issue his 'I told you so,' even though virtually nobody possessing political authority would have agreed that establishment was still a realistic or even desirable prospect for the colony.

Strachan's sermon, however, did not sputter out impotently in a diatribe of frustration. Rather, he attempted to draw the lessons of what had happened over previous decades. First, he drew a parallel between the failures of the governments in London and Toronto and those of the rulers of ancient Israel whom Hosea had denounced for their 'deplorable profligacy' and licentious 'Idolatry,' which had 'operated as a powerful inducement with this gross and obstinate people to quit the service of Jehovah and to forget his wonderful interpositions for their deliverance and advancement.' Strachan noted that 'this dereliction of duty was found no less impolitic than irreligious' because 'It split them into parties and enervated their character' at a time when 'union and National energy were essential to render them a match for their more powerful Neighbours.'

The allusion to the Canadian situation must have been clear to everyone sitting in the pews at St James' that day as they wondered whether the uprising would be successful and whether they would soon see Canada annexed to the United States. But Strachan offered them fresh hope when he lifted his sermon's focus to place the recent rebellion in a much wider context: 'But would you now desire an example from Modern as well as sacred and antient history?' He continued: 'Take one terrible judgement on account of which posterity will call this the age of revolution. Heavy was the judgement of God which France called down by her thirst of conquest and that gross infidelity which dissolved the bonds of domestic and social life and shook the foundations of truth & integrity. Inexpressible calamity has not only been the result to France but to all Europe and its consequences are still in operation.' Surveying the American and French revolutions, the Napoleonic wars, European constitutional crises of the 1830s, the Upper Canadian revolt, and all the other disasters that had beset the world in recent decades, Strachan commented hopefully: 'Yet we already perceive indications of ... it becoming a severe process of purifications for much that was noxious has already been swallowed up in the abyss of the wars & revolutions which have followed. Many of the most oppressive relations of society have been softened or removed' while 'prejudice is weakened and a corrector Knowledge diffused among the people & above all a deeper impression of the excellence of the Gospel and of the inestimable benefits which it is certain to confer when all embrace it.' He concluded his historical retrospect with these words: 'It is not easy for the most careless to cast their eyes over the history of the world during the last sixty years without being convinced that the judgements of God have been far more visible than in ordinary times.'

Next Strachan summed up many of the frustrations of his career within his own theological understandings: 'care should be taken not to judge rashly by regarding calamity as the measure of the guilt of those on whom it falls – nor aught we to forget that we are all sinners and therefore no person who is involved in any general distress can justly complain for he is not an innocent sufferer. Moreover God frequently visits the iniquities of the Fathers upon the Children who are comparatively less guilty & sends judgments not merely to punish but to prove.' Clearly the counter-revolutionary and fearful loyalism that had underlain the imperial government's hopes for establishment in 1791 still lived on in the archdeacon's mind, as in those of many of the province's Anglicans. But the politicians both in Toronto and in London no longer held these views, being in large part the legatees of the liberalizing trends that had paralleled the calamities of the previous six decades.[69]

The Erastian defeat is the key story that historians address when thinking about Strachan and his parish of St James'. In a sad way, one of Mackenzie's odious little diatribes turned out to be prophetically true for the John Strachan of history. Back in 1826, when Strachan set sail for England to lobby for a university, protect Anglicanism's interest in the clergy reserves, and advance the cause of establishment, Mackenzie had written him an open letter in the pages of his *Colonial Advocate*: 'the day will come when it will yield you infinitely more consolation if you are able to call to mind that you calmed with the words of everlasting truth, the troubled conscience of some poor perishing sinner, than that you were the favourite and prime minister of all the Lieutenant Governors on earth ... You will become the scoff and derision, the bye-word and reproach, of those for whom you shall have laid aside your gown and cassock, your bible and prayer-book, to turn dabbler in the impure and uncanonical mire of provincial party politics.'[70]

CLERGY AND PEOPLE

While the better-known story of John Strachan's Erastian crusade played itself out in Georgian Toronto, the comparatively quiet one of the daily work of the parish also unfolded at St James' as the church fulfilled its age-old tasks within a rapidly changing community from its unique position as the provincial capital's premier congregation. Tens of thousands of British immigrants poured into Upper Canada in the wake of the severe economic dislocations that followed the end of the Napoleonic wars in 1815. The population of the provincial capital grew from seven hundred in 1816 to twelve hundred in 1820 to nine thousand in 1834, when the province incorporated the community as the city of Toronto. Meanwhile the community moved far from its roots as a frontier outpost, developing into an up-and-coming commercial centre serving an expanding agricultural hinterland. Reflecting this growth, the church elevated York to the status of an archdeaconry in the diocese of Quebec in 1825, with John Strachan as archdeacon.[71]

In 1816, in response to the efforts of various laypeople, Strachan founded a second church north of the town on Yonge Street (now St John's, York Mills). He visited it one Sunday each month and sent one of his divinity students to officiate on the other Sundays. By May 1817, over eighty people had been baptized there. The presence of a church with regular services did much to advance the Anglican cause on Yonge Street and cut into the ranks of the Methodists, 'to their great annoyance,' as Strachan wrote in triumph.[72] In 1821, York Mills got its own clergyman. St John's was just the first of many parishes whose origins lay in the mission work of the original church at York.[73]

The 1807 church building in the town of York had come out of the War of 1812 in very poor condition and was too small for the growing congregation. These problems led Strachan to start a Sunday evening service at the neighbouring York District Grammar School for people who simply could not fit into the church. Given that these people were not pewholders, this congregation undoubtedly represented a more humble group of Anglicans than attended the morning service in the church, although it also included people with means who could not purchase pews in the tiny church because none were available. Strachan wanted to repair and enlarge the church but was not able to raise enough money to carry out the work until 1818, when he had the building enlarged to seat twice as many worshippers (Figure 1.10).

Yet the number of people who wanted to attend soon again exceeded the seating capacity. In the early 1830s some seventy families were willing to purchase pews but could not because there were none to be had. Strachan then began efforts to replace his wooden church with a much larger stone structure befitting the needs and pretensions of the growing provincial capital. In 1832 Lieutenant-Governor Sir John Colborne laid the cornerstone, and the next year a grand Neoclassical building opened with over two thousand people filling the pews for the inaugural service.[74]

Faced with the demands of an expanding congregation and a full public career, Strachan found that he needed an assistant. During the War of 1812, Richard Pollard from Sandwich (now Windsor) helped him while living as a refugee from the fighting in southwestern Upper Canada; and in 1824 Strachan placed one of the SPG's itinerant missionaries in the province, George Archbold, in charge of the parish when he went to England for a time. Strachan also got some limited assistance from his divinity students, the most famous being the high churchman Alexander Neil Bethune, who studied in York between 1819 and 1823 and who also helped out in the school.

The training of men for holy orders was a key concern for Strachan. He believed that there was a need to educate Canadians for the priesthood because he thought that a British education did not prepare candidates for the colonial environment and that old-country clerics might have difficulty adjusting to life in Upper Canada. He also doubted that men of real ability would want to leave the United Kingdom. A locally trained clergy, in comparison, would be more useful to their parishioners and more happy personally. In 1816, for example, there were four men studying under Strachan in York. Beginning in 1826, some of his students were ordained at St James' by Bishop Stewart.[75]

In a letter to one curate in 1833, Strachan outlined what he expected him to do, stating that he should assist 'in my stead as Garrison Chaplain in which capacity you visit the Military Hospital

1.10 Sketch of King Street, York, c. 1820, by James Cockburn. This is the only
contemporary picture of the first church (in the rear) as enlarged in 1818.

twice a week[,] baptise & marry & bury &c & perform divine service once every Sunday when
the troops do not come to Church at the regular Parish service.' The curate also was required to
take up to half the Sunday duties, assist in the Sunday school, and share the general parish work
and administrative responsibilities.[76] When he could, Strachan delegated most baptisms,
marriages, and burials to his assistants, reserving only those of the town's prominent people for
his own attention. One reason why he gave the curates these tasks was to augment their incomes
by allowing them to keep the customary fees.[77]

   A more or less continuous stream of ordained assistants began to appear in 1826 with the
arrival of Joseph Hudson and Thomas Phillips. While the historical record is somewhat unclear
about Strachan's other associates at this time, the signatures of the officiating priests in the

1.11 Cup made by William Stennett, a York silversmith, and presented to
the Revd Joseph Hudson, chaplain to the garrison and assistant minister at York, by
the congregation of St James' in 1833; now belonging to St James' Cathedral.

parish registers provide a rough chronology: Thomas Phillips from July 1826 to January 1833, William Boulton from September to November 1833, George Gwynne in February and March 1834, followed by Henry James Grasett, whose forty-seven-year tenure at St James' began in December 1835. Visiting clergy also helped out on an occasional basis. Joseph Hudson was a Cambridge graduate who took up duties as the garrison chaplain in 1826 and remained in the capital until 1833, when he accepted a chaplaincy in Quebec after the army decided to save money by reducing the post in York and transferring responsibility for the chaplaincy back to St James' (see Figure 1.11). During his time in York, Hudson and his wife were active in the life of the parish. Thomas Phillips, a widower, married Hannah Jarvis in 1828. William Boulton was the youngest son of Judge D'Arcy Boulton, but his short career ended when he died in 1834, leaving behind a widow and four young children. George Gwynne, an Irishman and son of a priest, lasted only a very short time because of homesickness. Strachan thought him an intelligent man and excellent scholar but, like most Irish priests, too evangelical. The most famous of the group was Henry James Grasett, the shy, low-church son of a military surgeon, who in 1837 married Sarah Stewart, daughter of the president of the executive council, and was destined both to follow Strachan as rector and to become the first dean of Toronto in 1867. Grasett found favour with the many Irish Anglicans in the city who did not appreciate the high-church tendencies of most of Strachan's English and Canadian clergymen.[78]

1.12 Upper Canada College, on King Street West; lithograph by Thomas Young, 1835. The clerical masters doubled as assistants at St James', and the 'westenders' of the congregation worshipped there after fire destroyed the second church in 1839.

The opening of Upper Canada College at the present corner of King and Simcoe streets (Figure 1.12) in 1829 was an important event for St James' because four new priests arrived in York to join the college faculty. These men regularly participated in the church's work. One was a Canadian, William Boulton; the others were English, Charles Dade, Dr Joseph Harris, and Charles Matthews. Two later college instructors – W.H. Ripley and Henry Scadding – would also serve at St James' (Figure 1.13). Thus the congregation of St James' and its outlying stations, week after week, heard sermons from a collection of the capital's most educated people. Most of these sermons were long and relatively sophisticated. While tending to skirt serious theological controversy, they regularly affirmed Anglican doctrines. More commonly, preachers explored issues of morality in general terms, either avoiding immediate local controversies or mentioning them only obliquely. They affirmed ideals of family life, goodness, and loyalty. The nature of God's creation and an individual's response to it were other favoured topics. Unlike Methodists and other dissenters, Anglican preachers tended to see an individual's spiritual growth in non-dramatic and rational terms, something centred in the mind rather than in the heart.

Besides preaching, the clergy at St James' offered frequent lectures, such as a series in 1816 in which Strachan expounded on the Creed, or another on the life of Christ delivered during Lent 1836, or one in Lent 1837 on the early history of the church.[79] One Presbyterian minister, feeling outnumbered, described the impact of Strachan and his assistants when he wrote in 1830 that York 'contains an episcopal church with several learned Doctors from Oxford to preach in it, who have been long striving by every honest means to prop up their cause, and as the Governor & dependants are generally Episcopalians that creed has become fashionable even among certain wealthy [Presbyterian] Scotchmen who have been overcome by Dr. Strachan's golden arguments.'[80]

1.13 Revd W.H. Ripley (l.) and Revd Henry Scadding (centre) in 1847, when they were classical masters at Upper Canada College, from a lithograph by T.H. Stevenson. Both also served as assistant clergy at St James'.

As from time immemorial, the clergy's primary activities were leading worship, preaching the gospel, and officiating at the two great sacraments as well as at weddings, churchings, and burials.[81] They also performed the age-old tasks of catechizing the young, supporting good works, and providing pastoral care. The main Sunday service took place at eleven o'clock and consisted of a marathon of Mattins, Litany, and Ante-communion, topped off by a sermon. Not everyone was able to pay attention through these long services; on one occasion, a parishioner observed that 'George Jarvis sat in Miss Crombie's pew playing the fool with her all the service.'[82] This routine was enlivened by the celebration of the Eucharist, at first only four times a year, but then with greater frequency as the impact of Tractarianism began to be felt in Toronto. After the morning worship, the clergy conducted more services in the jail and hospital, plus Evensong at three o'clock and a service in the plain environment of the school at seven o'clock for those who could not find space within the church itself. When parliament was in session, Anglican priests read prayers for the legislators' benefit every day. Some sense of the scale of effort comes from statistics printed in 1836, which noted that during that one year the clergy at St James' had performed 223 baptisms, solemnized ninety-eight marriages, and officiated at 142 funerals. The same list also noted that, in an age when many people did not choose to participate in the Eucharist, 350 people were communicants.[83]

With the great influx of British immigrants after 1815, the Church of England gradually grew into the largest denomination in the province, comprising twenty-two per cent of the population in 1841. This was a far cry from its status in the 1790s when it probably embraced less than ten per cent, but even with this growth it could hardly be considered dominant and could not reasonably claim demographic legitimacy for its aspirations to be the state church.[84] In Toronto, Anglicans formed a larger segment of the population than in the province as a whole: in 1841 the capital's 14,248 inhabitants included 6,754 Anglicans.[85]

A study of St James' surviving parish registers shows that people from every level of society called on the Church of England when they wanted to marry, have their children baptized, or bury their dead. In 1808, for example, George Stuart officiated at nineteen weddings. One was solemnized between Sarah Ann Robinson and D'Arcy Boulton, Jr, from the town's élite; but most of those who married that year were humble people, many signing their names with an X. Two decades later, the register shows a similar balance between the prominent and the obscure, the literate and the illiterate. In 1808, Stuart baptized thirty people – most notably, the son of James Givins of the Indian Department and his wife, Angélique, but the register also included the six children of Peter and Sarah Long, whom Stuart described as 'Africans,' as well as other people of modest station. From 1826 on, the clergy associated with St James' kept a separate register for the garrison chaplaincy. Between that year and 1838, they baptized about 190 individuals, mostly the children of the rank and file, and buried 106, the vast majority being common soldiers, their wives, and their offspring.

A survey of the 161 burials conducted from St James' itself in 1838, outside the garrison chaplaincy, confirms the picture created by the baptismal and marriage records. Several well-known families lost loved ones that year, including the Boultons, Powells, Ridouts, and Robinsons; but the bulk of people buried by the clergy were obscure, the most humble being 'a man unknown.' Some people's ranks or occupations were listed. They consisted of the retired chief justice of Bermuda; the retired secretary of the province; two 'ladies'; two 'gentlemen'; one serving and one retired army officer; three merchants; an apothecary; five farmers; one each of a millwright, tailor, shoemaker, butcher, gardener, and teamster; nine labourers; and nine lower-rank militiamen serving on a full-time basis because of the Rebellion crisis. The youngest person was Maria Thompson, whose little life lasted a mere seven days; the oldest was William Carruthers, who passed away at a majestic ninety-five years. Of those whose ages are known, twenty-nine were infants, forty-three children, nine teenagers, sixty-three adults, and nine what we would call seniors.[86]

While people from all levels of society called on the Church of England, social distinctions showed up in church attendance on Sundays. The congregation for eleven-o'clock worship included people from all levels of society, ranging from the lieutenant-governor to the rank and file of the garrison, but was heavily weighted in favour of the leading citizens, who owned most of the ground-floor pews, while humbler folk dominated the evening service in the school. Given the high degree of transiency in Upper Canada, we can assume that the evening worshippers had a more casual affiliation with the church than the morning group.

An 1822 list of pewholders for the ninety-eight pews is dominated by prominent court and government officials, with merchants and professionals owning most of the rest. One pew was set aside for the governor's servants, another for members of the legislative assembly, and a third for the legislative council, while sixteen pews were empty, presumably providing free seating in addition to the benches used by the garrison. Four women owned pews.

A record also survives of the pewholders in the new 1833 church; it lists about 280 pews, divided in a more complex manner than in the 1822 inventory, as befitted the growing diversity of the congregation. Government and commercial élites continued to dominate. In political terms, Tories outnumbered Reformers, although both could be found confessing their sins at St James'. Some prominent people owned both ground-floor and gallery pews, the latter presumably intended mainly for their servants. Most of the free or institutional seating was in the gallery. Of the designated pews, 130 were owned by individuals and thirty-six were leased to individuals; there were twenty-six for strangers, scholars, and others, twenty-two for the garrison, twenty vacant (and presumably open to visitors), fourteen as free seats, six pews for the bishop and clergy (other than Strachan), six for the choir (in the gallery in front of the organ loft), six for Upper Canada College, four for the lieutenant-governor and Government House, three for the legislative assembly, and one for the legislative council. Benches stood along the back walls of the galleries to accommodate the poor and Sunday-school children. Visitors appeared in the pews from time to time through their memberships in institutional and voluntary associations. For example, in July 1823, between three and four hundred Orangemen paraded to the church to hear 'an excellent sermon from the Hon. and Rev'd Dr. STRACHAN,' followed by a celebratory banquet.[87]

The religious education of the parishioners' children was never ignored, except during part of the War of 1812. In 1815 Strachan resumed catechizing. He described his methods: 'I make a few familiar remarks upon the questions in their order [from the Prayer Book Catechism] or sometimes select one for the day when it may call up observations more calculated from recent circumstances or events to make an impression.' With the construction of the Upper Canada Central School and the enlargement of the church in 1818, Strachan embarked on a more ambitious Sunday-school program. His pupils met for an hour before Sunday-morning worship and for another hour in the afternoon. The first hour began with a prayer and was followed by instruction and, if time allowed, a short exhortation before the children walked to church. In the afternoon, activities included reading of a New Testament lesson followed by memory work and instruction on scripture. In 1820, thirty girls and fifty boys attended the Sunday school in York and another served the people of the mission in York Mills. In town, the girls were instructed by three young women from the Powell family, under the patronage of the devout lieutenant-governor and his wife, Sir Peregrine and Lady Sarah Maitland.[88]

Charity in York was limited in this period. In addition to the church's concern to use philanthropy to support the established order, another basic assumption was that it should be available only to the deserving poor – that is, respectable persons who were willing to work if they could. Drunkards, in contrast, might be left to die in the gutter. Another assumption, typical of the period, was that charity must not be so liberal as to draw poor people to the capital from less generous communities. In 1817 the Society for the Relief of Strangers in Distress was inaugurated in the capital to provide more systematic care than had been available before, seeded with £212 from the Loyal and Patriotic Society's surplus. For many years it remained the primary agency of assistance in York. During one month in 1822 the Anglican-dominated Society for Relief of the Sick and Destitute at York cared for twenty-two 'cases' of one or more people, consisting mainly of the sick, the old, and the infirm who were unable to work, as well as one woman whose husband recently had died, leaving her and her child destitute. Another Anglican-dominated charitable enterprise, reflecting the interests of the period, was the Female Society for the Relief of Poor Women in Childbirth, founded in 1820 by Lady Sarah Maitland, Ann Strachan, and other prominent women. Ongoing fund-raising efforts by the people of St James' included such ventures as bazaars; one organized by Lady Elizabeth Colborne about 1830 used the proceeds to purchase blankets for the poor.[89]

In the wake of the cholera epidemics of 1832 and 1834, the people of St James' contributed about £1,176 of a total subscription of £1,263 for the Society for the Relief of the Widows and Orphan Children at York, founded by John Strachan. The amount raised rivalled the combined expenditures of the provincial and municipal governments in Toronto during the epidemics. Cholera killed four hundred in the town in 1832 and over five hundred in 1834; many were recent immigrants. The society's primary way of relieving distress was through binding out orphans as servants or apprentices.[90] 'In this manner,' Strachan hoped, 'much of the bitterness of this sad dispensation would be removed by Christian love.' While we might question Strachan's optimism, it is difficult to imagine what practical alternative the society could have pursued.[91] During the epidemics, Strachan had worked tirelessly. Without regard to his own health, he visited the sick in their homes, in hospital, and in jail, buried the dead, and conducted special church parades in the garrison because the troops were not allowed to go to town during the crisis. While toiling to improve the victims' lot, he also preached that the epidemic was a form of divine punishment and called on people to repent their sins and reform.[92]

Beyond these group enterprises, individual Anglicans shared their wealth with less fortunate people throughout the Georgian period, as in 1812, when Strachan wrote to one individual, soliciting his private patronage to help educate a young man for holy orders, noting in passing that he himself assisted the man and supported two orphans. York's Anglicans also financed mission activities, just as they themselves were sustained in part by the Society for the Propagation of the Gospel and other outsiders. In 1816 Strachan founded a Bible and Prayer Book Society centred in York, the first of several such organizations, Canadian and British, that the parishioners promoted during the Georgian era.[93] Another endeavour that Strachan undertook to advance the cause of Anglicanism was the establishment of a religious journal in York, the *Christian Recorder*, which appeared monthly between 1819 and 1821. He told Bishop Mountain that his objective in founding it was to 'gradually lead my readers in favour of the Church [of England] taking care to insert nothing particularly offensive to Dissenters' because 'the whole of the population not of our Church is ready to join against us.'[94] The parishioners of St James' supported various other efforts to expand and confirm the faith over the years, such as donating money to an organization that must have had one of the most patronizing names in Canadian history: the Society for Converting and Civilizing the Indians and Propagating the Gospel among Destitute Settlers of Upper Canada.[95]

The church's pastoral work in Georgian Canada remains something of a mystery, since most of it was necessarily confidential. However, we do have some glimpses of what happened. Strachan, for example, seems to have done most of his pastoral visiting in the morning to discuss people's problems with them privately. Another activity of the clergy was representing the cases of individuals when the demands of justice had been ignored. In 1822, for instance, a man was found guilty of stealing some wood planes in an effort to force his employer to pay his back wages. The court sentenced the thief to a public whipping in the market-place. In desperation, he turned to Strachan, who got the sentence remitted. Another time, the son of a parishioner ran away from school because he was about to be flogged for some offence. His mother was upset and asked Strachan to intervene. He interviewed the boy and then wrote to the school's headmaster, asking him to discipline the child orally and refrain from corporal punishment.[96]

On another occasion, Strachan wrote to a young man who was leaving home to continue his studies. He told him to write to his mother often, 'never do anything that you are convinced your excellent Father would have disapproved,' and to study French, dancing, and horse-manship.[97] He consoled one recently widowed woman with affirming words: 'In all your afflixions you have displayed a fortitude which could only be inspired by our holy religion [and] it is the contemplation of a future state where we shall meet again those we have lost that can support us under such afflicting calamities as yours.' He continued, 'The present world on such occasions ceases to interest us and we think it were better for us to die but when the feelings of nature have subsided and the agonies of a broken heart have almost annihilated the Soul[,] religion steps forward to raise our hopes and to present before us a happier place of existence where those we loved and mourned are waiting our arrival.' Continuing further – and perhaps pushing matters a bit – he wrote, 'Such reflexions bring us back to ourselves[,] they teach us resignation, and while they inspire us with a strong desire to join our departed Friends they render us anxious to render ourselves worthy. It is then that we perceive the intimate connexion between the present & future, how much it behooves us to attend to our duties here in order to insure our happiness hereafter ... We discover that we have still some duties to discharge[,] some labours of love that must be finished before we go hence.'[98]

Another time, Strachan tried to restore harmony between a mother and daughter in one prominent family by threatening to deny them Holy Communion if they did not make peace with each other, while at the same time he advised other members of the family and their connections to behave honourably and decently during a series of scandals that plagued the family.[99]

One known scandal provides a small amount of information about the church's pastoral care for people in distress. George Herchmer Markland was a prominent St James' parishioner, the son of a prominent Kingston merchant, and a protégé of Strachan's, having attended his school in Cornwall. He had once contemplated taking holy orders, served on the legislative and executive councils, held high office in the provincial government, and became secretary-receiver of the Upper Canada Clergy Corporation and registrar of King's College. In 1838 rumours began to circulate that he was a practising homosexual. The lieutenant-governor, Sir George Arthur, deputed several executive councillors who were also Markland's fellow parishioners to investigate the charge: William Allan, Augustus Warren Baldwin, William Henry Draper, John Elmsley, and Robert Baldwin Sullivan. Markland, presumably counselled by Strachan, tried to get the governor to let the archdeacon alone look into the matter. The governor demurred, and, largely through circumstantial evidence, Markland was accused of having sexual liaisons with several young men. What aggravated the charge was that he was supposed to have crossed class barriers, and abdicated his responsibility to his inferiors, by bestowing his favours upon common soldiers from the garrison. In the end, the inquiry was quietly dropped in return for Markland's agreement to retire to Kingston, where he lived out the rest of his life out of the public eye, and somehow, knowledge of the scandal did not get out. One wonders what role Strachan may have played in ministering to and advising Markland, caring for his wife, and lobbying the investigative committee. What we do see in the circumspection surrounding this incident is consistent with what we know about the archdeacon: he tried hard to mitigate the effects of private scandal and in his sermons addressed questions of morality in general rather than specific terms within an intellectual framework

1.14 View of King Street, Toronto, in 1835, from a watercolour by John Howard, showing the second St James' Church on the far right. Running forward from the church are the court house, the firehall, and the town jail. Both the uniform Georgian style and the juxtaposition of these public buildings typify and illustrate Strachan's ideal of unity of church and state. For plans see Figures 5.6, 5.7, and 5.8.

that accepted the limitations of personal human frailty. Politically, the timing of the Markland affair was particularly dangerous, coming as it did during the height of the Rebellion crisis when the legitimacy of the established order had come under violent attack. It would be wrong, however, to assume that Strachan's motives for handling it the way he chose to do were purely political.[100]

REFLECTION

The Toronto of 1838 bore almost no resemblance to the York of 1793. Instead of a military camp in the middle of a howling wilderness, it now was the province's premier city, the seat of government, and a significant commercial centre located within a large and expanding agricultural hinterland, although, as the Types Riot and Rebellion showed, it still was very much a raw colonial town. The church, too, had changed dramatically, from a fragile arm of the state, as represented by Lieutenant Smith's outdoor service, to a well established ecclesiastical body serving a large and diverse congregation through the ministry of well educated and dedicated clergy working out of several church buildings, the grandest of all being the fine stone structure at King and Church streets (see Figure 1.14).

The Church of England, however, never could have progressed as far as it did without government patronage. Yet this very support, this attempt to plant a church establishment in a colony where it could claim the support of only a minority of the populace, doomed the church to failure and a certain isolation. Perhaps it also provoked a poorer judgement from history than is warranted, given how well the church succeeded in meeting its core Christian responsibilities.

For the most part, history has remembered the Erastian crusade and judged the Church of England in Upper Canada harshly. Forgotten or subsumed in that judgement was the work of the church in preaching the gospel, administering the sacraments, and assisting those in need. Admittedly, the church fulfilled these functions within the limitations imposed by the flawed (or fallen) human nature of its agents; but it did its job, and did it with considerable energy and devotion in a diverse, complex, and rapidly changing society, in which both the institution and its people almost constantly faced some ravaging crisis, whether it was revolution, counter-revolution, threatened invasion, war, pestilence, or insurrection.

2

The Making of
an Evangelical Cathedral,
1839–1883

ALAN HAYES

IN 1839 ST JAMES' CHURCH stood as the very symbol of the Anglican establishment in Upper Canada. It was situated in the heart of Toronto, the capital city, then a colonial outpost of about thirteen thousand souls (Figure 2.1). It was the spiritual headquarters of the Family Compact, the little, intermarried group of high government officials, judges, and wealthy landowners who ruled the province. The church was securely under the control of its minister, John Strachan, who Sunday by Sunday from his pulpit exhorted his important flock to do their Christian duty, to value apostolic church order, to promote true religion as found most purely in the Church of England, and to maintain their commitment to what was in effect the Tory vision for society.

Forty years later, how thoroughly the character of St James' had changed! In 1879 it had become the spiritual home of the families of successful professionals and businesspeople in a thriving commercial metropolis of 100,000, the second city of a young nation. The Family Compact was no more, and Strachan's vision of Anglican social hegemony was a quaint memory from the distant past. The church was in the firm control of its leading laypeople, who were as a group not high-church Tories but Anglican evangelicals. Their rector was an evangelical of the old school; their assistant minister, who took the pulpit most Sundays, was an internationally known evangelistic preacher of the new type; and the evangelical seminary that would soon be called Wycliffe College had recently been launched in the parish schoolhouse.

This extraordinary transformation mirrored some sweeping changes in Upper Canadian society and some equally dramatic changes in Anglican thought and church order.

PARISH LEADERS IN THE NEW ERA

Three events mark the year 1839 as the beginning of a new era in the history of St James' Church. First, in January Britain's Colonial Office, having for some years endured the importunities of John Strachan and his supporters, finally announced that it would carve a new Anglican diocese for Upper Canada out of the huge diocese of Quebec and that Strachan would

2.1 King Street 1844–5 from a painting by James Gillespie. The spire of the first cathedral appears above the trees of the grounds on the north side.

be its first bishop (see Figure 2.2). As the bishop's church, St James' began to be called, 'by courtesy' though not by any formal act, the cathedral.[1] And so St James' became the most prominent church of the new diocese. Second, on 6 January a fire destroyed part of the church building. Somehow, somewhere in the edifice, a fire had begun; it had climbed up through a hollow column, spilled out onto the roof, and then swamped the building. Arson was not to blame; fires were common in a city with cold winters, hot furnaces, and wooden buildings. Strachan stood in the crowd watching – whistling, it was said, to relieve his sorrow. Third, Lord Durham's famous report on Canada appeared a few weeks after the fire. It advocated a constitutional overhaul that would uproot the Family Compact and put an end to Anglican privilege. Strachan was flabbergasted. And things got worse. In November a new governor arrived, determined to begin implementing Durham's reforms. Just as surely as fire had gutted the physical structures of St James' Church, so Lord Durham, his successor, Lord Sydenham, and their supporters began to gut its ideological structures.

On 4 August, while the new governor was making ready for his posting in Toronto, Strachan was in Lambeth Palace, the London residence of the archbishop of Canterbury, being consecrated bishop of the new diocese of Toronto. It was a moment of personal triumph. For years he had keenly wanted to be made bishop. Had he begun longing for it in 1817? That was when he began to build his mansion on what is now Wellington Street between York and Simcoe streets (Figure 1.7, p. 17); and his neighbour, seeing the grand red-brick Neoclassical building, the largest home in the province, with its sweeping view of the bay, its high wall around the estate, and the lodgehouse at the entrance to the grounds, said that it was a 'palace being built in anticipation of a mitre.' And in 1837, when the bishopric of Quebec fell vacant, Strachan felt bitterly disappointed to be passed over. But now he had beaten the odds; it was almost against

2.2 Rt Revd John Strachan at the time of his consecration as first bishop of Toronto
in 1839, from a portrait belonging to St James' Cathedral.

nature for a Scot of humble family origins to win a post usually reserved for English gentlemen, and at sixty-one years, his age had been against him too.

The good news was that he would finally be bishop. The bad news was that no one would pay his salary. Strachan conceded that neither the British government nor the Society for the Propagation of the Gospel (SPG – the English mission society) could be expected to commit itself to a bishop's salary until the current swirl of controversies around the church's share in the clergy reserve lands had subsided. So, until a permanent episcopal stipend could be arranged, the new bishop would have to continue as the rector of St James' as well. His annual remuneration, as he outlined it in 1840,[2] included £277 in rents from glebe land, £40 in 'surplice fees' (charges for marriages, funerals, and the like), £100 from the government for serving as chaplain to the garrison, £233 15s salary from the SPG as minister of St James', and £300 as archdeacon of York. His income had in recent years been greater: by losing appointments on the executive council, on the General Board of Education, and at King's College, he had given up £650 a year. Out of his income he paid the assistant minister at St James' £180. And to become bishop, he had to pay £250 for having the letters patent made out.

Those who see Strachan as a high churchman of the old school throughout his life, rather than as a high churchman who turned Anglo-Catholic in the wake of the Oxford Movement of the 1830s, would seem to have the stronger case. 'My opinions were settled long before the movements which have been for some years disturbing the Church had any existence,' he declared.[3] He knew the recent Oxford writers and could agree with much of what they had to say: yes, bishops were successors of the apostles; baptism effected the new birth; and salvation could not be found outside the church. But, unlike the archetypal Anglo-Catholic, he saw the Reformation as a triumph, not a problem, declined to place tradition with scripture as a theological authority, did not stake his theology on a theory of the development of doctrine, displayed little nostalgia for the Middle Ages, and reflected little of the poetic, even mystical bent of a Keble or a Newman.

Rolling through the five microfilm reels of his sermons in the Archives of Ontario, a modern reader senses that the gospel for Strachan had a great deal to do with the authority of the church, civil obedience, episcopacy, and moral duty. He had much less to say about God's grace abounding or about joy in the gospel. 'Whatever measure of grace we may think that we have already attained,' he explained a little discouragingly but typically to the people of St James' in 1841, 'we can only become the true Friends of our blessed Master by the strength of our Faith and the continuance of our obedience.'[4] Never far in the background was his conviction that Roman Catholicism was corrupted by its superstition, and dissenting (non-Anglican) Protestantism, by its reckless indulgence of private judgement. To confirm the right, Strachan was ready for both public controversy and backroom politics, and he took equal pleasure in both. 'I have the reputation of being fearless and decided,' he wrote the bishop of Nova Scotia, 'and whether correct or not, it saves me much trouble.'[5] *Caveo sed non timeo* was his personal motto: 'prudent but fearless,' he translated it.[6] But 'prudent' is perhaps not the right word for one whose outbursts were so frequently counterproductive.

As bishop, Strachan was so busy with the affairs of his huge diocese, and with provincial politics, that he left his parish work to the assistant minister, Henry James Grasett (Figure 2.3).[7] Grasett had arrived at St James' in May 1835 and would continue ministering there until his death almost forty-seven years later. He had been born in 1808 in Gibraltar, where his father, a surgeon, had been stationed as deputy inspector of British army hospitals. When his father was posted to Montreal in 1813 and Quebec City in 1814, the family moved with him. After the war young Grasett was sent to England for his early education, and he returned to the Royal Grammar School in Quebec City for further studies. He then won an SPG scholarship to study theology under Bishop Charles Stewart of Quebec, who, though not committed to any church party, was influenced most by evangelicals. Afterward he attended St John's College, Cambridge, from 1830 to 1834, receiving his BA. As a student there he was a devotee of Charles Simeon, the greatest of the Anglican evangelicals, at Holy Trinity Church. Returning to Quebec City, Grasett was ordained deacon in 1834 and priest in 1835 and served briefly as curate of the cathedral until Strachan invited him to St James', Toronto, as assistant minister. A parsonage (perhaps it was originally a hotel) stood on the church property (Figure 5.26, p. 211), and Grasett moved in and lived there until he died. In 1837 he married Sarah Maria Stewart, daughter of the Hon. John Stewart of Quebec, the president of the executive council of Lower Canada. He and his wife had eight children.

Grasett was a quiet intellectual with firm ideas. He loved to read theology; he was to receive the MA (1842), BD (1853), and DD (1877) degrees from Cambridge. He preached measured sermons noted for their cogent argument, beautiful expression, and solid theology, and he delivered them with scholar-like diction. Unfortunately, although he must have preached over two thousand sermons in his lifetime, they have not survived; and since he shunned literary theological polemic, we can no longer reconstruct what he had to say about grace and sin

2.3 Revd Henry James Grasett c. 1855. He served as Strachan's curate and then as his priest-vicar
before succeeding him as rector in 1847. In 1867 Strachan made him dean of Toronto.

and new life and ministry and prayer and sacrament. He served for some years as president of
the Upper Canada Religious Tract Society and the Bible Society, ecumenical groups that
high-church Anglicans shunned. His great love was education. For over thirty years he chaired
the Home District Board of Education, and he served on the Council of Public Instruction, the
predecessor of the provincial department of education. In his ministry at St James' what interested him most intensely was the Sunday school.[8] One of his few publications is a compilation
of about three dozen familiar hymns for use in Sunday schools, which he edited in 1876: some
entries are still familiar, such as 'Hark the Herald Angels Sing,' 'Just as I am,' 'What a Friend
we have in Jesus,' 'God Save the Queen,' and 'God moves in a mysterious way his wonders to
perform; / He plants his footsteps in the sea and rides upon the storm.'[9]

    Grasett appears to be in many respects Strachan's opposite. If Strachan was high-church,
Grasett was evangelical. If Strachan liked to be blunt, Grasett tried to be discreet. If Strachan
loved being a public figure, Grasett was retiring and, when he was required to speak extempo-
raneously, almost inarticulate. But perhaps Grasett was not so much Strachan's opposite as his
alter ego. They were bound together throughout their years by the bands of genuine love and
mutual respect. They shared a love for the Lord and a love for the Church of England, and
qualities such as principle, loyalty, and a pastoral concern for the people of God. The gruff
Dr Strachan did have a warm side, which friends such as Grasett knew. When the Grasetts'

three-year-old son died in early 1842, Strachan wrote him, 'The soul of infant innocence finds its way to the presence of the Saviour – who still delights to throw his arms of love around them. – You may rest assured that next to your own Family you have not more devoted Friends than Mrs. Strachan and your affectionate John Toronto.'[10] Grasett was Strachan's examining and domestic chaplain as well as his secretary and in effect his executive assistant. The Grasetts named one of their sons John Strachan Grasett; baby John's godparents at baptism included John and Ann Strachan. But the boy died in 1843 at the age of twenty-one months.

A remarkable indication of the relationship between Strachan and Grasett – their difference in temperament, their mutual affection, their unequal stations in the Anglican pecking order – is afforded by a letter of 1845.[11] Strachan had decided to require the cathedral clergy to preach in surplices instead of preaching gowns. Evangelicals maintained that preaching was a different office from ministering the liturgy and reflected a different authority and that for centuries the academic gown had been honoured ecumenically by both Anglicans and European Protestants as the badge of that office. Recently ritualists had decided to subsume preaching into the liturgy and were insisting that it should therefore be done in liturgical attire. Strachan simply thought that it looked clumsy and distracting when the priest took off the surplice and put on the robe before preaching, and took off the gown and put on the surplice afterward. Grasett remonstrated. Strachan replied:

My Dear Grasett,
    I have placed in you since we first met the most unbounded confidence and desired to treat you more like a Son than as one merely connected with me in affairs and we have hitherto proceeded in the greatest harmony; let me therefore implore you to reconsider the request you have made to me and withdraw it. The question is in itself nothing but if made one of conscience which in my opinion you are not justified in doing you will make it impossible to deal with it. Recollect that as my Assistant in the Parish, my examining Chaplain and Confidential adviser in the affairs of the Diocese I have a right to look for and to receive your cordial co-operation for where shall I look for respect if not to those who are as it were my own Household whose duty it is to afford it.

As Strachan and Grasett led St James' into the turbulent 1840s, their parishioners included a striking number of the province's political and social leaders, but the arch-Tories were at the centre of gravity. Most eminent among them was John Beverley Robinson, who turned forty-eight in 1839, the first year of our period. He was chief justice of the Court of Queen's Bench and perhaps the single most influential person in the province. From 1803, when the twelve-year-old Robinson had been tutored by Strachan at Cornwall, the two were intimately connected. One of Robinson's daughters married Strachan's son. Christopher Hagerman, forty-seven, a large, opinionated, belligerent man, and another former pupil of Strachan's, was the attorney-general. William Allan, sixty-nine, had retired as president of the Bank of Upper Canada, the financial instrument of the Family Compact, which the Reformer Robert Baldwin would call a 'dangerous engine of political oppression.' Allan's son married another of Robinson's daughters.

The Boultons and Jarvises were prominent in the Family Compact. Henry John Boulton, forty-nine, a lawyer, had just returned from Newfoundland, where he had been chief justice; his brother D'Arcy Boulton, Jr, fifty-four, another lawyer, built the Grange (now the Art Gallery of Ontario); and the latter's son William Henry, twenty-seven, was Robinson's nephew, a lawyer, and a city alderman. William B. Jarvis, forty, another former pupil of Strachan's, was sheriff of the Home District (York, Peel, and Ontario counties), or, in other words, the law-enforcer of the Family Compact. His cousin Samuel P. Jarvis, forty-seven, had in 1826 led the mob ransacking William Lyon Mackenzie's print shop. He was in charge of the province's Indian affairs but would be dismissed for mismanagement. He was in debt to the church for £198 for the purchase of pews.

Others as well belonged to the Family Compact. Robert Sympson Jameson, forty-three, vice-chancellor of the Court of Chancery, was a connoisseur of arts, of letters, and rather too much of drink. His wife, Anna, a feminist and author, had left him three years earlier; her *Winter Studies and Summer Rambles* of 1838 contains a memorable description of Toronto as 'a little ill-built town on low land, at the bottom of a frozen bay, with one very ugly church, without tower or steeple.' Henry Sherwood, thirty-two, another nephew of H.J. Boulton's, had been one of the vandals who destroyed Mackenzie's printing press in 1826. A lawyer and politician, he is described by a modern biographer as 'a man of intense egotism and ambition, ... affable but unloved.'[12] Young Clarke Gamble, thirty-one, would be a lawyer for the city for twenty-three years. His first wife, D'Arcy Boulton's daughter, had died two years earlier. Alexander Dixon, forty-seven, who had arrived too recently in Toronto (1830) to have a place in the Family Compact, already owned a thriving hardware and saddlery business, was a powerful city alderman for St Lawrence ward, and was active in the St Patrick's Society. The person who had owned the most pews of all at St James' – ten of them – no longer attended. John Elmsley, thirty-eight, Henry Sherwood's brother-in-law, gentleman farmer, member of the executive and legislative councils, bank director, and railway promoter, had become a Roman Catholic in 1833, provoking John Strachan to turn his pen to a stinging tract against popery.

Not all parishioners were high Tories. The Baldwin family, the leaders of the Reformers and earnest Irish Christians, also had their pews at St James'. William Warren Baldwin, sixty-four, a doctor, lawyer, politician, and Whig constitutionalist, is usually credited with developing the idea of 'responsible government' in Canada. This idea – that ministers of the government are politically responsible to a house of elected representatives – was instrumental in moving Canada and other British colonies into nationhood. His son Robert, thirty-five, another of Strachan's pupils, popularized responsible government and was one of the earliest theoreticians of Canadian biculturalism. He would serve as premier of the province twice in the 1840s. He was converted from scepticism to faith through reading the Bible with his wife.[13] William Hume Blake, thirty, a lawyer who had arrived in Canada seven years earlier, was also of Reform temper and would serve as solicitor-general in Baldwin's second government.

Situated politically between the arch-Tories and the Reformers were the more progressive Tories. One was Thomas Gibbs Ridout, forty-seven, cashier (general manager) of the Bank of Canada, who married into Robert Baldwin's family and whose eldest daughter wed one of H.J. Boulton's sons. His older brother George, forty-eight, a former pupil of Strachan's, was a lawyer. But the most notable of the progressive Conservatives was William Henry Draper, thirty-eight.[14] We see much more of him in this chapter. The son of an evangelical Church of England minister and scholar who wrote lectures on the Prayer Book, he ran away to sea at age fifteen, found his way to Upper Canada in 1820, and soon began studying law. He worked in Robinson's law office for a while and became a partner of Hagerman's. But, perhaps partly because his evangelical views distinguished him from the high-church Family Compact Tories, he was conciliatory towards non-Anglicans, which shocked his Conservative friends. He even became friendly with the Methodist leader Egerton Ryerson, Strachan's nemesis. By 1841 he was advocating responsible government in some form. Between 1844 and 1847, as government leader under an incapacitated governor, he would become virtually the first colonial prime minister. Later he would be appointed chief justice of the Court of Error and Appeal. He had a commanding presence, and his eloquence won him the nickname 'Sweet William.' He gave his protégé John A. Macdonald a vision for a new Conservative party, one that would embrace the idea of responsible government and seek to be moderate, inclusive, and popular.

We see a statistical snapshot of St James' in a table of information appended to a diocesan publication in 1844.[15] The total population of the parish is 24,100; the Anglican segment is estimated as 9,120. The cathedral will hold 2,000 people (at a stretch); average weekly attendance is 1,600; the average number of communicants is 250; and the greatest number of communicants at one celebration is 360. During the year there have been 243 baptisms, 101 marriages, and 157 funerals at the cathedral. There are seventeen other congregations in Toronto in addition to Anglican, including Presbyterians, 'white' and 'coloured' Methodists and Baptists, Roman Catholics, Congregationalists, Disciples, Millerites, Universalists, and Catholic Apostolicals.

STAFF AND FINANCE

The rector of St James' was not salaried or paid out of the church budget but received a good income from glebe lands and from the York rectory endowment – all grants from the government. The church's original land grant in 1820 of four acres north of King Street and east of Church Street was glebe, except for the part occupied by the church and churchyard, rectory, and stable. There were also two parcels granted in 1825 of about an acre each, one between King and Colborne at Toronto Street, and the other between Adelaide and Lombard west of Church Street (Figure 2.4). The rectory endowment was a huge grant of eight hundred acres of land in York Township, given in the final hours of Lieutenant-Governor Colborne's régime in 1836.[16] Ownership of these lands was deeded to the successive ministers of the parish, who were to receive all the rental income.[17] The validity of these land grants was not secure from legal challenge until 1857, and then in the 1870s, as we see below, the Anglican clergy of Toronto claimed a share in the income.[18]

St James' had a small staff of salaried workers.[19] One was the parish clerk, who in the early 1840s was receiving £50 a year. He assisted the clergy in robing, read the responses in church, attended at baptisms and funerals, kept records of burials, prepared the Lord's table when Communion was celebrated, and supervised the vestry room, including church plate, robes, and furniture. The beadle, who also received £50 a year, swept and dusted the interior, lit and extinguished fires, lamps, and candles, attended at the weekly distribution of alms, rang the bell for service on Sundays and holidays, tolled the bell at funerals, superintended the doorkeepers, and helped visitors find seats. The beadle also opened graves, earning a fee of ten shillings each time. On Sundays there were also five doorkeepers, paid one shilling each. The organist received £100 a year in the early 1840s. Her job included tuning the organ and finding a person to blow the bellows. All these salaries were adjusted downward in the course of the decade. A list of other expenses a few years later, in 1849, includes interest on a loan (£210, in

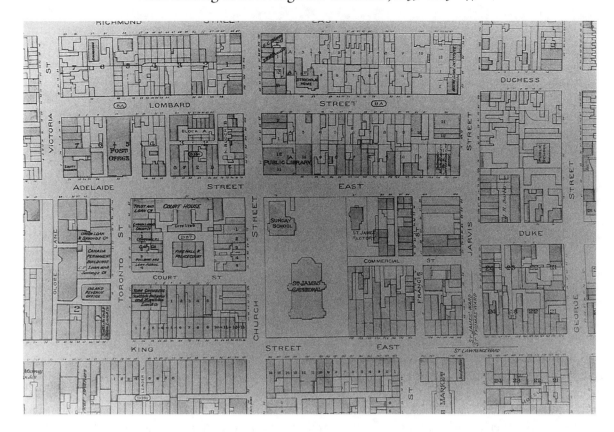

2.4 St James' Cathedral and its environs from Goad's Street Atlas (1884).
Besides the church precinct and the rectory grounds to the east, the church owned the lands
to the northwest, bounded by Lombard, Church, and Adelaide Streets and the lane
opposite the court house, and another tract south of King Street.

round numbers), commissions on collecting debts to the church (£25), insurance (£24), wood (£14), Christmas decorations (£3), cleaning snow (£1), and pew openers (£13). Total expenses for 1849 were £566 10 s 1 d.[20]

For most of our period St James' had only one source of operating income: pew sales and rentals. Weekly offerings were not taken until 1879, nor were appeals made to worshippers in the free pews. After the fire of 1839, Strachan observed ruefully, 'Great numbers who attended Church, for it was commonly full, contributed nothing towards its support.'[21] Pews came in three classes, depending on location: first-class pews cost £50, second-class £40, and third-class £25. The purchaser still had to pay rent to the church for the ground on which the pew stood. Ground rent on a first-class pew cost £3 a year. After the fire of 1839, it was estimated that, of 282 pews in the old church, 122 were sold, a few were let, eighty-four were reserved for the troops and for the poor, some were set aside for the organ, and about sixty could yet be sold. Some people bought pews in order to make a profit letting them. Inevitably disputes arose.

Sometimes people could not afford to pay their debts; and occasionally the churchwardens had to resort to persuasive tactics. In February 1844, for example, the wardens distributed circulars to those who were in arrears, threatening legal action.[22] The wardens might also remove the door of a pew whose rent had not been paid, to signify that the pew was not reserved. In 1853 a Mr Munro arrived in church to find the door of his pew taken off, apparently because he had not paid a pledge to the building fund. He sued. His lawyer said that the churchwardens had committed 'the most unwarrantable, oppressive, and insulting act that could be performed by any person pretending to be guided by any principles of propriety.' The wardens' lawyer said, 'If a man's religion consisted in having a door to his pew, it was of questionable character.' Munro on examination said that there had been a misunderstanding; he had pledged $100 but unaccountably the figure £100 had been entered in the pledge book.[23]

St James' also owned and managed a cemetery that was modestly profitable.[24] Its first cemetery was of course its churchyard, but this had become crowded, and parish leaders thought that a large cemetery outside the city would eventually pay for itself. In April 1844 the church bought sixty-five acres along the Don River from W.H. Boulton for a new cemetery. Only about fifteen acres proved usable, and the price of £1,000, plus several years' interest on a principal sum of £1,250, was advantageous to Boulton. The wardens had the property secured by a 'substantial board fence,' and in 1845, at their request, Bishop Strachan consecrated the land as a cemetery. But the first interment seems to have already taken place in July 1844. In 1847 an additional acre had to be bought as well. For the first five years this land was a liability. The expenses for the land and interest, surveying, fencing, erecting a house and sheds, paying a superintendent, receiving a vault, and so on, were about £2,743, while receipts totalled about £1,760. In later years, revenues outpaced expenses. Revenues included the sale of compost, sand, and wood, as well as more obvious fees. In 1857 the vestry would approve construction of a cemetery chapel (St James' the Less), and in 1863 a cemetery chaplain would be appointed to take services (the origins of St Peter's, Carlton Street). In 1872 another eleven acres was purchased for the cemetery.

In addition, St James' owned about fifteen acres of property in the area of present-day Parliament, Dundas, Sackville, and Queen streets; but in our period this land was hardly developed.[25] This land had been allocated in the original town surveys to a large park reserve. In 1831 the church received permission from the governor in council to buy several lots for the purpose of a burial ground, and in 1832 it completed the purchase from the trustees of the park reserve. But after St James' developed its cemetery on its alternative site up the Don River, it obtained permission in 1859 to use the land as its vestry might see fit. In 1871 the church had the acreage divided into building lots of an average size of 52 feet by 166 feet, plus the necessary streets and lanes. Some of this property was leased, though at very low rental. More time passed, and in 1886 ground leases were issued for periods of twenty-one years. The area was within walking distance of a factory district, and it attracted working-class tenants. The next two chapters recount how these 'Park Lots' became a slum and how St James' came to be accused of being a slum landlord (Figure 2.5).

CHANGES IN PARISH CULTURE

The institutional culture of St James' as our period begins was principally one of congregational passive dependence. Ministry was the work of the clergy; they were provided courtesy of the government and the Society for the Propagation of the Gospel (SPG). Pew revenues covered the reasonable necessities of heat, light, music, and cleaning. Outreach did not extend much beyond

A CHRISTMAS CAROL.
(AFTER DICKENS.)

The Dean stood deeply pondering.   " Please sir, would you spare a trifle to help the starv-
ing," said a poor weak voice.   All around were tumble-down dens of Satan.   And the good man
still stood pondering.   He might have been thinking of the long ago ; he might have been rumi-
nating on the chime of the Christmas bells.   Or perhaps he was thinking how good it would be
to devote some of the enormous income of the Rectorship of St. James to the moral and material
improvement of Lombard Street, the reproach of the city though the property of the Church.

2.5   Dean Grasett in Lombard Street; caricature by J.W. Bengough in *Grip*, 1882. By then
the church properties there had become one of the worst slums in Toronto.

regular almsgiving; the lay apostolate did not extend much beyond the churchwardens, who
administered property and received pew rents; mission did not go much further than correcting
the errors of papists and dissenters. Sermons offered a reassuring theological sanction for the
social vision of the ruling class; and Anglicans were comforted to be told that, wretched sinners
though they were, at least they were not Methodists. But by the end of the 1840s, several
circumstances had moved St James' definitively from its Family Compact, high-church past
towards its middle-class evangelical future.

First, the decline of arch-Toryism in Upper Canada in the 1840s ensured its decline at St
James' as well. In particular, the Durham Report of 1839, the blueprint for transforming Upper
Canada from colony to nation, also sounded the death-knell for Anglican privilege. Before he
read it, John Strachan and his friends felt confident that Toryism and Anglicanism were more
secure than ever in Upper Canada. The rebels of 1837 had been routed, and their reforming ideas

discredited by their extremism. Chief Justice Robinson had sentenced two rebels to death; Sheriff Jarvis had been required to carry out the sentence. A conservative reaction was in full bloom. As a bonus, the church was reaping the benefit of its newest endowment, the rectory lands. But Lord Durham, 'Radical Jack,' had found real problems in the province during his brief tenure as governor-general and had made them very public indeed. One of the biggest was the 'petty, corrupt, insolent Tory clique,' which meant Strachan and his friends. Another was the Anglican hold on public land, which meant the clergy reserves. Here was a cause of the rebellion, he thought, and an unceasing source of civil discontent.

During the summer and autumn of 1839, Upper Canadian reformers called together public meetings and demonstrations to rally popular support for Durham's recommendations. One of these 'Durham meetings' was organized in Richmond Hill on 15 October by one parishioner of St James', Dr W.W. Baldwin; it was put down by club-carrying Tories under the supervision of another parishioner of St James', Sheriff Jarvis. One person died in the 'Yonge Street Riots,' and the legislative assembly launched an inquiry. If the radicalism of a Mackenzie was discredited by its extremism, so was the arch-Toryism of a Sheriff Jarvis. Lord Sydenham, when he arrived as governor, turned away from the Family Compact and, in the new United Province of Canada, granted political preferments to younger, more moderate men. 'Church of Englandism became less fashionable' about 1840, an attorney-general reminisced in a letter of 1856.[26] Toronto's city council, however, remained fiercely Tory throughout the decade.

Two evangelical parishioners of St James' were particularly instrumental in dismantling the Family Compact edifice of Anglican privilege. Draper as early as 1839 wanted to distribute the clergy reserve land among all denominations, including the Roman Catholics; the very idea appalled Strachan and his Tory supporters. Equally shocking, a few years later he tried to secularize the Anglican King's College. He was thwarted by the wily Sherwood. But Robert Baldwin achieved the same end in 1849, using the endowment for King's College to create the non-denominational University of Toronto. Strachan sometimes thought that the Church of England's greatest enemies were inside the church.

Control of the land and control of education were linchpins of Anglican Toryism, and Strachan did not give them up without a fight. He protected the Anglican share of the clergy reserves as long as he could, and his response to the University of Toronto was to sail to England to raise money for a new Anglican university, Trinity College. Anglican evangelicals constituted a loyal opposition to the diocesan hierarchy, questioning the justice of its land claims and doubting the wisdom of a denominational university. For years afterward, the issues of landed endowment and Trinity College would pit St James' against the diocesan establishment.

While large political, legislative, financial, and cultural forces undermined the hold of the Family Compact over Canada West, more particular events and changes within the Anglican household accelerated its demise at St James'. For one thing, out of the ashes of the fire of 6 January 1839 grew a new Anglican congregation that emptied St James' of many of the stalwarts of the Family Compact and made room for a new class of Upper Canadian social leaders. Before the conflagration, Strachan had strenuously resisted founding a second Toronto church, for fear of 'dividing the congregation,' though he had envisioned chapels of ease on the west and east sides of the city. But after the fire there was now no building in the city that could hold everyone who had been accustomed to worship at St James'. He arranged for

2.6 The first St James' Cathedral, 1848; lithograph after Sir Sandford Fleming.

west-end Anglicans to worship in Upper Canada College (on King Street between Simcoe and John; see Figure 1.12, p. 30), and east-end Anglicans in the City Hall at the St Lawrence Market. He and Grasett alternated Sunday by Sunday between the two congregations. The west-enders liked the arrangement and wanted to make it permanent, and Strachan came to agree. They worshipped at a west-end 'station' until a church could be built. D'Arcy Boulton of the Grange offered a parcel of his land, and the new church building, St George the Martyr (a good British saint), was completed in November 1845. Many of the Boultons (though not H.J.), Robinson, Jameson, Sherwood, and others of the arch-Tory party gravitated to St George's, though some kept pews at St James' as well.[27]

The fire separated St James' from its past in another way: it compelled parishioners to take responsibility for their own church. Until recently, English mission societies had been endless-ly munificent, the Crown had brimmed over with largesse, and local authorities had blatantly favoured the Church of England. In recognizing that they now had to raise their own building funds, the leaders of St James' were putting behind them the Tory ideology of an established, favoured, publicly supported church. Strachan invited parishioners to a meeting on 9 January 1839 to discuss their responsibilities. They struck two committees – one for the building and one for finances. Significantly, it was W.H. Draper who chaired the Building Committee; the one who would do so much to decolonize Upper Canada was ready to move his parish church towards independence too. Meeting their own crisis, shouldering their rightful tasks, planning their own building (Figure 2.6), and raising their own funds gave lay leaders a sense of holding a stake in St James' and accustomed them to making decisions for it.

DECOLONIZING THE DIOCESE

In the wider diocese, too, the Anglican laity was learning to take more responsibility for the church, breaking out of a pattern of dependence on ecclesiastical authority. The people of St James' contributed to this development and were influenced by it as well. Strachan himself led his people in this direction. Though never mistaken for a populist, he was now sure that the financial health of the Church of England in Canada depended on the laity. The British Parliament had stopped giving grants to the colonial church in 1833; the SPG had announced its intention to reduce its benefactions; the church's interest in clergy reserve lands was being severely eroded; and legally enforced tithing was of course entirely out of the question. Strachan's mistake was to think that he could enlarge the laity's authority in temporal matters such as property and money while restricting it in spiritual matters such as doctrine, worship, theological education, and church discipline. The demarcation between the two spheres proved distressingly ambiguous.

While in England in 1839 for his consecration as bishop, Strachan had consulted with the archbishop of Canterbury and other authorities on how to set the temporal management of the church on a sound organizational basis with lay involvement. The Episcopal Church in the United States had set up synods of clergy and representative laypeople; but the Church of England in Canada was not independent of the British Crown and therefore needed enabling legislation from Westminster to take such a radical step. For at least the next fifteen years the problem dogged the bishop. Strachan first brought the laity into the constitutional government of the church through the Church Temporalities Act, which was passed by the provincial legis-lature in 1840 and proclaimed in 1841 (3 Victoria cap. 74). It gave the laity a clear legal role in 'the management of the temporalities of the United Church of England and Ireland' in Upper Canada. It made parish churchwardens a corporation with legal authority in temporal matters and provided for their accountability. It eliminated complications for laypeople who wanted to make gifts to the church. And it constituted parish vestries, which would include all pewholders and all those renting sittings. This provision enfranchised far more parishioners than the typical colonial 'select' or 'close' vestry, comprising a dozen members of the local élite.[28] It still excluded the poor, but it put middle-class gentlemen on a level with the scions of the Family Compact, made wardens accountable to most of the congregation, and even permitted those women who could own property (spinsters and widows) to participate. The first vestry of St James' met on Easter Monday 1842, inaugurated by a solemn public reading of the rather lengthy act. The historian has a particular reason for appreciating the new vestry system at the cathedral, for it opens a new window on the life of Victorian St James'.

Strachan's second step was the Church Society, which he announced when he held his first formal episcopal meeting with his clergy, or visitation, on 9 September 1841. In his charge to the clergy he recommended an Anglican organization to be managed by clergy and laypeople with the purpose of receiving contributions and allocating funds. It would have nothing to do with things spiritual, in which 'the Laity ought to have no voice.'[29] Such a body already existed in Nova Scotia and had proved its value. The new Church Society of the diocese of Toronto was duly organized at a public meeting the following April. Laypeople were to be involved in managing it, but always acting under the supervision of the bishop. Strachan promoted the new organization in a pastoral letter of 30 May 1842 and convened the first meeting on 7 June, 'after divine service in St James', a phrase revealing that cathedral parishioners were giving significant leadership to the new diocesan institution.[30] The following year the society was legally incorporated; it could now hold title to church property. One of its primary objectives, it seems, was to raise endowments for the bishop's salary and for the cathedral. It was also intended to evangelize Natives and settlers; circulate Bibles, prayer books, and other books and tracts; maintain churches and parish schools; pay clergy; support theological students; and assist retired clergy, widows, and orphans. Congregations were mandated to take up four offerings a year for its purposes and were even asked to consider taking up collections of money every Sunday, 'to lay up weekly a portion of our substance as an act of holy worship and a sacrifice of sweet savour unto God.'[31]

St James' Church was the real engine of the Church Society. In the first year, of total donations from across the diocese of about £1,836, almost £550 came from St James'.[32] Among the society's many vice-presidents figured several prominent pewholders at St James', including Allan, Robert Baldwin, H.J. Boulton, Dixon, Draper, and Sheriff Jarvis. The clerical members of the first Central Board included Grasett and the second assistant minister of St James', Henry Scadding (1813–1901), who was to win a reputation as a local historian, antiquarian, and writer. The first lay members included such St James' figures as Clarke Gamble and Alexander Dixon. In 1849, 142 members of the congregation also belonged to the Church Society.

In 1852 some unexpected and not entirely welcome legislation removed the government's authority to appoint Anglican rectors and gave the patronage (or right of appointment) to the Church Society. Strachan and his arch-Tory friends such as Robinson were highly annoyed; they wanted the bishop alone to enjoy the patronage, and they announced that the laity agreed. In fact, however, not all the laity did agree, and neither did all clergy. In particular, members of St James' displayed the spirit of dissent for which they would become increasingly notorious over the next several years. At a special meeting of the Church Society called to discuss the matter in November, one of the speakers was George Duggan, Jr, of St James', who, according to the official report, 'thought there was much feeling amongst the Laity, and a desire to have Lay influence introduced. It would have the effect of uniting the Clergyman and his flock ... There was at this meeting no opinion of the Laity. It was said they were unanimous in their approval of the course proposed. This was not so. There were many who he knew would not desire to transfer the patronage beyond the present Diocesan.'[33] The society decided that patronage would be vested in Strachan during his lifetime and then revert to the Church Society. Draper and Allan were made a committee to prepare a by-law to this effect.

A third step towards entrenching lay influence in the church was the introduction of the diocesan synod, which, unlike the Church Society, would be a representative institution with the authority to legislate for the diocese and 'to express [the church's] opinion, as a body, on the posture of her secular affairs.'[34] Strachan found the need particularly urgent in the 1850s, as legislation was looming to eliminate the clergy reserve lands; a diocesan synod, he thought, would be a powerful political voice against the government's plan to secularize the church's endowment. Consulting once again with the authorities in England, Strachan 'was at once met with the maxim, that no diocesan synod can be held without leave and licence from the Crown.'[35] He began the lengthy process of having enabling legislation prepared for the Imperial Parliament; but he could not wait long.

In 1851, before holding his regular triennial visitation of the clergy, he took the bold step of inviting lay representatives from each parish. The 1851 visitation marked 'the first time,' as Strachan declared, 'that the whole Church of this Diocese, lay and clerical, has assembled'; it was explicitly the prelude to a diocesan synod. The meeting voted a resolution against disturbing the present arrangement for the clergy reserves and another in favour of a diocesan synod. In September 1853 the bishop called together another visitation of the clergy with lay representatives; the people of St James' chose Dixon and Gamble as their representatives. On 13 October 1853 it was boldly moved, seconded, and carried, that this meeting of bishop, clergy, and representative laypeople, with spectators (including ladies, as members were 'pleased to see'), was in fact the synod of the diocese.[36] But it was not until 1857 that diocesan synods were explicitly authorized by law.

Some layfolk saw the synodical system as a kind of ecclesiastical 'responsible government', by which church leaders might be held accountable to the people. Strachan certainly did not see things in this way, nor did his successor Bishop Bethune, nor the bulk of the Toronto clergy. Increasingly we see St James' defending 'the rights of the laity' and synodical constitutionalism against episcopal prerogative.

Strachan resigned as rector of St James' Cathedral in 1847. No more fitting symbol could be found of the end of the Family Compact era at St James'. Finally Strachan could do without his income from the cathedral, for an unexpected surplus had developed in the annual clergy reserves account, and the SPG agreed to use it to guarantee Strachan a bishop's salary for the rest of his life. He would receive £1,250 a year, plus arrears. On 10 February 1847, he wrote the SPG to resign as rector of St James'.

By the same mail Strachan wrote W.H. Draper, as head of the government, to ask that the Crown might be pleased to appoint Grasett to the rectory: 'You know Mr Grasett too well to require me to say anything in his favour. I may however be permitted to state, that for more than eleven years he has discharged the duties of his Station in a way that has gained him my strong approbation and the esteem and affection of the people.'[37] The governor-general's letters presenting Grasett as rector of St James' arrived two weeks later. Strachan sent them to Grasett with the following covering letter: 'I send you the enclosed with great pleasure and my best wishes. It is a promotion of which I consider you well deserving, and my prayer is that God's blessing may ever be on you for good and you may rest assured that none of your Friends rejoice more in your Success than Yours most truly[,] John Toronto.'[38]

The same day, Grasett wrote Strachan: 'Permit me to offer you my heartfelt thanks for your most kind note accompanying the letters missive. Many and weighty are the obligations under which your Lordship has placed me by numerous acts of confidence, generosity, and paternal kindness ever since I had the happiness of being ministerially connected with

2.7 Revd Canon Edmund Baldwin, Dean Grasett's long-serving and much-loved assistant. He was the only working assistant at St James' to be styled 'canon' until Philip Hobson obtained the title in 1996.

you – but the distinguished mark of your favour which I have now received appears to have crowned them all. My earnest prayer to Almighty God is that I may be faithful to the important trust committed to me and that my future course may be such as to occasion your Lordship no regret for this disposal of your patronage. With feelings of gratitude, affection, and respect, Believe me, my dear Lord, your faithful and obliged servant, H.J. Grasett.'[39] At Eastertide, on 10 April, Grasett was formally inducted into 'the actual and corporal possession' of the first York rectory.

Three years later the position of first assistant minister of St James', which Grasett had so recently occupied, was filled by Edmund Baldwin (Figure 2.7), another pronounced evangelical, who was to remain in that position for over a quarter-century.[40] Baldwin was the nephew of William Warren Baldwin and thus cousin to Robert Baldwin the Reformer; he was a Christian gentleman of good inheritance and independent means. One of his brothers, Maurice, would later become dean of Montreal and bishop of Huron; another, Arthur, would become rector of All Saints', Toronto. Edmund was born in 1826 and educated at Upper Canada College and King's College. He was ordained in 1849 and served for a few months at St Mark's, Niagara, before moving to St James'. He married Grasett's sister. He was known to be a favourite of Strachan, who made him a canon of the cathedral. An obituary in the *Evangelical Churchman* portrays him as a person of earnest simplicity and integrity, unusually free of the 'professional manner and tone' of a Christian minister; the centre of a happy home circle, a practical preacher of the gospel, a calm voice in synod, a quiet and pastoral visitor in the sick chamber, and a consoling friend of the bereaved. He had charge of the Canadian grants of the Colonial and Continental Church Missionary Society, an evangelical English organization.

A NEW GENERATION OF LAY LEADERS

In the 1840s and 1850s a new generation of younger men, moderate Conservatives or Reformers, entered into influence at St James'. Members derived their social prominence and authority not from intermarriage with the colonial landed aristocracy but from business or professional work or popular politics. Unlike the Family Compact, they mingled freely with Christians of other denominations in business and government, in political parties, in the Board of Trade and arts organizations, in the Sunday School Association, the Young Men's Christian Association, and the Bible Society. As a result they were instinctive ecumenists, part of what William Westfall has called the mid-Victorian Protestant alliance in Toronto.[41] Protestant evangelicalism was part of the air that they breathed.

The two churchwardens in 1849 were Thomas Dennie Harris, forty-six, and Clarke Gamble. Harris was a merchant, insurance agent, and president of Canada's first telegraph company and would continue as warden to 1864. Clarke Gamble was developing the Toronto and Lake Huron Railway and was married to his second wife, a daughter of Henry J. Boulton. He had been churchwarden since 1841 and would serve again from 1866 to 1868 and from 1869 to 1881. Two sons of George Ridout, George Percival, forty-two, and Joseph Davis, forty, owned the city's most thriving hardware company, the predecessor of Aikenhead's, which until recently was a familiar Toronto landmark. Joseph was also first president of the Canada Permanent Building and Savings Society. We have already met George Duggan, Jr, thirty-six, arguing for lay rights at a meeting of the Church Society. He was recorder (a kind of magistrate) in Toronto and later county judge and was married to Egerton Ryerson's sister-in-law. He would be warden from 1862 to 1869. George Allan, William Allan's son, a waterworks commissioner, was 'president of everything cultural and horticultural that happened in Toronto.'[42] Frederic W. Cumberland, twenty-nine, had come to Toronto from England two years earlier. Trained as an engineer, he was now practising architecture. He was a cultivated gentleman with gifts of persuasion and was a Conservative in politics. He would marry Thomas G. Ridout's niece and enter into partnership with Ridout's son. H.J. Boulton, whom we met as a Family Compact Tory ten years earlier, had moved towards Reform and evangelicalism.

These figures reflected the new Toronto and the new St James'. Toronto in the early 1850s had a population of over thirty thousand, and its harbour, railways, industry, and government offices were making it a strong commercial centre. The city's élite and the new guard at St James' were people who had made their mark in government, trade, industry, and the professions; they were Conservatives of a moderate bent or Liberals in politics, of the low church and evangelical in theology. Many of the old high-church Tory Family Compact families had moved to St George the Martyr; others were dying away. The new rector of St James' and the senior assistant were evangelicals, committed to a doctrine of the priesthood of all believers and open to lay leadership. St James' had become a powerhouse in the new instruments of diocesan self-government, notably the Church Society and the diocesan synod, and its lay representatives were speaking up for the rights of the laity against the clericalists in the ageing diocesan establishment.

Intermittently during the period 1839–83, and sometimes rather intensely, St James' wrestled with what it meant to be not simply a parish church but also a cathedral, or at least something called a cathedral. What were cathedrals supposed to do or to be?

The cathedral idea was controversial among North American Anglicans in the nineteenth century. The Episcopal Church in the United States – the American counterpart to the United Church of England and Ireland – had no cathedrals at all until the 1860s. Some American dioceses, principally low-church ones such as Virginia, still have no cathedral. Some Americans considered the cathedral idea incompatible with republican institutions and the spirit of religious freedom. In 1782 William White (1748–1836), minister of Christ Church, Philadelphia, chaplain to the Continental Congress, and later first bishop of Pennsylvania, argued that the Episcopal Church constituted not an establishment but a voluntary association; its policy was set not by Crown or bishops but by representatives of the parishes; therefore power should be understood as flowing up from the people and the parishes, not down from the diocesan governments. From this premise followed the principle of 'an equality of the churches; and not, as in England, the subjection of all parish churches to their respective cathedrals.'[43]

If many political progressives were suspicious of cathedrals, so were many evangelicals. The very word conjured up the image of strongholds of effete piety, where idle priests intoned their liturgies in private chapels, bishops built power bases against the laity, and poor widows bought votive candles with their last pennies. But many high-church people were attracted to the idea: it was an icon of the church's mission to hallow the secular world, and it reflected the authority of the bishop and the honour due him. The great apologists for cathedrals were the Anglo-Catholics. An early advocate was George Washington Doane, one of John Henry Hobart's priests, who became bishop of New Jersey in 1832. He was inspired by Pusey, Keble, and other English Anglo-Catholic leaders – he was called 'the rankest Puseyite in the country.' The world's first Anglo-Catholic bishop, John Medley, founded the first Anglican cathedral establishment in North America at Fredericton, New Brunswick, in 1845.

Strachan himself was very content for St James' to be called a cathedral, in an honorific sort of way, as the church of which the bishop was rector and the mother church of the capital city. But it did not have the endowment or the style of government that a true cathedral was expected to have. Constitutionally it was a parish church; and because it was controlled by the rector and churchwardens and vestry, it could never function with the broad vision for diocesan service characteristic of a true cathedral. Even seating was restricted, since most of the pews were owned by pewholders. Moreover, St James' before 1853 did not even look the part. A cathedral, most progressive-minded Anglicans were agreeing by the 1840s, should be designed in Gothic style, with a long choir, wide transepts, a high roof on strong walls supported by flying buttresses outside, a clerestory, towers, and windows pointed at the top. Square, plain St James' looked nothing like that.

Strachan dreamed of a real cathedral for little Toronto. He reportedly sought a government land grant for one in 1841. One of the chief objectives of the Church Society, as soon as it was organized in 1842, was to raise funds for one.[44] It is said that Strachan gave some of his own land the next year to endow one.[45] The year after that, in his charge to a visitation of clergy, Strachan hoped that his new theological seminary at Cobourg, Ontario, would become the 'foundation of a still more extensive institution, to be attached to the Cathedral, as was the custom in former ages'.[46] The next year, in a letter of 6 September 1845 to Grasett, he wrote that he was hoping to introduce the whole round of cathedral service.[47]

A year later, on 10 August 1846, he wrote the SPG seeking an endowment to confer on St James' 'cathedral privileges and a cathedral establishment.' Could the SPG endow a dean, organ, canons, and a couple of archdeacons? St James' could then be something new in North America.[48] The next month he sent W.H. Draper a petition from his diocese for the grant of a suitable site for a cathedral. He pointed out that there was one three-acre lot vacant to the west of the parliament buildings and another to their east, and a portion of the square on which the jailhouse stood was also available. It was a disappointment for him that neither the SPG nor the government rose to the occasion.[49]

We can see what ambitious dreams Strachan was dreaming. Toronto would have a diocesan cathedral, built especially for the purpose in a central location, perhaps next to the legislature; it would be fully endowed, with a full staff, a full discipline of cathedral liturgy, and an extensive educational institution and school of clergy attached to it. This splendid institution would be a modern renewal of an ancient Christian tradition.

St James' was once again destroyed by fire on Holy Saturday, 7 April 1849, along with a sizeable part of downtown Toronto. The congregation began worshipping in Holy Trinity Church. Fires are unpleasant, but they do focus people's minds on priorities. 'The New Church might be erected in the Cathedral style & never as before as the Mother Church,' wrote Strachan.[50]

The vestry met on 9 April and appointed a Building Committee, including the rector and churchwardens, and Dixon, Draper, Ridout and Robinson. The committee, after some meetings, decided to advertise for designs in Gothic style.[51] Cost was a factor. With £8,500 in insurance coverage less £3,500 outstanding debt on the 1839 building, plus £959 unpaid debts owing to St James' less £400 owed by it to others, plus £2,238 new capital if pewholders were required to pay one-third of the purchase price of their pews, plus the value of the salvage from the fire and the possibility of £1,000 from the SPG and £1,000 from local donations, the parish would not be able to afford more than £10,000. That would cover a basic Gothic church for a congregation of two thousand, but it would not look distinguished.

St James' could afford something more expensive if it could collect rents on some of its land. The Building Committee recommended situating the new church on an east–west axis facing Church Street, freeing land on King Street for development. It could then subdivide the church's property, remove the remains of bodies in the churchyard, and lease the lots commercially. Those valuing primarily financial stringency supported the recommendation; those disinclined to disturb the dead, and those wanting to preserve the cathedral precincts from commercialism, disapproved. The bishop weighed in with the opinion that the important thing was to use the land for the glory of God; therefore commercialism was not ideal, but moving the dead so that the living could give glory was not desecration.[52] The debates during the next ten months, and the succession of procedurally intricate resolutions, amendments, and points of order at a series of overwrought vestry meetings, defy summary. The final decision was not to lease, in fact to exclude leasing for ever by moving the new church to a more central location on its property so that no land would be available for leasing. The old foundations would be abandoned, and bodies in the churchyard would be moved. From votes on resolutions on 21 December 1849 and 9 March and 23 March 1850 we can infer that those who wanted to make commercial leases on the cathedral property included Allan, Draper, Gamble, Harris, Jarvis, Robinson, and Vankoughnet, while those opposed included W.H. Boulton, Dixon, and four Ridouts.

Should the new house of worship be designed as a parish church, as a cathedral, or as a hybrid? As Shirley Morriss notes at greater length in chapter 5 below, each option had its supporters. Architect William Thomas had designed a parish church, cheap to build, unencumbered by transepts that made it hard for the congregation to see and hear the service. Architect George Smith had designed an impressive Gothic building according to the latest canons for an English cathedral, with a long choir and wide transepts. But who would pay for a cathedral foundation of dean and canons, and why would the vestry want to surrender its powers to the bishop? Frederic Cumberland submitted a hybrid.

Compromise seemed to appeal to Anglican tastes. On 21 December 1849 the vestry voted down a resolution that the parish church should be a cathedral. It resolved instead, by a majority of five, that St James' should remain a parish church but that, when it was rebuilt, 'His Lordship the Bishop be respectfuly invited to establish his throne therein until such time as a Cathedral of the Diocese be constructed[,] the congregation being desirous of maintaining the Honour and advantage of his presence.'

Another vestry meeting on 23 March 1850 reaffirmed the substance of the resolution and envisioned a 'handsome parish church in the gothic style to be denominated the Cathedral Church of St James.' Other hybrid designs had been submitted, but Cumberland's won the vestry's support. It perhaps did not hurt that he was himself a member of the vestry, with influential friends at St James', such as the Ridouts. His victory was far from a foregone conclusion, however. Those voting against it on 21 December included some of the heavyweights of the parish, such as Draper, Duggan, Gamble, Harris, Howard, and Robinson. Had the decision been left to a select vestry of the dozen most important parishioners, the present cathedral might never have seen the light of day.

Cumberland's design, scaled down somewhat, was given to contractors, and after various cost overruns and numerous unforeseen delays, and through the tireless efforts of Thomas Harris, the churchwarden, it was opened to worshippers on 19 June 1853 (Figure 2.8). Its cost was £18,803, much more than originally anticipated, forcing the vestry to authorize a sale of £9,000 in debentures.[53] The interest expenses crippled the congregation for years. And the building was still unfinished, lacking its tower, spire, five porches, turrets, pinnacles, and finials. There was no stained glass, apparently because too many parishioners objected to graven images.[54] But Strachan was serene. He thought the new church 'not perhaps surpassed in comfort, elegance, and architectural beauty by any in North America.' A historian observes that St James' Cathedral became 'a general model for new Anglican churches in the diocese of Toronto and a living expression of the new Anglicanism now flourishing in Ontario.'[55]

Pewholders naturally were particularly curious to see whether their new pews were in precisely the same location as in the former building. Many were disappointed. The addition of

2.8 The second St James' Cathedral as opened in 1853, from a photo by J. Hollinsworth.

two side doors had altered the position of some of the pews on the ground floor, some pews were narrower, some of the new pillars, being larger than the old ones, obstructed views, and the pews were generally two or three feet further removed from the chancel, and so on. These matters had to be patiently or impatiently addressed by various committees and meetings of vestry over the next several months.[56]

Some parishioners, annoyed for one reason or another, refused to pay their pledges. Mr Francis H. Heward, a Tory of excellent Upper Canadian lineage, had pledged £20 to the building campaign, but only on condition that the cathedral be built on the site of the old church and the graves in the churchyard be left undisturbed. When his stipulation was not met, he refused to pay his pledge. Moreover, when the remains of his brothers and sister were removed from the churchyard, he felt entitled to a refund of the burial fees. The wardens replied that they had a policy of keeping burial fees and that they had not heard of Heward's condition on his pledge, which was nowhere recorded. At their suit, the bailiff seized twelve barrels of Heward's flour to be sold by public auction.[57]

CONGREGATIONAL LIFE

The ministry of St James', as at most churches, was shaped by worship, preaching, music, pastoral care, programs, education, and outreach. William Cooke and Giles Bryant discuss worship and music below in chapter 6; the ministry of pastoral care generally leaves little historical record;

2.9 St James' Schoolhouse, with the Mechanics' Institute behind, from an engraving c. 1860.

texts of sermons, after Strachan and before Rainsford, are rare; programs do not seem to blossom until the 1870s. A word can be said here, however, about education and outreach in the 1840s and 1850s.

Education was particularly dear to the hearts of both Strachan, the former schoolteacher, and Grasett; and St James' had had an active Sunday school before our period began. Before the fire of 1849, members of the congregation were already thinking of building a new parish school-house, and at its meeting two days after the cathedral burnt the vestry determined to include one in its building plans. Cumberland designed it, and it was completed at the end of 1851 for £928 (Figure 2.9). By 1854, with the help of some unnamed 'benevolent ladies,' the debt was retired. The St James' Schoolhouse featured two airy school rooms, one for boys and another for girls, with desks, seats, and stoves, along with committee rooms and a basement residence for the master and mistress. The building was enlarged in the early 1870s.[58]

In the early 1850s between two hundred and three hundred children were attending the Sunday school every week at nine a.m. to receive instruction from volunteer teachers. The heart of the curriculum seems to have been the catechism. Connected with the school was a lending library of five hundred volumes, open Saturdays from 10 a.m. to noon to those paying an annual fee of five shillings. Most of the funding came from an annual grant from the Church Society.

In outreach, the wealthy clergy and laity of St James' took a paternalistic interest in the poor of the city. Week by week they gave alms. They also sought to expand the religious ministrations of the Church of England to the poor, who would probably not feel comfortable at St James', by opening two new churches. Trinity Church in the Park, as it was then called, or

2.10   St James' Cathedral in 1865, after completion of the bell chamber, with Schoolhouse in the foreground.

Little Trinity, as it is now called, was conceived on 12 July 1842 at a meeting of John Strachan, Alexander Dixon, William Gooderham (a miller and later a distiller), and others. It was to serve Irish Protestant labourers in the squalid area around its site near King and Parliament Streets.[59] In the west end, Strachan opened the Church of the Holy Trinity in 1847, through the gift of £5,000 from a woman in England who stipulated that all its sittings must be free so that the poor would feel welcome. Prayer books and Bibles were provided those unable to afford them, and donations of clothing were given to 'those who give sufficient evidence of their disposition to become permanent worshippers.'[60] Henry Scadding (Figure 1.13, p. 31), formerly the second assistant minister at St James', became its incumbent.

Education for the poor was provided on weekdays at the new schoolhouse after it opened in 1851. A schoolmaster and schoolmistress were hired to educate the children in reading, writing, arithmetic, scripture, and the catechism. About one hundred or one hundred and fifty young people attended. And the St George's Society, a major social and benevolent group closely connected with St James' in informal ways, also did charitable work among the poor.

2.11 Arrival of the bells for St James', 1865. A set ordered from England was lost at sea. The replacements came from Troy, New York.

Parishioners from St James' such as Cumberland, Draper, and G.P. and J.D. Ridout were prominent among its presidents through these years. One of its earliest charities was to bury the indigent dead in the St James' cemetery.[61]

THE DEATH OF STRACHAN

At the age of eighty-nine, John Strachan began to reflect that his lease on life was growing short, and he asked the diocese in 1866 to elect a coadjutor bishop, which is an assistant bishop with the right to succeed the diocesan bishop. The high-church and evangelical parties could not agree on a first choice, but as a compromise candidate the electoral synod unenthusiastically returned Alexander Bethune, a sixty-five-year-old priest who, as archdeacon of York, had been closely connected with Strachan theologically and administratively for several decades.

Perhaps wanting to deal equitably with the other priest who had been so closely associated with him, Strachan raised Grasett to the office of dean of Toronto a few months later, in

2.12 Bishop Strachan's funeral procession, 1867.

January 1867. Grasett was touched: 'My dear Lord, Many are the favours and tokens of confidence I have received at your hands while, during a long course of years, I have had the privilege and happiness of serving under you in the Ministry of the Church. Your offer now to confer upon me the dignity of Dean of your Cathedral I accept with the liveliest emotions of gratitude, not so much for the ecclesiastical promotion it brings, as for the assurance you so kindly give me that it is intended as a mark of your Lordship's personal regard. That regard, permit me to say, I esteem as my highest earthly honour, and it is my earnest hope that I may retain it undiminished to the end. Believe me, my dear Lord, With filial affection and respect, Your faithful and Obliged servant, H.J. Grasett.'[62] It may also be that Strachan was finally about to establish a full cathedral staff for the diocese and was beginning with a dean.[63]

Strachan died a few months later, on 1 November, and was buried in the chancel of St James' (see Figure 2.12). 'No one has provoked keener opposition, or has called forth more loyal attachment and co-operation,' the *Globe* editorialized.[64] He displayed, 'upon the whole, a singleness and, in general, an honesty of purpose, worthy of all respect; with a certain serene conviction that he was always right.' He might barely tolerate dissenters, the *Globe* continued, but with evangelical congregations in his own communion 'he not only did not thwart their wishes, but sought to meet them in a friendly, considerate way.' Thus it was that, for the rest of their generation, the evangelicals of St James' venerated the memory of the crusty old high-churchman from Aberdeen.

2.13 Sir Casimir Gzowski, churchwarden of St James' 1881–3, one of the leading evangelicals who founded the Church Association and Wycliffe College. He also designed the cathedral gates and fence (Figure 5.25).

NEW PROGRAMS

By 1867 or not long afterward another generation of evangelical laypeople with business and professional connections had grown up in or migrated to St James'. Edward Blake, who turned thirty-four that year, a son of W.H. Blake, was a lawyer and Liberal politician and would soon be the second premier of Ontario. A study published in 1975 represents him as a victim of the evangelical piety of his parents, for he never experienced the conversion that they desired for him, and while maintaining Christian appearances he felt a 'castaway' from the Lord.[65] He married a daughter of Bishop Cronyn of Huron. His brother Samuel Hume Blake, thirty-two, another lawyer, would become vice-chancellor of Ontario in 1872. He was as outspoken and belligerent as his brother was moody. He wedded another of Cronyn's daughters. James Kirkpatrick Kerr, twenty-six, a law partner of the Blakes and their brother-in-law, was another supporter of the Liberal party. He would be churchwarden from 1872 to 1884 and in the next century speaker of the Senate of Canada. Casimir Gzowski, (Figure 2.13), fifty-four, an exiled Polish freedom fighter, civil engineer, and member of the Conservative party, had made a fortune on railway construction and land speculation in the 1850s. He would be warden from 1881 to 1883. Daniel Wilson, fifty-one, was a historian and ethnologist and would later be first president of the federated University of Toronto. John George Hodgins, forty-seven, chief clerk in the provincial office of education since 1844, later (1876) appointed deputy minister of education, was closely connected with Egerton Ryerson's educational work in Ontario. He would become lay secretary of synod in 1870. William P. Howland, fifty-six, grocer and Reform assemblyman, was about to be appointed lieutenant-governor of Ontario (1868). His son Oliver A., twenty, was training for law and would later be a churchwarden of St James' and mayor of Toronto. Robert Baldwin, Jr, thirty-three, second son of Robert Baldwin the Reformer, was becoming active in evangelistic work and would be treasurer of the *Evangelical Churchman*. A member of the St James' branch of the YMCA, he organized a city-wide, non-denominational 'Y' in 1864.

In the next few years St James' finally completed its building. In 1867 the debt remaining from the building campaign of 1849–53 was $6,345; a committee including Edward Blake, Duggan, and Gamble was struck to solicit donations to retire it so that the church could be consecrated.[66] In 1870 the chancel was beautified, and in 1872 the leaders of the parish pushed to finish the tower, spire, and porches. More donations were solicited; a list of pledges displays familiar names: Grasett $5,000, Gzowski $2,000, Kerr $800, Draper $500, Edmund Baldwin $400, Gamble $250, and from Allan, Hodgins, W.P. Howland, and Wilson, lesser amounts.[67] The edifice was finally completed in 1875 (Figure 2.14). The spire was said to be the highest in North America. And in 1876, from a committee of citizens of Toronto, 'through the liberality of Christians of various Religious persuasions in the City,' came a grand clock for the tower.[68] The ecumenical gift perhaps symbolized that St James' was no longer seen as the stronghold of the Family Compact, but as the mother church of Toronto civic religion.

'One of the most conspicuous features of Ontario religious life during the last decades of the nineteenth century,' John Webster Grant has observed, 'was the multiplication of voluntary organizations.'[69] In this respect, as in so many others, St James' was an exemplar of mainstream Ontario Christianity. Its programming developed with particular strength in the 1870s, developing community life by drawing people together across socioeconomic lines within the congregation.[70] The parish YMCA was founded in 1861. The Cathedral Young Men's Association, through various committees, held readings, debates, lectures, and social functions, raised funds, and led cottage meetings with music and scripture at places around the city. In 1880 it opened a penny savings bank, to induce 'habits of saving' among the indigent, with the cheerful thought that 'much of the pauperism of Toronto is due to the too indiscriminate relief given by charitable persons and institutions.'[71] A Young Ladies' Aid Association, begun in 1877, organized bazaars, sponsored social events, took orders for bazaar items, and distributed the proceeds to worthy parish causes. The District Visitors' Society in 1879 comprised forty-two visitors, who among them that year made 8,878 visits, circulated 12,809 tracts, and distributed clothing to the needy. The choir reported fifty-nine members. The Dorcas Society met Tuesday mornings to make clothing for distribution among the poor. In 1877 some members of the church attempted to form a branch of the Church Missionary Society (CMS). This was, it was firmly declared, to be not a 'Society of Ladies', but one of women, men, and children. The ladies were, however, instrumental in recruiting, and they soon had 262 members enrolled. At a meeting in May 1878, leaders of this parochial chapter of the CMS included Baldwin, Sam Blake, Gamble, Gzowski, Hodgins, and Wilson. Soon they realized how complex it was to affiliate with a British society, and in 1879 they settled for an independent parish organization, which they called the Home and Foreign Mission Aid Society. Mrs Hodgins was secretary. This group became the parochial branch of the Women's Auxiliary to the Domestic

2.14 St James' Cathedral soon after its completion in 1875.

and Foreign Mission Society in 1889. In 1878 a Boys' Meeting for prayer was started, but it attracted only a handful. A Young People's Association was begun in 1882, and a parochial Temperance Society in 1883.

In the 1870s the annual Christmas entertainment was a popular event. The schoolhouse was decorated with evergreens and Christmas bells, the choir sang carols, the children sang hymns, someone (perhaps Daniel Wilson) read a poem, someone (perhaps Sam Blake) gave an address, and the ladies provided refreshments.

The Sunday school, too, continued to grow. By 1879 it enrolled 1,311 children, 'being now by far the largest Sunday school in the Dominion.'[72] Bible classes were also held, one for young men and one for 'young ladies.' The teachers met once a month for prayer. The superintendent was John Gillespie, later first rector of the Church of the Messiah. The annual Sunday school picnic in late spring was a splendid event. Thirteen hundred passengers piled on a steamer at Nairn's Wharf and sailed for Victoria Park in what we now call the Beaches.

From the late 1830s to the early 1870s Toronto had changed, and so had St James'. The cathedral still reflected the values and culture of the city's leaders, but those values and that culture had changed. The old order was agricultural; the new, professional and commercial. Toronto once had been an outpost; now, through railways and canal systems and telegraph wires, it felt very connected to the world. The Protestant culture of mid-Victorian Ontario was evangelical and ecumenical, progressive and humanitarian.

And St James' in the 1870s, with the largest Sunday school in Canada, a huge landed endowment, a powerful lay leadership, a magnificent building crowned with the tallest church spire on the continent, solid preaching, a large congregation, a busy program of activities, a growing conscience for mission and outreach, a historic past, and civic esteem, was at the pinnacle of its success. Unfortunately, it was also widely resented in the Anglican diocese of Toronto, chronically at odds with the bishop, rooted in a certain theological narrowness which the times were beginning to leave behind, and perhaps a little too proud. In the 1870s and early 1880s, one bishop sought to bring it under control and his successor simply picked up his episcopal throne and moved it elsewhere; the diocesan clergy worked to dismantle St James' endowment, and the evangelical laity began to migrate to other parishes.

PARTY STRUGGLES

The main reason why many in the diocese resented St James' was its highly adversarial role in a period of intense and bitter struggle between what Anglicans called the Church party (high-church sympathizers) and the Evangelicals. The Evangelical party supported ecumenical Christian associations, the University of Toronto, lay rights, and plain liturgy. The Church party supported Anglican societies, Trinity College, episcopal prerogative, and a measure of ceremonial in liturgy, and it blamed the Evangelicals for helping the dissenters destroy the landed endowment of the church. The struggle was at its most heated from Bishop Bethune's enthronement as diocesan bishop in 1867 to that of his successor in 1879. Although what happened in Toronto was simply a local skirmish in a theological war that engulfed the whole Anglican world, Bethune was part of the problem. He lacked Strachan's breadth and charm and skills at manipulation, and, being old and often sick, he delegated much of his work to his archdeacon of York, George Whitaker (1811–1882), provost of Trinity College and the nemesis of the Evangelicals. Bethune and Whitaker became the generals of the Church party in Toronto; the generals of the Evangelicals were members of the vestry of St James' Cathedral.[73]

Tensions had emerged in Strachan's day.[74] In 1860 Bishop Cronyn of Huron had created a storm by disparaging Whitaker's teaching at Trinity College as 'unsound and un-Protestant.' At least some Evangelicals, including Grasett, sympathized with Cronyn's charges. In 1865 W.H. Boulton of St James', again supported by Evangelicals, published newspaper articles demanding an accounting from John Hillyard Cameron, a high-Tory lawyer who served as diocesan chancellor. In the 1850s Cameron had borrowed diocesan money to speculate in the stock market, and in the 1857 crash he lost huge amounts of money, which he was never able to repay. Strachan protected him. The Church Society responded to Boulton's articles by expelling him and returning his membership dues. A fledgeling Church party supported Cameron, and the Evangelical party supported Boulton.

Party feeling escalated when church patronage returned to the agenda of diocesan government. With Strachan's death, patronage in church appointments reverted from the bishop to the Church Society, which in 1867 was incorporated into the diocesan synod. It therefore fell to synod to adopt a patronage canon. Bethune, Whitaker, and their supporters wanted to vest patronage permanently in the bishop, reflecting what they took to be the apostolic order that clergy should be sent not called; Sam Blake, W.H. Boulton, Gamble, and others sought to protect the rights of the laity in self-supporting parishes, on the English model, in which those who funded the ministry chose the minister.

In the synod of 1873, the Church party organized a ticket of candidates for diocesan committees, resulting in the total exclusion of Evangelicals. The next evening, outraged laypeople met in the St James' Schoolhouse and established what they called the Church Association. This group was to dominate diocesan life for the next seven years. It was clearly led by the people of St James': Draper was president, Grasett clerical vice-president, and Sam Blake lay vice-president. The Church Association published tracts and spawned a weekly newspaper, the *Evangelical Churchman*, which answered the weekly newspaper of the Church party, the *Dominion Churchman*. It raised funds to support Evangelical mission churches and Evangelical theological students. Elsewhere on the continent, where the same battles were being waged, discouraged Evangelical Anglicans were leaving the Church of England and the Episcopal Church for friendlier denominations or were breaking away into schismatic groups, notably the Reformed Episcopal Church, which was organized in 1873. It was perhaps chiefly the energy and the sometimes outlandish pugnacity of the people of St James' that prevented large numbers of Toronto Anglicans from forsaking their church.

In its fund-raising for Evangelical missions, the Church Association undercut the synod's fund-raising for diocesan missions and theological students. The bishop took particular umbrage at a statement put out by the association which opined that it was 'impossible ... to assist in maintaining a student's Fund for the support of young men who are carefully trained to look with aversion on our Church as a Church of the Reformation.' In 1874 the bishop announced that Grasett (initially with some other clergy) was being charged with depraving the discipline of the church and that he would be tried by a church commission. Hundreds of Church Association members rallied to his defence. Weeks passed while the diocese fumbled. During the Easter vestry meetings at St James', Gzowski took the chair and Duggan moved a resolution concluding: 'The Vestry tenders their heartfelt sympathy to their rector, assuring him of their unshaken confidence and regard and their determination to stand by him to the end against his accusers. Carried unanimously.'[75] The commission finally decided that Grasett and his co-defendants had violated no canon with force in Canada. Party warfare continued in the secular and church press, in the diocesan synod, and in all the relationships of the diocese.

The people of St James' helped found two new congregations for Evangelical Anglicans disaffected in high-church downtown parishes.[76] Ritual was advancing quickly at Holy Trinity, on the doorstep of St James', and in 1874 Evangelical members of that congregation organized a new parish called Grace Church. It completed its first church building on Elm Street near Bay in 1876. Its first incumbent, C.A. Matthew, had been assistant minister of St James'; Sam Blake was a churchwarden. (Grace Church moved to the northern suburbs in 1911 and became Grace Church on the Hill.) In 1875 disgruntled Evangelicals broke away from St George the Martyr to form 'the Church of the Ascension: Canon Baldwin Memorial Church' on Richmond Street West. Its sittings were entirely free, and it was deeded on the condition that it remain 'always strictly Protestant and Evangelical.' Its rector in the 1880s was H.G. Baldwin, son of Edmund Baldwin and his wife, Grasett's sister.

The conflicting economic interests of the rector of St James' and other Toronto clergy also contributed to party feeling. The rectory endowment of St James', whose income went directly to Grasett, began to increase in value quite delightfully in the 1860s, and in 1871 some of the clergy in Toronto began publishing anonymous notes in the press lamenting the fact that they eked out a meagre existence while Grasett lived in the lap of luxury.[77] The churchwardens tried to set the record straight by obtaining Grasett's permission to publish his accounts. His rental income had been $3,600 in 1866, $5,200 in 1870. But the Toronto clergy began to see an issue of principle here. The rectory endowment had been given to the rector of York Township; now the area that had once been York Township had many rectors, and they should all share in the endowment.

A resolution to synod in 1873 proposed that the provincial government should be asked for legislation vesting all rectory land in the diocesan synod, which could then distribute it to the rectors. Disputes and laborious negotiations ensued. In 1878 the legislature passed an act (41 Victoria cap. 69) with two major provisions. First, it gave the diocesan synod authority to sell a rector's landed endowment on his death, retirement, or removal. Second, it in effect limited future rectors of St James' to $5,000 annual income from the York rectory endowment and authorized synod to distribute the surplus. Grasett could keep the golden goose, but his successor would have to surrender it to the synod.

THE RAINSFORD MISSION

The outstanding event of the evangelical period at St James' was a preaching mission by William Rainsford in 1877, which led to his appointment as first assistant minister and, in 1882, to a new conflict between St James' and the bishop of Toronto.[78]

William S. Rainsford (Figure 2.15) had been born in Dublin in 1850, the son of a parish priest in the Church of Ireland who participated in its evangelical revival in 1859. In 1866 his father took a church in London, and the next year the teenaged Rainsford was trying his hand at Christian evangelism and social service in the east end of London. His father wanted him to be a minister and sent him to St John's College, Cambridge; after that young Rainsford was

2.15 Revd W.S. Rainsford, assistant under Grasett, who conducted
a very successful mission at St James'. Denied the rectorship after Grasett's death,
he became rector of St George's Church, Stuyvesant Square, in New York.

ordained and served a curacy in Norwich. At twenty-six, through the recommendation of a friend, he was invited by an Episcopalian minister in New York to take charge of his church during the summer. Arriving in New York, he discovered that he was also supposed to preach every evening under a tent on 34th Street and Broadway in the summer heat. Crowds came to hear him, and the experience made him determined to be a missioner – a person invited by parish churches to preach for a week or two of renewal services.

For two and a half years he held missions in the United States; then a Canadian cleric who heard him in Philadelphia invited him to London, Ontario; and he was invited thence to hold a mission at St James' Cathedral, Toronto. The Cathedral Young Men's Association distributed handbills, and an announcement appeared in local newspapers: 'Rev. W.S. Rainsford, of St John's College, Cambridge, will hold a series of special gospel services in the Cathedral during the week beginning February 26th, at 8:00 each evening excepting Saturday. He will also conduct Bible readings in the St James' Sunday School room at 3:00 p.m. same days. Seats free. A hearty invitation to all. Will you come?'[79] Three weeks before his arrival parishioners gathered for prayer. His first sermon was to be on Sunday morning, 25 February, and long before the eleven-o'clock service a continuous stream of people was filling the cathedral.

Rainsford strode into the pulpit. Over six feet tall, he was strongly built and handsome, with a winsome smile, kind eyes, a penetrating expression. He preached in simple and direct language, without affectation or sensationalist tricks; the overall impression he gave was that he was 'terribly in earnest.' Over the next few days he preached personal love of Christ, mortification, the new birth, and the life of holiness in Christ. He told people that God was on his knees, praying to them to accept their own value in Christ. He urged them to examine themselves. He asked: Has the mighty change of new life been wrought in you? He illustrated his message with powerful and touching images – to modern tastes, it is true, images laced with Victorian sentimentality, stories about children on their deathbeds bravely witnessing the faith to their parents, for example.

By Wednesday, all the pews of the cathedral had been filled, three hundred additional seats had been set up, hundreds of people were standing, and hundreds more were being turned away at the door. People said that nothing like it had ever been observed in the Church of England in Canada. Rainsford himself had never seen anything like it. One evening he invited any who would like to speak with him on personal religion to meet with him after the service in the schoolhouse. When he arrived, he found five hundred people on their knees. During the course of the week, hundreds were converted or quickened in their faith.

Parishioners urged him to stay. Grasett was going to England for four months; he offered Rainsford accommodation in the rectory and asked him to take charge of St James' for the interval. Rainsford agreed. He preached, taught Bible classes, organized groups, visited. He mentioned from the pulpit that the parish assessment for the Widows and Orphans' Fund had gone unpaid for two years; $400 was raised. Reporters for the *Evangelical Churchman* took notes and published his sermons. The vestry passed a resolution giving thanks to God 'for the season of great Spiritual blessing which they and the other members of the Congregation have lately enjoyed,' paying due notice to the preparatory labours of the rector.[80] Many more people came to the Lord's Table on communion Sundays. On Ascension Day two hundred were confirmed. Rainsford's last service was Sunday evening, June 14; four thousand people were counted coming in at the door. Rainsford was exhausted and 'preached out'; he returned to England and spent six months recuperating. He also married.

In the meantime, the Grasetts returned from England. The dean was clearly failing; he lapsed in and out of cogency; and the cathedral lacked a first assistant minister. Parish leaders naturally thought of Rainsford and repeatedly implored him to accept the position, promising that on Grasett's death or retirement they would elect him rector. Rainsford finally agreed to accept the position in January 1878.

The Rainsford mission accelerated a project that Toronto's Anglican Evangelicals had been considering for some years – the founding of a new theological college.[81] Grasett had chaired a committee of the Church Association on clerical education but had made no progress. Now, under Rainsford's preaching, several young men had recognized a calling to ordained ministry, and they wanted a place for training that valued the teaching of the English Reformation. Sam Blake and others in the Church Association found a parish priest in Nova Scotia who was a Hebrew and Old Testament scholar and invited him to be the founding principal of a new theological school. The churchwardens of St James' made the schoolhouse available to the new institution at moderate rent, and it was there (Figure 2.16) that the first class of what was to be called Wycliffe College met in October 1878 under its first principal, James Sheraton. Among the founders of the college were Robert Baldwin, the Blakes, Gamble, Gillespie, Hodgins, W.H. Howland, Kerr, Rainsford, and Wilson. Two years later, when the college erected a new building in Queen's Park, the ladies of the cathedral ran a bazaar that raised nearly two thousand dollars to furnish it.

2.16 Interior of St James' Schoolhouse as used for the first classes of Wycliffe College.

Rainsford was not surprised to discover that 'the Toronto clergy, with one or two notable exceptions, were not cordial,' but he was dismayed to find over the next three years that he was growing less acceptable to some of the leaders of his own congregation. He learned first that preaching every Sunday was extremely difficult. As a mission preacher, he had needed only about fifteen sermons, which he could perfect and recycle. But more important, he found himself increasingly questioning the affective conversionist evangelicalism and Biblical literalism that he had so long accepted. Nor could he be satisfied with the more cultured and intellectual evangelicalism that Grasett represented, though he rather admired it.

The heart of the matter was that he could not square new ideas of evolution and historical criticism with the old religion; and he was troubled by the evangelistic axiom that God's grace became effective at conversion but not before. He spoke to almost no one about his theological perplexities, but he began to seek ways to cast old doctrines into new forms and to build up the cathedral as 'a great free and open liberal church for the people.' But that was not what his congregation wanted. People came to him and said, 'You are not preaching as you used to preach'; 'Give us the old gospel you gave us with such power.' The ultra-evangelicals, led by Sam Blake, began suggesting to him that he should resign, and, at their instance, so did Grasett. His own sense of vocation began to be confused. He had once felt the intoxication of swaying thousands of people; now he faced patches of empty seats on Sunday morning.

Meanwhile, Bishop Bethune had died in 1879. At the meeting of synod called to elect his successor, representatives from the Church party and the Evangelicals engaged in some backroom politics to agree on a compromise candidate. The Church party would support a moderate evangelical if the Evangelicals agreed to disband the Church Association. The new bishop was Arthur Sweatman, a minister in Woodstock, Ontario. He agreed with the Evangelicals on the value of the English Reformation, but he was not prepared to let the laity usurp his episcopal prerogative.

THE END OF AN ERA

Grasett died 20 March 1882 and was buried under the communion table in the crypt of the church. The vestry expressed its sympathy to Mrs Grasett and her family and appreciation for the 'loved and venerated rector' – for his forty-five years of devoted ministry and for his faithfulness and consistency in proclaiming 'the pure evangelical doctrines of the Church of England.'[82] Fifty years later old residents of Toronto still remembered him, 'the kindly old gentleman, whose home in the old Rectory behind the cathedral was a centre of Christian culture and social hospitality.'[83]

Grasett died on a Monday. On the Friday, a delegation from St James', led by James Kerr, the churchwarden, waited on the bishop, Arthur Sweatman.[84] It had very firm ideas about who the new rector should be. The bishop, for his part, knew that the lay leaders of St James' took an altogether too exalted view of lay rights and had a very defective view of episcopal prerogative. And he knew that the patronage canon was on his side: it was he who had the authority to appoint rectors after consultation with the parish; the parish emphatically did not enjoy the power to name rectors after consulting with the bishop. The outlook for the interview was not promising.

The delegation wanted Rainsford. The bishop could think of at least two things wrong with Rainsford: he was hardly in his thirties, and he supported Wycliffe College against Trinity College. Perhaps given Rainsford's growing liberalism, the delegation was not unconditionally committed to him. It would gladly accept Maurice Baldwin, rector of Christ Church, Montreal, brother of their late first assistant minister and an evangelical preacher of considerable force. It was notorious, however, that Baldwin had recently defied his bishop on a matter of cathedral governance: he had refused to allow a diocesan event in the building on an evening when a parish event had already been planned. This sort of behaviour did not appeal to Sweatman. The bishop wanted time to reflect. Kerr wanted to consult with the vestry. The bishop, a former schoolteacher, who liked to be precise about texts, warned that the Church Temporalities Act gave no warrant for the subject to be raised at a vestry meeting. Kerr, a lawyer who also liked to be precise about texts, said that the patronage canon 'was intended to give the Congregation voice in the selection of the person to be appointed.' He consulted the vestry.

The vestry agreed with Kerr that the spiritual interests of the congregation, not the temporal interest of Trinity College, must be paramount. It passed a resolution, with loud applause, that the appointee must be 'in thorough accord with the teaching of their late departed Rector.' The bishop soon received a 'memorial,' signed by seven hundred members of the congregation, asking for Rainsford or Baldwin to be appointed.

In the meantime, a deputation of fourteen clergy and laypeople from other local parishes waited on the bishop. It reminded him that Grasett's death triggered a provision of the act of 1878 forcing distribution of income from the St James' rectory endowment. The bishop decided to think about this matter before considering a new rector and put off the wardens for the next two months. The matter of the rectory fund was decided by the diocesan synod on 16 June. The annual York rectory surplus would be distributed to sixteen rectors in the city of Toronto and five in the township of York,[85] subject to judicial approval.

On 7 June the bishop informed the lay leaders of St James' that he had offered the rectory to the Reverend Canon James Carmichael and that the latter had accepted, subject to approval by the congregation. Although Carmichael had supported Grasett during his trial, he now reportedly backed Trinity College, and he had quarrelled with the editor of the *Evangelical Churchman*. The congregation, through Kerr, told Carmichael very clearly that it did not approve at all. Carmichael wrote, 'My dear Mr. Kerr, In general answer to your last letter, I write to say that I have declined the Rectorship of St James', and that I have written to the Bishop of Toronto to that effect. I remain Yours sincerely[,] J. Carmichael.' At a special meeting of the vestry, members applauded the wardens and lay representatives 'in the respectful but firm representation to his lordship of the rights and wishes of the congregation.'

In mid-July the bishop summoned Gamble, Hodgins, and Kerr to meet with him and suggested Philip DuMoulin as their new rector. DuMoulin was at St Martin's, Montreal; an Irishman, he was a moderate evangelical who had been recruited and ordained by Bishop Cronyn of Huron (of whose evangelical credentials there could be no doubt); he was a man of retiring disposition in his 'ordinary relations' but eloquent in the pulpit. Rainsford would be appointed associate rector, with right of succession. Gzowski and Wilson, currently in England, were consulted by cable. Agreement was reached.

Sweatman asked Rainsford if he would remain as associate rector. Rainsford replied, 'Certainly not.' DuMoulin arrived in October 1882; Rainsford left in January 1883. Rainsford became rector of the floundering St George's, Stuyvesant Square, New York. He had been courted for several months by its senior churchwarden, J.P. Morgan, the wealthy financier and later the founder of the U.S. Steel Corporation. In the next few years he became one of the most celebrated liberal Protestant preachers in the United States and implemented a vision for the inner-city church that he had developed at St James', Toronto. Under his ministry St George's grew from about twenty families to a congregation of well over a thousand. His liberal evangelicalism, which emphasized God's love over God's judgement and recognized that scripture had developed in changing cultural contexts, had proved too advanced for Toronto in the early 1880s.

DuMoulin was immediately faced with a lawsuit. The Toronto rectors had got their way with the rectory endowment, and they now turned their hungry eyes on the 1820 and 1825 glebe grants to St James'. The bishop stayed aloof from the dispute, perhaps because he was planning a new cathedral and did not want to acknowledge St James' as the mother church of the diocese. Langtry v. DuMoulin was settled in 1884 in chancery, in favour of the plaintiffs, and that judgment was upheld on appeal.

The bishop was fed up with the *Evangelical Churchman*, Wycliffe College, and the vestry of St James'. He also shared Strachan's vision of a real cathedral, established for that purpose and governed under the bishop. He announced at the 1881 meeting of synod that he would like a cathedral where he and his canons and his other ecclesiastical dignitaries could lead services, design programs, teach clergy, and plan church development. The qualifier 'without unsolicited interventions from the laity' was understood. The synod supported the bishop's vision with their votes, though never, as it turned out, with their money. In 1883 the Ontario legislature incorporated the cathedral chapter of St Alban's, and in December 1884 the diocese secured four and a half acres for the church building where St Alban's Church now is, on Howland Avenue in the Annex north of Bloor Street West. St James' could keep the designation 'cathedral' as a historical tradition, but, if the bishop had his way, it would never again stand as the icon of the diocese or as the spiritual symbol of the city of Toronto, and certainly it would never again seek to give direction to its ecclesiastical superiors.[86]

Some at St James' would have been glad to make an effort at being a cathedral as well as a parish church, but they were a minority. Sweatman wrote Cumberland, 'Without committing myself to any opinion as to the feasibility of ever making St James' the cathedral church, I might remark that the obstacles to bringing this about are in the St James people.'[87]

The death of Grasett in 1882, the establishment of another cathedral in 1883, and the final gutting of the York rectory and glebe endowments in 1884 pushed St James' into a less confident future and left it with memories of a more glorious past. Over the previous forty-five years, reflecting the transformation of Canada from colony to nation, St James' had evolved from the spiritual headquarters of the Family Compact, pampered and manipulated by English governments and mission societies, into the self-supporting religious home of the city's professional and business classes. It was blessed with learned and worthy ministers of word and sacrament, who lived in harmony with generous, responsible, and canny lay leaders. It was entirely clear about its theological identity. It was articulate in defending the Reformation. It was housed in a splendid building that symbolized its vision for the gospel in the world. It ran the country's largest Sunday school. It worshipped according to the Book of Common Prayer, which Anglicans considered the purest of liturgies and one of the most excellent compositions in the English language. It never lacked funds, even if it was always in debt. It was vigorous in its congregational life and committed in its social outreach. It was on good terms with practically everyone, the bishop and the diocesan clergy excepted. It was, before 1882, everything that a mid-Victorian evangelical church should be, and even a bit more than that, because it was also the mother church of the city, the cathedral of the diocese, and the symbolic centre of the lay Protestant alliance of the province of Ontario. It had been a witness to Christ, a model of discipleship, and a beacon lighting the way for the Church of England in Canada.

3

Success
and Distress,
1883–1935

PAUL H. FRIESEN

S ST JAMES' CATHEDRAL rounded the century's end it had good reason to celebrate its success. Predictions of its demise, whispered two decades earlier, had proved not only premature but largely unfounded. The confidence of the congregation endured almost unshaken. The 'true' diocesan cathedral, St Alban's, imagined by Bishop Sweatman and endorsed by a resolution of the 1881 synod, was still not more than a barely begun spectacle in Toronto's rather new Annex. Disinherited it might be, but St James's perfect Neo-Gothic edifice still towered over King Street; its spire in old Toronto could be nothing less than 'a credit to the city, being the highest on the continent' (Figure 3.1).[1] Its plentiful congregation held court in the financial district of a financial city, and its British parishioners dominated the polite society of a very British city. And, after all, it really was still St James' *Cathedral*. People did not stop calling it that, in conversation or in print. Yet the successes of the Cathedral were by 1900 already mixed with some distress – battles lost, if not any wars – and with hints of greater trials to come. And they did come, especially in the years between the Great War and the end of the Great Depression.

A two-hundredth anniversary is a fitting time for both critical institutional evaluation and joyful celebration. So this chapter looks at the ebb and flow of the cathedral's fortunes over the half-century from the viewpoints of 'outsiders' and 'insiders' and those in between and does so under four headings. It offers first a description of the public perception and reputation of St James' in a changing Toronto; second, an analysis of its reputation among Anglicans in the diocese; third, a sketch of the plentiful parish activity of the cathedral; and fourth, an inquiry into the thoughts, hopes, and fears of the clergy and people who constituted St James'. This of course it cannot do without constant reference to the ongoing story of the congregation under the four successors of the legendary Henry James Grasett: John Philip DuMoulin (1882–96), Edward Sullivan (1896–9), Edward Ashurst Welch (1899–1909), and Henry Pemberton Plumptre (1909–35). Yet in many cases the leading laymen and women were every bit as significant. In fact it would be impossible to tell the story without constant reference to their lives, even if their names are sometimes too numerous to acknowledge.

3.1 King Street, Toronto, in the 1920s. The view of St James' spire, the tallest in Canada, now began for the first time to be obscured.

ST JAMES' AND TORONTO

It might be argued that St James' Cathedral had reached its peak in Toronto society some time before Dean Grasset died in 1882, when St James' dominated the life of a still-small imperial outpost with its canopied governor-general's pew at the front of the nave. But visitors to the city at the turn of the century could hardly say that they had seen the city if they had not seen St James' Cathedral. 'More closely than any other institution in Toronto, secular or ecclesiastical, is the Church of St James, linked with its inception, growth, and present condition,' they would have read in the promotional literature of the cathedral.[2] In their *Might's Directory* pull-out map, concentric lines orbited the large dot (the corner of King and Bay streets) that was a financial epicentre of Canada, second only to Montreal's business district.[3] And just a fraction of an inch to the right on the map lay the cathedral, well inside the borders of what has been aptly dubbed the land of the 'Plutocrats' (Figure 3.2).[4] And if new residents of Toronto approached the cathedral from the north down Jarvis Street on a Sunday morning, they would likely draw one conclusion quickly. In fact, it would be hard for them to dismiss the connection between the great church near the foot of Jarvis and the princely mansions that lined that grand avenue, which one enthusiast has called the Champs Élysées of turn-of-the-century Toronto.[5]

In fact those who approached the downtown core with eyes turned skyward would have been more impressed the further south they walked. There was, on Bond Street for instance, what one historian has called a late Victorian 'profusion of spires.' Bond Street Congregational, St Michael's (Roman Catholic) Cathedral, and Metropolitan Methodist formed a very new but impressive Neo-Gothic phalanx.[6] A few streets over, a sentinel of the same kind arose in the shape of Jarvis Street Baptist. But St James' took first prize in the nineteenth-century church-building contest. Not only was its spire the tallest, but its bells, a Toronto wonder, had been ringing since 1866, offering 'an instantaneous translation to the other side of the Atlantic.'[7] This was, after all, the acknowledged 'mother church' of the Church of England in Canada – at least west of Montreal – in a city that was still over 90 per cent British and 30 per cent Anglican.[8]

Entrance into the cathedral could overwhelm guests: it would at least impress them (Figure 3.3). Conversation with any of the more prominent members would reinforce in the mind of any inquirer the remarkable self-confidence of the 156 pewholding families.[9] And if visitors slipped by the crowds, they would see the silent message of God's providential ways with this congregation in the large windows that lit up the nave and chancel. Still in its first stages, the glass tale that gradually surrounded worshippers in the cathedral would be completed in 1931 and would remind visitors throughout the period of the church's pivotal role. The account commenced in the apostolic age with Jesus and his disciples, wound through the lives of the martyrs and saints, and culminated – quite naturally – with the creation of St James' Cathedral, Toronto. Yet it was a revelation taken in stride by the families who owned the pews and governed the vestry. This serene assumption of the cathedral's importance in itself surprised visitors as much as the claims of the windows.

It would not take one long to name the wealthy families who supported the cathedral and figured large in its decisions. The 'Subscriptions to St James' General Improvement Fund,' printed and distributed in the spring of 1889, was heavily supported by a small group of benefactors who were themselves a select group of pewholders.[10] Canon DuMoulin, the Gooderhams, the Grasetts, and five other men (W.R. Brock, R.N. Gooch, O.A. Howland,

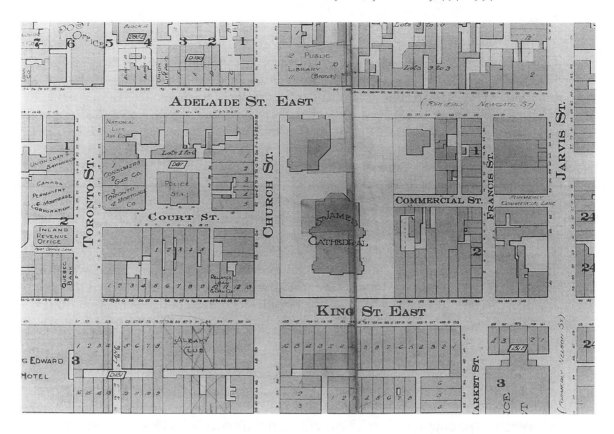

3.2 St James' Cathedral and its environs from Goad's Street Atlas, 1910.
The Schoolhouse and old rectory shown in Figure 2.4 have been replaced by
the Parish House and new rectory commissioned by Canon Welch.

A.S. Irving, and J.K. Kerr), who were all churchwardens some time between 1883 and 1919, provided half the amount collected. They were men of a significant reputation in the city, even if the glory days of their predecessors – men such as Sir Casimir Gzowski – were waning. And the total gathered for an 'enduring,' 'beautiful,' 'venerable,' and 'historic' refurbishment – $22,200 – was an enormous sum in the late nineteenth century, a little over the total cost of the first Wycliffe College building in 1882.[11] And almost equivalent funds were confidently requested of the congregation at the same time, to 'complete satisfactorily' the job begun.

A decade later the church's self-published *History and Directory* termed the pewholders' roster a 'List of Members,' as did every club and society of important people in the city.[12] Their names and addresses were often recognizable and usually admired, and they could be confirmed by a careful perusal of the readily available *Might's Directory* (1899), which revealed the occupations of almost all those listed and the vocational tendencies of entire neighbourhoods, street by street – even who was whose widow. The 'List of Members' abounds in presidents of banks, managers of huge enterprises, physicians, top civil servants, and partnerships of lawyers. On the first page, for instance, we find the first seven men under 'B' listed as W.H. Beatty of Queen's Park Crescent (a senior law partner, president of the Toronto Silver Plate Co.,

3.3 Interior of St James' in the 1920s or 1930s. The flowers were presumably for a wedding.

a vice-president of Gooderham and Worts Ltd., and associated with London & Ontario Investment Co.), George A. Boomer (a barrister), D.O. Brooke (a clergyman), G.W. Beardmore (president of Beardmore Belting Co. Ltd.), Walter Barwick (a senior law partner), W.R. Brock (president of W.R. Brock Co. Ltd., and of Canadian General Electric Co. Ltd.), and Edmund Bristol (a senior law partner). It was not surprising to Torontonians that a goodly number of St James' clergy and parishioners appeared in *The Canadian Who's Who* (and its predecessors) from the 1890s to the 1930s.[13]

The pewholders, and even their dependants, could not account for all the people that entered St James'. But there is a prior problem: exactly how many people regularly passed through its doors and the doors of its schoolhouse (later its Parish House) is as hard for us to determine as it would have been for a passer-by then. In the late 1880s, when renovations were taking place, there was some concern that taking down the galleries, which blocked 'the most impressive aspect of the interior,' would remove needed seating.[14] The Finance Committee responded that there were more than enough seats remaining (1,356) but that the new plan made room for even more: 1,348 sittings, with 174 additional free 'draw seats' proposed for the aisles in case of unexpected demand. The committee admitted that at that moment only 575 of 932 ground seats and 100 of 320 gallery seats were actually let out. It granted that some 'occasional attendants and strangers' could be found in the unlet gallery pews (and presumably in the few free seats), but not how many of those seats let out were actually filled Sunday by Sunday, though complaints about pewholders' absences were routine by the early 1900s. Quite apart from those who came or returned to midweek programs, as few as five hundred might be a fair estimate for a Sunday service in the 1890s, though occasional special services (synods, high points in the liturgical calendar, services with famous guest preachers, and so on) certainly attracted far more. Thereafter complaints about falling numbers are heard. But at least some observers must have noticed that even as attendance slipped, the number of communicants increased, a scenario consistent with rumours about 'high-church' enthusiasms. Easter communicants numbered only 313 in 1900, but over 650 by the mid-1920s, before declining to the low five hundreds in the mid-1930s, during the Depression.[15]

In fact there was a greater diversity of people than the 'Lists of Members' revealed or could be seen entering the church on an average Sunday. Of the seventy-nine infants baptized from 31 January 1886 to 30 January 1887, thirty-six came from homes where the father was a professional or a still wealthier man. The others had as fathers teamsters, labourers, machinists, shoemakers, butchers, and members of other trades. The same general welcome to parents of all backgrounds held throughout the period – even a 'private detective' presented his child for baptism! Of the twenty-six children brought for baptism in 1936, nine had fathers with professional occupations, and nine had fathers who were tradesmen or labourers.[16]

The marriage records show the same broad social diversity. Among the bridegrooms of 1896 we find an artist and sculptor, a machinist, a lawyer, a journalist, a motorman, and a carpenter. The bridegrooms of February 1906 to February 1907, a big year for weddings at the cathedral, included a clerk, two barristers, a shantyman, two merchants, three carpenters, a physician, two waiters, a labourer, a glassworker, a warehouseman, a civil engineer, a joiner, a teamster, a merchant's clerk, a railway employee, a physician, a bricklayer, and a manager.[17] It would seem that while the pewholders and their families were prominent Torontonians who attended in some numbers on Sundays, many of the local residents, who came for the celebration of their rites of passage, were in humble circumstances and were seldom seen in the church at other times. Others were probably recent immigrants who moved into other parishes as they found work and homes out of the city centre, and newer immigrants replaced them.

But it was not just social class that made the life of St James' seem inaccessible to a significant group of neighbouring Torontonians as the early decades of the new century unfolded. As the 'British' cathedral of the city, the church's credentials seemed impeccable. At a time when an overwhelming majority of Torontonians were of British descent (still over 80 per cent in 1931), many were British-born (still over 25 per cent in 1931),[18] and most of these remained nostalgic for the motherland, St James' delivered the best British-born and British-educated talent. The rector from 1899 to 1909, Edward Ashurst Welch, had taken a first-class degree from Cambridge. The incumbent from 1909 to 1935, Henry Pemberton Plumptre, had been educated at Harrow and Oxford. The organist and choirmaster from 1897 to 1933, Dr Albert Ham, arrived directly from England with his FRCO and doctorate of music in hand.

Decades after adequate and even exemplary educational and cultural institutions (on the British model) were entrenched in Toronto, St James' satisfied the nostalgic yearning that many of its citizens still felt for authentically British life and worship. During the pastoral vacancy in 1899, an important parishioner had suggested to the churchwardens that Canadian candidates should be considered. James Scott, a prominent manufacturer who was a warden from 1898 to 1902, wrote him back three days later: 'The Committee composed of the Churchwardens and Lay Delegates [to Synod] of St James' Cathedral believe in the principle of "Canada for the Canadians", but find some difficulty in carrying it into effect without sacrificing the interests of the Cathedral whose circumstances are such that a Rector of undoubted eloquence is absolutely indispensable. If such a man can be found in Canada, the Committee will give his name due consideration in their recommendations to the Bishop.'[19] And this was from an Irishman who had immigrated to Canada as a six-year-old – some fifty-four years earlier!

The congregation were enabled to hold out against the slowly growing irrelevance of their British credentials by the tonic of the Great War, Anglican sensibilities, and the enduring anglophilia of a largely British city. 'Of all the churches in Toronto, the atmosphere of St James' is most distinctively English – the intonation of the clergy's voices, the singing of the choir, [and] the appearance of a very large number of the congregation,' enthused one journalist in 1913.[20] But this 'atmosphere' was not so congenial to many who lived and worked within the parish bounds. By 1914, after an impromptu parish census, the church leaders were dismayed by 'small' businesses and 'small' factories that had invaded their blocks, for it had been generally agreed that the cathedral had a large sphere to go with its enormous spire. But they seemed appalled above all by European and Asian immigrants – 'a foreign population,' they lamented, which had 'driven away the English speaking people from the Neighbourhood.'[21]

St James' made a sincere but weak effort to adapt to this reality: an attempt at a Chinese Sunday school, for instance, met with enthusiasm from parishioners at first, but the project dwindled after a few years.[22] Being so terribly British was becoming a liability. The church bells that had transported Henry Scadding and so many British immigrants back across the Atlantic in the late nineteenth century may still have been ringing, but fewer and fewer were within earshot. Nor were British suburbanites so faithful as the rectors had hoped: even at Easter they would sometimes visit closer parish churches, leaving their paid-up pew boxes at St James' largely vacant. It took the tonic of a new model of the cathedral as a unique, gathered, devoutly liturgical congregation to create a new reputation for the church in the 1930s and 1940s.

St James' self-image was also shaken by a scandal that culminated in 1934. Its endowment properties had been problematic for years. A significant portion of them, situated not far from the church, known as the 'Park Lots' had been let at high rates to middle-class men and women of modest means who had then sublet them to tenants as a source of needed income. The Park Lots soon formed a large part of the degenerating Cabbagetown ghetto (Figure 3.4). Though

3.4 Some of St James' Park Lot properties. In the 1920s and 1930s
their condition became an embarrassment.

the properties continued to yield significant rents, some tenants were impoverished and erratic in their payments.[23] St James' worried about this annually early in the century and felt obliged to do something about it but ended up keeping the issue at arm's length for decades, postponing necessary renovations and hoping for an improvement in the real-estate market.[24] The vestry finally decided to sell some of the properties, in a tentative step towards getting out of the real-estate business.[25]

When the Depression hit, the irony was too much for the press to ignore. The wealthy cathedral had, through indecisiveness and a desire to secure maximum profits, become a slum landlord. Meanwhile one of its prominent parishioners, Dr Herbert Bruce, the lieutenant-governor, had headed a social-assessment commission of Toronto's slums. And the rector's wife, Adelaide Plumptre (Figure 3.5), was pursuing a well-recorded career as a social activist and civic politician.[26] Unfortunately the Bruce Report recommended rebuilding the run-down St James' properties as a civic social-service project – at the city's expense! Irony had become hypocrisy in the eyes of many Torontonians, though not everyone tried to make capital of it. 'Mrs. Plumptre's Mask' and 'Fat Salaried Clergy Babble as Property Falls into Ruins' screamed the headlines of Toronto's muck-raking *Hush* in the dying days of 1934.[27] This scandal could not help but push St James', in the next phase of its life, into a different model of social outreach and into a new concept of endowments.

ST JAMES' AND THE DIOCESE

It seemed to some zealots late in the nineteenth century that St James' relationship with the diocese was chiefly marked by liturgical controversy. Whoever wrote 'The Progress of Ritualism

3.5 Adelaide Plumptre, wife of Canon Plumptre, prominent Toronto politician and social activist.

in St James' Cathedral, Toronto!' in 1890 may have had other hobby-horses in his stable, for it appeared as one topic in a series of *Church of England Tracts for the Times*. Yet St James' provoked two sharply worded numbers.[28] The Anglican author had reviewed 'ritualism' in several parishes, presumably St Thomas's, Huron Street, perhaps St Matthias,' and one or two others. But he seemed most exercised by the erosion of what he believed had been radically Protestant Anglicanism. St James', he said, had been since the days of Dean Grassett 'quietly converted into a Ritualistic theatre for the propagation of semi-popery.' It would seem an odd charge, given that Benjamin Cronyn, later bishop of Huron and an adamant low churchman, had been responsible for bringing Grassett's two immediate successors at St James' (1882–99) – J.P. DuMoulin and Edward Sullivan – out from the ultra-evangelical Church of Ireland for missionary service in Canada.[29] Furthermore, not only was H.J. Cody, the growing giant of St Paul's, Bloor Street, and of Wycliffe College, still a visitor to the pulpit of St James' in 1899, but so was Dyson Hague, as Protestant as Wycliffe men came.[30] None the less, the firebrand author of the tract may have been putting his finger on what appeared to be the very slow drift away from zealous evangelicalism at the cathedral and in much of the rest of the diocese. What was emerging was a moderate churchmanship that, for instance, allowed Cody, still the rector of the evangelical St Paul's, Bloor Street, at least to consider the offer of the provostship of Trinity College in 1921.[31] In fact, the very gradual architectural and liturgical innovations that marked the entire period in part were due to St James' 'cathedral' ambitions and in part reflected similar architectural and liturgical tendencies throughout the Anglican world. Yet the drift was largely imperceptible; in the eyes of almost all Anglicans, St James' remained soundly Protestant.

There were in fact much bigger controversies in this period, which made the congregation's relationship with both the diocese and the bishop often unpleasant. It is an odd but telling fact

3.6 Most Revd Arthur Sweatman, bishop of Toronto 1879–1909 and primate of all Canada 1907–9, founder of St Alban's Cathedral. While he deprived St James' of its official status as cathedral and twice denied the church its preferred choice of rector, he warmly supported cathedral-style worship there.

that St James' had at the time no ecclesiastical right to call itself a cathedral at all. The less charitable and more pedantic in the diocese of Toronto may have on occasion argued that it was no more than a rather large, glorified Neo-Gothic parish church. It had a series of rectors, not deans; it had no complement of prebendaries, canons, or cassocked choir-boys gambolling on the lawns of a cathedral close. To be blunt, it lacked much of what a genuine English cathedral sported. Above all, the bishop's throne, cheerfully installed at St James' in 1870, was empty – at least as often as the bishops could manage.[32] Its rectors were in fact nominated only as sub-deans of the real diocesan cathedral, St Alban's, which threatened to rise majestically over the residences of the suburb north of Bloor Street (now known as 'the Annex'), hard by the new residence of the bishop of Toronto.

Yet there was good reason for St James' to insist on being called a cathedral. Quite simply, ever since the governor's box had dominated the old St James' building, the most important Anglicans in the province had been attached to the church – not the least of them the first bishop of Toronto, John Strachan, that robust and long-lived chaplain to the Family Compact. On his deathbed in 1867 he had fulfilled his dream of bequeathing a full-fledged episcopal establishment to the diocese by naming eight canons and a dean to St James'.[33] He also left them a huge endowment in the shape of the York rectory – properties which produced substantial annual revenues.

The next great bishop, Arthur Sweatman (1879–1909, Figure 3.6), thought better of trying to run a cathedral out of a parish church governed by a congregation of the most powerful

3.7 St Alban's Cathedral, Toronto, as conceived by
the original architect, R.C. Windeyer, 1883. Only the chancel was ever completed; it now
serves as the chapel of Royal St George's College, an Anglican boys' school.

businessmen and professionals in the city. He was determined to have a true English cathedral, independent of any parish's control – a glorious centre of architecture and music and education. Soon it was legally incorporated by a provincial act (1883), and its realization was publicly

3.8 The House of Bishops of the Church of England in Canada on
the front steps of St James' Cathedral, 1918(?).

advertised as one of his central objects. Somehow Sweatman even managed to present the first paper at the first session of the 1884 congress of the Church of England in Canada – 'The Adaptation of the Cathedral System to the Needs of the Canadian Church' – held on the grounds of St James' Cathedral![34] Ground was broken for St Alban's (Figure 3.7) in 1885, and some diocesan functions were held there from 1892, but economic downturns and other diocesan priorities slowed its erection to a crawl. Thus in 1893 almost all sessions of the first national synod of the Church of England in Canada were held at St James', which was allowed to keep the name 'Cathedral' as long as St Alban's was incomplete (in the end, only the chancel and the foundation for the nave were ever built). Thus St James' remained the effective centre of diocesan life and worship, its reputation and facilities unrivalled until new St Paul's was built on Bloor Street. Moreover, St James' maintained episcopal prestige through its rectors: J.P. DuMoulin left after fourteen years in 1896 to become bishop of Niagara, and his successor, Edward Sullivan, left the bishopric of Algoma for St James'.

By 1909 it was clear that Sweatman was losing the battle. He had scarcely been laid in his grave that year before Canon Welch, the soon-to-depart rector of St James', was offering the new bishop, James Sweeny, a double-edged sword – the assistance of St James', which he proudly announced as 'the Mother Church of [the bishop's] See City.'[35] Later that year

3.9 Most Revd S.P. Matheson, primate of all Canada, with others (perhaps members of
the executive committee of General Synod) in St James' Parish House, 1918(?). Although St Alban's was
then the official cathedral, diocesan and national church events continued to take place at St James'.

St James' succeeded in humilitating the new bishop: a diocesan committee, desperate to
stay the flow of thousands of dollars into the skeletal St Alban's, petitioned St James' directly,
over the bishop's wishes. Would it become the cathedral again? The authorities at St James'
were unmoved by the plea. They were quite happy as they were, they said, and would not
give up what they had in order to achieve what John Strachan had long ago said was rightful-
ly theirs. That is to say, they would not relinquish their congregational autonomy, 'so as to be
constituted as a Cathedral proper.'[36] The wardens and rector wrote with cocky self-assurance,
offering the committee only a slender, mocking hope: 'The time may possibly come, sooner or
later ... when St James' might be made available as the Cathedral of the Diocese.'[37] Meanwhile,
St James' assured itself that it could retain its independence, continue as the 'Mother Church'
of the diocese, and still be known as 'the Cathedral' nestled in the heart of Toronto, where it
had been for generations (see Figures 3.8 and 3.9). It really was *the Cathedral*, after all. H.P.
Plumptre, presiding as rector at his first vestry meeting, heard these proud words from the
leading laymen of the parish: 'Before and since the incorporation of St Alban's, with few
exceptions, all functions of a diocesan character ... have been held at St James', the expenses
incidental thereto being borne by the Parish.'[38]

The battles with the bishops, however, did not begin and end with the 'cathedral question.' It almost goes without saying that St James' was accustomed to getting the rector that it wanted on those rare occasions when the incumbent died, retired, or moved on. It had already breached the delicate protocols of Anglican episcopal etiquette by assuming that it would get one of its two choices in 1882 – ideally the young and charismatic evangelist W.S. Rainsford.[39] With its choices rebuffed, it ended up, after further disputations with the bishop, with J.P. DuMoulin (Figure 3.10), a fine compromise. The short-lived tenure of Bishop Edward Sullivan (Figure 3.11) as rector from 1896 to 1899 might have been uncontroversial to the pewholders: it could only seem right that if they lost DuMoulin to the episcopate of Niagara, they would get a bishop in return. They were parishioners, after all, of St James' Cathedral, whatever plan the bishop of Toronto might have. But the situation in 1899 was more tense. Sweatman, who was becoming a powerful, centralizing administrator, was developing St Alban's Cathedral precisely because of the powerful laity at St James'. He was wary of St James' ambitions and had grown weary of what he no doubt considered its pretensions and so asserted his full canonical right to make the final appointment regardless of the congregation's choice.

During the vacancy of 1899, which lasted almost the full year, the congregation had decided on the moderate evangelical John de Soyers, said by the former archdeacon of London to be 'an unusually eloquent, earnest and impressive preacher, well fitted to adorn any University pulpit' – and a well-published church historian besides.[40] But the bishop resisted this early conclusion and suggested other names, till in the fall of 1899 the churchwardens and leading laymen became impatient. Feeling that they had met the bishop's unsubstantial objections to De Soyers (who had apparently had a falling out with the bishop of Fredericton), almost all the pewholders signed a petition asking for his immediate installation.[41] Someone leaked it to the Toronto press, which immediately announced that the new rector had been chosen. The bishop was furious. St James' made its last plea for De Soyers on 29 November 1899, and then on 2 December the bishop announced that a different candidate would be installed. The new rector had never been considered by the wardens until perhaps just before the bishop's announcement – when, it would seem, he had given them an ultimatum. Edward Ashurst Welch, the provost of Trinity College, proved a logical and happy choice for all in the long run, but St James' had been reminded of the limitations that it shared with all other Anglican parishes. James Fielding Sweeny (bishop 1909–32; see Figure 3.12), Sweatman's successor and a bishop in his centralizing tradition, did not let St James' forget this limitation. And this came on top of another blow from fellow Anglicans. In 1908 the diocese of Toronto had, by procuring an act of Parliament, finally settled a sizeable chunk of St James' rectory endowment on other, more needy parishes.[42]

St James' status was further challenged by new developments in its relation to St Alban's. In 1909 St James' had rebuffed the diocese and had come close to insulting the bishop; by 1918, things had changed. By then the parish boundaries contained fewer and fewer of the sort of people St James' imagined should fill its pews. Givings had begun to dwindle. The vestry wrote to the bishop, trying to play on his financial difficulties with St Alban's without betraying their own panic: 'We are anxious to re-open the question of the use of St James' as the Diocesan Cathedral.' In what must have seemed, to the bishop at least, a rare display of magnanimity, they added, 'every effort will be made on our part to make such arrangements as may appear to be in the best interests of the Diocese.' When the bishop replied with a terse

3.10 Revd Canon John Philip DuMoulin, rector
of St James' 1883–96 and subdean of St Alban's
Cathedral from 1889. He left St James'
to become bishop of Niagara.

3.11 Rt Revd Edward Sullivan, rector of St
James' and subdean of St Alban's 1896–9.
He had resigned as bishop of Algoma
to come to St James'.

'the request you make is quite out of the question,' the churchwardens suggested that he should consult the 'Diocesan Authorities.' His tart response ended the match as he reminded them of the canonical reality behind the diocesan committees packed with the powerful laymen of the city: 'I am the only "Diocesan Authority" before whom such a matter could be brought.'[43] It was St James' turn to be humiliated.

Sweeny's death in 1932, however, when coupled with Canon Plumptre's retirement as rector in 1935, prepared the way for the final settlement of the (at times) tense relations between St James', the bishop, and the diocese. Significantly, it took not only a death and a retirement but years of financial frustration at St Alban's, new financial difficulties at St James' and rapid changes in its parish, and the Great Depression to force the issue. After a fifty-year hiatus, St James' would become the only cathedral once more. The 1933 synod created a joint committee of diocesan delegates and chapter representatives from St Alban's, which sat for two years.[44] Its recommendations were hardly unexpected: St James' ought to return to its status as a 'pro-cathedral' with a 'dean-rector.' The proposed arrangement struck a fine balance between the vestry of St James', the bishop, and, of course, the diocese, but St James' played its cards close to the chest for two years. The 1933 vestry report made no mention of the proceedings. The churchwardens buried a reference to the matter in the eighth paragraph of their 1934 report, affecting disinterest, with little more than an aside: 'Negotiations have been initiated by the Synod for the use of St James' as the Cathedral of the Diocese ... A resolution with respect to this matter will be submitted to you.'[45]

3.12 Most Revd James Fielding Sweeny, bishop of Toronto 1909–32,
archbishop of Ontario 1932. He steadfastly kept St Alban's alive in the face of mounting
diocesan pressure to end the project and restore St James' as the cathedral.

The actual resolution presented at the vestry meeting of 28 January 1935 was a little less detached and designed to guarantee a positive vote. It made it clear where the vestry thought the real power resided: it was the synod that was petitioning the vestry 'for the use of St James' as the Pro-Cathedral of the Diocese.'[46] Lest anyone in the diocese should suppose that the solution of the question left the vestry beholden to the diocese or to the bishop, the final word, in the 1935 report, was pushed even deeper into the churchwardens' report, behind a list of the faithful departed. Still they could not conceal a certain glee at their vindication: 'The necessary bill for the disestablishing of St Alban's will be presented to the Legislature next month, and we can look forward to the return of the bishop's chair to St James' probably in the early summer.'[47] Despite the financial difficulties that had twenty years earlier prompted St James' initiative in the matter, despite continuing financial crises that by the mid-1930s were occasioning annual dips into the endowment revenues, St James' had been a cathedral all along, though the vestry might allow itself to be a little gratified that the diocese had finally understood that fact.

It would of course be a mistake for anyone to depict all relations between St James' and the diocese in terms of bickering and power politics. The cathedral was the central symbol of Anglicans in the city and throughout the many rural parishes that stretched far into the countryside. Synods, conferences, civic functions (to commemorate royalty, to pray for success in the Boer War, to mourn the death of a sovereign, to honour the dead of the Great War, and for other events), and the beautiful presence of the building itself, made Anglicans proud of

St James' throughout this period. But this half-century was more fraught with diocesan tension than any other. It was with obvious relief that the congregation, the bishop, and the diocese confirmed the new arrangements in the mid-1930s. It is fair to say that in the ensuing decade the congregation was caught almost off-guard by its own enthusiasm for its recovered status and for its enhanced reputation as a 'legally constituted' cathedral. Almost at once, cathedral dreams sustained from the days of John Strachan, ambitions for beauty and dignity realized over the half-century just ended, and hope for a certain destiny combined to promise a new and vital life for St James' Cathedral.

PARISH LIFE

It hardly needs to be said that St James' was much more than the sum of its public or diocesan reputation in Toronto. Behind all of this lay a vital congregational life. The grand image of St James' was of course never far from the minds of those at the centre of its work. And to be sure, it was a concern that cropped up in sermons and vestry reports and numbers of the parish magazine throughout the period. But parish energy went to a great number of causes and forged the people of the congregation into a dynamic community. The worship of the church was its most conspicuous form of activity, and by most accounts one that was carried out with great care. This is not to say that the teaching office of the church was neglected. Sermons, lectures, and Bible classes were given in profusion, and debates and discussions regularly held. Likewise pamphlets and papers and books were circulated and discussed and libraries organized. But the period from the 1880s to the 1930s was a great age of working, of doing. The perpetual creation of new parish organizations, the revival of old ones, the nomination and election of officers and members and probationers, the holding of meetings and activities and banquets (and the reporting of as much of this as possible!) were the main occupations of the parish. Thus, worship, learning, and work were the trinity that made up the life of the congregation. But never far from these three concerns was the very practical and never-ending task of raising and spending great sums of money. It facilitated parish life and many parish activities and itself became the goal of others.

This preoccupation with money was hardly unique in an age that assumed voluntarism as the basis of most public life, whether the matter was religion or medicine or politics. But St James' was atypical among Anglicans west of Montreal (apart from St Paul's, Bloor Street, after its rebuilding) in the size of its facilities, the extent of its endowments, and the considerable wealth of a good part of its congregation. The general shape of the financial health of the parish is not hard to sketch. St James' depended on a combination of pew rents, property endowments (including its cemetery lands), investments, and 'open' collections (voluntary offerings received Sunday by Sunday). The early 1880s tended to be gloomy: 'The future of the church seems to be now assured; it stands in no danger of sale and demolition,' claimed the relieved churchwardens in April 1888: 'Its destruction, an event at one time so busily threatened would have been a calamity.'[48] This may seem pessimistic beyond belief, given that the tower and spire (of what the wardens were so bold as to call the 'Canadian Westminster Abbey' in the same report) were little more than a decade old. But these new features required a large mortgage. And the creation of St Alban's and the loss of most of the huge York rectory endowment to other city churches in 1882 had almost knocked the financial self-assurance out of the congregation. It was only on careful reflection that the wardens for that same year, W.R. Brock and O.A. Howland, regained their composure. They found that the 'Park Lots' – the principal portion of their remaining property endowments – were a 'more cheerful subject,' as they had through lease renegotiation, arbitration, and shrewd dealing guaranteed an astonishing 750 per cent annual increase in revenues, from $800 to $6,000. This revenue became the mainstay of the operating budget for years to come. It was likely the cheerfulness stemming from this change that within a few years allowed a proposal for a window to commemorate the thirty-some parishes carved out of St James', which were now in possession of a good chunk of its former endowments![49]

Still financial problems did not dissipate. The general economic downturn of the 1890s led the wardens to acknowledge both the decrease in the open collection and the difficulty in securing rents owed by the humble folk in the Park Lots and their other properties. On top of this, DuMoulin had 'intimated his conviction of the unsuitableness of the Old Rectory house for a residence' – an opinion that would be echoed in succeeding decades by other rectors. By 1895 the parish managed to avoid an operating deficit only by the expedient of an emergency canvass of prominent members. This borderline situation persisted, prompting the wardens to express scorn for 'trifling contributions' and to make repeated appeals for 'more liberal contributions' – the latter a habit many worshippers found hard to cultivate with the pew-holding system firmly in place.[50] With the return of economic prosperity at the end of the century, and the enthusiastic incumbency of Canon Welch, economic difficulties receded, allowing the Parish House (Figure 3.13) committee of 1908–9 to propose an expenditure of $80,000 on the project and to see it approved by vestry.[51]

H.P. Plumptre, Welch's successor, started his tenure with an optimistic outlook. But after the Great War, the churchwardens found themselves taking substantial amounts from endowment income (which the congregation had early in the century grown accustomed to ploughing back into investments) while they still owed $24,000 on a building mortgage.[52] With the onset of the Great Depression matters worsened. By 1930 the mortgage had $44,000 owing on it, and by 1931 St James' was selling some of its Park Lot properties, hoping to turn the proceeds into investments that would yield more certain returns than the intermittent rents of the poor. To this anxiety was added the knowledge that the cemetery was running out of lots to sell, and hence income to maintain it.[53] The situation had not improved by 1934–5, when the $7,000 repair bill for the spire and the operating deficit of over $5,000 were both charged to 'endowment income,' as operating revenues could cover neither.[54] Yet St James' was actually in good shape for a voluntary organization, and certainly for a downtown church during the Depression. The combination of pew rents, uneroded endowments and investments, public and private canvassing, and open offerings kept it throughout the period in what many other organizations must have seen as an enviable condition.

But how did the congregation spend the revenues generated from all its sources? Their priorities were in fact quite clear, and often they seemed to have little choice in their expenditures. The maintenance of the church building and Parish House, the staffing of the office, the cemetery property and rectory, and any building projects took the lion's share of the resources. Next in line came the professional staff of the cathedral. Finally, various forms of outreach – parish, diocesan, and overseas – received any remaining revenue.

One might see 1917 and 1918 as typical years, if not for total expenditures, then in terms of the ratios between priorities.[55] Of $16,135.17 charged to the general purposes account, about

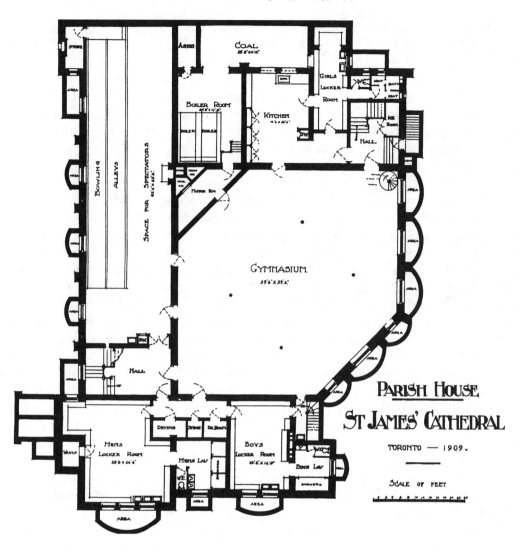

3.13 Basement floor plan for St James' Parish House, by Darling and Pearson, 1909.

$9,500 went to maintenance and support staff. The stipends of the rector's assistant clergyman (about $2,000), the deaconess (about $700), and the choirmaster and choir's allocation totalled over $4,200.[56] This did not include the rector's housing; from 1922 the church rented a house in Rosedale in lieu of Welch's 'new' rectory which was leased out for income.[57] (Alas, within a few years the tenant, the Union Jack Club, was to be raided by the police and its managing committee charged with keeping a 'common gaming and betting house.'[58]) Nor did these figures include the rector's annual salary, which was unlisted but was probably the $5,000 that came from the First York Rectory Fund, topped up with a further a $1,000 and the cost of a new car.[59] (Thus Plumptre's salary seems to have risen, during the First War to match that of the Revd H.J. Cody at St Paul's, Bloor Street.)[60] On the other hand, out of $11,817.50 of endowment income in 1917, $9,000 went to pay off the mortgage, and $2,817 was paid out as mortgage interest.

Of the total payments from the special purposes fund of $11,526.32, $3,654.87 was spent on overseas missions, $1,615.00 on the diocesan office, and $1,620.73 on 'Church Extension in Toronto.' Another $1,700 went to the rector's car and to 'cathedral improvement,' while the remaining outlays were quite small; they included $429.22 for widows and orphans, $282.56 for Trinity College and Wycliffe College, $297.23 for prisoners of war, $129.60 for the mission to the Jews, $5.00 for army and navy veterans. Nothing was spent of the $350.00 poor fund; it was passed on to the next budget year. Finally, out of 'Cemetery General Purposes' expenditures of $12,945.34, $8,094.63 went on maintenance, $2,499.96 on salaries, and the rest on repairs, supplies, and a reserve fund.

But parish life did not have as its chief end raising, investing, and spending money. Those organizations that did so did more, and many did much more. We can find a road into the complexities of life at St James' in part through the format of the vestry reports. The opening pages of the 1905 report list, one below the other, those who were ostensibly the backbone of parish life: the rector (Welch); the assistant clergy (Derwyn Trevor Owen and L.W.B. Broughall), the organist and choirmaster (Albert Ham), the vestry clerk (T.E. Rawson), the sexton (C.E. Millen), the churchwardens (J.H.G. Haggarty and A.H. Campbell), the sidesmen (thirty-seven men), the Tribunal Committee (the rector, the churchwardens, and two other men), the Finance and Consulting Committee (the rector, the churchwardens, and seven other men), the Investment Committee (the rector, the churchwardens, and three other men), the Musical Committee (the rector, the churchwardens, and seven other men – but not Ham), and the lay representatives to synod (three men). Under the last category, 'Chancel Guild,' women finally appear – nine in the choir section and sixteen in the decoration section.[61] Over the years the roster changed as a deaconess and then 'Directors of Boys' Work and Girls' Work' were added and removed, and with the coming of Plumptre, a sanctuary guild was formed.[62] But the list remained a fair sketch of the official face of parish life.

Yet parish life was richer, more creative (even chaotic), and less organized than these perpetual lists implied. Of the three great activities – worship, learning, and working – the first needs the least said about it here, being treated specifically in chapter 6. Time and again members of the congregation expressed great appreciation for their rectors, organists, and choirmasters, even as these men slowly coaxed St James' liturgical habits higher through the five decades. And they committed much effort to ensuring that worship was as good as they could imagine it to be. At the end of the century, for instance, the Musical Committee commended Dr Stocks Hammond, the recently deceased organist and choirmaster, for his 'brilliant services [which would] be long remembered,' even as they waded through 150 applications for the post of his successor, eventually choosing Dr Albert Ham. That same year the wardens appealed for increased givings so that worship would continue to be 'rendered in a way to maintain the prestige of the Parent Church of Toronto.'[63]

Likewise in Ham's second last year, during the Depression, he and the choir were praised for maintaining 'the high standards so long enjoyed at St James'.'[64] This work had included the great service that celebrated the church's centenary (after some debate about the correct year) in June 1904, as well as other great civic occasions.

Of course Welch and Plumptre both worked hard to improve the liturgy and to scold parishioners for skipping out of Holy Communion services. 'We have a large number of seatholders and other regular attendants who apparently never have been, and never intend to become, communicants,' Welch complained at Easter 1903, in the midst of some modest liturgical revision: 'It is quite one of the most perplexing problems with which I have to do.'[65] A decade later Plumptre praised regular communicants, commended the efforts of several ladies to secure another frontal for the communion table, and voiced his displeasure over the pewholders' irregular attendance and the 'almost universal neglect of Lenten observance.'[66] But on the whole worship seemed a strongly promoted, if slowly evolving, aspect of parish life.

By contrast, education in all its manifestations was a side of parish life vigorously and unreservedly promoted by all the clergy and all the people. One issue of the *St James' Cathedral Magazine* early in the century, for instance, listed (besides sermons at Morning and Evening Prayer, and at Communion) many such opportunities, which were typical for the era.[67] There was the young men's Bible class at half past two, and Sunday school and Bible classes at three o'clock every Sunday. The confirmation class took place every Wednesday evening at eight, and the rector's Bible class every Thursday at three. Along with the educational objectives of the parish magazine itself, there were hosts of lectures and discussions at the meetings of the myriad parish organizations. Missionary activity was a favourite subject (as for all Anglicans and indeed all Protestants), with the interest in diocesan and Canadian missions being joined late in the nineteenth century by a growing concern with overseas projects. The Women's Auxiliary (WA) in its many manifestations held frequent educational sessions, featuring travelogues, stories of conversions, and anthropological talks of far-off mission stations, in hopes of eliciting contributions to the great cause of the mission of the church. 'The terrible condition of our wintry roads in the backwoods of our Diocese was dwelt on,' wrote the WA correspondent after one meeting, 'and three pairs of snowshoes were at once promised to enable the clergy to visit their sick and dying parishioners.' A week earlier the ladies of the auxiliary had experienced a mishap of their own: 'A missionary lecture was given by the Rev. Arthur Lea of Gifu, Japan, and he told us many interesting things and showed us some beautiful views of the country. Unfortunately, the lantern was not in good working order – as seems frequently to be the way with lanterns.'

But the educational topics and opportunities extended far beyond the WA's diligent efforts. There were parish libraries, for instance: the Sunday school had its own library, which at one point had a heavy turnover of books.[68] Many of the other organizations that rose and fell through the half-century also had an educational purpose. In 1889 the Boys' Guild replaced the flagging, temperance-based Band of Hope and promised 'to give the boys a thorough, accurate, and systematic knowledge of Holy Scripture.'[69] And the Young People's Association, born in the energetic years of Canon Welch, put intellect at the front of its pursuits – its goals were 'edification and fellowship.' In its first month of its existence, members presented papers on the life and works of Charles Dickens. In its third month, the group heard a lecture on Rudyard Kipling by the senior curate, listened to a round-the-world travelogue and saw the accompanying slide show, and started a series of debates on the issues of the day. The first was this: 'Resolved that trades' unions as they now exist are to the best interest of the working classes.' It was a spirited contest: 'Mr. Kirkpatrick and Mr. Plant worked hard to show the evils of unionism, but in spite of their efforts the judges gave the decision to the affirmative.' The following month promised a less heated, but no less captivating event: a Trinity College professor would deliver a lecture on

3.14 'At St James' Parish Hall' in the 1920s. The boy holding the ball is Wynne Plumptre, the rector's son.

the 'Holy Grail.'[70] Finally, other organizations still had an educational component. The Mothers' Union promoted the *Mothers in Council* magazine and held informative talks to help its members understand their domestic role. The rector, for one, 'gave an address on "The Home: A Kingdom, a School, and a Sanctuary."'[71]

Quite apart from these liturgical and educational endeavours, parishioners worked for various causes and – what was almost as important – set up auxiliaries, guilds, associations, committees, and clubs to accomplish their ends. These formed the great interconnected web on which the social life of the parish depended (Figure 3.14). The 'Calendar' posted for the month scarcely revealed a day when at least one or two bodies would not be meeting. Activities and clubs appealed to the power-brokers of Toronto and their dependants – but not just to them. Many were aimed at those who lived within the parish bounds, and from the 1880s to the 1930s more and more of these were from humble backgrounds, and not all were British. But for the historian, to separate the activities aimed at middle-class parishioners from those that targeted the poorer is not always easy. The sheer number of organizations was staggering, and they were constantly changing: some reported sporadically, some were named in budgets but never really discussed or described. Others seemed not to be parish organizations but to always meet in the parish, and others were allowed to die, some being resuscitated and some replaced by new groups. Some organizations were known by several names over the years. Some met only for the season (October to Easter), while others met year round. But though it is difficult even to name or classify them all, much less trace their fifty-year fortunes, it is possible to get an overview of the many-sided splendour of St James' at work.

On the whole, parish organizations tended to fall into several groups. Those oriented towards middle-class parishioners at the centre of cathedral life often separated men, women, and children or youth. Of those targeting the parish population, most supported either temporary relief projects or ongoing 'improvement' programs. There is no doubt that most of the officers and decision-makers who directed parish life were well-established gentlemen of the parish, often the heads of families or extended clans. They were in charge of a host of committees listed at the head of every parish report. Some were directly involved in leading organizations devoted to boys and young men. But in fact the great burden of parish life rested on the ladies.

The queen of all organizations from the 1880s to the 1930s was, of course, the Women's Auxiliary (WA; see Figure 3.15). It was the most influential of all the women's groups, and the mother (formally or informally) of most of them. Without it, parish life would have withered. The most notable ladies in the parish, often but not always attached to the most important men, were its chief officers. It turned its many hands to a variety of projects, often raising money for worthy causes of its own choosing or for those pressed on it by the rector or the leading men of the congregation. The WA report for 1899–1900 occupied the last third of the vestry report and witnessed to a wide range of activities.[72] In this particular year the money had gone to (among others) Anglican missions in Algoma, Athabasca, Calgary, Mackenzie River, Moosonee, and Rupert's Land as well as to several overseas missions for Bibles, medicine and hospitals, and missionary work. The money had been raised by a variety of means: members' fees, the renting out of their rooms in the Parish House, leaflet subscriptions, the Extra-Cent-a-Day Fund, North-West pledges, and the direct canvassing of individual members. The WA presented bales of clothes and toys and other amenities to mission projects. Other activities included a service of thanksgiving, the inevitable lectures, and business meetings. Under the senior branch were arrayed others, with their own slates of officers: the Young Women's Auxiliary, the Junior Branch of the WA, and the Girls' Auxiliary (also known as the Forget-me-Nots). The Willing Workers were listed without their own slate of officers; they seem to have been local girls who did not belong to parish families. A few years later the charmingly titled Twelve Little Daughters of the King appeared – apparently a retitled continuation of the Circle of King's Daughters, which aimed at encouraging very little girls to make and collect clothes and toys for various missions.[73]

The WA supported many other activities as well and heavily subsidized other organizations. When the Guild of Service was formed in 1914–15 'for patriotic work of all kinds,' one can be sure that the WA supplied both its members and its energy.[74] In 1935 the WA was still in fine form. Its shape had changed somewhat – there was now an evening branch – and it was more oriented towards the parish projects of the Depression. The borderland between its Dorcas projects and those of the Mothers' Union is unclear, but that parishioners made dozens of outfits of clothing in both is certain. In any case, the WA remained the clearing house for much parish activity.[75] But for the authors of its 1939 history, there was more: 'Great stress [had been] laid on the

3.15 The Daffodil Luncheon of St James' Women's Auxiliary, 1905.

spiritual side of the work.' The WA had been the parish life of its hundreds of members for sixty years, and so had lived up to its motto, 'The love of Christ constraineth us.'[76]

Of the youth organizations, a number were for the boys and young men from the well-entrenched families of St James'. A choirboys' guild existed through the early years of the period but remained largely inactive, owing (as one year's report put it) to the 'greater frequency of practices of church music.' It had been convened once, ostensibly to cultivate 'brotherly sympathy and love' – no small feat, as the rector's address to it had ambitiously outlined 'the behaviour which should mark choirboys in the sacred edifice and during divine service.'[77] At the beginning of the period there seem to have been three main organizations: the Boys' Guild, which had a Bible-knowledge mandate; the Young Men's Association, of a literary and social character; and the Brotherhood of St Andrew, much favoured by the rectors and leading men of St James' as a cultivator of the next generation of parish leaders.[78] The last was the most enduring, though its activities and reporting had become sporadic by the late 1920s. It pledged itself to 'the spread of Christ's kingdom among young men,' and as the years went by it dedicated itself annually to the rules of prayer and service. This involved visiting other young men and inviting them to Brotherhood meetings and services at St James' and eventually included visits to the growing number of hotels, homes, and boarding houses within the parish bounds where young men of British extraction were settling after they immigrated to Canada.

In Welch's years, just after the turn of the century, the number of organizations for adolescents and young adults swelled. Besides the innovative Anglican Young People's Association (AYPA), which allowed mixed-sex meetings and outings for single adults, there were a variety of clubs for cricket, football, tennis, and other sports. It was originally hoped that the Parish House, completed in 1910, would serve in part as a clubhouse for youth of the parish families, but their flight to the suburbs made that more and more difficult even before the First World War.[79] Of the various clubs that rose and fell, the AYPA was the most successful, reaching its peak before the war. One of its debates summed up much of its success: '"Is single life preferable to married life?" Not very many points were brought out on this subject from either side, but those shown by those on the negative, without any preparation, were quite sufficient to drown all those given by the affirmative.'[80] Young men and women were there to meet each other, and as the years passed, social events seemed to push intellectual matters into the background.

But the parish devoted a significant portion of its energy to the growing number of humble folk and recent immigrants in the neighbourhood. Of those projects that stressed 'improvement,' as opposed to 'relief' the Sunday school was the most consistent and most prominent. Though intended for all parishioners, it became as parishioners migrated northwards more of an outreach to parish residents. In 1889–90 the morning Sunday school alone had a total of 578 on its roll (almost all from children's classes), thirty-seven teachers, and nine officers, with an average attendance of four hundred 'scholars' each Sunday.[81] Unfortunately, enrolment declined steadily: by 1917 it was down to an average total attendance of 104, and soon afterward statistics were no longer released and it began to close for the summer.[82] Yet the Sunday school continued to do much good. Homes were visited, lessons taught, and contributions to missionary and other projects undertaken. Even in its later years many teachers organized their classes energetically, both teaching lessons and identifying domestic needs. There were other forms of outreach. Before the turn of the century, for instance, the St James' chapter of the Church of England Temperance Society was hard at work among the classes that it considered most liable to succumb to the evils of drink. Parishioners were urged to help with the meetings: 'To cheer an hour or two once a month in weary and monotonous lives, and to light up worn and poverty stricken faces with smiles is certainly acceptable work.'[83]

The most thorough attempt to 'improve' those within the parish bounds came through the great Parish House project, begun by Canon Welch, who had a vision not unlike that fostered by the many 'institutional church' efforts of Protestants in the United States and Canada at about the same time. 'It is quite obvious, as my predecessor clearly saw,' Plumptre said in his 'Rector's Report' of 1910, 'that it is time to take a forward step in what may be called the social work of the church.'[84] Yet almost from its opening, with its gymnasium, clubrooms and kitchen, boxing equipment, and host of programs, the original vision seemed plagued by doubts and difficulties. It was hard to find staff, and fewer and fewer of the pewholders' families used the facilities each year. Some years it was seen as both a success and a failure in the same report – most often a failure in helping to pay for itself from membership fees, as it had been intended to do. By 1916 its reports had disappeared from the annual St James' Cathedral Report. Theories to account for its failure as a club for the adolescent children of middle-class families varied. Some blamed declining membership on competition from the YMCA, YWCA, Victor Mission, and similar bodies; others cited the fact that the respectable young men and women in the congregation increasingly preferred to spend their weekends near their families' new homes in the suburbs. The rector complained of both suburban migration and 'opportunities of cheap amusement, picture-shows and cheap theatres,'[85] sounding for a brief moment much like the pugnacious fundamentalist pastor T.T. Shields up the way at Jarvis Street Baptist Church.[86]

Yet the Parish House was not a failure in its outreach to the neighbourhood, even if the congregation lost touch with many of its efforts, and it increasingly became a facility for meetings of long-established parish organizations. During its first decade its permanent, front-line secretary noted that it was reaching young, lonely, and transient newcomers to the city and was helping them to find employment and to deal with other matters – things that it continued to do for some years.[87] In the 1920s it also became a recreation centre for impoverished youth of the parish under the 'Directors of Boys' and Girls' Work.' Though many of these young people had little to do with the cathedral itself (one Cabbagetown veteran of the clubs recalls that this was because the church really belonged to the 'Rosedale crowd'), they enjoyed the sports clubs immensely.[88] It was only with the tragic drowning of the director of boys' work and ten campers from the Parish House program in July 1926 at Balsam Lake that the athletic club, which had been aided by the Brotherhood of St Andrew, was terminated.[89] Even then, the Parish House continued some of its old functions and evolved new ones when the Depression hit.

But much of the work of St James' came necessarily in the form of 'relief.' In the 1890s the District Visitors' Society (composed mostly of women) started its operations, making as many as a thousand visits a year and giving some necessities to the 'deserving poor.' On occasion it received the help of the Brotherhood of St Andrew, 'who took in the more difficult districts, namely, Jarvis, York and Queen Streets.'[90] But the greatest work came from the successive parish deaconesses who from 1897 had their own annual reports and from 1911 were listed immediately after the clergy in the annual reports to vestry. They were in continuous contact with parish organizations, giving basic help to those whom they saw as the respectable poor, especially during the depression of the 1890s, when Miss Dixon lamented the 'scarcity of employment.'[91] Of their work, and the other work of relief, the rectors were generally quite supportive: Plumptre lamented the 'enormous amount of preventible and undeserved suffering, which might be alleviated by more sympathy and more self-sacrifice,' and prodded the congregation to act.[92] Soup kitchens, meal tickets, and clothing distribution were all taken up at various points. The greatest systemic endeavours took place in the early 1930s, when St James' kept its own poor fund and relief efforts going and contributed for a few years to both the Anglican Unemployment Fund and the Parochial Relief Fund.[93] One might wish that the amounts given had been greater and the effort more sustained, but in fairness St James' had its own struggles. From 1935 it was caught up in the matter of becoming the diocesan cathedral, which challenged both its parochial character and its priorities.

THE MIND OF ST JAMES'

Beneath its public image, its reputation, and its sometimes frenetic parish life lay St James' intellectual core. If not always consciously, the rectors, wardens, and people of the cathedral expressed many of their deepest convictions about God on many occasions and in a variety of ways. One might say that their opinions fell into two categories: those about God, theology, belief, and worship on the one hand, and those about humanity, society, politics, and life on the other. While the two classes were of course related, they were not always in harmony with each other. Parishioners most certainly disagreed with each other at points. But in retrospect, clear patterns of thought can be detected, though they were by no means consistent or stable through-out the half-century between the 1880s and the 1930s. It would seem that the parish as a whole went through roughly three stages. The 1880s and 1890s can be seen as a time of a moderate but lively evangelicalism and increasingly unfounded cultural confidence. The period up to the end of the war, or even the early 1920s, was characterized by a softer, broader evangelicalism, typified by cultural and theological re-integration. The final period was one of broad Protestantism and cultural secularism.

Before the turn of the century, a wag might well have said that cathedral folk believed in the God of Wycliffe College and held to the theology of the Church Missionary Society. Wycliffe was a college formed with the strong assistance of the men and women of St James'; it had met at first in the church's schoolhouse, and it continued to be supported by individual parishioners as well as by the parish collectively after it got its own buildings.[94] Though the college's evangelical stance was variously defined by the members of its faculty and its supporters, its outlook largely mirrored that of contemporary St James'. The parish confessed conversion and a lively, experiential faith buttressed by a conservative, nineteenth-century interpretation of the Protestant reformers and a strong desire to protect the scriptures. This stance was buttressed by cottage meetings, temperance gatherings, 'personal work,' and missions to convert the Jews. The spread of the 'Master's Kingdom' or the 'Kingdom of God' (slippery phrases in hindsight) most certainly involved a strong desire (as seen, for instance, in the brotherhood of St Andrew) to 'bring some one young man within the hearing of the Gospel of Jesus Christ every week.'[95] This evangelicalism entailed culling the Sunday-school library of dangerous and 'condemned' books and defending Holy Writ, 'in an age when attacks [were] being made on the Bible from all sides and even from within the fold of the Christian Church itself,'[96] and it precluded slipping into 'a shallow sense of sin [which] leads to a low estimate of pardon.'[97] Likewise guilt, confessions of redemption, and on occasion even public weeping, formed part of life at St James'.[98] It was later said (and probably with truth) that Canon DuMoulin had helped St James' to soften its prejudices against Trinity College and catholic liturgy,[99] but St James' evangelicalism, if moderate, remained firmly held down to the end of the century.

About the world around it St James' had few doubts. Society was ordered by God, with all people and institutions set in their proper stations of life under the sovereign of the British Empire, and all relationships were understood in terms of duties and rights. The congregation sincerely believed that their first duty to God, even in a time of economic depression, was to get from their investments as much as was justly possible, 'to ensure that the Church's work shall be fittingly performed, and its services rendered in a way to maintain the prestige of the Parent Church of Toronto.'[100] God had put St James' where it was for a purpose – which was to nurture those who would govern, whether mayors, politicians, or great manufacturers. The fate that might await it far down the road, 'to become a church chiefly for strangers and the poor,' was too foreign to its calling to consider seriously.[101] But those holding the levers of power had a responsibility to 'the poor of the parish' – a phrase often repeated in their various reports.

As everyone but radicals had agreed all through the nineteenth century, social class was ordained by God. Thus parish leaders believed that the very poor were not to be raised out of their class but rather cheered on their way if God called them home from their hopeless lives. Alternatively, they were to be 'relieved' by visits and soup kitchens and so on, especially during times of economic distress, and particularly if they were 'respectable' in their unwearying self-help and 'deserving' by their patience and humility under their unavoidable suffering.[102] There was no cruelty intended in any of these attitudes; they simply flowed from certain assumptions about the hierarchical nature of society and the providential ways of God.

The next intellectual phase of the parish's life, lasting roughly, from 1900 to the later 1910s, was one strongly influenced by a persuasive rector, Edward Ashurst Welch (served 1899–1909; Figure 3.16) and his assistant Derwyn Trevor Owen (1902–8), later primate of all Canada. Welch was a priest's son and a graduate of Cambridge University, after which he had come under the direct influence of the great scholar and notable moderate churchman Bishop J.B. Lightfoot. He came to St James' from Trinity College, Toronto, where as provost he had established cordial relations with Wycliffe College for the first time in the 1890s.[103] His churchmanship was tinged with Anglo-Catholicism, but he could not be considered either a theological extremist or a diocesan partisan. Owen, though not nearly the scholar that Welch was, had felt the influence of the moderate and progressive Anglo-Catholicism of the great theologian Charles Gore in England, after having been converted in Toronto under the influence of the great American evangelist D.L. Moody.[104] At St James' these two clerics contributed to the softening of evangelical theology and evangelical attitudes – a softening that characterized mainline Protestants elsewhere during the period, as did the other speakers and assistant clergy that came through the cathedral during Welch's rectorship.

On the whole the congregation did not find this intellectual shift objectionable. Nor do Welch's liturgical tendencies seem to have upset many of his parishioners. He could say by 1905, along with his congregation: 'Revivals, of which we are hearing much just now, are commonly thought to be almost ... confined to other Communions.'[105] If at times Welch preferred to talk and write in terms of stagnation and lethargy versus stretching, progress, and cultivation, rather than in the Calvinistic terms of sin and redemption, he remained by most definitions christocentric and orthodox.[106] He professed himself alarmed at the 'insidious growth of a sceptical habit of mind.'[107] But he was not dismayed by critical scholarship itself, and this stance allowed him to work within the broader, softer evangelicalism of St James'. The congregation was not interested in the fundamentalist offensives that other Anglicans had either launched or joined. Welch was not even inclined to 'defend' the Bible: 'It would be well if we could all realise that this moral and spiritual power of the Bible is unaffected by the "Higher Criticism,"' he wrote. 'Criticism has its own perfectly legitimate sphere ... Fear of consequences seems to me to indicate a most timorous soul or a weak-kneed faith or both.'[108]

St James' vision of its role in society also began to change. Debates on the benefits of trade unions, the value of the monarchy, and other 'settled' matters were gradually permitted, even among the youth of the parish family. The church also began to see its duty as going much further than merely serving as a nursery for politicians, professionals, and captains of industry – it was to help regenerate society. This was not an unusual ideal in the era when Anglicans came as close as they ever did to embracing the Social Gospel – a movement that

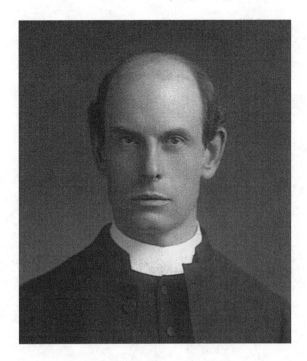

3.16 Revd Canon Edward Ashurst Welch, provost of Trinity College 1895–9,
rector of St James' and subdean of St Alban's 1899–1909. He returned to England to become
provost and vicar of Wakefield Cathedral, another dual cathedral and parochial church.

reached its first peak in Canada at about the onset of the Great War.[109] The Brotherhood of St Andrew began to talk less of religious conversion and more of 'outcast and homeless men, for whom, until very recently, the Church of England in this city … has done almost nothing.'[110]

At a more systemic and theological level, Welch enthusiastically explained to the parish that the new printings of the Prayer Book rearranged the commas in the Lord's Prayer, with the result that the 'coming of the Kingdom' was associated with earth in the present as well as heaven in the future.[111] This became an important theme at a time when the Protestant church – of which St James' was a conspicuous example – suddenly began to realize that its culture-shaping role was being eroded by hosts of new 'secular' (non-Christian) public institutions. This secularization – the forcing apart of church and society, or the separation of Christian belief from public welfare – was something to be resisted.[112] St James' buckled down to re-create an integrated Christian parish in Toronto, the city of which it had once been the hub. And at the centre of its plans was the new Parish House, which, Welch said, would be St James' step forward 'for righteousness and clean living in [the] community.'[113] 'This House,' wrote Plumptre in his foreword to the architect's plans, 'will touch all sides of life in the Parish – spiritual, intellectual, social and physical.'[114]

The final intellectual phase of this era, from the late 1910s to the mid-1930s, is somewhat harder to chronicle.[115] It would seem that the broad sympathies of Henry Plumptre (rector 1909–35; Figure 3.17) – that is, his 'liberal tendencies in theology and churchmanship,'[116] – flowered at St James' as the congregation followed the broad Protestant road through the complexities

3.17 Revd Canon Henry Pemberton Plumptre, dean and chaplain of Wycliffe College 1901–3,
rector of St James' and subdean of St Alban's 1909–35, reading at the eagle lectern in St James'.

of Canadian life from the late 1910s onward. He was a promoter of 'Protestant co-operation, if not unity.'[117] The themes of his preaching were not surprising: 'to further the cause of Christian unity [and] to develop the sense of social responsibility.'[118] A silent but eloquent testimony to this broad Protestantism was the growing preoccupation of both Plumptre and the congregation with the institutional character of church life – with statistics, programs, and administrative detail – often to the exclusion of coherent spiritual expressions of the cathedral's reason for existence. When it was expressed, the raison d'être of the parish could sound exceedingly vague. The rector's prayer for 1913 is an example of the direction in which St James' theology and understanding of society would soon be headed: 'That, as in the past, so in the future, St James' Cathedral will stand for all that is best in our holy religion, and will be a faithful witness for truth, justice and charity in the City of Toronto and throughout the Dominion.' These had been the characteristic values of the previous period, but they had then been tied to more specific spiritual confessions about God and the world with which Plumptre was not terribly concerned. In fact, his sympathy for the religious scepticism of the 'scientific youth' of the 1920s got him into trouble for a while, especially when he listed among the debatable issues the doctrines of the Virgin Birth and the Trinity.[119]

3.18 Dedication of the memorial cross to parishioners fallen in
the First World War, 1924. For an account of the cross see pp. 213–14.

One could not, however, argue successfully that spirituality at St James' declined in this period; both the service registers and snatches of spiritual conversation would confound such a notion. However, one might say that the community of worship and prayer became detached from the community at work in the parish. The Great War aided this blurring process for the cathedral (and many other churches) as Canadians pitched into a very broad national effort. The end of the war (see Figure 3.18) left St James' with no clear sense of how its worship and work fitted together – a disjuncture that ended in growing secularization. For St James', as for many Protestant churches, this secularization fostered a growing sense that the church's chief end was to worship God and (at arm's length) simply to bless all efforts to help the unfortunate. One of the chief signs of this new attitude was the placing of the programs of the Parish House in the hands of professional 'workers' (from 1923) instead of those of clergy and lay volunteers. Moreover, the director of boys' work was instructed not to convert souls (as one might have expected DuMoulin to require) or spread the Kingdom of God (as Welch would have expected), but merely 'to stop the leakage of teen aged boys from the organizations and influences of the church.'[120] Soon national organizations (neither Anglican nor offically Christian) such as the Rangers, Brownies, Scouts, and Cubs were filling the Parish House and the annual reports.[121]

Inevitable though they were, it would be unfair to say that professionalization and secularization completely characterized the mind of St James' in the 1920s and 1930s. Older parish organizations carried on, if in an attenuated form. Lay volunteers did help in various programs and introduced strangers (often recently immigrated or out of luck) to the worship of the church.[122] But by the 1930s the congregation of St James' had accepted the concept that its primary role was to be a well-endowed community of worship with a spiritual and aesthetic mission. All other programs were to remain clearly secondary to this goal and to belong to a different sphere. By 1935 St James' was quite prepared to be the diocesan cathedral, to be recognized for what it had learned to do so well, and finally to take steps forward to explore both the possibilities and the limits of this new role.

4

The Beautiful
Downtown Cathedral,
1935–1997

C. THOMAS McINTIRE

CATHEDRAL AGAIN

THE UNANIMOUS DECISION by the synod of the diocese of Toronto on 16 May 1935 to abandon St Alban's and for the second time make St James' the seat of the bishop generated new life for St James' (see Figure 4.1). The transfer occurred during hard times for Toronto and the capitalist world, still sunk in severe economic depression. St James' experienced the return of her glory and the achievement of the goal she had contemplated since at least 1909 and actively sought since at least 1918.[1]

People at St James' were relieved, and some at St Paul's on Bloor Street annoyed, that the synod had not made St Paul's the cathedral, as might have happened. St Paul's was the largest and wealthiest parish in the diocese and with its stone Gothic massiveness had the more majestic edifice. Its completion in 1913 had played a large role in the collapse of St Alban's. But, in contrast with low-church St Paul's with its focus on preaching, St James' still carried the cathedral tradition, symbolized by her having never relinquished the title and many cathedral-like functions. She also bore the impression of the higher standing of old Toronto society over those still regarded as the nouveaux riches gathered on Bloor Street. St James' had more of a feel of antiquity, and she was connected with the origins of the English settlements in this region and the creation of the diocese. Indeed, the bodies of John Strachan, the first bishop, Henry James Grasett, the first dean, and Sarah Maria Stewart, the first dean's wife, lay buried beneath the chancel. Archbishop Derwyn Trevor Owen (Figure 4.2), the fifth bishop of Toronto (1932–47) and former bishop of Niagara, acknowledged St James' as 'the Mother Church of Old York, and of Toronto,' which had given birth to the other churches and nourished them as well as the city.[2]

St James' became the cathedral again, but not in the same sense as St Alban's had been. Officially St James' became a 'pro-cathedral,' which meant that she had a dual identity, doubling as a cathedral and a parish church. The cathedral question that had beset the diocese for fifty years was not closed for good. The diocese explicitly left open the option of creating a proper cathedral later. This decision put subtle pressure on St James' to keep on proving that she really embodied everything that a cathedral should be.

4.1 St James' Cathedral in downtown Toronto at the time of the world Anglican Congress in 1963. The Parish House appears on the left, with the Diocesan Centre, built for the congress, adjoining.

In old English usage and Strachan's vision, a cathedral was a self-governing, self-financing, and self-contained corporation composed of a dean and a chapter of canons, independent of the vagaries of parish concerns and control, and devoted to the service of the diocese as a whole. This vision was what had failed at St Alban's after fifty years of blundering and left stone remains that recalled the ruined choirs of England. As a pro-cathedral, St James' was what

4.2 Most Revd Derwyn Trevor Owen, bishop of Toronto 1932–47 and primate of all Canada 1934–47. He had served as a curate at St James' under Welch and restored it to cathedral status in 1935.

the synod cathedral committee styled 'a church used instead of, or as a substitute for, a cathedral church.' In this St James' was like every other cathedral in Canada, except Quebec City's earlier and Victoria's then, as well as most cathedrals created in England since 1836, including Ripon, St Alban's, Truro, and Wakefield.[3]

The synod envisaged that an act by the legislature of Ontario might be necessary to make St James' the pro-cathedral, but none was secured. The legislature simply dissolved St Alban's as a cathedral corporation, effective 9 April 1936. This date may be taken as the moment when, by virtue of the synod decision of 16 May 1935, St James' the parish church formally also became St James' the pro-cathedral.[4]

The title 'pro-cathedral' stayed with St James' in *Crockford's Clerical Directory* into the 1970s. Every once in a while, the churchwardens or the dean raised a question about the ambiguity of the legal and financial status of St James' as a pro-cathedral, but nothing changed. Just about everyone forgot what 'pro-cathedral' meant and simply took for granted that St James' was the cathedral.[5] It seems that few people gave much attention to these technicalities, even in 1935. Although the original text of the memorandum of agreement between the archbishop and St James', by which the archbishop actually constituted St James' as his cathedral, was negotiated and approved in 1935, the final and revised text was not signed until 15 March 1940. It did not occur to anyone to consecrate St James' as the cathedral until preparations began for the one-hundredth anniversary of the diocese in 1939.[6]

The transfer to St James' happened invisibly, without anyone acknowledging it. Nobody thought to move the bishop's chair from St Alban's to St James'. Officials at St James' simply kept using the throne made in honour of Bishop Strachan in 1870, which had never left St James' and continued to sit at the west end of the communion table. The restored bishop's throne was the most important symbol in the whole transaction: St James' was the cathedral because it was the official seat of the bishop of Toronto. The throne indicated rather well the presence of the bishop in the cathedral: the bishop was rarely there in person, but he was present symbolically at every service and at all times, day and night. The memorandum defined his powers. He had the right to take part in any service of the cathedral as he desired and to preach up to six times a year. He could use the cathedral and the parish hall for diocesan services and meetings and other special events, provided that he consulted the rector in advance and paid for them. He had authority over such occasions, except for the music, which remained under the rector's authority, while the rector made all the arrangements. The agreement could be terminated by either side on only one year's notice.[7]

The bishop gave St James' the traditional accoutrements of a cathedral. He appointed a dean, Charles Edward Riley (see Figure 4.3), but not until 1937, and without any powers. The title was 'Dean of Toronto,' not 'dean of the cathedral' or 'dean of St James.' His powers within St James' derived from his position as rector, the incumbent of the parish. It later became common to speak of the dean in an honorary way as the senior priest of the diocese. The bishop also gave St James' a 'chapter' of canons, ten carried over from St Alban's and twelve new ones appointed in 1937 and 1938, for a total of twenty-two at the start. They had no powers either, and not even cathedral duties. In the coming years, bishops replenished and added to the body of canons, with the number rising to a peak of fifty in 1972. The title became an honour bestowed for loyal or exceptional service.[8]

The only corporation that the cathedral had was the parish corporation, composed for some purposes of the two churchwardens but for others of the rector and the churchwardens meeting together. From the 1960s, they were joined by one or more non-voting deputy wardens. The minutes of the corporation recorded the affairs of these meetings.

The prospects for St James' as cathedral were stunning. People were well aware that, even then, Toronto was the largest, wealthiest, and most influential diocese in Canada and that its cathedral might expect to provide leadership for the diocese as well as for the whole Church of England in Canada. Owen's own pre-eminence reinforced the point: he was at once bishop of Toronto, metropolitan of the ecclesiastical province of Ontario and hence archbishop, and, from 1934, primate of all Canada.[9]

To this was added the position of St James' as something like an official church for the city, the province, and the Crown in this region of Canada. At the very moment when St James' was becoming the cathedral, King George V died. The memorial service at St James' in January 1936, held on the day of his funeral in England, was attended by the lieutenant-governor, the prime minister of Ontario and the cabinet, the mayor and the city council, and the judges of the high courts of Ontario. At the end of that eventful year, the churchwardens expressed 'sincere regret' about the 'constitutional crisis' ending with the abdication of King Edward. Referring to George VI, they added immediately, 'To our new King we offer our homage and fealty. Long may he reign over us.'[10] After the accession of his daughter to the throne as Elizabeth II in 1952, his former consort, as Elizabeth the Queen Mother, worshipped in St James' several times over the years during visits to Toronto, as did Queen Elizabeth II herself.

4.3 Revd John Ames Coombs, assistant 1951–61 (l.) and Very Revd Charles Edward Riley, dean of Toronto and rector of St James' 1936–63 (r.), in their Canterbury caps and funeral copes, standing at the memorial cross in 1955.

CATHEDRALIZATION

Transforming Building, Liturgy, and Music, 1935–82

The people and clergy of St James' became captivated by cathedral consciousness, and they occupied themselves with the demands of the cathedral side of their now dual identity. They undertook the project of creating for their beloved parish church a distinctive cathedral culture. They took deliberate steps to render St James' more cathedral-like. They followed a social and theological image drawn vaguely from the great cathedrals of England. It mattered to them that St James' had a dean and chapter, because that was what a cathedral should have. It also mattered that St James' had deep connections with civic society, because a cathedral ought to express the integration of the spiritual with the whole of life. They wanted the cathedral to be a house of prayer that was fit to be the house of the bishop.

To reach this goal they focused on shaping the building, liturgy, and music. Their actions during the following decades pushed the worship, sound, and look of St James' persistently towards greater embellishment and magnificence. The ideals guiding them were beauty and majesty. They found these in Psalm 96:6, appointed for evening prayer in the 1918 Canadian revision of the Book of Common Prayer which the cathedral then used: 'O worship the Lord in the beauty of holiness: let the whole earth stand in awe of him.'[11] The theology underlying the ideals stressed the centrality of dignified, lovely, and feminine worship directed to a high, powerful, and masculine divine monarch, king above all kings, elevated even above the king of Great Britain and emperor of India. The cathedral was the mother, and God was the father whose presence the bishop and clergy represented. The aesthetic vision played with two traditions, a classical notion of beauty as order and harmony, and an eighteenth-century conception of the sublime as the exalted and the awe-inspiring. In the worship leaflets, in sermons, in annual reports to vestry, in the corporation minutes, in successive editions of the guide to St James', and no doubt in their conversation, both clergy and people alike remarked that the things that they accomplished rendered the building, the services, and the music ever more beautiful and majestic, done according to the highest standards of excellence. This they repeated again and again, for years to come, at every turn, as these symbols became enveloped in what it meant for St James' to be the cathedral. Once the churchwardens nearly thanked the vestry clerk, the auditors, and all the employees of the cathedral and St James' Cemetery for 'their beautiful co-operation throughout the year.' But they caught the text in time, blacked out 'beautiful,' and inserted 'helpful' instead.[12]

The St James' project contrasted remarkably with the reconstruction of the Metropolitan United Church nearby at Queen and Church streets during the same period and under similar social and economic conditions. After a disastrous fire, the church, already known as the 'Methodist cathedral,' was rebuilt on a grand scale in 1928 to be something like the 'Toronto cathedral' for the newly created United Church of Canada. Over the coming decades the clergy and congregation, in keeping with their theology and social policy, concentrated their efforts on preaching, social outreach, and music, and these became the marks of their church. Their work showed that there was more than one way to make an important ecclesial presence downtown and, by contrast, accentuated the distinctiveness of the cathedralization of St James'.[13]

At St James' the officials started with the interior and made several immediate changes to enhance her character as a cathedral. The renovation of the baptistery in the east porch in 1935 made the locus of baptism more glorious. Large benefactions in 1936 by William and Maude (Beatty) Cawthra, from two old Toronto families, magnified the sacred space and moved functional features out of sight. With part of the money, the cathedral removed the choir vestry from the southeast vestibule and closed the choir room underneath, a legacy of the days when the choir sang in the gallery overhead. In the vacated vestibule space, they constructed St George's Chapel, 'so beautifully conceived and embellished' by Maude Cawthra. This gave the new cathedral her first chapel. Its white, red, and gold vitality contrasted vividly with the dim look of the nave. The new stained-glass windows of the chapel symbolized 'the Christian amity' formed by 'the union of the Church of England and the British Empire under the Crown.' With the rest of the money they removed the clergy vestry from under the west organ next to the chancel, and in the vacated space installed the sacristy, reached through a new door opened from the chancel. They created a new vestry for the choir and clergy as well as a new choir room in renovated space in the lower level of the Parish House. The gift included 'the subterranean passage-way,' later called 'the tunnel,' joining the cathedral building and the Parish House.[14]

Becoming the cathedral gave the impetus to the reconstruction of the organ in 1936 and the installation of a four-manual console. The churchwardens exclaimed that the organ was now 'worthy of the Cathedral.' They praised 'the excellence of its mechanism and the beauty of its tone.' The choirmaster and the choir of gentlemen and boys likewise 'have risen to new heights in the excellence of their portion of the services.'[15] In May 1937 the choir began to wear blue cassocks and white surplices, with white ruffles for the boys, but they foresaw immediately that this enhancement would not be enough. The corporation asked Owen, in his capacity as primate of Canada, to apply to the Crown for permission for the choir to use royal red for their cassocks, as even more befitting a cathedral. The clergy continued to wear their black cassocks and white surplices in the services. Within less than a year of becoming the cathedral, St James' was already, said the churchwardens, 'adequately fulfilling its diocesan functions.' They believed that the services have 'never been more beautiful' and the music never more 'excellent.'[16]

Except for new grass and planting of ivy, they left the dark exterior of the building largely untouched, hoping that the ivy would 'add a mantle of green to the walls of the Cathedral.' The building sat within the former parish burial ground, surrounded on all sides by a low brick fence with posts surmounted by miniature towers of ironwork, connected by a chain hung with porcupine balls. The city paid the cathedral for the upkeep of the grounds – a token of the civic connection of the cathedral.[17] The Parish House at 65 Church Street, on the northwest corner of the grounds, still contained the vestry office, the house chapel, the meeting rooms, the social rooms, and the gymnasium, which served the parish, and the auditorium used by the diocese. The Synod Office, housed since 1931 in the former St James' rectory, sat on the northeast corner of the grounds at 135 Adelaide Street. To the east, extending to Jarvis Street, and to the south, opposite the front façade, were dense networks of commercial buildings, factories, warehouses, houses, and lanes. People found this vista picturesque, suggestive of the streets of old Quebec.[18] St James' still possessed and operated St James' Cemetery, with the lovely Chapel of St James the Less, at 635 Parliament Street, north of Wellesley Street. This grand and luxuriant site, long a burial ground for the élite families of old Toronto society, amplified St James' character as a cathedral.

The resignation of Henry Plumptre as rector, effective at the end of December 1935, cleared the way for the archbishop to choose his own candidate to run the new St James'. But Owen had difficulty getting the man he wanted right away, and the transition to cathedral status occurred without the benefit of a rector or dean. It is remarkable that the initiative for the work and the symbolism for the new cathedral came very much from the churchwardens and people, not from the diocese or even the clergy. Arthur Briarly Browne, the assistant priest since 1926, acted as rector-in-charge for 1936 and half of 1937. William Wells Hewitt, new in 1933, remained as organist and choirmaster. Charles Edward Riley had been Owen's dean in the diocese of

4.4 The cathedral staff at Dean Riley's farewell dinner in 1961: l. to r., Revd Kenneth Hill,
Revd John Coombs, the Dean, and Miss May Cameron, parish worker.

Niagara. He became rector of St James' in July 1937 as well as dean of Toronto – a title that
Owen had kept unassigned when he became bishop of Toronto in 1932. The dean and the
rector were now the same person, representing the diocese and the parish.[19]

Riley had an assistant cleric, as had Plumptre before him; from 1951 there were usually two
at a time (see Figure 4.4).[20] From the 1960s on some of these had the title vicar, associate, or
precentor. Riley immediately added a deaconess to the staff, restoring a position that had been
occupied most years from the 1890s to 1925 but had since lapsed. There were two deaconesses
in his time, Elizabeth D. Gulliver (1937–44), and Florence Lea (1944–58), who became Florence
Lea Goddard after she married the vestry clerk, H.E. Goddard, in 1950. They were followed by
a parish worker, May Cameron (1958–61), who did many of the same things as a deaconess.
Riley also appointed two honorary assistants in 1939, one being Plumptre. Thereafter St James'
had from one to five honorary assistants, usually people with primary appointments elsewhere
who helped carry the worship duties of the parish and were paid small stipends.

Riley was the first rector of St James' educated in Canada. He was also the first who held a
theological degree from Trinity College, Toronto, the college founded by Bishop John
Strachan. Briarly Brown, the priest, who had also been Plumptre's last assistant (1926–35), as
well as Robert Seaborn, Riley's first assistant (1937–41), also held Trinity College degrees.

Thereafter, every rector until Douglas Stoute in 1994, and nearly all the assistant and associate clergy through 1997, including all but one of the vicars, had degrees from Trinity College, which indirectly gave the college extraordinary liturgical and theological influence in the cathedral's life after 1935.

Cathedralization continued unabated as Riley joined the project of embellishing St James'. During 1937 the Cawthra family gave a prayer desk. Parish members offered a processional cross in 1937 and funds for a credence table in 1938, but the acceptance of both was postponed in a momentary display of hesitation about where the cathedral project was leading. In 1938 officials placed a Canterbury cross near the baptistery. It was mounted on stone taken from the walls of Canterbury Cathedral in England and sent from Canterbury in 1935 to all the cathedrals of the British Empire as a symbol of spiritual and imperial unity. In anticipation of the formal consecration of the cathedral in 1939, the interior was cleaned and redecorated and the marble steps at the altar were raised. The churchwardens observed, 'These changes have added greatly to the beauty of the Cathedral, while maintaining its mellow appearence.'[21]

The consecration, on the evening of Tuesday, 17 October 1939, long in planning, fell just weeks after the start of the Second World War. The occasion coincided with both the centenary of the diocese and the fiftieth anniversary of the Woman's Auxiliary (WA) at St James'. The churchwardens and the leaders of the WA joined together to mark the event. It was a moment to position the cathedral in the course of the ages. A centenary leaflet on the history of St James' was circulated in advance of the celebration, and the order of service itself contained a historical narrative by T.A. Reed of Trinity College and a detailed chronology running from 1796 to 1939. They told 'the story of the cathedral' from the days of Muddy York to the foundation of the diocese and the consecration that night. St Alban's was missing from the tale as if it had never existed. The pictorial history of the church displayed in the glorious stained-glass windows of the nave, from Pentecost to the formation of the diocese, took on new meaning. The process of forgetting about St Alban's was under way, and the reconstructed memory easily fashioned St James' into the only cathedral that the diocese had ever had. The event was a solemn and mighty display, with attendance recorded at 1,050. It began and ended with a procession, and featured the signing of the sentence of consecration and a sermon, but not holy communion. Holy communion occurred in a separate service that morning with ninety communcants.[22] Two months later the wardens approved the offer of the silver processional cross, which they now said was much needed to enhance the beauty of such services. It was set in a holder on the left side of the chancel and carried for the first time on Christmas Eve 1939.[23]

The churchwardens and Riley gave their support during 1939 to a substantial project of enlarging the chancel. The aim was to serve better the cathedral image and functions of St James'. Riley attributed the vision of a magnified chancel to Strachan, and his evidence was the image of the church in the front nave window to the west of the pulpit. The enlargement, they said, would better suit the presence of the bishop and accommodate the dignitaries of the church at diocesan events as well as providing space for the choir at all times and generally adding dignity to a beautiful building.[24]

Special services and diocesan events were numerous and significant. Chief among these were the elections and consecrations of bishops, diocesan celebrations, and services for the annual synods of Toronto. The business sessions of diocesan synods convened in the auditorium of the Parish House. Ordinations of deacons and priests occurred in the church, as did confirmations and the induction of canons and the archdeacon of York. Diocesan organizations, such as the WA, as well as civic groups, such as St George's Society of Toronto, came to the cathedral for their annual corporate services.

Royal and military connections were important to the cathedral. Royal commemorations and memorial services were held there. Members of the royal family attended when they visited Toronto. A grand rendition of the royal coat of arms continued to be displayed prominently on the south gallery below the organ casing, visible to all as they left the nave. In 1940 this was repaired and cleaned.[25] Because of the war the associations of the cathedral with the military increased. The Royal Regiment of Canada deposited their colours and those of their forerunner units there in 1940. St James' already had a few colours mounted on the west wall. The new colours and some of the older ones were immediately hung from the pillars of the nave. Others were added after the war, resulting in an array of military colours hanging throughout the nave and from both the east and the west walls. The Royal Regiment, following the tradition established in the 1860s by their predecessor unit, the Royal Grenadiers, continued to recognize St James' as their regimental church. On Remembrance Sunday each November they attended worship in their scarlet full-dress uniforms. The Governor-General's Horse Guards came annually as well and eventually deposited their standard in St James' in 1971. The cathedral at the time welcomed the military associations as expressions of her on-going civic role, and the people and clergy commented on how much the colours added to the beauty of the dim interior.[26]

The cathedral opened a fund for the chancel enlargement in 1939, and the corporation commissioned a design to show the congregation at the vestry meeting in 1941, but war led to postponement. Members could not, however, wait for the war to end before continuing their cathedral project. During 1941 they moved the bishop's and dean's chairs to what they called their correct places at either end of the choir on the east side. They put a bishop's mitre in the sanctuary to mark the bishop's seat. They finally acquired the credence table offered earlier and placed it in the sanctuary. In the previous year they had placed a litany desk partway back in the centre aisle of the nave. In 1943 they installed a loud-speaker system and removed the sounding-board over the great pulpit, opening up the look and feel of the chancel. About this time they discontinued the occasional placement of short pew benches facing frontward down the length of the centre aisle. The women of the Chancel Guild, led by Mrs Hedley C. Macklem, began a long-term project to provide needlepoint cushions at the communion rail and in the chancel, following the model of English and American cathedrals.[27]

When the war ended, the dean and the churchwardens moved quickly to embellish the chancel in keeping with their image of a proper cathedral. It was also a time of transition towards use of liturgically heightened language. After the vestry meeting of January 1946 gave approval, they replaced the communion table in the sanctuary with a new one, more majestic than before. It was massive, measuring twelve feet long by three and a half feet deep, a full five feet longer and a little deeper than the old one. They removed the Gothic wooden reredos in order to mount riddel posts to the sides and a new dorsal curtain at the back, better suited to their image of cathedral-style worship. A new superfrontal came soon after, as did a silver cross, silver candlesticks, and silver vases for the new communion table. They began to call the new communion table the 'main altar,' and this soon transmuted into the 'high altar.' They acquired a movable Glastonbury chair for use at ordinations and confirmations when the bishop needed to sit at the top of the chancel steps. They affixed a wooden cross to the wall behind the pulpit, in full view of the congregation during the sermon. In the middle of all this, St James' received a visit from the archbishop of Canterbury, Geoffrey Fisher, in September 1946. He wore an elaborate cope and mitre, which made a deep impression. The annual report for the year proudly displayed the photograph of the archbishop in his cope, but no Canadian cleric dared to imitate this fancy dress at St James'. By 1950, as a memorial to the many members of St James' killed in the two world wars, the corporation placed two sets of three ornate seats, called sedilia, on either side of the high altar under the great windows, for the use of servers, clergy, and visiting bishops.

The dean and churchwardens next created another altar. They moved the old communion table – the memorial to Bishop Strachan from 1870 – to the north end of the east aisle, removed the nearest pews in that aisle, and added a prayer desk and a communion rail. They named this the 'side altar' or the 'east altar,' dedicating it in 1947. By 1953 they were calling it the 'Lady Altar,' or the Chapel of St Mary the Virgin.[28] St James' now displayed three altars, two of them created since resumption of cathedral status: the high altar, the Lady Altar, and the altar of St George's Chapel. Besides these were two other chapels: the House Chapel, located in the first room on the west side of the first floor in the Parish House, and rededicated as the Chapel of the Holy Spirit in 1952, and the Chapel of St James the Less in St James' Cemetery. Altogether five altars now came under the jurisdiction of St James'. Archbishop Owen celebrated at the new main altar on several occasions before his death in 1947. His successor, Alton Ray Beverley, the sixth bishop (1947–55), did not come to the cathedral as often as Owen.

After all those years, the drive among the clergy and people of St James' to beautify and enhance the cathedral did not slacken. During 1953, the centenary of the cathedral building, they erected a grand vestry building, attached to the northwest corner of the chancel, to accomodate the increasing collection of vestments and the greater number of clergy vesting for all those special services. Inside it resembled an elegant gentleman's sitting room. The location facilitated the ever more elaborate processions of clergy moving to and from the chancel.[29] Then in 1955 officials extended the floor of the chancel into the nave over the steps, created a low stone screen 'rising from the floor of the nave to about 27 inches above the floor of the choir,' brought the communion rail eighteen inches forward to enlarge the sanctuary, paved the sanctuary floor with marble, constructed eight ornate canons' stalls with canopies at the back of the choir on each side to match the sedilia, added two prayer desks, remodelled the bishop's throne to match the stalls, and moved the lectern to the far left side behind the new stone screen. These changes, said the churchwardens, have 'considerably enhanced the interior of the Cathedral.'[30]

The question of the extension of the chancel remained, however, since this was not quite the work that Riley thought Strachan had envisioned. He tried again in 1960 and 1961 to rally support for a still larger chancel. It looked at first as if he had the funds, but the project failed when the bishop apparently persuaded the donor to give the money for church extension in the diocese instead. The most obtained was the removal of two rows of pews at the front of the nave in 1968 to allow for more movement by the clergy during elaborate services. More pews came out later for the same reason – those in the front half of the west aisle in 1971, and all the remaining side pews in the renovation of 1979–82. A new door nearer the sanctuary and the organ console was cut in 1963 between the chancel and the sacristy to facilitate the flow of clergy and servers during the Eucharist.[31]

The achievement of 1955 marked the end of the continuous process, extending over twenty years, to embellish and enlarge the sanctuary and chancel (see Figure 4.5). It finished the look of the central worship space. The results appeared suitably magnificent to the people and clergy, who readily likened their church to the cathedrals of England.

The transformation of worship proceeded in unison with the beautification of the building and furnishings from 1935 to 1955. To the people and clergy, the work done with the sacred environment meant something only in so far as it became a worthy vehicle for liturgy and music that were beautiful, dignified, and most excellent.

The round of services in 1935 and 1936 featured Morning Prayer at eleven every Sunday morning with Holy Communion added at least one Sunday a month. The centre of the service was the pulpit and the sermon, not the communion table and Holy Communion. The eight-o'clock morning service was always Holy Communion. Evening Prayer was at seven, and there was a service for children in the afternoon at three. Easter Day, however, was a special occasion when people were expected to receive communion. To accommodate the need, in 1935 and 1936 Holy Communion was received at five different services – seven, eight, nine-thirty, twelve-fifteen, and eight-fifteen – but with Morning Prayer still featured at eleven. During the week there were no regular services of Morning and Evening Prayer in the church, nor of Holy Communion.[32]

By 1937, after St James' had become the cathedral, Riley added more services of Holy Communion, more choral services, and, very soon, more services of Morning and Evening Prayer. The church authorities tended to call these daily offices 'Mattins' and 'Evensong.' They were implementing their image of the English cathedral, which involved the saying of the daily offices, more celebrations of Holy Communion, and greater use of the choir. The total number of services soon rose dramatically. From about four hundred a year during the 1920s and 1930s, the figure increased to around nine hundred in 1945, surpassing all others in the diocese.[33]

By 1940 a new pattern was operating. Mattins still dominated the service schedule on Sunday at eleven o'clock, but on two Sundays of the month there was a choral Holy Communion, one of which followed a shortened version of Mattins. The eight o'clock morning service continued to be Holy Communion every week. Riley added a nine-fifteen communion service on the second, fourth, and fifth Sunday of the month. Evensong was at seven, and the afternoon Sunday school and Bible classes for the older children met at three. During the week, Mattins became daily in the house chapel, Evensong thrice weekly, including a choral service on Friday, and Holy Communion twice weekly plus on saints' days. During the Second World War there was added a daily twenty-minute service of 'instruction and intercessions' at lunchtime. Mattins with a sermon was the still the principal service of worship for most people of St James'.[34]

Riley had a reputation for his fine preaching, although to the eyes of at least one young person it seemed funny when he looked out between the high pulpit and the sounding board overhead, wearing his half-glasses.[35] The choir was present each Sunday, but even with the addition of choral services, the clergy and churchwardens continued to speak of the choir's role as belonging to 'the musical portion of the services,' not fully integrated with the liturgy. They expressed gratitude to the choir and the choirmaster for continuing 'to add beauty and reverence to the services.'[36]

St James' adopted the new version of the *Book of Common Praise* in 1938 as soon as it was published by the General Synod of the Church of England in Canada, replacing the 1909

4.5 Interior of St James' as refitted under Dean Riley in the 1950s. The new furnishings,
intended to suit the church for its restored role as cathedral, were mostly memorials to parishioners
fallen in the two great wars. This picture appeared in the *Pilgrim's Guide* (1958)
captioned 'Worship the Lord in the beauty of holiness.'

version then in use. The Bible on the lectern was the Revised Version of 1884 in the edition with the Apocrypha from 1898. The copy of the King James Version given to St James' by Edward, Prince of Wales, in 1860 continued, however, to receive the signatures of visiting royalty and other dignitaries.[37]

After the war, from 1946 to 1955, worship was embellished and enhanced in association with the creation of the more glorious sanctuary and chancel. The total number of services per year increased to thirteen hundred or more and the pattern of worship became more complex. The Sunday schedule remained about the same, except that Mattins was said at eight-thirty on the two Sundays a month when the Eucharist was at eleven. The service at eight in the morning remained weekly communion. At nine-fifteen Holy Communion was now celebrated every Sunday, and on weekdays Evensong joined Mattins as a daily service, Monday through Friday, and Holy Communion occurred at least three times a week. During some seasons, notably for Lent and Holy Week, Holy Communion also became daily, except on Saturday. Accompanying this increased attention to the liturgy, the language of worship was heightened. What the people received at Holy Communion was routinely called 'the Blessed Sacrament.' Communion at nine-fifteen and eleven was most often called 'the Eucharist,' and on feast days it became 'Sung Eucharist' or 'Choral Eucharist.' For Christmas Day 1952 and Easter Day 1953, for instance, the eleven-o'clock service was identified as 'Mattins, Choral Eucharist and Sermon.'

The services were grander, with greater integration of the music. The choir and the choirmaster were repeatedly thanked 'for their untiring efforts in adding to the beautification of the Cathedral services.' The celebrant stood prominently at the high altar, facing the same way as the people, with priest and people together looking upward towards the transcendent God. The priest acted as a mediator between the people and God in the service of worship. People remarked on how magnificent the high altar looked with the new set of dressings: red during most of the year, violet during Advent and Lent, and a white frontal with cream and gold curtains on the sides and behind for Christmas, Easter, and other great festivals. The red and white frontals were made by Queen Mary's Royal School of Needlework in England.[38]

The clergy gave more of their time to preparing and carrying out the worship services. This was the moment when Riley increased the staff to two assistant clergy, besides the deaconess. In 1951 John A. Coombs began ten years (1951–61) as senior assistant cleric and John Bothwell (1951–4) became assistant curate. Bothwell remembered Riley as a fine preacher, but also as a sacramentalist.[39]

Riley wrote a new guide to St James', published in 1953, which used the image of pilgrimage to present an integrated theological understanding of the building, the liturgy, and the music. The image recalled the tradition of the Apostle James as the patron saint of pilgrims and the scallop shell as his symbol. A visit to St James' could become more than a tourist's tour; it could become a spiritual act. The scallop shell became a recurring symbol for the cathedral.[40]

Riley also produced a pamphlet, entitled *The Cathedral*, in which he represented a cathedral as 'preeminently a place of worship.' He now spoke of the provision of the daily offices and choral services as marks of a cathedral. He continued, 'The worship of a Cathedral should be so rendered as to set an example to other churches. For this reason particular care is taken that everything be done "decently and in order."' The music ought to be of 'the choicest kind' and entirely integrated with the sequence of worship. He called the cathedral 'the principal church of a diocese.' St James' was the Mother Church, not, as before, because she was the original church of the region, but because she was the cathedral. He reported proudly that, as part of her cathedral character, St James' had 'maintained its position in the general life of the city.'[41]

Riley was quite aware that the style and practice of worship at St James' were changing. He asked parishioners for sympathetic consideration in order 'to steer a course between the Scylla of rigorism and the Charybdis of licence and avoid the shallows of mediocrity.' Having said this, he eliminated the time-honoured procession and recession of the choir during the opening and closing hymns. He had in mind a more basic change. He intended to replace the traditional Book of Common Prayer (BCP), which had served parishioners since 1918, with the new book being prepared by the General Synod of the Anglican Church of Canada. Riley was a member of the liturgical committee of the national church and helped lead the work of revision. He took steps to instruct the congregation about the changes, but in general he simply created the assumption that the people would accept the new book. In April 1960, on his recommendation, the corporation ordered five hundred copies of the revised BCP, which the general synod had authorized in 1959, to take final effect in 1962.[42]

After 1955 attention at St James' shifted away from the chancel to the rest of the building. The dim nave and dark exterior enveloped in ivy, once praised for their mellow look of antiquity, suddenly seemed incompatible with the glory of the liturgical centre. In 1957 the corporation installed a completely new lighting system and entirely redecorated the interior. The next year they provided exterior lighting for the chancel windows, which made them appear bright from the inside during evening services. Said the churchwardens, 'We believe you will agree that this work ... has considerably enhanced the beauty of our Cathedral.' In 1958, consistent with the embellishment of the chancel, they added an elaborate and colourful wooden tester over the altar in St George's Chapel. In 1963 came large glass vestibule doors, surmounted by three stained-glass windows depicting the Trinity. In 1964, to the right of the chancel steps, the corporation placed a stone carving by Aisa Koperqualuk, an Inuit priest and artist of Povingnatuk, to commemorate the ordination at St James' in 1960 of Armand Tagoona, the first Canadian Inuit priest. The carving symbolized the long and continuing connection between the church in the Arctic and Toronto diocese and especially the cathedral's WA. The carving was later moved to the entrance of the nave.[43]

Turning to the rest of the property St James' leased some land to the diocese at the north end for construction of a diocesan centre. This opened in 1959 to serve as a more imposing and functional base for the bishop and diocese and for the preparations for the Anglican Congress in 1963. A parallel project included completely renovating the Parish House and connecting the two buildings together. The diocese kept its lease on the auditorium. St James' also sold the Synod House – the old rectory – to the city, and by agreement the city demolished the house in order to convert the land into a small park. Also by agreement the city tore down the ornamental iron fence that had surrounded the cathedral grounds, leaving a only small stretch remaining along Church Street in front of the Parish House. With the fence gone, the cathedral grounds and the little park appeared as one space and gave St James' an expanded setting. The corporation then completed the floodlighting of the exterior, including the clerestory, the bell tower, and the spire. As the churchwardens reported, 'We have had a great many comments on how beautiful the Cathedral looks at night.'[44]

But these efforts were not enough. The building was aging and needed constant repair. Year after year the need for repairs and restoration pulled on the time and attention of the cathedral staff and corporation. The perpetual drive to beautify the building, coupled with the unceasing urgency of repairs, led to extensive restoration of the exterior in 1970 and 1971, including removal of the vast growth of ivy and over a century of the effects of pollution. The building changed colour from black-red to cream-yellow and appeared immeasurably lighter, provoking criticism that the look of antiquity was lost. As a further saving on maintenance, the cathedral sold the clock in the tower to the city for one dollar.[45]

At the same time, the city permitted demolition of nearly all the old buildings between the cathedral and Jarvis Street and extended the land of the park, now named St James' Park, to fill all but the southeast corner of the block bounded by King, Church, Adelaide, and Jarvis streets. The cathedral had earlier played a role in preserving the park. In 1962 and 1963, the city planning board had proposed using the assembled land for an enormous civic complex, including an immense centre for the arts. Both the cathedral and the synod opposed the plan, noting that the synod had sold the old rectory to the city for a park. It appeared that the complex would go ahead in spite of the protest, until the city backed away, making the expanded park possible.[46] By 1970 the cathedral grounds and the park together virtually matched the original grant of land for a church in the late 1790s. The entire perimeter of this reassembled heritage was marked by the rise of a slight curb, distinguishing the sidewalk from the grass and framing the cathedral, and all this was maintained at city expense. Walter Gilling, the new rector and dean since 1961 (Figure 4.6), rejoiced in the outcome, '[T]he gem that now shines forth brightens all of King Street between Yonge Street and Jarvis Street.'[47] Adjacent to the cathedral to the northeast, the York rectory lands remained intact on Church Street between Adelaide and Lombard and still produced income for the diocese and a portion of the salary of St James' rector.[48]

Then between 1979 and 1982 St James' carried out a still more massive restoration. This effort included renewing the ceiling, the exterior stone pillars and window ledges, and the crypt, redecorating the walls, removing the remainder of the side pews, extending the red-tile floor under the pews and throughout the side aisles, upgrading the lighting, and installing ceiling illumination to accentuate the wooden beams. Hugh Stiff, rector and dean since 1974, took the opportunity to remove the regimental colours from the centre of the nave, rehanging most of them with the others on the side walls. This shift reduced their prominence and signalled a desire for both a liturgical focus in the nave and a de-emphasis on the military aspect of the cathedral's identity. St George's Chapel was redecorated with what the cathedral's newsletter described as 'gorgeous yet beautifully subdued colours and furnishings.' The cathedral was rededicated in a stunning service on 24 October 1982. While there were people who thought that the interior looked 'bland,' the newsletter praised the results. The acoustics were different, with 10 per cent more reverberation, producing 'grand and glorious choral effects,' and the interior was 'beautiful.' The historical chronology mounted on the west narthex wall recorded that in these years the cathedral was 'externally restored' and 'internally beautified.'[49]

Simultaneously, in 1981, the landscaping of St James' Park was completed to Jarvis Street. This included a Victorian garden next to the cathedral, dedicated by Dean Stiff in the presence of the mayor of Toronto. The garden was given by the Garden Club of Toronto, a civic group that maintained a relationship with St James', notably by mounting exquisite flower festivals for important occasions. During the early 1970s the cathedral had helped save the Victorian

4.6 Women of St James' WA presenting a ewer for the baptistery to
Very Revd Walter Joseph Gilling, dean and rector 1961–73.

buildings facing the cathedral on King Street and opposed the construction of high-rises there.[50] Between these buildings and Front Street, a complex of residences, shops, and courtyards opened in 1981 with the name Market Square. This included St James' Lane, a walkway that permitted views of the cathedral tower and spire from the south. A sculpture garden opened opposite the cathedral at the same time. By 1981, after a decade of living with vacant land to the east and parking lots to the south, St James' now sat within what felt like vast cathedral grounds, visually splendid from all sides. The building, both inside and out, appeared more majestic and even larger, as well as lighter and more ethereal. The stature of St James' as a cathedral for the diocese and the city had grown immeasurably.

The liturgical wave continued with exuberance through the 1960s and after. As before, the changes were regarded as belonging to the enhancement and beautification of St James' as a cathedral. Now, however, conflict arose over some of them. The Book of Common Prayer of 1959–62 replaced the 1918 version and immediately became the tradition, and only the very alert could tell much difference. It fell to Gilling, who succeeded Riley in 1961, to implement the new BCP. Gilling had served as a military chaplain in the Second World War and as rector of St Luke's in Peterborough, Ontario. Since 1956 he had been director of church extension for the diocese of Toronto, working out of the diocesan offices next door, and he first became associated with St James' as a canon. In addition to the assistant clergy on staff, he agreed at first to have a deaconess, but then eliminated the position and instead used the services of a volunteer parish visitor, Gwendolyn Lodder (1964–74).[51] John D. Hooper continued as organist and choirmaster (1956–65). By 1961 the newly catalogued music library contained some five hundred choral pieces, the largest in the Canadian Anglican church.[52] From 1964 to 1973, Warren Eling, one of the assistant clergy, took considerable responsibility for the liturgy, particularly for the integration of the music with the rest of the service. He received the title of precentor in 1968, taken from English cathedral tradition, in recognition of his new role. Gilling also appointed two honorary assistants representing churches and practices in other parts of the Anglican world – Ian R. Culpitt (1967–71) of the province of New Zealand and David Appavoo (1967–71), a south Asian of the Church of South India.

The cathedral moved deliberately towards more Eucharists and greater emphasis on liturgical theology. Sermons became shorter. By the early 1960s, Holy Communion became daily, including Saturday, all year long, and Mattins and Evensong were also extended to Saturday. Evensong shifted to four-thirty instead of seven. Following the practice in English cathedrals, St James' was kept open every day for devotions and visits. A new and briefer *Pilgrim's Guide*, written by Zita Barbara May, again presented the cathedral as the Mother Church of the diocese.[53] Gilling announced in 1967 that he would end the practice of midday Lenten preaching by invited clergy, deans, and bishops – a custom at St James' since 1943; such preaching, he said, 'had now lost its appeal and ceased to be a worthwhile venture.' The next year, he added, there would be noon-hour organ recitals and more Eucharists, since these were becoming popular.[54] By 1972, Holy Communion, or the Eucharist, was celebrated at the eight- and nine-o'clock services each Sunday, twice daily Monday through Friday, and once on Saturday. The schedule for Sunday at eleven called for the Eucharist on the first, third, and fifth Sundays, which in most months meant, in practice, every Sunday but one, and in some seasons every week, as well as on all feast days. The worship focus of the cathedral completed the revolution from Mattins and the sermon to the Eucharist.[55]

There was more care given to planning the services, there were more rehearsals for services, liturgical processions occurred more often, more vestments appeared, the clergy began to be addressed as 'Father,' the bishop came more often to St James', and diocesan services became more elaborate. Parishioners did not fail to notice that the cathedral was becoming 'spikier,' and there was vocal resistance to more Holy Communions.[56] Hooper introduced the Advent carol service from England, which quickly became 'one of the Cathedral's most beautiful services.' The year 1966 was an important one. New green frontals arrived to replace the red ones during the 'green season.' Gilling began to wear a cope, twenty years after the archbishop of Canterbury had appeared in one at St James'. The practice of the bishop's coming to the cathedral to celebrate the Eucharist at Christmas and Easter, only recently begun by Frederick Wilkinson, the seventh bishop (1955–66), was praised as 'our tradition' by the newly created newsletter. The installation of George Snell as the eighth bishop (1966–72) was staged as an enthronement with three especially commissioned fanfares by Godfrey Ridout of the St James' congregation. The newsletter called the enthronement 'one of the most thrilling events in many a year.' Meditations on the liturgical year appeared more frequently in the service leaflet. Reflecting on 1966, Gilling reported: 'As I stand at the Cathedral front doors each Sunday after service, I am thanked by so very many for the excellent ordering of the service and the music.'[57]

Other liturgical innovations followed. Under the impact of an ecumenical movement for liturgical renewal and especially of the Second Vatican Council (1962–5), many denominations

4.7 Synod delegates at the election of Bishop Garnsworthy as diocesan at St James', 1972.

throughout the world began experiments with liturgical change. These were guided most notably by what some liturgical scholars regarded as practices common among the early churches, a theology of the church as the community of the people of God, and a desire for greater scriptural emphasis in worship. Gilling attempted to introduce some of these new features at St James'. In 1964, well before the Second Vatican Council closed, he wrote a paper entitled 'Functions of a Dean and Cathedral in the Inner City,' which revealed his dream for this new liturgical and theological direction. On at least one occasion that year he had apparently used a movable altar for the nine-o'clock Sunday Eucharist, placed in the crossing of the nave at the foot of the chancel steps, with the priest facing the people. He explained that the idea was to symbolize the gathering of the people of God in worship. With the high altar so far away from the people, congregational participation was limited. This was the first time that the Eucharist at a major service had been separated from the high altar.[58] Loud protests arose, and he backed away from the practice. At the vestry meeting in 1965 he appealed to the parish to follow a 'course which, under the guidance of the Holy Spirit, will lead us into new paths, set us new goals and give us courage to attempt new things without being accused of wrecking the Church, or St James', in particular.' It would entail 'a new attitude of charity in the church,' and the laity would 'take over much more of the actual functioning of the church so that Christianity will be lived all week.'[59]

Gilling tried again later. He and Eling both sat on the diocesan liturgical commission which was then leading the exploration of new directions for worship. They put aside the BCP at the eleven-o'clock service twice in both 1967 and 1968, and then again for a series of Sundays in 1969, using instead the new liturgy of the Anglican Church in New Zealand, which, as they explained 'incorporates much contemporary thinking with regard to the revision of the Church's worship, and will give us some preview of the probable "shape of things to come."' For these services they moved the high altar away from the wall and the celebrant faced the people. The experiment provoked strong resistance and was perceived as an attack on the BCP, which had only just been revised according to the older model. It was not repeated, although Godfrey Ridout, now a churchwarden (1969–70), expressed his disappointment that it was not. Gilling made another impassioned plea for change: 'It is my hope that all of us together can spend some time thinking about change – change in our worship, change in our ministry, change in our organization, and not forgetting, also, change in our attitudes.' But once more he backed away, and the BCP remained securely in place. In 1973, at the end of his tenure, he assured the cathedral, 'We still stand at the altar with our backs to the people, and make no apology for it, and are still wedded to that wonderful Book of Common Prayer.' In his final sermon he admonished the congregation several times, 'Hold fast the Christ; hold fast the Book of Common Prayer.' St James' also retained the 1938 hymn book and declined to use the new red hymnal published jointly by the Anglican Church of Canada and the United Church of Canada in 1971, finding it unsuited to a cathedral style of worship. Thus the cathedral effectively withdrew from giving leadership to the diocese in the ongoing renewal of liturgy and worship, and chose instead to offer a pattern for how to render traditional services meaningfully and well.[60]

Cathedral consciousness at St James' was heightened immeasurably by four special occasions in the 1960s and early 1970s. The first was the world Anglican Congress hosted by the diocese, which brought to the cathedral a thousand clerical and lay delegates from around the world, including a huge array of bishops. Bishop Snell recalled, 'For ten days in August 1963 St James' Cathedral was the heart of the Anglican Communion.' The event instilled cathedral pride in the clergy and people of St James'; and to express this feeling permanently, the corporation afterward placed an emblem of the global Anglican communion, done in 'beautiful colours,' in the centre of the chancel floor. The churchwarden who proposed the project reasoned, 'The Cathedral of Minneapolis had a mosaic tile in their floor to commemorate the Congress of 1954, and it would be nice if we had such an emblem here.'[61] The second event was the annual diocesan confirmation service initiated by Snell. Instead of going to the candidates throughout the diocese in keeping with previous practice, the bishop restored the ancient practice of bringing the candidates to him at St James'. He remembered, 'When I came into the Cathedral I was faced with a host of white veils as far as the eye could reach down one side of the centre aisle with almost as many boys on the other side.' These services made a visual impression of the centrality of the cathedral in the diocese.[62] The third event was the 175th anniversary year in 1972, marking the founding of the congregation in 1797. The special events and the weekly worship leaflets during the year reiterated St James' position as the Mother Church and reaffirmed her antiquity and pre-eminence in both the diocese and the city. To mark the anniversary, parishioner Sydney H. Watson decorated the pulpit with five quatrefoil plaques representing the four evangelists and St James. A group of women led by Mrs Herbert A.

4.8 Cathedral staff with Rt Revd Lewis Garnsworthy, bishop of Toronto 1972–88, soon after his election. L. to r.: Revd W.N. McKeachie, associate; Revd M.H.H. Bedford-Jones, assistant; Aubrey Foy, organist and choirmaster; Dean Gilling; Bishop Garnsworthy; Revd J.W. Eling, precentor; Revd R.H. Pursel, associate; David Stuart, verger. In front: Margery Clough, vestry clerk; Eileen Martin, secretary.

Bruce and Mrs George Edison created needlepoint cushions for the sanctuary and choir; this, they said, would complete a project begun in the 1940s and match the practice of many cathedrals in England and elsewhere. The Friends of the Cathedral was founded, after the pattern of similar groups functioning at English cathedrals since the 1930s, to attract support from people in the city. The money that the group raised would go to restore the building and acquire 'items that would enhance the Cathedral or the Cathedral services: stoles, vestments, copes, and the like.' As a souvenir of the anniversary, the nineteenth-century pews were removed at this time from the lower side aisles and cut up to make limited-edition plaques.[63] The fourth event was the installation of Lewis Garnsworthy as the ninth diocesan bishop (1972–88), also during 1972, which was even more ornate and imposing than Snell's in 1966 (see Figures 4.7 and 4.8). The presentation of the new bishop to the people evoked thunderous applause, which rocked the building.

Music and the choir of gentlemen and boys became the centre of conflict during 1965 and 1966 in connection with the appointment of Norman W. Hurrle as organist and choirmaster. Hurrle put forward some demands for himself and the music of the cathedral, and St James' responded with a markedly increased commitment to music as integral to her identity as a cathedral. After a series of volatile meetings involving the corporation and the advisory board, the corporation made the music position full-time, considerably increased the choirmaster's salary, raised expenditures for the music budget, approved a larger number in the choir, and agreed to renovate the organ. The new policy was 'to provide the very best of music' and 'to have the finest choir possible for the Cathedral.' The corporation acknowledged, 'We are only making this decision because of the great importance which we attach to the music of the Cathedral both as it contributes to the beauty of the service and enhances the participation of the congregation.' But for reasons of finances, rather than want of desire, the cathedral finally drew back from Hurrle's proposal to create a cathedral choir school on the English model. In search of an alternative source of boys, St James' pursued talks from 1966 to 1969 with St George's College, a private Anglican boys' school recently founded on the site of old St Alban's Cathedral.[64] The conflict with Hurrle nearly brought about the collapse of the choir. The new choirmaster, Aubrey M. Foy (1969–78), had to rebuild it from the low of six men and four boys at the end of Hurrle's tenure to the twelve men and sixteen or eighteen boys, plus probationers, which became the standard from the 1970s onward, and St George's did become something like a choir school for the cathedral. The importance of choral Evensong as a mark of the cathedral probably dates from Foy's arrival in the late 1960s and he began the Wednesday choral Evensong that was added in 1971.[65]

In 1974, when the deanship and rectorship passed to Hugh Stiff, the advisory board and the corporation were very sure of what they expected of their new head. The advisory board requested the corporation 'not to economize in connection with the music and the choir because of its importance and the asset it is to the special place and function of the Cathedral.' The churchwardens responded with a clear statement of policy for the vestry in February 1975: 'that the Cathedral should function in all respects in a manner consistent with its position as the premier Church of the Anglican communion in Canada.' They added, 'We are firm in our conviction that its classic liturgy is one of the main bulwarks of the Anglican Church, that its presentation with music which is appropriate and excellent is of the essence, that together they are a legitimate and necessary function of worship and the life of the Church, and that any efforts directed to their advancement are well directed.' This statement signalled a rejection of the liturgical experiments of Gilling's time and a divorce from the trends in the diocese towards liturgical change. It was an affirmation of the 1962 BCP and what St James' took to be the English cathedral musical tradition as central to the cathedral's identity. It also constituted a statement of clear boundaries for any changes and an undertaking to guard St James' carefully constructed and particular cathedral character.[66]

Like Gilling before him, Stiff introduced many innovations in liturgical style and practice, but in his loyalty to the BCP he did not disappoint anyone. He had been chosen in part because of his experience with cathedral culture; he had been dean of the cathedral in Calgary and later bishop of Keewatin and had a known predilection for cathedral-style ceremony. In his first sermon he vowed 'to aim at a high quality of worship,' to 'maintain a Choir of a calibre second to none in the city and in the country,' to 'perpetuate the simple glory of our Cathedral,' and to develop St James' as a centre for diocesan life, the arts, counselling, devotional expression, and more.[67] In 1977, after having been elected metropolitan of Ontario, Garnsworthy asked Stiff to serve as an assistant bishop in the diocese, in order 'to regularize the work he already does for

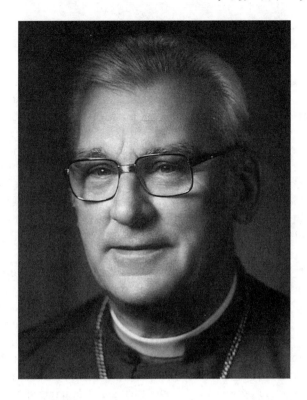

4.9 Rt Revd Hugh Vernon Stiff, dean and rector 1974–86.
He resigned as bishop of Keewatin to become dean.

the Diocese and the National Church.' Stiff left most of what he called the 'proper management' of the liturgy and music to others, notably the priest-sacrist Robert Pursel (1975–7) and the two vicars, Glenn Pritchard (1976–81; vicar from 1977) and David Bousfield (1982–8), as well as the two choirmasters, Foy (until 1977) and Giles Bryant (from 1978).[68]

Stiff immediately enhanced the cathedral by creating another chapel. In 1975, he took the old altar from the Chapel of the Holy Spirit in the Parish House, which had been deconsecrated in 1970, and placed it near the north end of the west aisle. Stiff explained that this new altar of St John the Evangelist joined with the Lady Altar on the opposite side to flank the high altar as John and Mary had flanked Christ on the cross.[69] With the high altar and the three other altars now within the body of the cathedral, St James' seemed all the more like the cathedrals of England, with their multiple chapels and hidden spaces. Stiff began the regular practice of moving the St John's altar to the crossing of the nave for the nine-o'clock Eucharist. For the sake of the music, the organ, thoroughly renewed in 1967, received a new four-manual console in 1979 to replace the 1936 model.

Worship on Sunday and during Advent, Christmas, Epiphany, Holy Week, and Easter became distinctly more elaborate, with splendid vestments and ceremonial. Copes seemed to be everywhere. The number of services stabilized at about 1,450 every year, which translated into an average of twenty-eight per week, the highest figure in the diocese. The year 1975 witnessed the first Easter Vigil and the Ceremonies of the Easter Fire and Paschal Candle, held at five-thirty p.m. rather than nearer midnight. Even the Sunday worship leaflet increased in size to a double fold. From the early 1980s the term 'Holy Communion' virtually disappeared, replaced by variations on 'Eucharist.'

Bishops came to St James' often, and there were more of them to do so. During 1960–6 and 1968–71 the diocese had three bishops, and between 1977 and 1980 two, besides Stiff. All took their turns in services at St James'. In 1981 a reorganization of the diocese created five episcopal areas, with four area bishops and the diocesan bishop forming a college of bishops; this added three new bishops, for a total of five, plus Stiff.[70] All five visited the cathedral from time to time; for instance, during Lent, Holy Week, and Easter 1981, all the area bishops then in place came to preach, and the archbishop celebrated once and preached twice, on Good Friday and Easter Day.[71] After the restoration and rededication of the cathedral in 1982, the setting became even more majestic. The sight of so many mitres and copes, so often, amid so much ceremony and music, and in such a building, set within spacious St James' Park, created an extraordinary image of what it meant for St James' to be the Mother Church.

In 1978, Stiff instituted the use of a reordered version of Holy Communion in the language of the BCP as the standard liturgy on Sunday at nine o'clock. This new liturgy, sometimes called the 'Toronto Rite' or the 'Blue Book,' represented a conservative attempt to incorporate some elements of the liturgical renewal movement while rejecting others. This was the service for which the moveable St John's altar came into use, and from 1977 on it was often sung by a congregational choir. For every other service, the BCP continued as the norm but about the same time the altar in St George's Chapel was moved out from the wall, and the clergy began the practice there of facing the people while celebrating the Eucharist.[72]

These acts marked the beginning of the use of two rites and two liturgical practices at St James' and revived the strong defence of the classical liturgy voiced by the churchwardens when Stiff became dean. The trace of a cleavage surfaced over the vision of a cathedral. For the majority of the people the classical liturgy and music of the eleven-o'clock Sunday Eucharist, festival Eucharists, and choral Evensong became the potent symbol of cathedral identity. Others, however, welcomed the innovations; and for some of the clergy a quest began for a new symbol that would associate cathedral identity with both tradition and innovation and with a diversity of liturgy and music. Pritchard as vicar suggested the metaphor of a mosaic, widely used in new Canadian discourse and the Anglican Communion, and he attached it to the very character of a cathedral. He wrote in the Newsletter, 'Worship in a Cathedral is perhaps best described by the word "mosaic" ... for the worship in a Cathedral is multi-faceted.' He continued, 'High altar, nave altar, said or sung, traditional or modern, simple or elaborate – a Cathedral must allow room for all of this under its roof. At this point we realize that we are not simply a parish Church.' A cathedral therefore both maintains tradition and fosters change.[73]

Five statements in 1980 and 1981 epitomized the cathedral consciousness of St James' and indicated the understanding of God that it embodied. Pritchard wrote in the newsletter, 'Since the Cathedral belongs to the diocese it must be dedicated to exemplary worship. Worship at a Cathedral is more splendid than anywhere else, awe inspiring, transporting.'[74] Giles Bryant, organist and choirmaster, observed in the annual report for 1981: 'The choir has continued to provide a Cathedral type music for two major services each Sunday and for quite a number of special services during the last year.'[75] Stiff, the dean and rector, spoke to the vestry: 'But of course, we are much more than a parish church – we are the Cathedral of the Diocese of

Toronto – our only rationale for the amount of money this place spends on ministry, music, restoration, maintenance, and works of art, I should say beauty. We hear that the Cathedral is the Mother Church of the Diocese. I must admit in all honesty, that that title does not turn me on!! I would like us to be known as the leading Cathedral in Canada – the leading church in the Diocese – leading in good liturgy that is offered to God and uplifts the people – leading in sound biblical preaching – and having a real concern and taking an active part in the life and witness of the Diocese of Toronto.'[76] Stiff in the newsletter referred to the practice of daily Eucharist: 'One of the great things – perhaps the greatest thing – about our Cathedral is that it is right here on the job as morning comes to Toronto.'[77] Pritchard, again, wrote in the newsletter: 'We can all speak much about worship because there is so much of us in it. But, strangely enough, a Cathedral's worship first and foremost takes us out of ourselves to bring us into direct encounter with that awe-filled and holy mystery, divine transcendental reality. There is no single way in which a Cathedral accomplishes that for you or for me, for rulers or for ruled.'[78] This was a cathedral theology of beauty and awesomeness.

Two Cathedral Visions, 1980s and 1990s

The publication of the Book of Alternative Services (BAS) by the Anglican Church of Canada in 1985 was the catalyst for articulating the two different visions of the cathedral's character. One vision centred on the Book of Common Prayer as the norm for cathedral worship and emphasized tradition. The other focused on the contemporary rite in the BAS and evoked possibilities for diversity and change. Neither vision appeared unalloyed, but rather as differences in emphasis; initially, the divergence was liturgically blurred. It was not a simple case of the BCP's being challenged by the BAS, for the liturgy that Stiff used at eleven o'clock on Sunday was not the BCP straight from the book but a slightly rearranged version that he preferred. Similarly, the liturgy he used at nine o'clock was not the contemporary rite from the BAS, but its second rite, entitled 'Holy Eucharist (1962)' – reordered but still cast 'in the language of the Book of Common Prayer,' and closely resembling the Toronto Rite that had been employed at nine o'clock for the previous six years.[79]

Ironically, it was the bishop and the diocesan services at the cathedral that delineated the distinction more clearly. The bishop upheld both visions of a cathedral at St James'. When Garnsworthy presided at diocesan services, he used the contemporary rite in the BAS and represented St James' as the agent of diversity and change. Yet when he attended regular cathedral services, he mostly chose to come not to the innovative nine-o'clock services but to the eleven-o'clock, where he used the classical liturgy that carried the traditional identity of the cathedral.

The deans who followed Stiff sought to juggle both visions, even as the distinction between them grew sharper. They maintained the alliance of the building, the liturgy, and the music, with the special emphasis on the eleven-o'clock choral Eucharist, festivals, and choral Evensong, which most of the people believed were bound to the cathedral identity of St James'. But they also implemented the vision of the cathedral as the bearer of diversity and innovation. Some of the most persistent defence of the traditional vision came from parishioners who were active as members and officers of the Prayer Book Society of Canada, a national body that organized support for the classical liturgy of the BCP.

Before Duncan Abraham became dean and rector in 1987, he was approached by the representatives of St James' and asked for a commitment on two points: that he would not fiddle with the tradition of the 1962 BCP on Sundays at eleven o'clock, and that he would respect the musical tradition. This was a request to honour the particular way in which the cathedral identity of St James' had been constructed over so many decades. Abraham knew both the diocese and the cathedral. He was already a canon and as such celebrated or preached frequently at St James'. After eleven years as rector of St Clement's Church, he had been serving since 1981 in the diocesan office next door as director of church development. He was also the first and so far the only incumbent or equivalent to have been born in Canada; most of his predecessors had been born in the British Isles, while George Okill Stuart had been born in the Thirteen Colonies, Grasett in Gibraltar, and Abraham's successor, Douglas Stoute, in Barbados.[80]

Abraham made the commitment requested, and, although the changes he helped to effect during his time were considerable, he kept the agreement.[81] He followed the policy of beauty and excellence in the trilogy of building, liturgy, and music, and frankly defended the immense sums expended on them. In a sermon on the uniqueness of the cathedral in 1988, he quoted the conventional support from Psalm 96.9: 'Worship the Lord in the beauty of His holiness; let the whole earth stand in awe of Him.' He continued, 'Now at the Cathedral, worship is at the heart of our corporate life, worship that is carefully planned and reverently offered, worship that is the blending of the dignity and colour of Anglican ceremonial, the majesty of the Prayer Book, beautiful music and, we hope, high standards of preaching. Let's face it, a Cathedral style of worship is not everybody's cup of tea.'[82]

Douglas Stoute, like Abraham, came to St James' from the rectorship of St Clement's, by then the parish with the largest average Sunday attendance in the diocese. In the conversations with Stoute before he took over as dean and rector in December 1994, some members of St James' made the same appeal for no changes that they had made to Abraham. But Stoute indicated that, unlike Abraham, he made no such promise. Abraham, in retirement, said that he would not have made such a commitment in 1994 either, because times had changed. Some confusion arose over what to expect from Stoute. Certain parishioners got the impression that no significant changes would occur at least for a couple years, while others felt unsure about Stoute, believing that, even if he had made the promise, he was not inclined towards the traditional and in any case would be under pressure from the wider church to change the eleven-o'clock service. Stoute was prepared to treat beauty and excellence in building, liturgy, and music, rooted in the classical tradition, as central to the cathedral's mandate, but he was equally convinced of the necessity for some change in these areas; he wondered, for instance, how much longer the celebrant at the eleven-o'clock could stand at the altar with his or her back to the congregation. He agreed that a cathedral should offer leadership but thought that her leadership should be more venturesome. The cathedral should help to move the whole diocese forward in liturgy and lead in the creation of new music as well as in a variety of other areas: preaching, the arts, outreach, theological reflection, lay ministry, social justice, and spirituality. As an example, he urged support for a canon theologian for the diocese.[83]

The minutes of the vestry meeting in 1996, after Stoute's first full year as dean and rector, recorded this exchange: 'Mr. Desmond Scotchmer asked that the Dean not make changes to the traditional liturgy and music of the 11:00 service. The Dean said that he could not promise not to change the service but that he would listen to people's concerns and would work to strengthen the life of the Cathedral.' While some older proponents of the traditional vision of cathedral identity felt confident that there would be no major changes at eleven o'clock or in choral Evensong in their time, their confidence was not shared by some younger traditionalists.[84]

By 1997 no major changes had had been to the building since the rededication in 1982, or to the musical tradition since the founding of the congregational choir in 1977. The contours of public worship had remained constant since the use of two rites began in 1978, but there had been some significant modifications within those contours. Further liturgical embellishment took place, such as the introduction of incense and the habit that some of the clergy and servers got into of calling the Eucharist on feast days at the high altar 'High Mass.' In 1987 the contemporary rite in the BAS replaced the 'Holy Eucharist (1962)' at the nine-o'clock service, making a sharper contrast with eleven o'clock. In 1993 the BAS replaced the BCP for weekday Mattins, with the BCP remaining in use for weekday Evensong, but by 1995 both offices had lapsed on Saturdays. At the same time, Mattins vanished from the eleven-o'clock Sunday schedule altogether, leaving a brief Mattins at the Lady Altar at ten-fifteen, sandwiched between two Eucharists. Sunday evensong remained as the only choral Evensong. There were now three Eucharists every Sunday, two a day Monday through Friday, and one on Saturday. In September 1995, at eleven, a large double-fold liturgical leaflet containing the complete text of the words and some of the music took the place of the actual prayer books that parishioners had been accustomed to hold in their hands. The text was not the straight BCP but the slightly rearranged version that had been in use since Stiff's day. This gave supporters of the BCP certain misgivings, which they did not hesitate to voice; they were left without the clear use of the traditional liturgy.[85]

By 1992 there was a different altar arrangement for each Sunday Eucharist, each implying a different theology. At eight a.m., for the said BCP, the St John's altar was moved to the crossing of the nave, complete with its reredos, and the priest celebrated facing away from the people. At nine, for the contemporary rite of the BAS, the altar stayed at the nave crossing and was pushed forward on its platform, but the reredos was removed, so that the celebrant could face the people. In 1994 a small eucharistic table replaced the St John's altar for the nine-o'clock services and was placed at the top of the chancel steps, with the celebrant still facing the people; at other times this was stored behind the St John's altar, where only the very observant would notice it. At eleven, for the choral service with the slightly modified BCP, the high altar remained against the wall, with the celebrant facing away from the congregation. For weekday Eucharists, the altar of St George's Chapel continued to stand away from the wall to allow the clergy to face the people.

The journey that the cathedral had embarked on at the end of the 1930s, when Riley added a few more services of Holy Communion, had arrived at the complete triumph of the Eucharist by 1995. Mattins and Evensong had declined to second position, though paradoxically they had also risen in status by becoming daily offices, except for Saturdays. The eleven-o'clock Sunday service, with its modified classical liturgy and its all-male choir, continued as the main service, around which most debate and anxiety circulated. Overall, limited diversity in the practice of worship was the rule.

The Bible used on the main cathedral lectern in 1997 was a copy of the 1957 Revised Standard Version with Apocrypha, given for St George's Chapel in 1959, not the gender-inclusive New Revised Standard Version of 1989. The hymnal still in use was the 1938 *Book of Common Praise*.

The cathedral had skipped a generation of hymn books, and there were voices who insisted that it should also bypass the new hymnal approved by the Anglican Church of Canada for publication in 1998 and instead adopt a modern book better suited to cathedral-style music such as the *New English Hymnal*.[86]

The clerics who worked with Abraham and Stoute included Donald Butler (1989–90), priest on staff; Carol Langley (1990-2), assistant curate; and Jane Watanabe (1992-7), associate priest. Of the vicars in this period, Bousfield (until 1988) and Philip Hobson (1992-7; also precentor from 1996) gave particular attention to carrying out the liturgy, as did John Gibaut as priest-sacrist (1987–94). Like Stoute, Hobson affirmed the vision of the cathedral as a sanctuary of balanced diversity, while desiring it to give leadership in other areas besides the classical liturgy and music. He envisioned new liturgical and musical explorations, an emphasis on spirituality and faith, a greater role in theological education and the promotion of theological thinking, and effective social outreach.[87] Watanabe combined respect for the traditional cathedral heritage with some impatience for new forms of expression; she wished the cathedral to be known above all for the depth and range of its ministry to people of all kinds.[88]

Giles Bryant, organist and choirmaster from 1979, made his preference for the classical tradition evident, and pointed out the intrinsic link between the BCP and the corpus of the Anglican musical heritage. He expanded the choir library to six hundred pieces, including forty settings of the Eucharist, forty-five settings of the Magnificat for Evensong, and one hundred anthems and motets, so that there was now little repetition in a yearly cycle. He remained strongly committed to the English cathedral tradition at the eleven-o'clock Sunday Eucharist and in choral Evensong. None the less, he willingly supported the clergy in creating excellent BAS services for diocesan events. He also continued to expand the St James' role in the musical life of the city, with thirty-six weekly lunchtime organ concerts a year and more special musical events and recordings.[89] The boys in the choir knew their role in maintaining the cathedral tradition, and one of them, Bernard von Bieberstein (choir, 1990–2), summarized it this way: 'Being the cathedral, we had to be that much better in the choir part than the rest of the churches. Maybe we were more important. We had to be good. We had to know our stuff.'[90]

The tenth bishop, Terence Finlay (from 1988), came to the cathedral frequently from the diocesan offices next door. Besides the diocesan services and the high services at Christmas and Easter, he celebrated the Eucharist on the rota about once a month, attended Morning Prayer often during the week, and came to Evensong when possible.[91] He ensured use of the contemporary Eucharist of the BAS for diocesan events, with the high altar pulled away from the wall and the priest facing the people; some parishioners and staff were convinced that the diocese would have liked to see similar changes at eleven a.m. on Sunday.[92] The 150th anniversary of the diocese in 1989 was celebrated to the full with an immense service in Toronto's SkyDome under cathedral leadership. A large wooden sesquicentenary cross was carried from parish to parish across the diocese throughout the year and came to rest in the southwest corner of the west aisle at the cathedral. That same year St James' hosted a major festival of contemporary and traditional liturgical art.[93] The staff sought new ways to draw in the people of the diocese, including Diocesan Cathedral Days and Ash Wednesday events for children.

For some of the most significant diocesan services, however, the cathedral lost her place to St Paul's, Bloor Street, because of her smaller size. After the side pews were gone, the

4.10 Children of St James' Sunday school assembled for the visit of
the Prince and Princess of Wales, 27 October 1991.

4.11 HRH the Prince of Wales signing the Royal Bible given in 1860 by
his great-great-grandfather, Albert Edward, Prince of Wales (later King Edward VII). With
the Prince are Princess Diana, Prince William, Prince Harry, Dean Abraham, head sidesman
Andy Ritchie, and (in rear) churchwardens Edwin Hawken and Barbara Hawkins.

permanent seating in the nave could hold 550, with three hundred in chairs on the sides and perhaps another hundred in standing room and the chancel, for a maximum of 950. Enthusiastic counts for special occasions, such as the Easter Vigil, stretched the tally to eleven hundred.[94] By contrast, St Paul's could accommodate two thousand. A large ordination service had gone to St Paul's as early as the 1960s. The consecration of the three new area bishops in 1981 was planned for the cathedral, but when Garnsworthy realized belatedly that St James' was enveloped in scaffolding, he moved the service to St Paul's; in any case, St James' could not have held the two thousand people who attended and received communion. While the election of Michael Bedford-Jones and Victoria Matthews as suffragan bishops in November 1994 took place at St James', they were consecrated in February 1995 at St Paul's. Meanwhile the business sessions of synods had moved from the auditorium of the Parish House to a hotel convention centre on the outer edge of Metropolitan Toronto.

The civic component of St James' cathedral identity continued strong. For example, the cathedral and the city remained conjoined in St James' Park. Terence Finlay's enthronement as diocesan bishop was attended by the lieutenant-governor, the premier, the mayor of Toronto, and the chairman of Metropolitan Toronto, and the bishop formally blessed the city in their presence. The Prince and Princess of Wales and their children worshipped in the cathedral on Sunday, 27 October 1991 (Figures 4.10 and 4.11), the occasion of the 150th anniversary of the Faculty of Divinity of Trinity College, when the Prince read a lesson. In December 1994, both Bob Rae, premier of Ontario, and Barbara Hall, mayor of Toronto, participated in the installation of Stoute as the sixth dean, and Rae read a lesson. Stoute emphasized that the relationship between church and state that the occasion symbolized was one of mutual benefit, which the cathedral intended to maintain. The Governor-General's Horse Guards, whose associations with St James' reached back to 1822, donated a three-light stained-glass window for the southwest façade in 1997. During the two-hundredth anniversary of St James', Queen Elizabeth II and Prince Philip worshipped there on 29 June 1997, two days before the British Crown turned over control of Hong Kong to China. The dean made an exception to the cathedral's long-in-the-making liturgical mission in order to accommodate the queen's requirements: the eleven-o'clock service that Sunday was Mattins rather than the Eucharist.[95]

In celebration of the bicentenary, the Friends of St James' raised funds from the wider church and the people of the city to acquire and augment a set of historic bells from London, England, and in 1997 these twelve English-style free-swinging bells were installed in the tower (see Figure 4.12). They complemented the set of American-style fixed bells struck by hammers activated electrically by a keyboard, which had hung there since 1865. The Friends explained the meaning of the project: 'The bells of a great cathedral church do not ring for its parishioners alone. As one of the oldest churches in Toronto and one at the centre of the old town of York, St James' has a role to play in the civic life of Toronto and all of Canada. Because bells ring with a richer voice when swung for change-ringing, the new twelve bell peal's message will carry much further and more prominently.' The bells were ready in time for the Queen's visit, and parishioners and clergy alike felt that they made a beautiful and wonderful crown for the cathedral.[96]

A special section of the Toronto *Anglican*, the diocesan newspaper, issued for the anniversary, carried a hint of the tension between the two visions of the cathedral. 'The cathedral,' it said, 'maintains traditions that have largely disappeared elsewhere in the diocese, and it reflects the diversity of diocesan life today.'[97]

4.12 Clergy and parishioners gathered at the Toronto docks for the arrival of
the new change-ringing bells from England, 1997.

PARISH, PEOPLE, AND FINANCES

The other side of the dual nature of St James' was her identity as a parish. Like Christ's human and divine natures, her roles as cathedral and as parish were utterly inseparable; but, as in orthodox Christology, it is very important to draw the distinction between them. Each gave life to the other. Long before 1935 the people and clergy of the parish of St James' had desired their church to become the cathedral again in order to save the parish, and the diocese had hoped that attaching the cathedral to the parish might preserve a cathedral for Toronto. Becoming the cathedral would give St James' a role that might safeguard her immediate future and offer her a longer-term mission. At the same time, the parish possessed the building, the heritage, a people, and a financial base that the diocese needed to maintain a cathedral. Joining the cathedral to the parish initiated a long-term project of mutual salvation as an alternative to euthanasia.

The first aspect of the St James' project, as we have seen, was the deliberate movement to shape the building, liturgy, and music according to a particular image of a cathedral. The second aspect, which we now look at, was the equally earnest effort to ensure enough people and economic resources to sustain and enliven the parish supporting the cathedral.

The Downtown Parish

In 1935 the great problem about people was the depopulation of the historic centre around the church. St James' was well aware of it. The churchwardens were convinced that the parish was dying a slow and painful death. When they described St James' as a 'downtown' church they meant by 'downtown' the expanding central business district of the city, which offered fewer and fewer possibilities for residence. The people who had long been part of St James', and especially the pewholders, had moved out of the district and could be counted on less and less for either regular attendance or financial support. Within living memory, Grace Church on Elm Street to the northwest had folded in 1911 and moved to a new site in the wealthy Russell Hill area as Grace Church on the Hill. Then in 1932 the neighbouring parish to the west, the Church of the Ascension at Richmond and York streets, had closed and moved to north Toronto, and nearby to the east, St Augustine's at Parliament and Spruce streets, had shut its doors in 1933. The churchwardens of St James' pictured the day when their parish and the Parish House might not be needed or wanted in the downtown.[98]

The formal boundaries of the parish followed Queen Street to the north and Sherbourne Street to the east and included the Toronto Islands to the south. The west bound had been Bay Street, but with the demise of the Church of the Ascension, it was moved westward to John Street. The south boundary was redrawn at the lakefront with the creation of the parish of St Andrew by the Lake on the islands in 1950. It appears that the west bound moved eastward to Spadina Avenue about 1965 and further east to University Avenue by 1984.[99]

By 1935 these boundaries and the adjacent areas already contained the stark polarity of wealth and poverty that was to characterize the downtown through to the 1990s. Awareness of these realities was omnipresent in the on-going deliberations both before and after 1935 about what to do with St James'. During the day, the wealthy and well employed worked and shopped downtown, and some of them returned on Sunday to worship at St James'. By 1935 the parish enclosed one of the two most powerful centres of corporate and financial capitalism in Canada (the other being St James' Street in Montreal) and from the 1970s the most powerful such centre, along with the offices of lawyers, stockbrokers, accountants, and other ancillary professions of capitalism. It also contained a wealthy commercial area, the chief rail-transport centre of Canada, leading hotels, warehouses, and, into the 1950s, considerable manufacturing. After the Second World War, however, the face of the downtown changed rapidly. Demolition proceeded briskly along Jarvis Street, physically annihilating most of the architectural glory of the street whose creation had once yielded the immense wealth that the Cawthra family had used to benefit St James'. During the 1960s whole city blocks in the heart of the former town of York were demolished, south, east, and west of the cathedral. The façade of the early city hall on King Street and the old St Lawrence Market on Front Street were threatened. From the late 1960s onward, stunning new building towers appeared around King and Bay streets, within the boundaries of the parish, and presented an emphatic display of the wealth and status of the big banks and big corporations. They dwarfed the spire of St James', still the tallest in Canada, and symbolized the shift in cultural and social power from the church and land to materialism and liquid capital wealth.

By 1935 the downtown also enveloped areas of deep poverty, dilapidated housing, vacant buildings, and vacant land. Here, day and night, lived many who were poor, unemployed, recipients of public welfare, and transient. They were served by Christian missions to the destitute, notably the Salvation Army and Fred Victor missions, and few if any of them, it seems, were parishioners of St James'. The once comfortable houses south of Bloor Street – especially around Jarvis, Carlton, Sherbourne, and Wellesley streets – were emptied of their St James' families and converted into rooming-houses or other uses. Most of the lesser houses remaining between Queen and Carlton were rated as fourth-class residences and occupied by poor families and single men. In 1978 the churchwardens fought, but failed, to get the city to install public toilets next to the cathedral 'in an effort to prevent the winos and transients in the park from spoiling the grounds.' In the 1990s the area was still among the poorest in Toronto. The church continued to keep the inner doors of the Parish House locked during office hours, and anyone wishing access then had to be known to the staff or make inquiry through a small sliding window looking into the vestry office.[100]

Beyond the parish boundaries, but still nearby, St James' in 1935 continued to own the Wellesley Lands at the end of Wellesley Street, next to St James' Cemetery, and the Park Lots, a large assemblage of houses and stores in an area bounded on the west by Parliament Street, on the north by Dundas, on the east by Regent, and on the south by Sydenham (later Shuter). The eastern bounds had once followed Pine Street (later Sackville). St James' had purchased the land from the Crown in the 1830s for use as a cemetery but had soon found the soil unsuitable. In 1935 the cathedral owned about 120 buildings that had been built on these lands. Of these, about ninety were substandard, but occupied by tenants, while the remaining thirty were designated unfit for habitation or simply vacant. The cathedral controlled the mortages on another two hundred or so buildings.[101]

The Park Lots were a slum, and the cathedral was a slum landlord. The news of this broke into the public press in December 1934 and January and February 1935, at the very moment when the negotiations for St James' to become the cathedral were in progress. The city was still in deep economic depression and eager to clean up the slums when the former rector's wife, Mrs H.P. Plumptre, a critic of slum housing, won election to city council in 1935. The churchwardens complained, 'Increasing stringency of the (city) Welfare Department regulations make the handling of this property more difficult each year.' Each year until 1938 city inspectors issued a summons to the churchwardens for non-compliance with city housing-standards. The churchwardens declared that the Park Lots brought in little or no income and responded partly by making some repairs but chiefly by evicting tenants, demolishing houses, and selling off properties. The annual report on cathedral revenue still showed income from 'Wellesley Street and Park Lands' in 1943, and it took until at least 1945 for St James' to extricate herself from the financial complications.[102] In the 1950s the city completed a huge demolition project in these blocks and built Regent Park South to join Regent Park North as the largest public-housing development in Canada.[103] The cathedral transferred the Wellesley Lands to the city in 1945 and 1947 for use as a playground. The motive behind the gift was to divert the children of the neighbourhood poor from the cemetery, where 'their mischievous behaviour' was 'the cause of annoyance' and 'costly damage to gravestones and other property.' The results were Wellesley Park and, apparently, an end to complaints.[104]

In 1963 and 1964 Dean Gilling appealed to the parish to become more deliberate in serving both the wealthy and the impoverished. By then the 'downtown' was also being called the 'inner city' – a term that highlighted the poverty and repression of the people still living there. In a report on the role of the cathedral in the inner city, Gilling noted that, compared with other areas, the inner city held 'a higher percentage of unemployed, school dropouts, alcoholism, prostitution, drug addiction, grasping landlords, and problems of colour and ethnic groups.'[105]

While the city of Toronto was still gaining in numbers, the distribution of people had been shifting from the historic centre around St James' to regions north of Bloor Street, especially east and west of Yonge Street, and outward to the new suburbs. St James' knew by the late 1930s that her parishioners were widely scattered and drawn from across the city, though judging from the baptismal registers, some still lived south of Bloor. In 1964 Gilling reported that only two house-holds were living downtown. One large share of the congregation resided in Rosedale, Forest Hill, and Russell Hill, wealthy areas north of Bloor served by St Paul's, St Simon's, and Grace Church on the Hill. Another large share lived on either side of Yonge Street around St Clair and Eglinton, in comfortable neighbourhoods with a high Anglican population who were well served by St Clement's and other parish churches. The rest came from the suburbs. By 1970 only one household lived within the parish bounds – the choirmaster and his family, living in one of the flats in the Parish House.[106]

The clergy followed the trend. After moving out of the rectory on Adelaide Street in 1921, Plumptre resided at various addresses 'uptown' in Rosedale. In 1937 the cathedral leased a house for Riley at 52 Roxborough Drive in north Rosedale; then in 1945 it purchased 8 McKenzie Avenue in south Rosedale, which served as the rectory or deanery until 1987. There Riley, Gilling, and Stiff resided in upper-middle-class style among the well-to-do of the parish. Over the years most single assistant clergy lived in the Parish House, but the married ones tended to follow the rector's example in living away from downtown.

Meanwhile a large percentage of the new non-British immigrants to Toronto settled in much of the housing that remained south of Bloor. Within the city of Toronto, the pool of people of British heritage from which the cathedral continued to draw virtually all her congregation was evaporating. In 1931 about 80 per cent of the city population of 631,000 were British. In 1951 the British share was 68 per cent of 675,700, and in 1981 only 33 per cent of 599,000; most growth occurred in neighbouring municipalities, twelve of which joined the city in Metropolitan Toronto in 1954. As the British moved out of the city centre, they were replaced, by 1951, by Jews, Ukrainians, Poles, and Italians, and by 1981 by Portuguese, more Italians, Chinese, Greeks, and others. Very few of these newcomers, if any, were attracted to St James'.[107]

During the 1970s, however, the depopulation of the centre started to reverse, and the parish took immediate notice. The city fostered new residential developments with the Southeast Downtown Urban Renewal Scheme in the 1970s and the East Downtown Planning Study from 1988. Beginning with the late 1970s and continuing through the 1990s, a vast complex of cooperative housing and comfortable condominium residences took shape around St James'. Most notable were the new neighbourhoods around Crombie Park, southeast of the St Lawrence Market, restored in 1977, and Market Square in 1981. St James' soon began to feel the effects. In 1991 eighty-six parishioners' households, or 17 per cent, were to be found within the downtown area south of Bloor. About fifty of these were within or near the actual parish bounds, twice as many as now lived in Rosedale, and the figures were rising. For the rest, the old pattern persisted: 42 per cent north of Bloor and to the west and east of the downtown within the city limits, 30 per cent in the suburban areas of Metropolitan Toronto, and 11 per cent in the outlying cities and regions from Oakville to Pickering. By 1996, the cathedral could report that about 30 per cent of her parishioners again resided downtown, and one of these new neighbours, Alfred Apps, entered the governing circle in 1997 as a deputy warden.[108]

The clergy followed this trend back downtown. At Dean Abraham's request, the cathedral sold the deanery in Rosedale and purchased a condominium residence in Market Square as the deanery. The perceived tie of the clergy with the wealthy had sent particular messages to parishioners and the city, and Abraham said, 'I didn't think it was appropriate for me to live in Rosedale.' Because Dean Stoute needed a family house, the cathedral sold the Market Square property and in 1995 acquired 44 Rose Avenue, in a socially mixed neighbourhood near Wellesley and Parliament, south of Bloor and not far from St James' Cemetery. In 1992 the cathedral bought a house for the vicar at 211 George Street, within walking distance of St James', replacing one at Kew Beach. From 1992 onward, all three full-time clergy lived downtown.[109]

The long-standing anxieties of both churchwardens and clergy about the future of St James' as a parish were well founded in attendance figures. The numbers for average Sunday attendance in Table 4.1 may serve as a gauge, provided we remember that it factors in the large numbers that came for festivals and that attendance on ordinary Sundays would be considerably lower.[110]

Table 4.1
Average Sunday attendance, 1920–96, including all services, by five-year intervals

Year	Average Sunday attendance	Year	Average Sunday attendance	Year	Average Sunday attendance
1920	1,200	1950	525	1980	601
1925	1,150	1955	488	1985	600
1930	950	1960	586	1990	521
1935	800	1965	510	1994	503
1940	700	1970	411	1995	527
1945	624	1975	579	1996	566

When St James' resumed her status as the cathedral in 1935, average Sunday attendance was apparently one-third lower than it had been in 1920. The numbers continued to drop at a steady rate until the mid-1950s, but by the end of the decade the decline had been arrested. From the 1960s onward into the 1990s, numbers rose for a time, then fell, and rose and fell again. There was some hope that they might rise again when 1995 showed 527 and 1996, 566.

Overall, these figures revealed an apparent absolute decline from the 1920s to the 1990s, and until the 1950s St James' relative position within the diocese also declined. In 1935, it was the sixth church in average Sunday attendance, well behind St Paul's. As people continued to shift away and the Anglican population generally moved outward, it fell further to sixteenth place in 1950. St Clement's, Christ Church, Deer Park, and Grace Church on the Hill – all in the comfortable, strongly Anglican areas north of Bloor – now vied with St Paul's for the top positions. The decline in numbers at St James' was disconcerting to people and clergy alike, as was the rise to pre-eminence of the parishes of north Toronto and the suburbs, and the annual reports repeatedly said so.[111]

Parishioners

These numbers reflected a sea change between the late 1930s and the 1990s in the kind of people who attended St James'. In the 1930s the parishioners seem to have spanned a broad range of social classes, from the élite of the old Toronto families to manual and industrial workers. The élite and the upper-middle-class well-to-do formed the core of the pewholders, divided into those who possessed pews by leasehold, paying annual ground rents, and those who rented seats in pews. The pewholders controlled all the best positions in the nave and acted as the financial and governing class in the parish. The pew boards mounted at the rear of the nave recited their names and pew numbers – a reminder of their social standing, wealth, and power. Their money enhanced the cathedral, and their names, as well as those who married into their families, continued after 1935 to be added to the memorials on the walls, the furnishings, the windows, and the list of benefactors: Beatty, Brock, Cawthra, Denison, Gooderham, Jarvis, Kirkpatrick, Laidlaw, Nordheimer, Northcote, Ridout, Strathy, and Wilkes. Many of these same names appeared on the list of churchwardens in the same period.[112] The pewholders came to St James' as families; they sat together in the same seats week by week and year after year saw the backs of the same heads. Many of their children attended Upper Canada College, Havergal College, and Bishop Strachan School, the schools for the social élite.[113] They valued tradition, loyalty, empire, connection, and wealth, and they were politically conservative.

There were also people at the other end of the social scale, although it is difficult to tell how many or how attached they were to the parish. The baptismal register for 1935 and 1936, in listing the fathers who brought their children to baptism or the adults who were themselves baptized, also gave their occupations. Of the forty-three entries, perhaps twenty-one were manual labourers and industrial and trade workers. They listed their occupations as baker, caretaker, chauffeur, cleaner, labourer, mechanic, messenger, postal helper, roofer, soap presser, and truck driver. The other twenty-two were spread across the middle classes, from barrister to secretary. There were evidently some poor and unemployed among the parishioners as well, for in the late 1930s the annual Easter offerings continued to be devoted 'to the relief of poverty and distress among the members of this congregation during the coming year' and to supplement the income of those on public welfare provided by the city.[114]

From the 1940s to the 1960s regular worshippers were well aware that the kinds of parishioners who made up St James' were changing. The pewholders were a measure of the shift; the corporation complained increasingly that they were not keeping up their rents and that their pews were usually vacant. The discrepancy between those who held pews and those who actually came for worship grew increasingly noticeable. The churchwardens very nearly abolished the pew system in 1956 and again in 1959 but pulled back each time for fear of giving offence. They did remove most of the lockable book boxes from the pews in 1959, while retaining the latched pew doors, and they campaigned for pewholders to deed their holdings back to the church. The Ridouts, after four generations in St James', had given up pew 110 in 1946. The Jarvis family donated pew 77 in 1962, with the provision that the Jarvis sisters, Augusta Jarvis and Bertha Jarvis Bedford, could occupy it for the rest of their lives. The Cawthras, who had owned a pew since 1803, relinquished pew 70 in 1968. The symbolic end of the era came in the early 1960s, when the corporation took the pewboards down. Yet a shadow of the tradition lingered on, for as late as 1983 the financial report showed income from pew rents of $485. In 1987 some sidesmen were reserving pews for regular parishioners, and the corporation acted to stop the practice, saying that it excluded other members and visitors and 'has cast a poor image of the Cathedral to many people.' Still the practice persisted into the 1990s; pew contracts were still being discovered in family papers in the 1980s and 1990s, and the pews donated to the parish. When the cathedral was renovated in 1979–82, one double box pew, pew 137, was retained as a memento of the earlier age.[115]

Meanwhile, new people were arriving, and the church first noticed their presence as visitors. In January 1937, after St James' first full year as restored cathedral, the churchwardens, W.W. Denison and Elliot G. Strathy, reported that the number of visitors was growing rapidly and that, because of the pew system, it was difficult to place them in good seats. They encouraged pewholders to welcome people into their pews and to make the cathedral feel more friendly to outsiders. After the Second World war the churchwardens again remarked that visitors were increasing in number. In January 1957, Riley reported that about half the families on the parish list and about one third of the individuals not belonging to families were new since 1937. In the 1960s the churchwardens acknowledged that on many Sundays the visitors outnumbered the core of regular parishioners.[116]

These 'visitors' were part of a regenerative process which replenished the parish. They were of four types at least: some came to try St James' and converted into regular parishioners; others were seasonal attenders, especially at services around Christmas and Easter; some came occasionally for particular services, notably the eleven-o'clock service on Sunday or choral Evensong; and others were once-only tourists from outside Toronto, some of them from other countries, coming mostly in summer. There were also people who came only for special diocesan and civic events – celebrations, confirmations, ordinations, the annual corporate worship of various societies, commemorations, synods, or notables' funerals. But some of these, too, returned as visitors and then converted into parishioners.

By the 1960s the changeover in the body of parishioners was remarkable. Joyce Sowby attended St James' from 1938 until she left the city in 1951. When she returned to Toronto and St James' in 1965, she noticed that nearly everybody was new. The old élite families were largely gone; their children, grandchildren, nieces, and nephews had gone elsewhere or had stopped attending church.[117] The reports to vestry recorded the deaths of parishioners year by year and, in slow motion, displayed the passing of the old social order. Most of those at the other end of the social scale seemed to have gone as well. When a survey of the parish in 1970 reported the occupations of the parishioners, about 50 per cent were retired or housewives and the rest were distributed as follows: 11 per cent law, finance, and management; 4 per cent doctors, dentists, and engineers; 13 per cent education, health care, and social services; 4 per cent marketing; 7 per cent secretarial; 4 per cent artists and artisans (in the sense of craft workers); and 4 per cent students. Apparently there were no manual labourers, industrial workers, or artisans in the sense of workers at a hand or machine trade, such as shoemakers. The baptismal register showed one such worker, a tool and dye maker, out of the fifteen entries given for 1965, none out of thirteen for 1970, and none out of seventeen for 1981. The parishioners seemed to have lost both the top and bottom ends of their social scale and become distributed within the ranks of the upper-middle, middle, and lower-middle classes.[118] Conservative politics still seemed to prevail; when in 1971, a long-standing parishioner, Margaret Scrivener, was elected to the provincial legislature for the Conservative party to represent the constituency that included Rosedale, the cathedral expressed much pleasure.[119] St James' appeared to have become more upper-middle-class and middle-class, and more Conservative, than the rest of the diocese.[120]

A majority of the parishioners were female, comprising about 55 per cent of the parish list. About half of these women lived alone, as compared with about one third of the men. The parishioners were predominantly an older lot: 75 per cent were over forty, and about 60 per cent of these were over sixty. There were fewer families, fewer children, and more individuals living alone. By 1950 only about half the households were families, with single-person households making up the rest. By 1960, more than half the households were single-person and by 1975, two-thirds. Sunday-school enrolments mirrored the decline in the number of children. The Sunday-school report for 1952 recalled that in 1891 enrolment had been over twelve hundred. In 1940, the afternoon and morning sessions together totalled 165 pupils, with twenty teachers and officials. The records showed seventy-six children in 1955, sixty in 1960, and forty-nine in 1964, with many fewer coming regularly. The parish seemed to have a larger percentage of individuals living alone and older people than the rest of the diocese, but about the same proportion of women to men as the rest.[121]

The Appeal of St James'

The clergy and people were usually confident of the appeal of St James'. Newcomers tended to be united in their attraction to the cathedral as cathedral, and especially to the particular way in which St James' shaped her cathedral identity. In January 1963, the churchwardens reported their assessment to the annual vestry meeting: 'For the past twenty-five years St James' has continued on its rather anomalous path. It is a parish church with all the obligations of a parish church. It is a cathedral with all the responsibilities of a cathedral, but it has none of the immunities and privileges of a cathedral ... We believe that the Cathedral's future lies in its becoming – as it well may, for it has the potential – an outstanding cathedral on this continent. While we do not think that St James' will ever regain its former glory as a parish church, it should always have an active and happy parochial life carried on by parishioners few in number but loyal and devoted.'[122] In 1970 parishioners indicated overwhelmingly that their top interests in St James' were the music, the liturgy, and the building, along with the general atmosphere. Very low on their list were the sermons, the clergy, parish visiting, and the newsletter.[123] There were, however, moments of doubt; in 1969 the corporation minutes recorded a concern that the music might not be attracting people as hoped.[124] The clergy throughout the period spoke often of the centrality of the tradition of building, liturgy, and music. In the 1990s they sensed that the cathedral shaped by this tradition manifested a rootedness and a weightedness that gave many people a place of safety in a world and a church where everything else seemed to be changing.[125]

The testimonies of some of the parishioners who joined St James' about 1960 confirmed that they came and stayed because of the building, the liturgy, and the music. Moira Esdaile began attending in 1959 and Helen Watson in 1963, and a generation later they both unequivocally agreed: 'It's the combination. The music is excellent. The building makes you feel you are in worship. The liturgy is perfection.' Barbara Hawkins, who started in 1962, concurred that the vast majority came for the beautiful church, worship, and music and, she added, because they felt that St James', as the cathedral, was important.[126]

We may look again at the attendance figures from 1935 to 1996. While the numbers did fall, the drop did not continue towards zero. By 1955, the average attendance on Sundays had fallen below 500 to 488, but then it rose to 586 in 1960. After a further fall to a low of 411 in 1970, it rose again to 601 in 1980, before falling and rising once again, but staying above 500.

In other words, over the long run of forty years from 1955 to 1996, attendance has fluctuated in a general range above and below five hundred, and since the mid-1970s it has remained above that figure. The statistics suggest that St James' found a relatively stable supply of people to keep her going. If we judge by these numbers, it was usually the second largest parish in the diocese. Attendance began to stabilize during the 1950s, when St James' was embellishing the chancel, the liturgy, and the music. With further liturgical heightening from the mid-1970s on, and greater enhancement of the building and St James' Park by 1982, stability continued into the 1990s. St James' rank within the diocese rose dramatically; from sixteenth place in 1950, she had moved up to second by 1975 and since then has usually kept that rank among all parishes in the diocese, right behind St Clement's.[127]

If another set of figures is added to these, the picture becomes more complete. In the 1970s and 1980s the cathedral reported the total annual attendance at all services. Besides the regular Sunday services, this figure included daily services throughout the week and special liturgical services and diocesan services throughout the year. These were all services mounted by St James'. Adding in these figures increases numbers significantly. For instance, in the course of 1983, after the rededication of the cathedral, the regular Sunday services drew 30,724 people, for an average Sunday attendance of 591, a figure on the high end of the stable range. To these were added 7,546 people at daily Mattins, Evensong, and Eucharist during the week. The special services – notably the Good Friday Liturgy, the Easter Vigil, the Advent carol service, and the first Evensong of Christmas – with other well-attended events attracted another 6,064 people. The special services of the diocese and diocesan groups – such as ordinations, which moved to Sunday afternoon, and the annual service of the Diocesan Chancel Guild – counted another 4,760. The total annual attendance for 1983 then became 49,094, and the clergy administered the bread and wine to 30,260 people. We could add other kinds of figures as well: during 1971, for example, 33,400 people attended services of worship, five to six thousand attended cathedral concerts, perhaps two thousand visitors toured the cathedral, two thousand children made educational visits, and still more people used the premises for one purpose or another during the week. These numbers placed St James' far ahead of all other Anglican churches, with the highest annual attendance in the diocese as well as the most people using the church building.[128]

In other words, St James' found enough people. By becoming the cathedral again in 1935, and by enhancing the beauty and majesty of the building, the music, and the liturgy over the decades into the 1990s, St James' survived the loss of her former parishioners and attracted and maintained new adherents and users as both parish and cathedral.

Economic Resources

The economic problem in 1935 was bound up with the issue of parish population; for if parishioners left St James', income would fall. The difficulty was exacerbated by the capitalist depression. At this very moment, when St James' was becoming the cathedral, income from all sources was dropping severely, as it had been since 1929. Between 1929 and 1935 contributions from regular givers dropped by 43 per cent, pew income by 17 per cent, and investment income by 44 per cent, while the operating deficit increased by 200 per cent. It seemed an open question whether St James' would survive financially. Over the next sixty years there were periodic financial troubles, and the churchwardens repeatedly spoke of economic difficulties and at least once of financial collapse.

Half the problem was that expenditures went up during some periods, while in absolute numbers the average Sunday attendance was declining. Table 4.2 displays the actual expenditures from 1929 to 1996, highlighting the years when important changes occurred in the total amounts.[129]

Table 4.2
Expenditures (adjusted) for selected years, showing changes in range of amounts

Year	Expenditures($)	Year	Expenditures ($)	Year	Expenditures ($)
1929	32,800	1957	83,400	1981	439,600
1931	29,300	1959	114,800	1984	589,800
1935	25,600	1960	130,400	1987	692,700
1937	30,300	1970	175,200	1988	728,900
1939	33,600	1973	195,000	1990	856,600
1943	38,400	1974	218,600	1991	905,700
1950	43,000	1976	262,700	1994	1,139,800
1952	50,000	1978	282,200	1996	1,315,100
1955	62,500	1979	317,100		

Expenditures fell by 23 per cent from 1929 to 1935 and did not recover to the pre-Depression level until 1939. Only a slight increase occurred during the Second World War, to a level that lasted until 1949. Then, abetted by an expanding economy and driven by higher costs during the 1950s, expenditures rose unimpeded, jumping by large amounts each year in the middle and late 1950s. The churchwardens were sometimes apologetic about the increased spending, and expenditures levelled off during the 1960s until 1969, as they fought to keep spending at the same levels as in the previous decade. Then began an unending and meteoric rise from 1970, but especially from 1976, fuelled by inflation and relatively greater costs. The two periods of the most rapid increases matched the times when the parish's expectations for the grandeur of the cathedral were rising remarkably – from the end of the 1940s under Riley, in connection with the main work of extending the chancel, and from the mid-1970s under Stiff, when everything became considerably more elaborate. In the 1990s the cost of operating at the level needed to maintain the cathedral's identity surpassed one million dollars a year.

The expenses comprised the same kinds of items throughout the whole period; but the percentage spent on particular items sometimes varied, as did the issues and concerns affecting them. A look at five different moments in Table 4.3 helps us understand the constancies and shifts.[130]

Salaries and wages for the clergy and staff remained a remarkably constant share of the whole. This means that their pay increased, often under pressure from the diocese, and kept pace with the overall dramatic rise in expenditures. In 1982, for instance, salaries increased 12 per cent for the three clergy, the vestry clerk and the office secretary, the verger, and two other members of the maintenance staff. Operations included everything needed to run the cathedral and the Parish House and to provide for worship and parish life. This share varied in relation to the amounts assigned specifically to music, restoration of the building, and the diocese. Local outreach pertained to the work of a new committee established in the 1980s to focus the attention of the whole parish on the needs of impoverished people in the immediate neighbourhood; until then, what help there had been for local needs had come almost entirely from women's groups with separate budgets and not from the general parish budget.

Over the long haul, music accounted for a fairly constant share of the parish budget, averaging around 13 or 14 per cent. But there were fluctuations, as is suggested by the unusually high amount shown in 1937. This occurred within a depression year and represented once-only outlays made for things such as books, surplices, and care of the organ which were incurred

Table 4.3
Expenditures, by item and percentage, for selected years, 1929–96

Item	1929 (%)	1937 (%)	1957 (%)	1976 (%)	1996 (%)
Salaries: clergy, staff, and housing	26	28	24	28	29
Operations: cathedral, parish house, rectory	41	31	30	45	31
Music including salaries, choir	16	22	12	15 plus choir fund	13
Building restoration	3	3	15	1	10
Diocese allotment	9	14	20	12	12
Local outreach	0	0	0	0	5
Other	3	1	0.2	0.6	0
Total expenditures ($)	31,600	30,300	83,400	262,700	1,315,100

on St James' resuming its status as the cathedral but charged to the regular budget. Music costs went down to 9.5 per cent in 1961, but the commitment in the mid-1960s to make Hurrle full-time choirmaster and put more into the program drove the share up to 20 per cent in 1967. The figures include the hourly wages paid to the men and boys as well as the salaries of the choir-master and an assistant organist. In 1982, the total number of people on salary at the cathedral was ten, plus those on wages. From the 1970s to 1995 the figures did not include the choral scholarships paid to boys enrolled in St George's College, but in 1996 they did. Although the music share might have been expected to decline as salary and maintenance costs escalated, in fact music expenditures rose, animated by the continually high expectations for the contribution of music to the cathedral's identity.[131]

The clergy and churchwardens as well as outsiders often complained about the amounts spent on music, but St James' usually rallied around this commitment. Two particularly volatile moments stood out. The protracted battle between the corporation and Hurrle over the music program evolved into a complaint about the high cost of music and poor returns for the effort. After St James' had come close to firing him, Hurrle resigned in 1969 and left on bad terms.[132] Another conflict broke out with Foy in 1976 over his duties and what critics regarded as excessive music expenditures; this blended into a dispute over music costs in 1977 between Stiff and Sydney Wrightson, a churchwarden, which led Wrightson to resign in mid-year – the only such resignation recorded in the long list of churchwardens since 1807. The choirmaster's position had ceased to be a completely full-time one because of the connection with St George's, which put first Foy and later Bryant on the school's staff as well.[133]

Compared with the 13 to 14 per cent spent on music at St James', a parish church that did not specially feature music yet maintained a commitment to good music, including an organist and paid singers, might commit 9 per cent of its budget to music, while a parish that considers music important but maintains a Sunday-only organist and voluntary musicians might assign 3 to 4 per cent to music. St James' usually spent more on music than she gave to the diocese and much more than she did on outreach, while two of the comparison parishes each gave the diocese two to five times the amount of their music budget, while the second parish committed at least four times more to outreach. The cathedral was sensitive about this matter – so much so that at one point the newsletter published an article on cathedral music as outreach. St James' probably had the highest music expenditures in the Canadian Anglican Church.[134]

The figures for building restoration reflect the usual practice of postponing major repairs and then mounting extraordinary campaigns for special funds to pay for large-scale work. The years were punctuated by immense campaigns for building restoration: 1951–5, 1971–2, and 1979–82. Special expenditures on the building around the 1971–2 campaign totalled about $400,000, and the tally around the 1979–82 campaign came to about $800,000.[135] Routine repairs were charged to the regular budget, as is indicated by the shares for 1929, 1937, and 1976. The accounts for 1957 and 1996 reflect the resolve after the campaigns in the 1950s and 1979–82 to build large amounts into the regular budget for major work. In the late 1950s and 1960s the corporation was trying to put aside an extra five to ten thousand dollars a year for repairs and renewals. In the 1980s and 1990s Barry Graham was citing figures ranging from $75,000 to $175,000 per year for continuous building restoration. Starting from 1981 Graham served four years as deputy warden and churchwarden and then in 1985 became permanent volunteer property manager, charged with care of the building fabric.[136]

The diocesan numbers reflect recurrent tension between the cathedral and the diocese over funds. The diocesan share increased steeply during the Depression and the Second World War, reaching the 14 per cent shown for 1937 and 35 per cent in 1943, then settling around 25 per cent until 1956. These figures mirrored the enlarging role of the diocese in church affairs. Over the years, in effect, St James' subsidized the diocese by serving as the cathedral, but the terms of their financial relationship varied. In 1957 St James' reneged on her diocesan commitment – a reversal of roles, for until then the diocese had depended on St James' financially. As one sign of this dependence, in 1934 St James' waived the mortgage payments that the diocese owed to her on the synod office, housed in the old parish rectory, and she finally cancelled the mortage in 1939.[137] From 1957 on, St James' failed several times to meet her annual payment to the diocese, especially the outreach portion. The corporation often protested that the payment required was too high or unfairly assessed. This happened four years running in the early 1960s, again for several years in the early and mid-1970s, yet again in the early 1980s, and from 1989 through the early 1990s. The corporation's minutes were dotted with suggestions that the diocese or the bishop of the day did not really care about the cathedral. St James' and the diocese fought over access to wealthy Anglicans in the parish in 1970, over a lease to the C.D. Howe Institute in 1984 and 1985, over payment for the services of the verger, over how to calculate the diocesan assessment, over payment for diocesan services at the cathedral, and over other matters.[138] For three years – 1991, 1992, 1993 – St James' acted unilaterally to apply income from special funds to regular expenditures in order to reduce the assessable base used for determining the parish's obligations to the diocese for outreach and other purposes. The diocese responded by revising the formula, and St James' stopped this practice. The complaints and protests over the years worked. Each time, as for 1996, the diocese brought the amounts down to the range of 12 per cent or lower. After years of having the highest assessable base in the diocese, the new calculations placed St James' second to St Paul's, though still higher than St Clement's.[139]

The other side of the economic problem was the constant need to secure enough income. The parish managed to meet expenditures each year, but not without difficulty and only by making large changes. Table 4.4 suggests how this happened.[140]

Table 4.4
Income sources, by percentage and dollar amounts, for selected years, 1929–96

Sources	1929	1938	1957	1976	1996
Offerings	69%	70%	54%	48%	31%
Collections	*17%	*13%	*15	*8%	*7%
Envelopes	*52%	*58%	*39%	*40%	*21%
Special purpose					*3%
Pews	10%	9%	4%	0.2%	0
Investments:	17%	17%	42%	52%	59%
General	10%	*7%	*34%	*43%	*49%
Trusts	*0.1%	*0.2%	*8%	*1%	*10%
Land/property*	*7%	*9%	?	*8% est.	?
Cemetery payment	2%	2%	0.4%	0.2%	4%
Other	3%	2%	0	0	5%
Operating income	$31,600	$32,000	$83,400	$261,800	$1,315,800
Parish groups and other income	$17,000	$12,800	$57,300	$58,600 + ?	$27,000 + ?
Total income	$48,722	$44,800	$140,700	$320,400 + ?	$1,342,800 + ?

In 1929 pew income accounted for more than the receipts from the Sunday-morning collections, or investments in stocks and bonds, or land investments. By 1938 the proportions were changing, so that pews generated about the same as land and less than the Sunday-morning collections, and stocks and bonds were ascending. Pew income remained in the range of 8 to 10 per cent into the 1950s, until the pew system collapsed around 1960. Thereafter only a minuscule amount from pews lingered in the budget. The category 'other' became important in the 1990s, when the cathedral realized that film and television companies would pay for use of the building and grounds; this brought $56,000 in 1996, but it was an unreliable source.

St James' found unusual 'other' sources to draw on for special appeals, which, while not appearing in the general budget, released parish funds that might otherwise have gone to special purposes. Notable among these was the Wintario Lottery grant of $124,000 for restoration of the building in 1981–2. The cathedral actively sought the grant, threatened legal action against the government to enforce payment, and then used the money to beautify the building, at a time when Anglican ethics generally opposed lotteries.[141]

The cemetery payment covered administrative services provided by the parish in managing the accounts of St James' Cemetery. In the 1930s and 1940s the cemetery was earning barely $50 a year after paying its staff and operating expenses. As early as 1931 the corporation realized that it would become a financial liability once land for grave sites was exhausted and actively considered building a crematorium to increase income. In 1945, after the war, the cemetery installed the crematorium underneath St James' the Less, and in 1948 a columbarium, with more to follow. The name changed to St James' Cemetery and Crematorium. This shift was well in advance of the changes in theology and social custom that eventually established cremation as a widespread practice. Anticipating good results, in 1951 the corporation consolidated the investments of the cathedral and the cemetery, except in the case of certain trusts, thereby permitting the cathedral to benefit directly from any gains. The number of cremations rose dramatically, and casket burials declined. By the 1960s the crematorium was earning thousands of dollars a year, while, as predicted, the cemetery proper lost money. George Durdy presided over these transformations as manager for forty years (1927–67). In 1996 St James' performed 2,700 cremations as compared with thirty-eight casket burials. The cathedral had a new source of funds. The corporation channelled large sums from the crematorium into investments, amounting to $300,000 in 1996, and increased the cemetery payment due the cathedral to $10,000 by 1980 and nearly $60,000 by 1996, or 4 per cent of total income. The churchwardens constantly remarked on how much time they gave to cemetery business, including negotiations with the staff, which was unionized in 1948; but financially they had little choice.[142] Meanwhile, in the 1960s, the name of the cathedral passed to St James' Town, an enormous complex of high-rise apartments with the highest population density in Canada, located across the street from the cemetery.

The offerings of parishioners used to carry about 70 per cent of the budget, as in 1929 and 1938. The Depression had reduced the offerings to 42 per cent in 1937, which, together with the alarm over the depopulation of the downtown, contributed to the huge fears for the future. A vigorous campaign in 1938 to visit parishioners in their homes to ask for funds, called the Every Member Canvass, and the introduction of the duplex envelope system – the black side for parish maintenance and the red for diocesan missions – restored parish donations to the accustomed level. Giving stayed around 65 to 70 per cent into the mid-1950s, dropped to fifty per cent in 1958, but returned to normal for 1959 after two intense financial drives, which were now called 'stewardship campaigns,' reflecting a change in both theology and fund-raising stragegy. But contributions declined steadily again in the 1960s. Even the introduction of pledge cards in the mid-1960s and the simpler weekly single-envelope system in 1967, to replace the old duplex method, failed to stop the fall. In both 1970 and 1971, parish giving paid for less than half the expenses, at 42 per cent, and in a difficult period of transformation in the parish's population, St James' seemed to be in financial free fall.[143]

The clergy and churchwardens had responded at first with a call for the spiritual and financial revival of the parish – Renewal '69 and Renewal '70. They conducted an 'inventory of parish resources' to find out what kind of people the parishioners were and what their prospects were for higher giving. They produced a set of financial forecasts for the next decade and in March and April 1971 the wardens reported their conclusion to the parish and the diocese: the cathedral was going bankrupt. 'The future of St James Cathedral' they wrote 'is bleak at best. If the various forecasts of operations hold true all general fund (investment) income will be dissipated in nine years, and the Cathedral will have to close its doors.' The options that they suggested to the diocese included heroic parish fund-raising, large-scale reductions in costs, redeveloping the cathedral grounds for income, a diocesan take-over, and closing the cathedral.[144]

St James' did not close; nor did the diocese take over, being financially incapable of doing so. Instead many parishioners gave heroically. The envelope offerings are an indicator: in 1971 9 per cent of envelope users gave 42 per cent of the gifts; in 1976 9 per cent gave 41 per cent; in 1989 9 per cent gave 46 per cent; and in 1991 7 per cent gave 45 per cent. The figures showed progressively more givers, higher receipts, and greater giving from the most wealthy.[145] Yet congregational giving still accounted for less than half of the church's needs during the 1970s and 1980s and then fell to 37 per cent in 1987 and 31 per cent through the 1990s. The diocese did reduce St James' assessments for diocesan work, but rather than cutting costs across the board, the parish actually increased its financial commitment to the building, music, and liturgy – the things that mattered most to the cathedral's identity and drew the most people there. The amount applied to local outreach also increased sharply in the 1980s. From at least 1987, the cathedral seriously investigated participating in the redevelopment of the site of the Parish House and the Diocesan Centre, together with the York Rectory lands across the street, to be coupled with selling the cathedral's density and air rights to a developer. Nothing viable had emerged by 1997, but the question stayed very much alive.[146]

In financial terms, the biggest factor that kept St James' from closing was her investments. In the mid-1960s the churchwardens began telling the congregation, 'The future of the Cathedral must inevitably depend more and more on its investment income.'[147] They appealed for people to leave bequests, so that the congregations of the past could help sustain those of the future. Many did so, and the annual reports acknowledged their legacies to the general fund or special trusts. For instance, Pauline Langstaff left $137,000 in 1987, and the musical tradition was well supplied with three funds or trusts: F.J. Coombs Clergy Retirement Fund (1957), expanded to include music (1989), and later devoted to music as the St James' Music Trust (1996); the Choir and Music Trust Fund (1978); and the John Coombs Memorial Music Trust (1990), endowed with $730,000. Added to these were the financial successes of the crematorium. Led by Colin M.A. Strathy, a former churchwarden (1949–53) and long a member of the investment committee, the parish approved a new by-law in 1976 that wrapped the administration of certain special trusts into that of the Consolidated General Investments, allowing for more flexibility in applying income to parish needs appropriate to the trusts' purposes.[148]

Above all, however, the investments increased in value through astute and relatively conservative management of the endowment, riding on the back of the extraordinary successes of the stock and bond markets of the early to mid-1980s. In 1970, the corporation reported that the unrestricted capital endowment available for general operations was about $930,000. In 1990, even after the stock-market crash of 1987 and the beginning of a protracted recession in the capitalist economy, unrestricted investments reached about $3.2 million; and with the consolidations and new flexibility in the administration of the trusts, total investments for cathedral use were valued at $6 million. By December 1996, total cathedral investments stood at $10 million – an increase of nearly one million dollars during the previous year. Expenses exceeded revenue by $770,000, but the investments covered the difference, or nearly 60 per cent of total income for the year. With a further 9 per cent from the crematorium and 'other,' nearly 70 per cent was carried by sources other than parish giving – exactly the reverse of the income profile in 1938.[149]

A noteworthy change in the investment portfolio since 1935 was the decline in the role of landholdings. The funds gained from the sale of the Park Lots after 1935 were reinvested directly into bonds and stocks. The Park Lots dated from the early years of the parish, and their end symbolized the end of the régime of land in St James' finances.[150] St James' did not, however, leave property investments completely behind; for instance, she still received rent from the diocese and after 1985 from the C.D. Howe Institute, and in 1976 she held mortgages on eleven houses in the suburbs or farther out.[151]

The bulk of the investments from the late 1930s to the 1990s were in bonds and stocks, in the ratio of about 60 to 80 per cent for bonds and about 20 to 40 per cent for stocks. For most of this time the portfolio was managed by Dominion Securities, originally an independent firm, but later controled by the Royal Bank, Canada's largest bank. The relationship with the cathedral came through the Strathy family, particularly J.G.K. Strathy, long head of the firm.[152] The kinds of investments chosen remained remarkably constant. From 1937 to 1939, St James' had holdings in Canada, Ontario, and municipal-government bonds and in bonds or stocks in big banks and big companies, notably in railways, gas, communications, manufacturing, and mines.[153] The investment portfolios were nearly identical in 1976, 1984, 1989, and 1996, with only a few pieces altered here and there.[154] The portfolio for 1984, for instance, contained bonds from governments and government-related corporations (Canada Export Development Corporation, Government of Canada, Ontario Hydro, Province of Ontario, and Province of Saskatchewan) and three big banks (Canadian Imperial Bank of Commerce, Mercantile Bank of Canada, and Toronto Dominion). It also contained stocks in some of the very biggest corporations, and biggest profit-makers, in Canada – top-rank members of the *Financial Post* 500.[155]

Table 4.5
Corporations in which St James' Cathedral held stock, 1984

Banks
Canadian Imperial Bank of Commerce, Nova Scotia, Royal, Toronto Dominion (not Montreal)

Oil
Gulf, Imperial, Shell, Texaco

Mines
Alcan, Cominco, Dome

Energy
Interprovincial Pipelines, Trans-Canada Pipelines

Communications
Bell Canada Enterprises (BCE), Northern Telecom, Southam, Thomson

Manufacturing
Dofasco, General Electric, Moore

Food processors
Canada Packers

Conglomerates
Canadian Pacific, Imasco

As St James' came to depend more and more on investments, the stability, growth, and well-being of these giant corporations became necessary to the continuing existence and financial health of the cathedral. St James' was structurally intertwined with some of the most powerful members of the capitalist economy. The lawyers, corporate managers, and financial people who acted as churchwardens and members of the Investment Committee took the relationship to be natural, since their own weekday work was intertwined with the same sort of business. St James' operated within the high-finance world of 'blue-chip thinking.' The tie was poignantly revealed by the stock-market crash of October 1987, in which St James' stocks instantly lost about 9 per cent of their value. But because St James' had invested in some powerhouses of the economic system, the loss was relatively contained; by comparison, the Toronto Stock Exchange price index (TSE index) lost 24 per cent overall.[156] With such dependence on the chief operators and beneficiaries of the economic system, St James' was not in a strong position to reflect critically on, or act freely with respect to, the structural factors that helped produce the rising number of hungry and homeless people, cast off by society, who survived within the sound of the cathedral bells on a Sunday morning.

This tension surfaced in 1977, when Anthony Ketchum appealed to the parish to confine its investments to companies that honoured human rights; the cathedral, he said, should be concerned with more than merely profits. Discussion of the issue percolated through the parish, focusing particularly on investment in South Africa and corporate damage to the interests of Native peoples in northern Canada. The investment committee eventually responded with a policy statement, which was approved by the corporation and distributed to the vestry meeting in 1982. The document affirmed the long-standing practice: 'to maximize the financial return' on investments while taking very little risk, and to do so without regard 'to controversial social, economic, and political issues.'[157] But partly because of pressure from the diocese, the question did not go away, and in 1987 members of the Investment Committee attended sessions arranged by the diocese on alternative investments. In 1990 the corporation approved the new diocesan guidelines on investments and agreed that the cathedral's policy needed to be reconsidered. Their rethinking included looking at the options for 'ethical investment' – an approach that assessed the human effects and social policies of companies as well as their financial performance.[158] They noted that there would be perils ahead, however, if the cathedral followed this ethical route, for it would mean tampering with a financial strategy that had worked and worked well. The traditional policy of seeking profits above all, within the bounds of low-risk investments, had, after all, succeeded in filling the gap opened by the retreat of the older sources of parish income.

In other words, St James' had found the economic resources to sustain it both as parish and as cathedral, although not quite in the way that people had at first expected.

In spite of the tensions, the symbiosis of cathedral and parish had proved beneficial to both. St James' the parish had succeeded in finding and maintaining enough people and financial resources to save the cathedral for the diocese; and St James' the cathedral had provided an identity and a mission that saved the parish.

PARISH LIFE

Throughout the whole period since 1935, virtually all the people who have participated in St James' have come in order to worship, whether within a Sunday service or a special service. The great majority have had no connection with parish activities during the week, although many do. The life of the parish has involved worship above all, as well as an elaborate matrix of activities and groups that goes beyond worship.

Worshippers

Amid the overall shifts in attendance, the role of each of the four main Sunday services changed over the years. The place of the Sunday-evening service continued to decline, and the importance of the morning services increased markedly. Whereas in 1920 the average Sunday congregation in the morning was 550, with 650 in the evening, by 1935 the popularity of the services was reversed, with 450 in the mornings and 350 in the evenings. In 1965, the average numbers were 400 in the mornings and 110 in the afternoons, and in 1990, 440 in the mornings and perhaps 80 in the afternoons. Among the three morning services, the two early congregations grew. In the late 1930s, perhaps ten to twelve people on average attended the eight o'clock, and twenty the nine-fifteen. In 1965, the average was perhaps twenty at the eight o'clock and fifty at nine, and in 1990, fifty at eight and sixty at nine. The eleven-o'clock Sunday morning service, by contrast, experienced overall decline, from an average of about 400 in 1935 to 350 in 1965 and 300 in 1990. The regular weekday services remained small throughout the whole period, with perhaps five to eight people for Mattins, four to eight for Evensong, and eight to ten for the Eucharist.[159]

In spite of the relative numerical decline of its congregation, the eleven-o'clock Sunday-morning service received markedly greater liturgical attention than any other service. A change in the liturgical behaviour of the people accompanied enhancement of the liturgy and alterations in the social composition of the congregation. From 1935 through the 1950s, St James' continued within the tradition enjoined by the Prayer Book of 1918, which remained in use. Printed there for all to read was a clear warning: Holy Communion was only for those who were 'religiously and devoutly disposed' and who examined their own lives, learned to 'bewail' their sinfulness, and were purified before God. Holy communion was 'dangerous to them that will presume to receive it unworthily.' In practice, the warning induced hesitation and still worked to discourage people from taking communion frequently or as a matter of course. The result was that most people who attended at eleven on the Sundays when Communion was appended to Mattins did not receive the sacrament. The worship leaflet printed the following advice for the congregation: 'An opportunity will be afforded after the Prayer for the Church Militant, for those who desire to leave. It is earnestly requested that all who communicate will remain until the whole service is concluded.' At the appointed moment there was a hymn and fully 50 to 60 per cent of the congregation departed in a vast exodus. Contrary to the request in the leaflet, some of those who did communicate left as soon as they had received. A similar request to stay to the end appeared in the leaflet for the nine-fifteen service. Ordinations to the diaconate and the priesthood, which were major diocesan occasions, were set within the regular eleven-o'clock service on Sundays, which included Holy Communion. At these times, the people who were not relatives or friends of the ordinands were urged not to communicate because of the length of the service, which added to the proportion of those not receiving communion. This practice at ordinations continued into the 1960s.[160]

The liturgical structure of the services combining Mattins and Holy Communion may have contributed to the high numbers of people not receiving the sacrament, but it also permitted a new emphasis on communion without making the congregation feel pressure to conform. The 'earnest request' to remain to the end suggested that many among the congregation treated communion as merely an individual, even a private experience. This practice did not meet the expectations of the clergy, who desired greater emphasis on its corporate character and on the integrity of the service.

4.13 Worshippers going up for communion and back on Easter Sunday, 1997.

By the 1960s the emphasis was shifting towards greater participation in the Eucharist as well as more frequent communion. In the 1950s people were being urged to communicate. The Lenten Services leaflet for 1950, for instance, published 'the Church's Rule,' found in the Book of Common Prayer: 'Every parishioner shall communicate at the least three times in the year, of which Easter to be one.' The advice about when to leave the service disappeared, replaced by the acknowledgement that some will have received communion at an earlier celebration and that they might leave after the prayer for the church or when the choir communicated. During the 1950s the proportion of actual communicants was higher but still amounted to only half or fewer of those attending at eleven o'clock on Easter Day. By the end of the 1960s nearly everyone stayed and received. Consequently the number of Easter communicants rose significantly over the years, from around 550 in the late 1930s to over 900 after 1975, in some years well over one thousand. In the course of the whole year 1983, for instance, the figures show that of all those attending a Eucharist at St James' nearly 90 per cent communicated. With the eventual displacement of Mattins by regular Sunday Eucharist, worshippers had to become accustomed to receiving communion virtually every time they went to church.[161]

This change in liturgical behaviour, coupled with the regular presence of so many visitors, required new measures both to keep order and to encourage people to come forward. Previously, following the great exodus after Mattins, the people who remained would leave their pews at the appointed moment and crowd towards the front during communion. In the late 1950s, with a higher percentage staying for communion, the sidesmen began the practice of moving row by row down the nave, unlatching each pew door, and signalling when people should step out. The practice continued through the 1990s (see Figure 4.13). The clergy felt that special instructions were necessary amid the changes. On Easter Day 1967, for instance, the worship leaflet invited communicants to fill up all vacant spaces at the communion rail, requested ladies to remove their gloves and their veils when receiving, asked people to guide the chalice to the mouth with one hand holding the base, and directed those on the Gospel side to leave by the door to the sacristy.[162]

Men's Activities and Women's Activities, 1935–1965

From 1935 to the early 1960s, worship on Sunday and in the special services may have been the only thing that the great majority of people did at St James', but many did more. Sunday worship was contained within a dense network of activities and organizations involving many people, both on Sunday and throughout the week. The names of the groups and of the principals involved in the parish network were displayed in the annual reports to vestry.[163] Except for ordinary participation in public worship, nearly all activities for people above age eight were organized by sex: men and boys did one thing, women and girls did another. There were, however, a few exceptions. One was the special fund-raising campaign of 1934, called 'The Way of Renewal,' which was directed by a central committee composed of ten men and nine women. Another, until the 1950s, was the Anglican Young People's Association, which included both men and women in their twenties.[164]

Into the 1960s the male network centred on the control and leadership of public worship, and on financial and political decision-making and administration. The principals at worship were all males – the clergy, the choir of gentlemen and boys, the choirmaster and assistant organists, the sidesmen, the verger, the Servers' Guild (from 1946), and the Sacristans' Guild (from 1978). Financial and political affairs were conducted by men – the rector, the churchwardens, the Finance and Consulting Committee (to 1952), the Advisory Committee (1953–63), the Advisory Board (from 1963), the Investment Committee, the lay delegates to synod, the vestry clerk, and the Cemetery Advisory Board (from 1940). The clergy controlled education in the parish, with an assistant cleric serving as the superintendent of the Sunday school. The afternoon Sunday school, which was the main one, held separate classes for boys above age eight, taught by male teachers. The parish sponsored Boy Scout Troop 78 and Cub Pack 78 until about 1950 and for a time thereafter the St James' Boys' Club for boys in the district.

Many men served with great devotion and for very long hours and many years. Among the churchwardens, Elliot Strathy (1935–40) and W.W. Denison (1935–9) oversaw the transition to cathedral status. Elliot Strathy, George Denison Kirkpatrick (1944–8), Alexander Ramsey (1956–62), Robin Merry (1963–7), William J. Anderson (1964–9, 1973–4), and James Harvie (1968–72) all served five or more years as churchwardens, and many others served four years. But these terms were reduced from the seven to nine years common during the previous generation, or the fourteen to twenty-three years known before that. Colonel H.D. Lockhart Gordon convened the investment committee for some thirty-five years until stepping down in 1962. Parallel to this, Jack Manley sang in the cathedral choir for thirty-eight years before retiring in 1965, making the claim that Manleys had served the choir in succession for 142 years. An invisible but very audible man associated with worship was the bellringer, the carilloneur. The parish honoured Walter Lye in 1959 for his seventy years of service. Beginning with his father and extending briefly to his son, the Lye family rang the bells of St James' for ninety-four years until the family tradition stopped in 1960.[165]

The most obvious duty of the sidesmen was to act as ushers. They dressed in black morning coats, or, after the Second World War, black jackets with pin-striped trousers or, later still, dark business suits. From 1957 onward the two churchwardens stood prominently at the head of the centre aisle and led the sidesmen in regulating the flow of people to the altar. At St James' the sidesmen were expected to retain the traditional role of overseeing the congregation, which included noting who was absent, looking for newcomers, and learning who was sick, although they were not consistent in this. They also organized the Every Member Canvass, or the Sidesmen's Visitation, when one was held. In the late 1930s there were about fifty sidesmen, led by conveners for each of the three aisles. In 1945 they created the Sidesmen's Association with extended activities and meetings during the week, designed to match some of the women's activities in the parish. Through the 1940s and 1950s there were about ninety members, with an executive committee and special committees for seating, envelopes, special fund appeals, and entertainment. They worked hard, but the group did not have the same drawing power for men as the women's groups did for women.[166]

In contrast, the female network operated outside the dominant power structures and largely out of public view. The main women's groups had their own budgets, with independent sources of funds, and provided their members with milieux for leadership and service that were unavailable to them in the general parish structures. For decades, many women participated in the various groups with loyalty and devotion. The Woman's Auxiliary (WA), the principal organization, celebrated its fiftieth anniversary in 1939 and its seventy-fifth in 1964 and sponsored two histories of its activities, one by J.S. Grasett in 1935 and another by Beatrice H. Kirkpatrick in 1964.[167] The WA was elaborately organized. In the late 1930s, the Afternoon Branch, which was the senior and larger group, and the Evening Branch, for women employed during the day, comprised together about 190 members, besides the Junior Branch for girls and the 'Little Helpers' for the smallest children. There was a Morning Branch, also called the St James' Study and Service Group, from 1956 to 1963, and for a time a Teen-Age Branch, with a reorganized Junior Branch to accommodate young girls. By the early 1960s, the combined adult women's membership stood at about 135. The president of the Afternoon Branch was treated as the chief woman leader in the parish, and the bishop's wife and the dean's wife were the honorary presidents of the two main branches.[168]

The WA functioned something like a church within a church. The women engaged in prayer, religious devotions, and corporate communion; they gave spiritual, financial, and material support for missions and social service for women and children; and they participated in education. They raised sizeable amounts of money for social-service institutions in Toronto, missions in the north of Canada and overseas, and the bishop's emergency fund. They supported some Toronto institutions for decades, including Strachan Houses for aged men and women; Humewood House, a teenage maternity home; and Georgina House, a boarding house for women. They financed missionaries – most notably Miss Adelaide Moss, who grew up in the parish and served in Japan until 1941; after she resettled in Toronto, the WA made her president (1947–57). Under the name of the Dorcas Department, they sought to follow the beloved woman in the Bible who was 'full of good works and almsdeeds' and made 'coats and garments' for people in need. WA women met every week for decades to sew clothes for children and women in downtown Toronto and the Canadian north. They maintained long-term support for 'Indian and Eskimo' pupils in Anglican residential schools in northern Canada and frequently sent whole bales of clothes to northern children. They made hundreds of visits annually to the sick and to young mothers in St Michael's Hospital, near the cathedral. They assisted the Downtown Church Workers' Association, and their representative participated in the Neighbourhood Workers' Association of Moss Park, a public housing project near the parish boundaries.[169]

There were other women's groups, some related to the WA, some not. The Chancel Guild, renamed the Altar Guild from 1947, had ten to twelve members who prepared and cleaned the altar linens and silver and polished the brass communion rail. A committee on Sunday flowers (Figure 4.14) purchased the flowers and decorated the church according to the season. Mabel Henderson was head of flowers for forty years, until she stepped down in 1965. The Guild of St James cared for the cassocks and surplices of the clergy, servers, and choir, collected clothing for people in the neighbourhood, and in 1939 founded a day nursery school in the Parish House for downtown children and women. From 1937 on, some version of a day nursery school operated almost continuously into the 1990s. The Mothers' Union, later the Mothers' Club, with about forty members, met weekly to make quilts and layettes and hear talks on family life, such as 'The kind of house we should make for our children.' The Service Club began in 1940 to prepare clothing, food, and seed parcels for poor mothers and children in Twickenham, England; many of its founders stayed together for over forty years, engaged in social service. The Business and Professional Women's Club, formed in 1947, gathered about fifteen 'unmarried and profession-ally engaged women' each week for purposes similar to those of the WA. Until about 1950 girls had the Girl Guide Company 23 and Brownie Pack 23. The afternoon Sunday school had a full set of classes for girls with women teachers, and women taught the smaller children, in both afternoon and morning.[170]

The two successive deaconesses during Riley's time served as paid staff members in a tertiary capacity to the dean, after the assistant clergy. Their duties followed a profile similar to those of the women's organizations. They dealt especially with social service to the poor and the old, the education of girls and small children, relations with women's groups, and parish visiting. In the 1930s and 1940s, the deaconess headed the morning Sunday school, the primary department of the afternoon Sunday school, and sometimes the Sunday school for St Andrew's on the Toronto Islands, while the assistant cleric was the superintendent of the main Sunday school in the after-noon. With the changing make-up of the parish and the decline in the number of children, the afternoon Sunday school disbanded in 1951, leaving a morning Sunday school for children whose parents attended the eleven-o'clock service, which was renamed the church school. The clergy put the deaconess in charge of the church school, with a staff of mostly women teachers. The deaconess also worked with the Junior WA, the Teen Age WA, the Mothers' Union, and the Business and Professional Women's Club. One deaconess, Florence Lea, was jointly appointed to the cathedral and the Downtown Church Workers' Association.[171]

There was one sense in which the deaconess blurred the gender division of parish life and labour: despite having a lower status, she was acknowledged as belonging within the ministe-rial group. For instance, the Sunday worship leaflet in the 1940s listed the deaconess in the section with the clergy. From at least 1943, Riley and the churchwardens referred to the

4.14 Flower Committee with Canon Hobson (l.) and Dean Stoute (r.), 1997.

deaconess in the same breath as the assistant clergy. The annual report to vestry sometimes contained such a sentence as this: 'The Dean and his assistants, the Rev. G.E. Moffatt and Miss Gulliver, are continuing to render a splendid service in the Cathedral and throughout the parish.' The deaconess – and later the parish worker – appeared with the clergy as signatory on the annual Christmas card. In the 1940s Elizabeth Gulliver took over the Parochial Relief Fund from the assistant cleric. Florence Lea was very visible: she stood at the entrance of the cathedral and greeted people every Sunday.[172]

Inclusive Parish Community, 1965–1990s

Between the mid-1960s and the late 1980s, the gender-defined network of parish activities and organizations broke down as clergy and parishioners deliberately worked to create and stabilize new forms of parish life. The most tangible and persistent signs of the change were the incorporation of women into activities and organizations previously assigned exclusively to men and the founding of groups comprising both women and men. These were matched by the adoption of an inclusive vision of Christian community, associated especially with the metaphor 'family.' A new parish network emerged that managed to retain some elements of the old, and it continued through the 1990s. The life of the parish and the list of parish organizations changed remarkably, but the transition was not straightforward and not made without conflict. The process was driven chiefly by the needs arising from the changing character of the parish but was made possible by parishioners' acceptance of new roles for women and by the persistent desire to nurture community.

The impediments to building a new kind of parish community in St James' were considerable and appeared at every turn. Most worshippers lived at a distance from the church. Most came to the church only for worship on Sunday, and not every Sunday, and only a minority participated in other activities. The number of new faces in the pews was always high. As the various services underwent change, it became clear that on the whole each kind of service attracted different people. With perhaps some overstatement, the report of the parish planning day for 1991 likened St James' to 'a multi-point parish with four regular and distinct congregations' and the parish profile in 1994 spoke of the need to build community 'within the four congregations of St James'.' Moreover, the very things that drew people to the cathedral could also work against community. Jane Watanabe observed that the majesty of the building could also be scary, and the beautiful activity and music occurring up front and carried out by others could seem distant. When people attended worship at eleven o'clock in the 1990s they were first met by a greeter, then ushered down a long aisle by a sidesman who guided them into a pew and shut the door behind them. In such an ambience, even with the most friendly intentions, people's behaviour tended to be reserved and proper.[173]

Early indications of the change in parish life came in administration and governance. In 1963 Marjorie Clough became vestry clerk, the chief administrative officer for the parish, following a long line of men. Her manner apparently gave the vestry office an atmosphere of friendliness, and Gilling began to talk about the feeling of the staff members that they 'belong to a very happy family.'[174] She served for twenty-seven years until her retirement in 1990, surpassing by a year the long service of C.F.W. Talbot (1918–44). Irene Thomson took over many of the duties and in 1993 received the title as well. When she retired in 1996, the corporation discontinued the use of the classic title 'vestry clerk' and appointed Elizabeth Boland as 'administrator and director of finance.'

Also in 1963, and following the lead of the new statutes of the diocese, Gilling strengthened the role of the Advisory Committee, changing its name to the Advisory Board. His stated aim was to extend lay participation in running the affairs of the cathedral and the board became a secondary decision-making body, advisory to the dean and churchwardens. Gilling appointed Beatrice Kirkpatrick to the Advisory Board in 1965. She was a past WA president, able and loyal, and much supported in her pioneer role by her connection with two old Toronto families, the Denisons and Kirkpatricks, and by her wealth. She had just funded a new colourful window for the mid-west porch as a memorial to her husband, George Denison Kirkpatrick, the last of the long line of windows memorializing members of the élite. She represented the transition: she belonged to the old St James' but she was an initiator of the new. She immediately pressed the dean and churchwardens to include more women as members of the board, with the result that Mrs Ian Cameron, the immediate past WA president, and Mrs J.A. Rhind, wife of a member of the Investment Committee, were added in 1966.[175]

More changes rapidly followed. The churchwardens acknowledged in 1968 that the cathedral lagged behind other parishes in sharing power with the Advisory Board and parish groups, and accordingly a new board structure, implemented in 1969, incorporated representatives of parish organizations, two of them women's groups, bringing the number of women on the board in that year to four. In 1975, each recognized parish group received a seat, in addition to the members elected by the vestry and appointed by the rector. The 1994 board counted eleven women and fifteen men. Stiff cited this broadening of membership as evidence that 'lay involvement in the Cathedral is growing.' More particularly it showed how the character of parish community was changing.[176]

From 1975 into the 1990s, parish conferences were a regular feature of life at St James', acting like an extension of the Advisory Board. Twenty or thirty women and men of the parish would go away for a weekend to discuss significant issues and suggest new ideas. House groups also met in various forms off and on from 1975, drawing women and men together in small groups for prayer and reflection on parish needs.[177]

An early expression of the new inclusive form of parish community was the inauguration of the coffee hour after the eleven-o'clock Sunday service. It began in 1966, sponsored initially by a new group of women and men called the Tour Guides' Association and prompted by a desire for members of the parish to meet visitors. Until then new people had been greeted by the sidesmen, the clergy, or, at one time, by the deaconess and, if female, perhaps invited to the meeting of a parish woman's group, while visitors had been offered cathedral tours under various sponsorships since the clergy had introduced the practice in 1952. The coffee hour was held in the basement dining room of the Parish House; it attracted few parishioners at first, but slowly more came. From 1967 onward an invitation appeared regularly in the Sunday leaflet.

The coffee hour created unexpected results as both the theology and the social mores of parish life changed. It brought together men and women as well as children to socialize with each other every Sunday. It drew in newcomers and made them feel welcomed. The featuring of coffee served from an urn, together with tea from a tea pot, in an open and informal setting became a fitting way to embody a more inclusive ideal of parish community. It marked the decline of the formal upper-middle-class culture centred on tea served in fine china from silver tea servers within enclosed groups. A Coffee Hour Committee of both sexes soon took over, and during the 1970s the coffee hour became a parish event, disconnected from the tours and tour guides and promoted by the clergy, with hospitality given by a Women's Coffee-Hour Group. The clergy called it 'the family setting' of the parish. The churchwardens noted with pleasure in 1978 that the event was 'now so big and active' and it has continued through the 1990s as a very popular occasion, with a second now added after the nine-o'clock service in the southwest narthex of the church.

The Sunday leaflets regularly invited everyone to participate in other social occasions that became common over the years. These included lunch before the annual vestry, coffee after special occasions, and a Eucharist and dinner before most evening mid-week events. These functions were intended for the whole 'parish family' and were put under the care of a hospitality convener, an office held from 1980 into the 1990s by Iris Lowe. Looking back years later, some parishioners felt that it was Stiff more than Gilling who 'got the people moving as a parish.'[178]

Another early sign of the emergence of inclusive parish community was the parish newsletter. From 1965 to 1970 the cathedral published one issue per year before Advent, and thereafter two or more issues in most years through the 1990s. The newsletter began at Gilling's suggestion in connection with the parish financial canvas[179] but was eventually transformed into a means of building parish community. It aimed to reach everyone connected with St James' with information about parish life and to raise important subjects for reflection. It started under clerical control but then passed to lay editors, most of whom were women: Anne Wills (appointed 1976), Joan Young (1980), and Pamela Stasiuk/Guy (1987).[180]

The newsletter tended to take over the informational function of the annual reports to the vestry meeting. Since the nineteenth century, the annual reports had been very thorough, published as a finely printed booklet whose formal appearance matched the upper-middle-class social style of the churchwardens, the sidesmen, and the annual meetings of the WA. The last of these printings was the report for 1968. Its demise was explained as an economy measure, but it was also a sign of the social change in parish life.[181] The annual reports thereafter were incomplete and unevenly done by typewriter and mimeograph, and later by word-processor and photocopier, without concern for social style, and only the auditors' reports and financial statements continued until the 1990s to appear on fine paper. The newsletter was relatively thorough in its coverage of parish activities, and while the look varied, it was usually neat and approachable, befitting a more open style of parish community.

Beginning in 1968, the clergy and concerned laity deliberately broadened the educational efforts of the parish to involve people of all ages with both sexes working together. The 'Church School Report' became the 'Christian Education Report.' Michael Bedford-Jones articulated the new approach as assistant cleric (1968–75); in the newsletter he explained that there was 'an educational dimension in all aspects of Cathedral life' and that education needed to be appropriate to each stage of a person's life, from childhood through the adult years. 'Christian education' he continued, 'is designed to help a person to learn and live the meaning of his baptism. The educational process is one in which a person matures as a member of the Body of Christ.'[182]

The Church School remained the central vehicle for the education of children, but its instruction was revitalized, in keeping with new theological thinking about the Church as the people of God, and the teachers employed a more participatory pedagogy. The work was led for a while by the Church School Working Group, composed of men and women of the parish. At the same time, new efforts to provide Christian education for the boys of the choir were undertaken. The Church School met during the eleven-o'clock service, and over the years various patterns were tried, including occasional separate Eucharists for children and having them rejoin their parents for the main Eucharist at the high altar. Boys and girls were educated together at all levels. Yet in spite of increased efforts, the number of children declined and attendance was irregular. The figures for 1994 reported forty-two children on the roll but an attendance of only twenty-five. The difficulties induced the parish weekend conference in 1976 to conclude, 'A Cathedral is not essentially a family church, nor should it be.' The clergy then resumed the leadership of the Church School until 1988, when Brother Michael Stonebraker of the Order of the Holy Cross became its coordinator, serving until 1997.[183]

As for adult education, the wider parish discovered how much of this was already occurring, above all in the women's groups. The newsletter frequently included articles on some aspect of Christian education for adults. The clergy strengthened the role of the Sunday service leaflet as a mediium of theological education. Both clergy and laity directed 'Christian education programmes at the adult level,' for both sexes together, which, according to a service leaflet in 1986, 'are offered from time to time depending on congregational interest and availability of leaders.'[184]

Educational themes changed over the years, reflecting the changing theology and ecclesial concerns in the wider church. In the 1970s, following the lead of the diocese, the parish studied the relation of confirmation and baptism, and later the admission of children to the Eucharist. During the 1980s, Bible study became more common, the baptismal ministry of the laity was a

4.15 York Group of St James' WA at a baby shower, April 1994.

frequent theme, and there was a series on world religions, including a lecture on Hinduism. In 1990 a special topic was women in the church, and in 1992 and 1993 it was homosexuality. A 1995 series examined the diversity of Christian spirituality, and several offerings in 1997 featured prayer and spiritual life.[185]

The corporation established the cathedral archives in 1975, supervised by a committee of women and men led by William Cooke, who became honorary archivist. Their work was based in the former Chapel of the Holy Spirit until 1985, when they set up the archives in space previously used as the balcony of the Parish House auditorium. There was hopeful talk in the 1970s about establishing a cathedral treasury either in the tower or in a new building to the east of the chancel, opposite the vestry, but these schemes were shelved because of concerns about both security and climate control as well as lack of funds.[186]

The two women's groups initially tied into the Advisory Board were the Anglican Church Women (ACW) and the York Group (Figure 4.15). The ACW began at St James' in 1968 as a branch of the new diocesan body established the previous year. The aim was to collect all women's organizations and activities within one structure. The creation of the ACW was, paradoxically, a symptom of the decline of gender-based groups in the church. The women of the WA in St James' agreed to join, but for reasons of sentiment as well as financial realpolitik, they retained their identity and separate financial endowment as the York Group. The composition of the ACW evidenced the fluidity of the new kind of parish life, including some groups that proved stable and ongoing and others that came and went with the times. In 1968 Betsey Merry, the branch president, reported that the ACW included the Altar Guild, the Service Group, the Flower Group, a group connected with the Church School, a group for prayer and intercession, and the Study and Action Group. The newsletter in 1973 listed the groups as the York Group, the Altar Guild, the Service Club, the Flower Committee, the Coffee-Hour Committee, the Choir Mothers' Group, the Knitting and Sewing Group, and the Group of Young Women. The ACW's report to vestry for 1981 listed the York Group, the Altar Guild, the Service Group, the Flower Committee, the Coffee-Hour Group, the Hospitality Committee, the 'Christmas at the Deanery' Group, and a replacement for the old Evening Branch of the WA, called the Lincoln Group. Initially the

York Group was much larger than all the others combined, but by 1975 the number of women in the other groups combined was about equal and eventually surpassed the York Group, in keeping with the shift to other activities in the parish.[187]

From 1969 onward, when the parish undertook special campaigns for funds or parochial revitalization, both men and women served on the steering committees. The lists of their names were a gauge of the changing cohort of parish notables. For instance, the committee for Renewal '69 included fourteen men and ten women, chaired by W.L. Gordon James, and both men and women led the workshops inaugurating the events. Margaret Scrivener chaired the sequel, Renewal '70, with eight women and eight men forming the committee. She continued to serve the parish in various ways, notably as treasurer in 1979 of the Restoration Appeal, the extraordinary drive for funds to repair and renew the building. The committee for that effort included eight women and twenty men.[188]

Women entered other realms of erstwhile male power. The corporation, the stronghold of financial and political power, had already moved to include others in the ruling group, as well as to lighten the workload, by adding an assistant to the churchwardens for 1961 and 1962. From 1967 on there was at least one deputy warden per year. These secondary officials met with the corporation and, while non-voting, shared many of the duties of churchwardens. From the mid-1970s on the usual terms of office of churchwardens were shortened to two or three years, and the position was treated as something to be shared around. Dean Stiff appointed Kathleen R. Lewis as deputy warden for 1975 and 1976, and then Jill Smith for 1977. Jill Smith became a lay delegate to synod from St James' in 1977, and women served virtually continuously in this capacity thereafter. Mary Nesbitt and Sybil Symons sat on the investment committee in 1982, while other women became members of the Cemetery Committee and the Public Relations Committee.

When Dean Abraham (Figure 4.16) appointed Barbara Hawkins (Figure 4.11) as deputy warden for 1987 and again for 1988, it had been ten years since a woman had held that position. Meanwhile it had become usual for a male deputy warden to succeed as a churchwarden after two years, but parish resistance to having a woman in that position was still great, even though women had been churchwardens in the Canadian church since before St James' resumed cathedral status and in England for centuries before that. With characteristic shrewdness, Abraham kept Mrs Hawkins on as deputy warden for a third year, 1989, so that he could appoint her as rector's warden for 1990 and 1991, thereby avoiding the risk that the vestry might defeat her if she stood for election as people's warden. She was a new kind of leader at St James' – not a corporate or financial figure or a lawyer, but someone who had come up through the women's network in the parish and contributed to the formation of the new type of parish community. Since joining the parish in 1962 she had served as a leader in the Church School, the Altar Guild, and the Flower Committee, as well as head of the York Group and president of the ACW, and had also helped found and lead a new-style committee for local outreach. She experienced difficulties as a woman churchwarden yet testified that most parishioners accepted her. She noted afterwards how she felt it necessary to dress in a dark jacket, white blouse, and grey striped skirt, to match what was expected of male churchwardens in the centre aisle.[189]

In his final year as dean, 1994, Abraham appointed another woman deputy warden, Pamela Stasiuk (later Pamela Guy). She too had risen through parish organizations. Under Stoute, she continued as deputy warden for 1995 and then, by election at vestry, became people's warden for 1996 and 1997 in what amounted to a clear affirmation by the parish of women's leadership. At

4.16 Cathedral staff, 1987. In front (l. to r.) are Revd John Wilton, assistant; Very Revd S. Duncan
Abraham, dean; Revd David Bousfield, vicar; behind are (l. to r.) Norman McBeth, suborganist;
Giles Bryant, organist and choirmaster; and George Nightingale, verger.

the 1996 vestry meeting, two men were nominated for the Parochial Tribunal, but, as the minutes
record, 'After some discussion about female representation, it was decided that Mr. (Edwin F.)
Hawken would step down to allow Ms. Pamela Guy to be nominated for the Tribunal.' She and
William J. Anderson were duly elected.[190]

Women's groups continued to provide a substantial share of the work and funding coming
directly from St James' for missions and social service to the poorest and most vulnerable people
in society. By about 1967, under the impulse of the diocese, these activities began to be called 'outreach.' From the 1970s through the 1990s, the York Group and the ACW used the income of
bequests from former members for outreach projects, at least $20,000 annually. The York Group

4.17 Revd W.N. McKeachie with clowns at a children's festival in the cathedral grounds, c. 1973.

continued to meet weekly to sew clothes, make diapers, and knit warm items of clothing for children and mothers in Toronto. In 1995, Margaret Peel, who had worked on these projects for forty years, explained the motivation: 'These things are much needed. It's missionary work. It is our way to help people who need them.'[191] There were other long-standing sources of outreach that continued. The corporation made outreach grants from the income of bequests designated for the purpose, notably from two large funds established by women of the parish, Nora Drayton and Anna Maude Brock. In 1980 the grants totalled $7,000. St James' mandatory payment, via the diocesan assessment, for the outreach projects of the diocese and the national church increased from about $14,000 in 1967 to $66,000 in 1989.[192]

Next to these, new avenues opened up as parishioners and clergy sought ways to make outreach a direct and conscious concern of the parish as a whole (see Figure 4.17). For a while in the mid-1970s an Urban Ministry Committee, chaired by Fred Rainsberry, brought women and men of the parish together on projects that helped the surrounding neighbourhoods. Seeking a more structural approach to dealing with poverty, Rainsberry drafted a letter to the provincial government, then in Conservative hands, requesting 'better financial assistance for work in depressed areas of the city,' but the corporation blocked it.[193] At the same time, some outreach projects financed by the diocese devolved to the revitalized local council of St James' Deanery, composed of the Anglican parishes in the downtown core. This link gave St James' a direct attachment to the social ministries of All Saints' Church at Dundas and Sherbourne streets and a food bank at St Peter's Church on Carlton Street, as well as to chaplaincies at downtown hospitals. Men and women from St James' became very active in deanery projects over the years, with special emphasis on food and shelter for homeless people in the area, and in 1992 the vicar, Philip Hobson, became the regional dean for downtown Toronto.[194]

4.18 Outreach Committee at a tree-planting in the cathedral grounds
on Earth Day (21 April) 1991.

The most visible and active new group was the Local Outreach Committee, a parish-wide group founded in 1983 with Rainsberry as chairman. Funding appeared from a surprise source in 1984 and 1985 when the cathedral and the diocese disagreed over the maintenance of the Parish House auditorium, which the synod had been using for its annual meeting. The corporation leased the space to the C.D. Howe Institute without diocesan agreement, in a deal that left relations between Dean Stiff and Archbishop Garnsworthy rather strained. The main floor of the auditorium became the Howe Institute's offices, and the balcony the cathedral archives. Simultaneously, the dining room below the auditorium was renovated for enhanced parish use and for the St James' day nursery school. After a strenuous debate in the parish, the corporation, with vestry approval, assigned the annual rent of about $30,000 to the Local Outreach Committee, who had lobbied vigorously for the money.[195]

The committee members deliberately sought to base their activities on a commitment to social justice, rather than a sense of noblesse oblige, as it might have been under the former parish style. They focused on individual social projects for marginalized people in the neighbourhood of the cathedral. They tended not to ask structural social questions, such as whether the production of poverty in the downtown had a connection with the production of wealth in the capitalist economy, as represented, for example, by the investment portfolio of the cathedral. By 1989, the committee had a membership of eight women and four men, with sub-committees on affordable housing, food, education and social development, and recruitment of volunteers. The Committee made grants to area groups, including All Saints' Church Cornerstone Residence for Women and Street Outreach Services (SOS) for street youth. But at various times the members also engaged in direct action for local people: they sent volunteers to assist teachers in Market Lane Public School, employed a summer worker to help street people in St James' Park, opened a drop-in centre on Tuesdays where homeless people could find food and someone to talk to, conducted a literacy program in the Crombie Park neighbourhood, and hired an addiction counsellor. They participated in the Victoria–Shuter Non-profit Housing Project and persuaded the churchwardens to make St James' one of the sponsors. This led to the opening of a large low-income housing complex at Dundas and Church streets in 1996. Through the newsletter and Sunday leaflets, at parish conferences, in conversations with parishioners, on occasions such as Earth Day (see Figure 4.18), and, from the time when Barbara Hawkins became churchwarden, in the corporation, the committee promoted outreach, and leadership in outreach, as primary functions of the cathedral.[196]

The effective role of the sidesmen was shrinking during the late 1960s, and recruitment became harder. In 1967 and 1968 they reported to vestry that they had nothing to report except their Sunday duties as ushers. The corporation tried to induce them at least to advise the clergy when regular parishioners were missing, especially the elderly, so that pastoral visits might be arranged, but these and other attempts to revive a broader role brought few results. A parish weekend conference in 1975 finally recommended opening the ranks to women, but fourteen years passed before the corporation responded. In their 1989 report to the vestry they acknowledged that it was becoming difficult to recruit enough men as sidesmen, and when the WA/ACW at St James' marked the centenary in May of that year, the corporation allowed women to be sidesmen for a special celebration at the eleven-o'clock Sunday service – but, after second thought, only in the side aisles. The following year, for want of men, women were finally permitted to join the Sidesmen's Association, and from then on they worked together with the men every Sunday. By 1992 they were referring to their members as 'sidesmen,' 'sides-women,' and 'sidespersons.'[197]

The Sunday greeters started in 1990 as a supplement to the sidesmen, a group of fifty men and women who took turns welcoming people as they entered and left the eleven-o'clock service and the four-thirty evensong. They actively recruited new members for the parish. A stewards' group for the nine-o'clock service was established in the mid-1980s, as a core of women and men to welcome people and give support for worship, a continuation of repeated efforts made since the mid-1970s to create a spirit of parish community within the nine-o'clock congregation. The congregational choir of women's and men's voices, which had been singing in that service since 1977, expressed the same spirit.[198]

As a good pastor, Stiff became concerned about the erosion of specifically male roles in the cathedral. He knew that the trend was towards creation of inclusive parish groups – what he called the 'new interest groups' — but at vestry in 1975 he announced that he was founding the Dean's Men, designed to mirror the ACW and its associated groups. 'Outside of the Sidesmen ... and membership on the Advisory Board,' he remarked, 'there is no organized way in which the talents and gifts of many men may be used to serve the cathedral' — this despite the fact that men — or at least certain men — still controlled the liturgical, musical, pastoral, political, and financial life of St James'. The new group took the name Men of St James'. It provided some of the opportunities for fellowship and wider service that had once been available in the sidesmen's association and served to recruit men for leadership in parish life from a wider circle than previously. The men usually held four meetings a year, with dinner and a speaker, and supported various projects, until the group's demise soon after the retirement of its patron in 1987. According to one member, 'The social side of its activity was especially welcomed by the growing number of unattached men in the congregation.'[199]

The role of women in ministerial leadership within the parish actually underwent a reversal before reappearing in a new and more comprehensive form. There had been a woman on the paid ministerial staff continuously from 1937 until 1958, when Riley replaced the deaconess with a volunteer parish worker. After Gilling permanently discontinued the deaconess position in 1961, his appointment of a volunteer parish visitor in 1964 still kept a woman prominent in the ministry of pastoral care of the sick and aged. When Stiff discontinued that position in 1975, however, only the male clergy remained as leaders of ministry, taking over most of the duties that women ministers had been fulfilling since the 1930s.

At the same time, however, both the diocese and several branches of the Anglican Communion were moving the other way. In 1969 a woman was ordained deacon in the diocese of Huron, with many more to follow throughout the Anglican Church of Canada, including Toronto diocese. Between November 1976 and November 1977 eighteen women became Anglican priests in Canada, including one in Toronto diocese. St James' became the normal setting for the annual ordinations of women and men to the diaconate.[200]

Gilling did not support this trend, even though he facilitated the movement of women into lay leadership positions. He liked to cite maxims in his reports, and some of these betrayed his ambiva-lence about women's roles. For instance, when he said: 'Never underestimate the power of women,' he acknowledged the success of the women who organized the cathedral flower festival in 1973 but implied that their accomplishment was something of a surprise. With 'Behind every successful man stands a woman' he praised the invisible work of Marjorie Clough, the woman vestry clerk, while reinforcing the role of the male clergy and corporation, who held the power and received the credit; was it a mere coincidence that Marjorie later posted a sign beside her own desk reading 'Behind every successful man stands a woman – telling him he's wrong'? Gilling had a strong sense of the fraternity of the clergy and in 1973 told the vestry, 'We are, indeed, a happy band of brothers.' He could say this with particular fervour then because he no longer had to deal with what he called a 'feeling of revolt' from his vicar, John Barton (1968–71), whom he had asked to leave the staff.[201]

Stiff was pointedly resistant to women as deacons and priests. He praised the women 'who work week in and week out' in their traditional roles to dress the altar, arrange the flowers, and pour the countless cups of coffee, and he, too, facilitated the admission of women to new roles of lay leadership. He appointed lay women as well as men to be scripture readers and intercessors on Sunday at eleven o'clock when the time came for that in 1976. The parish readily welcomed the move. The list of trained readers in 1995 included thirteen women and thirteen men. The nine-o'clock Sunday service included both women and men in these roles as well.[202] But the inclusion of women in the leadership of worship was a different issue for him, and the attempts proceeded amid controversy and with mixed results. He made it known that women were not appropriate for the Servers' Guild, and while the pulpit was opened on occasion to women clergy, they were not welcomed either to assist or to celebrate the Eucharist in St James'. Stiff was widely quoted among parishioners and the clergy as saying, 'There'll be no women in the chancel.'[203]

Members of the Servers' Guild, joined by members of the new Sacristans' Guild in 1978, were well aware of Stiff's opinions about women. Under the leadership of Ian Storey as head server (1974–88), they felt particularly responsible to ensure 'that our corporate worship is carried out with great beauty, reverence and meaning.' Over the years a few became adamant about the male identity of the group and the necessity of male-only presence in the chancel. They were upset when Duncan Abraham authorized two women to act as servers at the nine-o'clock service in October 1987 (Figure 4.19) dressed in full cassock and surplice, and again shortly before Easter 1989, when he announced that women would be admitted to the guild. The new head server, William Sewers, resigned over the issue, and three younger members resigned out of loyalty to him. They and other members also voiced some dissatisfaction about the way in which the dean had announced and implemented the change. In October 1989 six women and some new men were formally admitted to the guild and thereafter acted as servers at the eleven o'clock and as sacristans after the two guilds merged. The newsletter observed that 'a new era began in the life of the Servers' Guild.' Mary Jane Tuthill recalled that some of the men labelled the women 'serviettes' and in this and other ways made them feel uncomfortable. But, she said, the women tended to work still harder to be sure that the high standards of the group were maintained. In 1993 the guild included eleven women and twelve men, led by head server Paul Seddon. They had to cover all the Sunday and special services, using thirteen servers for an extraordinary festal solemn high mass at eleven.[204]

The corporation later agreed to ask approval for parishioners to be licensed as lay chalice-bearers. Three men and one woman began their service at the eleven o'clock in September 1991, with another woman and man added the following year. This was new for St James', where there were usually several clergy on hand to help administer the sacrament at the main Sunday communion, but it had been a practice elsewhere in the diocese for about twenty-five years.[205]

4.19 Mary-Jane Tuthill (l.) and Melanie Egan-Lee, two of the first women servers at St James',
with Revd Douglas Graydon, associate priest, in October 1987.

The two choirs in the parish took different paths. The congregational choir at the nine-o'clock service, active since 1977, reflected the community gathered there and included both women's and men's voices. The main cathedral choir continued as an all-male institution, with twelve men and eighteen boys, plus probationers, and kept relatively distant from the congregation. The readmission of women to the main choir – of which they had been members until 1898 – had become an issue in 1967 and 1968. The recruitment of enough boys year by year seemed to be ever more difficult, and women's voices seemed to be an option. But the idea was rejected in favour of strengthening the choir of gentlemen and boys.[206] Supporters believed that a boy's voice possessed a special purity lacking in a woman's or a girl's voice and counted maleness as part of the English cathedral choir tradition. After 1969, the linkage with St George's College helped supply voices. Both Foy and Bryant, as successive choirmasters, used their connection with the music program there to channel boys into the cathedral choir. Some St George's boys were funded on choir scholarships, while all the men and the other boys were paid. Although some boys came from cathedral families and a few men were or became active parishioners, the majority of both boys and men were recruited from outside St James' and seldom made contact with parishioners; the post of a lay clerk at St James' Cathedral was one that gifted male singers found fulfilling whether they were devout Christians or not. In some parts of the Sunday morning services they provided musical leadership for the congregation, while in other parts they sang for appreciative hearers. Choral Evensong put the service mostly in the hands of the clregy and the choir and gave the congregation the role of listening, which was what the parish and the many visitors wanted. When the question of women in the choir came up again in 1989, exemption given the choir from the norm of the inclusion of women in all aspects of parish life permitted continuation of the traditional male choir into the 1990s. Over the years the newsletter acted as a primary medium by which the musical leaders, the churchwardens, and the clergy promoted the musical tradition.[207]

In the spirit of parish inclusivity, a way was nevertheless found to recognize the musical talents of women at the cathedral. The St James' Choral Society, a chorus of women and men formed for the two-hundredth anniversary year, while not singing in worship services, did join with the choir of men and boys for special performances during that year.[208]

Women deacons and priests were the crux of the matter of leadership in worship at the cathedral. Notwithstanding his opposition to their sacramental role, Stiff did invite women priests to preach at St James': for instance, Elizabeth Kilbourn preached in a mid-week service in March 1980, followed by a Eucharist with Stiff as celebrant, and Ansley Tucker preached at Sunday Evensong in April 1984. Kilbourn worked on the diocesan staff from 1980 to 1988 as coordinator of chaplaincies, and her office was next door in the diocesan centre. Once when Stiff was away in the summer of 1985, the celebrant scheduled for the midday Eucharist failed to arrive, and the verger, George Nightingale (1977–88), ran across to the diocesan offices, found Kilbourn, and insisted that she should take charge. She was thrilled. She hurried over and celebrated the Eucharist in St George's Chapel with Nightingale as server but did not sign the vestry book. Thereafter, when Stiff would go away, he would tell the vicar, David Bousfield, 'Don't let Betty Kilbourn near the place.' A few months later, in October 1985, Tucker celebrated the Eucharist at the high altar for the annual meeting of the diocesan chancel guilds; Stiff did not oppose this, because the invitation had come from a diocesan group, not from the cathedral. Bousfield remembers being struck by the sight of red lipstick at the high altar. Tucker did sign the vestry book. When Abraham became dean, he invited Kilbourn to celebrate at the high altar for the Ash Wednesday Eucharist in 1987. She admitted that she was nervous and awestruck as she stood before that huge altar over the tomb of Bishop Strachan. After that she became a regular celebrant at St James' and in 1989 an honorary assistant.[209]

By 1988 the question of the role of women permeated parish life and tensions over their inclusion ran high. The parish weekend conference that January recommended many things, including new emphasis on spirituality, clarifying the image of St James' to other parishes, attracting new parishioners from the downtown, and extending help to the surrounding poor. The report on the weekend mentioned these themes and then turned to the subject of women in St James': 'Much heat but little light was generated by this subject which popped up continually during the discussion of most of the other topics.' The report called for the parish to give special attention to the participation of women.[210]

In response to a request by the Advisory Board, initiated by Mary Jane Tuthill, the dean established a task force on the role of women in the cathedral. The resulting recommendations, issued in June 1989, outlined some theological principles and set the following goal for St James': 'the integration and mutuality of women and men in the work and worship of the Cathedral.' This would mean in practice a woman priest on staff, visible mutuality in all aspects of parish life, and equal opportunity in decision-making. The Advisory Board endorsed the principles, and the corporation accepted the recommendations. Abraham gave reassurances to parishioners: this change would not affect the BCP tradition in the cathedral, and the traditional male choir would be exempted from the goal. One prominent male parishioner suggested in a letter to the corporation that some of the findings of the task force implied heresy.[211] It was within a year of this that the six women joined the Servers' Guild, Kilbourn became honorary assistant, Barbara Hawkins became churchwarden, and several women became regular sidesmen.

During this time racial consciousness also became a minor issue within St James' when Donald Butler, a newly arrived priest from the Caribbean nation of Antigua, became the first black member of the clerical staff (1989–90). Bishop Arthur Brown facilitated his appointment to the cathedral, which came soon after the Lambeth Conference of 1988, when people suddenly noticed the huge number of black bishops in the Anglican communion. A few blacks then attended services at St James', but apparently most of them were not active in the parish. Butler felt that most people welcomed him and appreciated his ministry; but, as he said, 'It only dawned on me slowly that there was some racist feeling here.' He first grew aware of it when he noticed that one parishioner would always cross to the other side of the communion rail 'to avoid taking communion from me.' Some people seemed uncomfortable around him because of his colour, or at least with having to talk about it; instead of saying the word 'black' they would refer to 'people like you.' His year at St James' coincided with the sesquicentenary of the diocese in 1989, when the enormous crowd attending the anniversary Eucharist in the SkyDome witnessed to the presence of a vast number of blacks from Toronto parishes. Butler later felt that not only people at St James' but Toronto Anglicans generally were only then beginning to cope with the reality of racism in the church.[212]

Attention turned to the issue of adding a woman priest to the clerical staff. Anticipating this, William Somerville, a member of the investment committee and a former churchwarden, sought to rally the opposition. He moved at the meeting of the congregation in February 1990 that a secret ballot of all parishioners should be taken on the subject. The dean in the chair ruled the motion out of order, on the grounds that the Anglican Church of Canada, of which St James' was a part, had already decided the issue. William J. Anderson, also a former churchwarden and a retired Ontario Supreme Court judge, challenged the ruling. The meeting upheld the dean's ruling in a vote that amounted to a parish decision to accept a woman priest.[213]

Abraham acted quickly. At Archbishop Garnsworthy's suggestion, he interviewed Carol Langley. 'You will need the heart of a dove and the skin of a rhinoceros,' he told her. After her ordination as a deacon in May 1990, Langley joined the staff in June and stayed until 1992. The newsletter featured her picture when she was priested at St James' with three other women in 1991 (Figure 4.20). This was fifteen years after the priesting of women began in the Canadian Anglican Church. After thirty-two years of absence, a woman was back as a paid member of the ministerial group at St James'. She overlapped briefly with Donald Butler, and he later came to believe that his presence as a black priest at St James' had helped to prepare the way for a woman cleric. She felt that most parishioners accepted her readily, especially the members of the ACW, but there were those who did not. Three more members of the Servers' Guild resigned at that time because 'we felt we could not in good conscience serve for a woman celebrant and would be in an awkward position if we made that a condition for continuing to serve.' Carol Langley was very aware that a few parishioners would shift to the other side when approaching the high altar to avoid receiving from her during the Eucharist.

'Gender-inclusive' language also became an issue, as it had briefly in 1987. It sometimes fell to Langley to say the 'comfortable words' after the absolution during the service of communion, and in place of the verse from St John as given in the BCP, 'If any man sin, we have an Advocate ... ,' she would say, 'If anyone sin.... ' The male clergy had begun to make the same substitution, but people only noticed it when she did, and vigorous objection arose in the Advisory Board. She carried on, as did the other clergy, and judicious use of inclusive language soon became routine. People did not know what to call her, since the cathedral's tradition of addressing the assistant clergy as 'father' would not do. Some called her 'Carol,' most called her nothing, while most referred to her superior as 'the Dean' or 'Dean Abraham.' This contrasting usage made her lower status clear, but it also made her more approachable. She felt that pastoral care was a special feature of her ministry. She found that people would come to her for help who might otherwise hesitate to approach a male priest, especially people who had been abused as children or adults, and those dealing with their sexual orientation. Abraham observed that this experience convinced him all the more of the need for a woman priest on staff.[214]

Jane Watanabe, who became associate priest after Langley left, had experiences similar to Langley's. Most people accepted her readily, but she observed and was told that there were some who would stay away when she preached or celebrated the Eucharist, would cross over at the Eucharist to avoid receiving from her hands, or would not receive when she celebrated. Her work put her very close to the spiritual, pastoral, and social needs of parishioners. She won over some of those initially resistant who came to know her as 'a hardworking, capable, and valued member of the clerical staff.' The parish profile prepared in 1994 stated, 'Although a great deal of progress has been made with regard to the issues of inclusion there are still concerns, witness the absence of several members whenever a woman is either Celebrant or Preacher.'[215] Judy Rois continued the new tradition of a woman cleric on staff when she became vicar in 1997.

Meanwhile, the wider church moved to another level on women's issues and leadership in ministry with the election of Victoria Matthews and Michael Bedford-Jones as suffragan bishops at St James' in 1993. Matthews became the fifth woman bishop in the Anglican Communion, and in 1997 she was chosen bishop of Edmonton. To replace her in Toronto, an electoral synod in June 1997 at St James' chose Anne Tottenham as suffragan – the second Anglican woman bishop in Canada and the tenth in the world. The ordinations to the diaconate at St James' in May 1997 foretold the future role of women priests in the diocese: the ordinands numbered two men and six women.[216]

The question of homosexuality erupted publicly at the cathedral during 1992, when a parish priest in the diocese who acknowledged having a partner of the same sex was tried before the Bishop's Court. The clergy at St James' treated the question as a matter of parish inclusiveness and community, much like the role of women and the question of race. The parish held workshops and educational events on the subject in 1992 and 1993, and discussions occurred in various settings. Parishioners scarcely doubted that the issue related to them. Some people active in St James', whether in the Servers' Guild, the choir, or other groups, or in one of the various congregations, already were or now became open about their gay or lesbian identity. Many recalled Stiff's apparent preference for men. The deaths of three people important to the cathedral brought the question unmistakably home. First in 1992 Norman McBeth, recently assistant organist (1979–90), died of AIDS, then James McCue, a former assistant curate (1979–83), followed in 1993. That same year Warren Eling, who had been an influential assistant

I.1 Exterior view from northwest.

I.2 Exterior view from northeast.

I.3 Memorial cross and west wall.

I.4 View from rear gallery showing nave and chancel.

II.1 View of nave looking south.

II.2 The baptistery, as fitted up by Samuel and
Edith Nordheimer in memory of their two sons.

II.3 Detail of rear organ case, with the royal
arms of Queen Victoria.

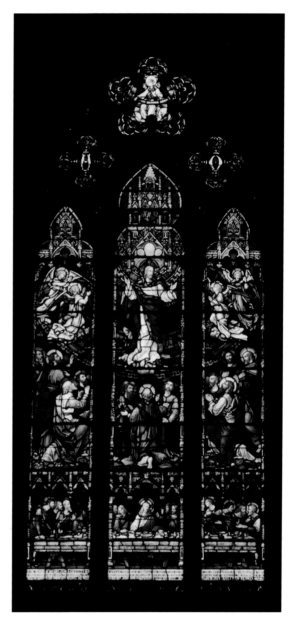

III.1 Window by Lady Altar showing the descent of the Holy Spirit on the apostles.

III.2 High altar window (c. 1890), showing the Ascension and the Last Supper.

IV.1 Window in St George's Chapel, commemorating the silver jubilee of King George V in 1935.

IV.2 View of midwest porch. The small marble font is the only surviving fixture from the 1839 cathedral.

V.1 The Chapel of St James the Less from southwest, as designed by Cumberland and Ridout; perspective drawing (c. 1858), attributed to William Storm.

V.2 Interior of chapel of St James the Less, as designed by Cumberland and Ridout; perspective drawing (c. 1858), attributed to William Storm.

VI.2 Laying up of regimental colours by the Royal Regiment of Canada at St James' Cathedral, in the presence of HRH Princess Mary, colonel in chief, 24 June 1962. The Royal Regiment and its predecessor, the Royal Grenadiers, have a long association with St James'.

VI.2 Liturgical procession on Easter Sunday, 30 March 1997.

VII The choir of St James' Cathedral with Giles Bryant, organist and choirmaster, and Christopher Dawes, suborganist, 1996.

VIII Cathedral staff, 1996. L. to r.: Revd Orville Endicott, honorary assistant; Brother Michael Stonebreaker, OHC, head of the Sunday school; Revd Jane Watanabe, associate priest; Revd Elizabeth Kilbourn, associate priest; and Revd Philip Hobson, vicar. Behind: Dean Douglas Stoute.

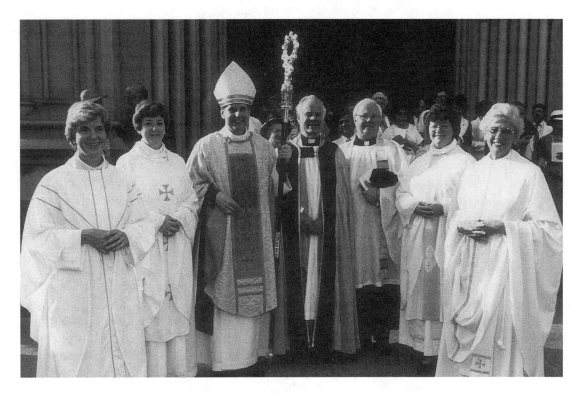

4.20 Newly ordained women priests with Bishop Finlay, Dean Abraham, and Peter Slater, dean of divinity of Trinity College, on the cathedral steps, 1991. The second from the left is the Revd Carol Langley, first woman cleric to serve at St James'.

cleric and later precentor (1964–73), died violently in Montreal, and St James' held a memorial service for him attended by a large number of the Toronto gay community.[217]

After these vivid and very human experiences with blacks, women, and gays and lesbians, parish life changed all the more. The self-assessment prepared by the parish workshop in May 1994 was hopeful: 'As a congregation, we have made significant strides in the area of women's roles in the Church, understanding homosexuality, accepting all people regardless of race, colour, gender, or class.'[218]

The way in which the church celebrated its two-hundredth anniversary in 1997 expressed the inclusiveness of Christian community that the parish had sought since the 1960s. Just about every group within the parish found a way to join the celebration, and the parish also reached out to the neighbourhood and the city. The membership of the Anniversary Committee itself reflected the inclusive image of the parish: an equal number of women and men, a cleric, the choirmaster, people from most of the parish organizations, and worshippers from the different congregations. The bells project drew in the city, the multimedia production of 'Pilgrim in Time' involved members of many other parishes in a historical drama about St James', a book produced by the York Group with two hundred special recipes sold well beyond the parish, a new gift shop in the west narthex catered to the hundreds of visitors, and many other special events included the parishioners, the diocese, and the city in the activities of St James'.

This book on the history of St James' from 1797 to 1997, written independently of cathedral control by historians from outside the parish and knowledgeable participants from within, marked the cathedral's willingness to look candidly at herself. This time the historical depiction included St Alban's.

THE EXPECTATION

In 1997 Toronto had an Anglican cathedral whose role in the diocese and the city was considerably more prominent than that of St Alban's had been before 1935. The people of St James' were carrying out a mission at least as effective as anything the congregation had seen throughout the previous two centuries. The continuities with all the preceding generations were irrepressible; yet the people who came to St James' were remarkably different from their predecessors, and what they did together was in many ways unlike, even contrary to, what had gone on before. Since 1935 St James' had known the joys, satisfactions, conflicts, and inconsistencies that befitted a human community engaged in service to God and neighbour.

Parishioners and clergy were well aware that people in other churches as well as the city at large had divergent images of St James', even as her own members engendered at least two visions of themselves. There were more voices than St James' cared to admit, even within the parish, who spoke of the cathedral as rigid, hopelessly traditional, perhaps even retrograde, incapable of leadership for a church entering the twenty-first century.[219] Yet there were also many voices, including even those of critics, who knew a growing fondness for their cathedral, or felt the thrill of an extraordinary service of ordination on a Sunday afternoon, or experienced the excitement of the pageantry at Easter, or testified of communion with God because of the ministry of St James'.

Since 1935 St James' had experienced unanticipated transformations, yet they were changes that the clergy and people had themselves helped to effect. They had modelled St James' on their image of the English cathedral, but what they had produced was their own creation and not a likeness of something elsewhere. In any case, cathedrals in England varied among themselves, and they too had altered along their own trajectories during the same period. By 1990, for instance, most used the contemporary eucharistic liturgy of the Alternative Service Book of the Church of England for their principal Sunday-morning service. Both St James' and other Anglican cathedrals throughout the world were affected by movements and trends that embraced yet transcended them all.[220]

Perhaps more changes had occurred in St James' since 1935 than during any other comparable period in its history. High among these was the emergence of the expectation, in theology and in action, that St James' would continue to transform both as parish and as cathedral.

5

Architecture

SHIRLEY MORRISS WITH CARL BENN[1]

THE FIRST CHURCH: ANNE POWELL'S 'GOOD BUILDING,' 1807–1833

EVEN THOUGH JOHN GRAVES SIMCOE founded York (Toronto) in 1793 and the government set aside land for a church four years later, Anglicans in the provincial capital had to wait until 1807 to worship in a proper church building. It took another three years before such essentials as a pulpit and a gallery were installed. Then, after only a short period, the congregation lost its house of worship entirely when the army converted it into a hospital during the dark days of the War of 1812. The building was damaged and vandalized in the war, and only in 1818 was it repaired and enlarged to meet the needs of the growing community. Some of the choices that the congregation made during those renovations proved to be unfortunate, and in 1820 and 1821 they altered and improved the structure once again. They continued to praise God in their little wooden church until 1833, when they moved into a much larger masonry building and sold the old one for its salvageable construction materials.[2]

In 1807, Anne Powell, wife of Judge William Dummer Powell, described York's new church as a 'good building.'[3] A good ecclesiastical building in the early nineteenth century was not a Gothic Revival structure, with its sense of the mystical and transcendent, such as came to dominate religious architecture later in the century. Rather, Anglican churches built in this period normally reflected the logic and light of Neoclassical architecture – a style inspired by Roman and Greek design as interpreted through Georgian eyes. However humble the construction materials and the size of the building, the finished edifice was supposed to communicate a sense of proportion and dignity. Presumably Anne Powell's 'good building' did a reasonable job of conveying these images in its own modest way.

With the installation of the gallery and the pulpit by 1810, the frame and clapboard structure was completed. It faced east (i.e., the altar was at the east end of the church). It was not large: sixty by forty-two feet, and twenty-two feet high, exclusive of the stone foundation, which probably added another two or three feet to the height above grade. It had eight rectangular windows along the sides in two rows of four, likely four or five panes wide and six high. Each pane of clear glass was eight by ten inches. The west end of the church probably had a single door at the entrance (possibly with a fanlight or single row of windows over it), no windows on the first level, but three on the second, plus a small fanlight at attic level (Figures 5.1 and 5.2). The east end of the church likely had a window over the sanctuary to balance the door at the west end and possibly had three windows at the upper level to balance those on the west wall.[4]

D. GRAYDON

5.1 Reconstructed front elevation of the first church at York, 1807; drawing by Douglas Graydon.

As there was no vestry and probably no separate narthex, the rectangular shape of the structure did not suffer any interior divisions. A tall, impressive pulpit dominated the worship space from its strategic location in the centre aisle, about three-quarters of the way from the door to the sanctuary. A sounding board hung from a pole in the ceiling above the pulpit. Reading and clerk's desks stood in front of the pulpit. All were painted white (Figure 5.3). At the east end, hidden behind these commanding features, was the sanctuary, enclosed on three sides by an altar rail. The sanctuary itself likely stood a step or two above the floor and housed a small, almost square 'altar-table,' which did not look much different from contemporary domestic tables (Figure 5.4). The earliest reference to altar and pulpit accoutrements at York dates from 1819. Although we cannot be certain what furnishings were provided in 1807, those known to have been in use somewhat later were typical of the period, consisting of a rich crimson cloth covering for the altar (which probably reached the floor) with matching damask cushions for the pulpit and reading desk.[5] (The colour sequence now generally observed for altar coverings in Anglican churches, imitated from continental European usage, had not yet obtained a foothold in the Anglican Communion.) On the comparatively few Sundays when the Eucharist was celebrated, a white linen cloth covered the altar. Although two candlesticks may have stood on the altar, that is unlikely, and there would certainly have been no cross.[6] Besides an altar,

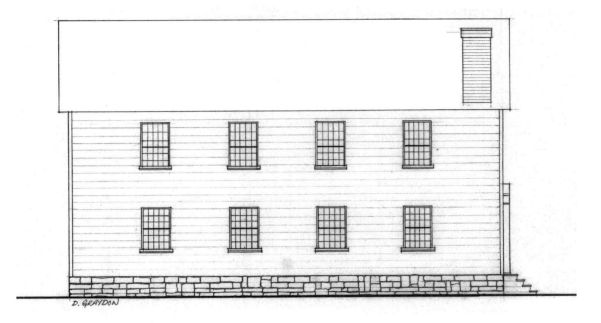

5.2 Reconstructed side elevation of the first church at York, 1807; drawing by Douglas Graydon.

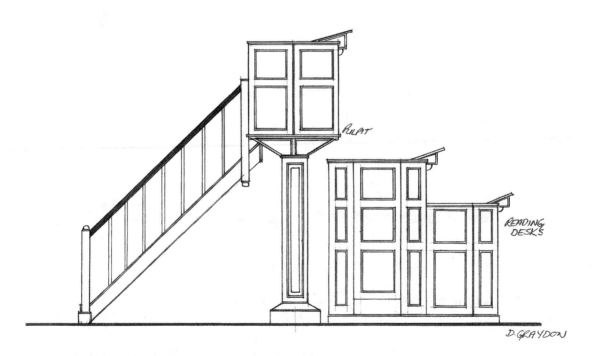

5.3 Elevation of pulpit and reading-desk as they might have appeared in the first church at York;
drawing by Douglas Graydon.

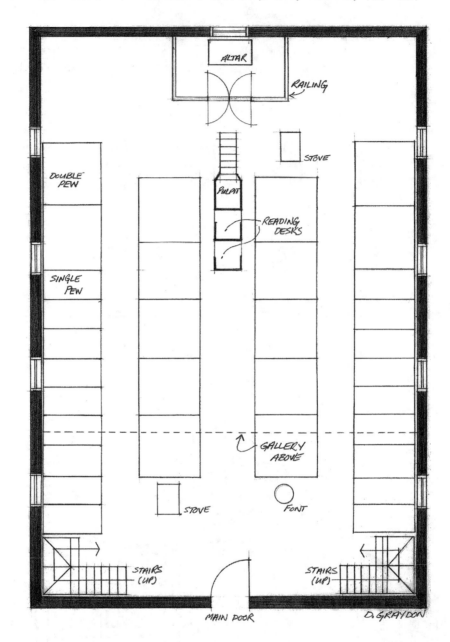

5.4 Reconstructed floor plan of the first church at York; drawing by Douglas Graydon.

an Anglican church would not have been complete without provision for baptisms. While the historical record is silent on a font at York, fonts usually stood near church entrances, as canon law required.[7]

Draft-excluding panelled box pews provided seating on the main level, while pews or benches served those who sat in the gallery at the west end of the church (Figure 5.5). The main-floor pews were laid out in four rows: two along the side walls, flanked by aisles four feet

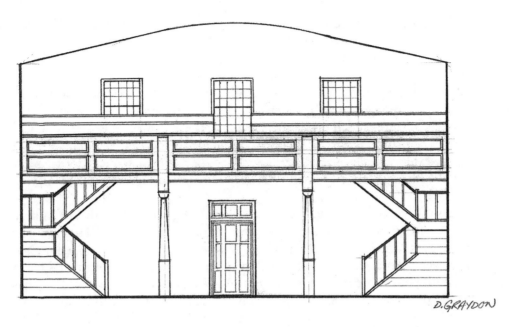

D.GRAYDON

5.5 Reconstructed interior elevation of the gallery in the first church at York, 1807; drawing by Douglas Graydon.

four inches wide, and two central rows, separated by a six-foot main aisle. There were thirty-two pews on this level: eighteen singles (3.5 x 6.5 feet each) and fourteen doubles (each 6.5 feet square). The exteriors of the pews probably were painted yellow or buff, with black trim along the top rails and black numbers painted on the sides. The interior colour seems to have been left to the discretion of each pewholder, who also may have added kneelers, footstools, cushions, foot-warmers, and possibly an extra chair or two. The tops of the pews, at least by the 1820s, had small gimlet holes for inserting evergreen branches at Christmas. One or two cast-iron box stoves, mounted on sheet-iron platforms, provided the building with heat.[8]

The interior walls and ceiling were lath and plaster; the colour they were painted is unknown for 1807, but in 1814 they were whitewashed. Normally Anglican churches at this time were outfitted with the royal coat of arms, along with the Ten Commandments, the Lord's Prayer, and the Apostles' Creed, painted either on the plasterwork or on wooden or canvas tablets. We have no mention of these features for the earliest days of the church, although it would have been odd for it not to have had them. It also is possible that there were tablets or other memorials mounted on the walls, as was done at the same time in Montreal and elsewhere.[9]

The War of 1812 brought on a period of abuse and destruction for the church fabric, beginning in 1813, when American troops looted the building during their brief occupation of York. When the British returned, the army used the church as a hospital in 1814 and 1815. By the end of hostilities, Anne Powell's 'good building' was in a very sad state: the pews had been dismantled, the walls were filthy, the windows were broken, and the fence around the cemetery had been torn down for firewood on two occasions.[10] Even if the building had escaped the war unscathed, it was too small to accommodate the growing community. Therefore John Strachan raised £1,700 to double the seating capacity and improve his little church.[11]

The building was expanded in 1818 to sixty by sixty-six feet by moving the north and south walls. The main door was now placed on the south side of the structure, which opened on to an impressive twenty-by-thirty-foot porch, which may or may not have been covered. The windows at gallery level were given rounded tops; and the window over the altar was raised, given a rounded head, and flanked with side lights in the Palladian style. The exterior also could boast a short, square tower on the south side, bearing a circular bell turret, surmounted by a small, tin-covered spire, added probably in 1821. The bell, however, was heavy enough to shake the building when rung. Blocks of wood to imitate stone decorative details were added to the corners of the exterior walls; and these, along with the window frames, doors, and trim details, were painted white to contrast with the light blue paint applied to the clapboards (see Figure 1.10, p. 28).[12]

To address the internal structural needs of the building, the old north and south framing was replaced with turned pillars to support new north and south galleries. These posts consisted of two sets of pillars, one from the floor to the gallery, the other from the gallery to the ceiling. The ceiling over the part exterior to the gallery was divided into four semicircular vaults, which met at a central point. The old east door remained in place for the use of the garrison soldiers who sat along the west wall.[13] Alexander Neil Bethune first saw the church in 1819 and described its interior: 'As you entered you found yourself in a building almost square. The aisle leading from the front door was bounded northwards by the Governor's large square pew: and midway it was intersected by ... [the original centre aisle] running east and west. Bounding this on the east was the chancel, in front of it was the pulpit, reading desk, and clerk's pew.'[14] The lieutenant-governor's pew on the main floor had a canopy over it, supported by four thin pillars, and was ornamented with the king's arms. Besides the addition of the galleries on the north and south sides, the old west gallery was enlarged. At least some of the galleries had pews: William Dummer Powell's gallery pew had a high back lined with dark green baize to keep out the draft.[15]

The new arrangements were not totally satisfactory, particularly because it was so difficult to heat the building, and in 1819 a committee proposed moving the altar and pulpit to address the problem. Probably the liturgical focus shifted to the north, and the north gallery moved to the east wall in 1820 or shortly thereafter.[16] The historical record is a bit unclear, but period documents suggest that the postwar renovations were not of the best quality because of problems with workmanship and materials. Furthermore, the renovated blue-and-white structure, with its tin spire, may have looked a little too gleeful and unsophisticated for many parishioners as architectural tastes changed and as York grew into a large and important provincial town. Presumably members of the congregation found relief in 1833 when they moved into their new and much more impressive masonry church.[17]

THE SECOND CHURCH, 1833–1839

In the spring of 1830 John Strachan and the parishioners of St James' Church petitioned the British government for financial assistance with the erection of a new church, arguing that the old one was dilapidated and too small. A much larger structure was needed to accommodate the growing congregation, the masters and students of 'the Public Seminaries as belong to the Established Church,' and the children of the thriving Sunday schools. As well,

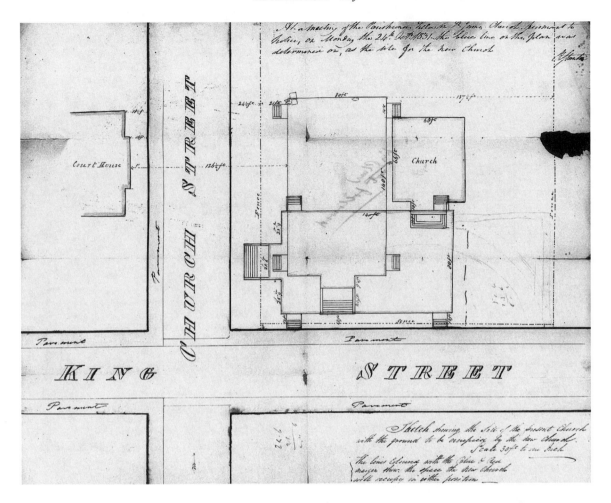

5.6 Site plan showing the old church (upper r.) and two positions for the proposed new church, 1831.

the lieutenant-governor and members of the legislature, judiciary, and military required suitable pews.[18]

The Colonial Office responded with a promise of £1,000.[19] Strachan and his vestry promptly set about raising the necessary additional funds through the sale and rental of pews.[20] The Building Committee commissioned plans from Thomas Rogers, an English-trained architect who had established himself in Kingston.[21] Strachan would have known him as the architect of St George's Church in Kingston and also of the parliament buildings then under construction on Front Street in York. Though the committee had contemplated a 'plain brick building,' the tender calls placed in newspapers in June 1831 were for a stone structure 140 feet in length (exclusive of its tower) and eighty feet in width.[22]

The new church was sited just a few yards west of the old one, with the main entrance still on the south fronting King Street, though a return to its original east–west orientation had been considered (Figure 5.6). John Ritchey was the builder, and James Chewett, a member of the Building Committee, superintended construction, acting in Rogers' absence as 'architect for

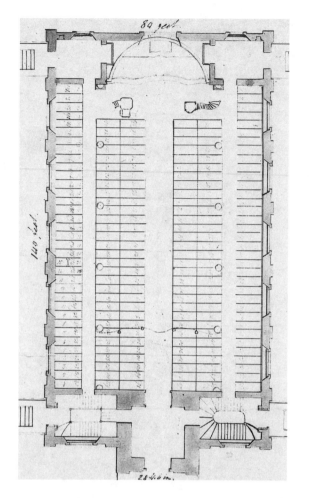

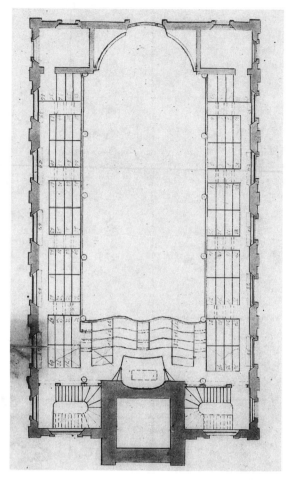

5.7 Ground-floor plan for second St James'
Church by Thomas Rogers, 1831.

5.8 Gallery plan for second St James' Church
by Thomas Rogers, 1831.

the time being appointed.'[23] Unhappily for Rogers and confusingly for many since, the form used for the laying of the foundation stone on 7 June 1832 misleadingly named Chewett as architect.[24]

Rogers bestowed on his compact design the same classical repose as characterized St George's, Kingston (Figures 5.9 and 5.11). St James' was also very similar in plan, if more modest in scale. Nevertheless it was more than twice the size of its dismantled predecessor and provided more than triple the seating (Figures 5.7 and 5.8). The walls were constructed of Kingston limestone, and the roof was shingled. There were tall round-headed windows to either side of the main entrance, a larger one in the sanctuary, and five similar ones along each flank separated by pilaster strips supporting an architrave (Figures 5.9 and 5.10). The principal entrance was through the tower, which projected about nine feet from the façade. It was graced with a pediment echoing the façade's broad gable. Side doors at the south end gave access to the stairs leading to the galleries and, from stair halls, to the side aisles. Another pair of doors at the north end opened into what must have been the vestry and sacristy.

5.9 Front elevation of second St James' Church by Thomas Rogers, 1831.

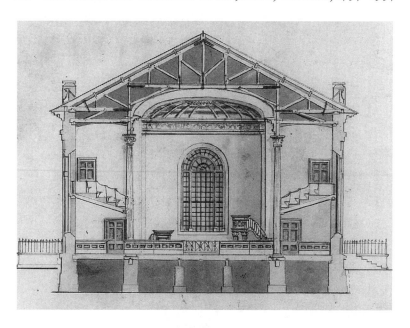

5.10 Transverse section of second St James' Church by Thomas Rogers, 1831.

5.11 View along King Street, Kingston, near St George's Church, from a watercolour by James Cockburn, 1829. The church, on the left, is shown without its intended portico.

5.12 All Souls' Church, Langham Place, London, England, designed by John Nash and built in 1822–4;
from an engraving after Thomas H. Shephard, 1827.

The interior was divided by a centre aisle; a U-shaped gallery supported on tall columns
extended over the side aisles and the rear of the nave. The shallow communion recess was
contained within the basic rectangle of the church. The service of the period required nothing
more elaborate; St James' was, after all, an 'auditory church,' where parishioners expected to be
able to observe the service and hear the spoken word with ease.[25] Although the Ionic order was
specified for the tall columns supporting the gallery as well as the diminutive four bearing the

pulpit, the contract with joiner John Lacey mentioned Corinthian capitals (as Rogers' sectional drawing seems to illustrate; Figure 5.10). These were to be carved from black walnut, also specified for the furnishings and much of the woodwork. A letter from John Strachan to Mrs James Brown, a friend, confirms that this material was at least used for the pews and gallery fronts.[26] A local artist, John Craig, designed the large painted window that dominated the communion recess. Mrs Anna Jameson, wife of the attorney-general and well-travelled author, thought it to be in a 'vile, tawdry taste,' although she found the interior of the church 'rather elegant.'[27]

Rogers intended the church to have a conical spire – a 'candle snuffer' rising from a Corinthian colonnade encircling the third stage of the tower (Figure 5.9). It would have made a striking landmark when viewed from King Street or from the lake, had financial constraints not prevented its construction. In designing it he had borrowed unashamedly from John Nash's Church of All Souls, built a decade earlier in Langham Place, London, England (Figure 5.12). In spite of the omission of the spire, Strachan rejoiced in his 'superb church' as it neared completion in the fall of 1833, having cost approximately £7,000 to erect.[28] About the same time the York *Courier* noted: 'The English Church ... which, although not remarkable for the taste and elegance of its architectural design, is fitted up within with great neatness, beauty and simplicity; and is altogether a noble building.'[29]

THE THIRD CHURCH AND FIRST CATHEDRAL, 1839–1849

Barely five years later, on 6 January 1839 – the Feast of the Epiphany – fire severely damaged the second church. An investigation into the cause proved inconclusive, but it was conjectured that the fire had spread rapidly because one of the columns, 'being in a great degree hollow, acted like a funnel and carried the flame instantly to the roof and in a few minutes set the whole ablaze.'[30]

The congregation, still struggling to rid itself of the debt incurred by the building's construction, consulted local architects Thomas Young and John Howard about restoring the church. Both concluded that it could be done economically. In response to the members' request to look into increasing the height of the walls and raising and dividing the windows into a double range, both suggested the solution adopted by the eminent English architect, Sir John Soane – division of the windows into upper and lower compartments by a solid transom. A device used in 'several of the Metropolitan churches of Great Britain,' this was really a way of dealing with the visual conflict between galleries and windows in the interior; it also facilitated the structural incorporation of the gallery into the wall at the level of the transom.[31]

Howard went on to propose a far more ambitious design for reconstruction – modification of the Georgian form by 'introducing the Gothic or English style of Architecture, and raising the nave ... to admit another range of windows above the roof of the Galleries.' In fact he was recommending an ambitious type of church with a clerestory – one in which the upper wall of the nave opens into windows and is supported on arches by piers that separate the nave from the aisles. Even if this clerestoried type had appealed to the congregation at this nascent stage of the Gothic Revival, it would have been deterred by Howard's estimated cost of £12,000. Still, the Gothic seed had been planted and would bear abundant fruit in less than a decade.

Perhaps alarmed by what they may have regarded as Howard's radicalism, the church's Building Committee had Thomas Young prepare plans; John Ritchey was hired to rebuild.[32] Having trained as an architect and engineer in England, Young had emigrated to Upper Canada

5.13 View of King Street, Toronto, by Thomas Young, 1835, showing the second St James' Church. The spire was never built, and the design shown here was Young's own addition to the picture.

in 1834 and soon obtained a position as 'ornamental drawing Master' at Upper Canada College. Today he is best known for his series of Four Views of the City of Toronto, painted in 1835 and lithographed by Nathaniel Currier. His view of King Street included the second St James', which he considerately provided with a spire, thus enhancing his composition (as artists of cityscapes frequently did), while advertising his architectural capability (Figure 5.13). Though Young is known to have designed only one other church before St James' – a frame structure for the Presbyterians of York Mills in 1836 – he was the architect of the celebrated Wellington Buildings, completed the same year at the northwest corner of King and Church streets, and was commissioned to prepare plans for King's College in 1837, though construction was delayed until 1842.[33]

Young's design for St James' was not much of a departure from its predecessor. (Compare Figures 5.14 and 5.15 with 5.7 and 5.9). It seems to have been a given that the church was to be reconstructed in stone above the sound portions of the walls. The grey stone that was used for rebuilding was painted to resemble freestone (an easily worked, fine-grained stone), probably to mask the fire's scars and the join of old masonry with new. The roof was tinned, no doubt as a precaution against fire.[34] The Building Committee rejected the more imposing of Young's alternatives for the façade, with its panelled parapets to either side of the tower (Figure 5.15),

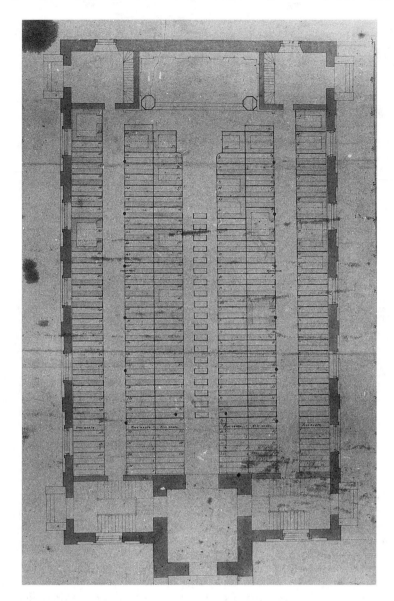

5.14 Ground-floor plan for first St James' Cathedral, 1839, by Thomas Young.

as well as the addition of a ground-floor room at the rear of the church, probably because of the additional expense (Figure 5.14). Young substituted a hipped roof for a pitched one in the rebuilding. By retaining only the frieze of Rogers' design, he obtained the height needed to raise the windows and divide them with panelled transoms without serious changes to the building's proportions. To maintain consistency in the flanks he added blind-arched recesses above the side doors.

The Building Committee disregarded Young's design for the steeple, adopting instead a sketch that had been submitted by John Spragge, one of its own members.[35] Neither of these

5.15 Young's proposals for façade and north end of first cathedral, 1839.

survive, but Young's lithograph of 1835 (Figure 5.13) gives some idea of what he might have proposed. Whether or not he modified Spragge's suggestion, the steeple that was raised late in 1839 (Figure 2.6, p. 51) resembled that of James Gibbs' influential St Martin in the Fields, built in 1722–6 in London, except that the former was made of wood. Had finances permitted, the congregation might well have added a reduced version of St Martin's stately portico. As it was, Young simply reproduced Rogers' classically detailed main entrance.

The Building Committee was adamant that the seating plan maintain 'the same situation and accommodation' for each pewholder as before and permitted few internal changes, for fear of inviting extreme discontent and risking the loss of much-needed revenue.[36] Young squared the curve of Rogers' communion recess and lit it with three windows. He used cast iron – a material less vulnerable to fire – instead of wood for the slender gallery supports.

Having to work within Rogers' plan and its structural remnant, while incorporating the design features imposed by the committee, considerably limited Young's contribution. The restored church represented a compromise in design, and in function too. Strachan's consecration as bishop of Toronto in August 1839 meant that the Church of St James had evolved into that colonial hybrid – a parish church and a cathedral.

On 22 December 1839, from the pulpit of the reopened church, the bishop commented on the 'wonderfully improved' interior: 'There is more light, and a better distribution of sound than in the old church: and the substitution of a gracile [slender] style of pillar has contributed to relieve the obscurity so much felt before.'[37] Early in 1842, the insertion of a 'mitre in stained glass ... in the middle window of the three over the altar' signified St James' cathedral status.[38] Unperturbed by Mrs Jameson's caustic criticism of his earlier work, John Craig replaced the mitre the following year with a painted window that incorporated the royal arms and depicted Christ healing the sick in the Temple, based on a work by Benjamin West, an American artist who rose to prominence in Britain.[39]

Though loyalty to the auditory type of church remained generally steadfast, taste at home and abroad was to change during the next ten years. A.W.H. Rose, an English visitor with a Gothic bias, conceded that St James' was 'comfortably, even handsomely fitted up inside.' He lamented, however, that 'instead of the decorative style which they of the dark ages knew so well how to employ for sacred purposes, and which has been of late years so happily copied in England in many of our new churches, the building as it stands is one with the commonest possible round-headed windows and but for the ill-proportioned stumpy attempt at a spire, might answer as well ... for a corn exchange.'[40]

FROM GEORGIAN TO GOTHIC REVIVAL

In the early morning of 7 April 1849 a calamitous fire destroyed a large area within the city's main commercial section. Shortly after the ringing of St James' bells warned of the danger, a flaming wind-borne shingle lodged in the louvers of the church's wooden belfry; within hours the third building was a smoking ruin.[41] Occurring on Holy Saturday, the day before Easter, the disaster was all the more devastating. The following morning the distraught congregation celebrated Easter at Holy Trinity Church, then rallied once again to the task of rebuilding. A committee appointed to decide on the best measures to be adopted recommended following the old plan and dimensions so as to seat two thousand; to build for a larger number would mean that 'all could not hear distinctly.'[42]

Bishop Strachan's main concern was that the church should have a 'Cathedral-character,'[43] and John Howard's proposal of 1839 had already nudged the congregation in the direction of Gothic. Thus when the committee proposed that the 'style of Architecture be Gothic' it evidenced a belated desire to follow developments at home and abroad.[44] By the early 1840s Toronto architects, including Howard, had already turned to Gothic for local churches.[45] All were representative of the early stage of the Gothic Revival but still Georgian 'preaching-boxes,' featuring openings with pointed arches. A pinnacle here and a buttress there produced a Gothic effect, even if any real understanding was wanting of the principles of the style and the structural precepts that governed them. Recognizing that these attempts were already outmoded, and lacking a local source of authoritative architectural advice, the committee considered sending to England for plans and elevations 'of two or three of the most admired and approved Churches among those recently erected.'[46]

Committee members probably thought to consult England's Ecclesiological Society, which had made the building of Anglican churches (both at home and abroad) one of its main concerns. Formed in 1839 and first known as the Cambridge Camden Society, it had emerged as an architectural parallel to the theology and liturgy of the high-church Oxford Movement. The society was motivated to seek reforms by what its leaders considered the decadence of congregations as manifested in the laxity of liturgical practice and the inappropriate design of new churches. Through its publications, especially the *Ecclesiologist*, it came to exercise a profound influence on church architecture wherever Anglicans worshipped.[47]

Following the lead of English architect and theoretician Augustus Welby Pugin, the society rejected all classical references in church architecture because of their association with the ancient pagan world. Instead, it called for a return to medieval ideals and the architectural settings associated with them in order to encourage a renewal of truly Christian values. Ecclesiologists dealt with all aspects of church design and took as their model the English parish church from the late thirteenth century to the middle of the fourteenth (known as 'Middle-Pointed' or Decorated Gothic). Each component of the building was expressed in the plan and in the outward form as a three-dimensional metaphor of the faith, with Christian symbolism invested in every detail. Within, a high-pitched roof of heavy timbers, exposed to view, sheltered a long nave and spacious chancel. The focus was emphatically directed towards the east end; the atmosphere inspired reverence and awe. This theme had been picked up by the *Church*, the local unofficial Anglican weekly, in which a contributor pleaded for 'the propriety of making our churches ... correspond in appearance with the solemn and sublime realities of our faith and worship.'[48]

The yearning towards the sublime and the transcendental experience, and the desire to return to the forms and ideals of an earlier age, were aspects of the romanticism that by now infused much of Western literary and artistic activity. And within the Anglican community at large it represented the church's search for a new role for itself in a changing social structure. In Toronto, the church's turning away from the classicism and rationalism of the built forms of recent years reflected the erosion of the 'alliance of church and state,' as exemplified in the move towards the secularization of the provincial university and the Anglicans' loss of more than half the clergy reserves.[49]

A Design for the 'Metropolitan Church' of Western Canada

In June 1849, the Building Committee at St James' decided on the risky device of competition as a means of acquiring plans. John Howard composed the notice that was placed in Toronto, Montreal, and New York newspapers requesting plans for a church 'in the Gothic style,' at least as large as the late church (149 feet long by eighty feet wide, and holding eighteen hundred persons). The materials were to be 'white brick, with cut stone dressings, cost not to exceed Ten Thousand Pounds. Exclusive of TOWER and SPIRE which should be of cut stone and sufficient to bear a full Peal of Bells.' The successful competitor would receive £75, if not employed afterward to superintend the building; second prize was £50, and third, £25.[50]

On 13 September 1849 the Church announced that F.W. Cumberland of Toronto had won the first premium (Figure 5.16). It later emerged that John Ostell of Montreal had come second, and Kivas Tully, also of Toronto, third.[51] Frederic William Cumberland was born in London, England, in 1820. A student at King's College School in London, he went on to a four-year apprenticeship with William Tress, a civil engineer and architect, and then to jobs with the railways and as an engineer with the Department of the Admiralty. A connection through marriage to Thomas Gibbs Ridout, cashier of the Bank of Upper Canada, and dissatisfaction with his Admiralty work prompted him to emigrate and resettle in Toronto in 1847.[52] His winning the premium for St James' was his first notable success in Canada. Unexpectedly, it embroiled him in a complex controversy that was to involve the larger community. Foremost among the issues that arose was whether the church was to function as a parish church, a cathedral, or both. The question had come up in the pages of the *Church* as early as 1842.[53] By 1844 some type of cathedral service had come into use at St James'.[54] The *Ecclesiologist* had already explained that a cathedral was cruciform in plan, with transepts suggesting the arms of the cross, and with the choir and nave equal in height.[55] It had tentatively examined the colonial solution to the problem – the union of the two forms – without much expectation of success.[56] In its review of the competition the *Church* had asked, ' ... are we to have a Parish Church or a Cathedral?' And it went on to complain that some of the designs were deficient 'in some of the leading qualifications that ought to attach to the latter.' It insisted that 'massive dignity' should be kept in view in the erection of an Anglican cathedral – even though a new country 'cannot duplicate the glories of ancient edifices ... much may be within the reach of a refined and elevated taste.'[57]

Members of the vestry held differing views on what was wanted. The conservatives, including rector Henry Grasett, preferred 'a large square parish church similar to the one destroyed.' They strongly opposed transepts. What might be regarded as the progressive and 'High Church' party, including the bishop, favoured a cathedral-like structure of more imposing design.

The progressives were greatly impressed with the submission of George Smith, who had described himself as professionally educated in England and the architect of St Andrew's Presbyterian Church under construction in Montreal.[58] Smith had sent in his design as a non-competitor, thus releasing himself from the restrictions imposed by the Building Committee. Both Smith's and Cumberland's proposals included transepts and a central tower at the (liturgical) west end; Cumberland also offered the option of a two-towered façade.[59] His plan, necessarily smaller in scale than Smith's, had a proportionately wider nave and shorter chancel.[60] It seems that the first premium had gone to Cumberland as a compromise between two opposing points of view.

Since Smith's entry had 'recommended itself more strongly ... than any of the others' to the committee, he was invited to prepare new drawings so as to enable a 'just comparison' between the two submissions.[61] As part of the process of comparison, the committee had block plans of the two designs drawn side by side on the same sheet of paper (Figure 5.17). While this may have been only one of several such comparisons, no others are known to survive. Allowing a tantalizing glimpse of the two projects, it illuminates the committee's quandary. Smith's scheme was clearly the more elaborate of the two. Greater in overall length by sixty feet, and with longer though narrower transepts, its sanctuary was externally expressed by an apse, a form generally regarded as continental rather than English and particularly associated with French Gothic.[62] But what a distinctive feature, what a pleasing alternative! The commission was now offered to Smith. A letter to the *Globe* claimed that this was done on the understanding that the transepts were to be divided from the body of the church by panelled screens. 'Thus the Vestry will be called upon to spend £5,000 more than they had originally contemplated in order to please the Bishop, by providing transepts which, to please the Rector they have afterwards to shut up!'[63]

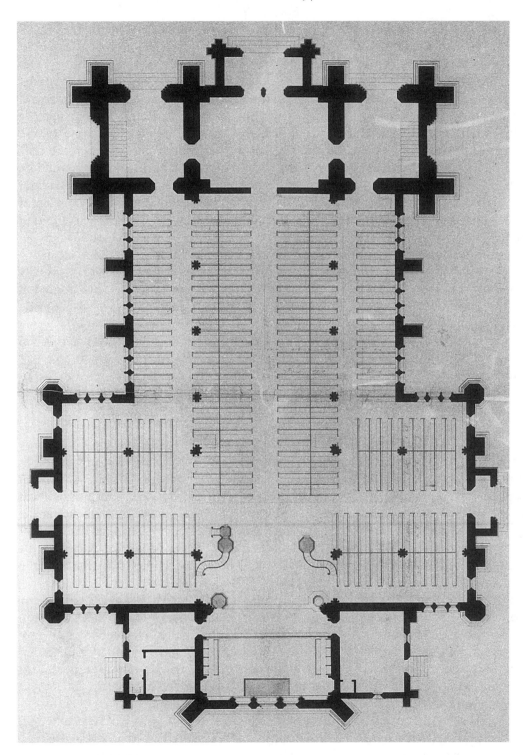

5.16 Frederic Cumberland's competition design for second St James' Cathedral, 1849.

This decision only added to the threatening storm of protest connected with the vestry's intention to augment the building fund by leasing its King Street frontage, a move that would have permitted commercial development there and necessitated reorientation of the church in an east–west direction.[64] In spite of this being the more traditional alignment, many in the congregation were offended by the proposed secularization of the church property and desecration of the burial ground adjacent to the church. Seeking to reduce costs and avoid such an expedient, this group asked William Thomas, a leading Toronto architect and one of the competitors, to investigate reusing the damaged walls of the old church. He had been the only competitor whose design had exploited this possibility, and he now confirmed that it could be done.[65] His report led Kivas Tully, winner of the third premium, to claim that his design could also be 'applied' to the old walls but that he regarded such a course as unsafe. Had he realized that he was allowed to depart from the competition requirements, he too could have submitted a more cathedral-like plan.[66]

Faced with Tully's complaint and the possibility of protests from other competitors, a compromise was reached at an acrimonious vestry meeting on 21 December 1849. With the expectation of income from insurance on the third church, pew rentals, and sales, and assured of £1,000 from the Society for Promoting Christian Knowledge, the vestry approved adoption of Cumberland's plan for a structure that would serve a dual function.[67] A public meeting organized to forestall desecration of the church's burial ground, and substantial donations to the building fund conditional on 'preserving the ground untouched,' forced the vestry to abandon its proposal to lease the King Street frontage.[68] Cumberland was then instructed in April 1850 to provide a new design in 'Early English' with a clerestory and side porches, to be erected on the old site, using the old foundations.[69]

In this architectural tussle Cumberland had finally come out on top. Employing a strategy increasingly resorted to by church architects, his new plan in June 1850 called for construction in stages, as funds became available. The first stage, which could be built for £11,463, would lack tower, spire, porches, and pinnacles but would be 'enclosed and fit for service.' This proposal was accepted, subject to the church's being centred on the King Street frontage (thus retaining the north–south orientation), thereby preventing any leasing of the frontage.[70] The final details were approved in November, and the prominent builders Metcalfe, Wilson & Forbes, who had just completed St Lawrence Hall to the east on King Street, received the contract to construct the church.[71]

The disparity in the types of plan submitted points up the confusion both within the Building Committee and among competing architects as to what the colonial situation demanded. The design submitted by Gervase Wheeler had a 'triple row of lights' that gave the building 'the air of a three-decker.'[72] The plans proposed by William Thomas and several others lacked clerestories. Thomas had obviously hoped to please those who wanted a parish church by planning 'an open church of one span' without entrance porches on the façade and without transepts – not so different in form from that destroyed in the fire.[73]

Frank Wills' entry – he had been the architect of the 1845 design for Christ Church Cathedral, Fredericton – disappointed the *Church*. His nave and chancel were described as 'coldly correct', and his spire as a mere copy of Fredericton's (which was itself copied from the fourteenth-century St Mary's Church at Snettisham in Norfolk).[74] While his proposal might be suitable

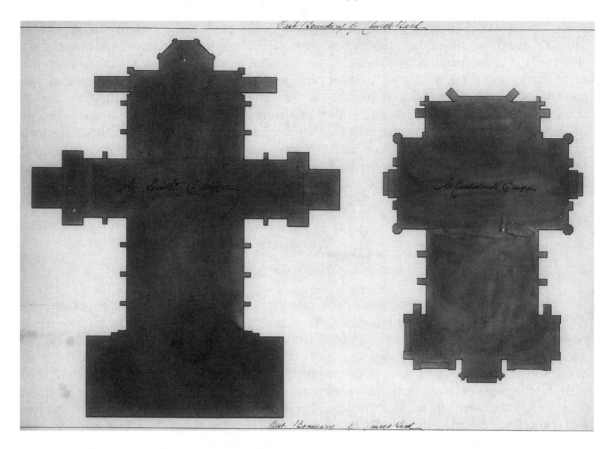

5.17 Comparison of block plans of Cumberland's competition design for second cathedral (l.)
and George Smith's (r.).

'for a country Parish Church situated close to some rugged shore of the mother country,' the *Church* thought it hardly a 'fit model for the metropolitan Church of Western Canada.'[75] Stung by criticism that he considered unjust, Wills took the same tack as Tully, pointing out that the Building Committee's detailed instructions had stated that a design for a parish church was wanted, yet incorporating a tower, transepts, and 'finely imagined turrets and finials' – an absurdity, he declared, in view of the imposed limit of £10,000 on the cost.[76]

William Hay's submission arrived too late for the competition; it was sent from St John's, Newfoundland, where he was superintending construction of the early stages of George Gilbert Scott's Cathedral of St John the Baptist. Although not questioning the choice of Cumberland as architect of the new St James', the *Church* reviewed Hay's design in January 1850 and explained that its form – a Latin cross with an apsidal chancel and a spire springing from the intersection of the arms of the cross – approached 'nearly to perfection' the ideal cathedral plan.[77]

The *Ecclesiologist* offered only a tardy comment on St James' in 1857 when giving a generally favourable review to Frank Wills' design for Christ Church Cathedral in Montreal.[78] Comparing the two structures, it noted merely that the new cathedral at Toronto 'is as yet unfinished, and on (we believe) a much inferior and less correct plan.'

Ecclesiologists' primary objection would have been to pews and the inclusion of galleries. They had fought an ardent campaign against pews, apparently failing to understand the colonial church's financial dependence on the pew system.[79] Pew rentals made up a significant portion of St James' building fund, and parishioners guarded their locations in the seating plan jealously. Galleries were required so that the new church might remain faithful to the old seating plan and provide the same number of sittings. In his address to the vestry in 1853, Bishop Strachan reported that the wish that 'all should be placed in the new church exactly as in the old' was 'gratified to the very letter.'[80] Cumberland had met the potential pitfalls with flexibility and sensitivity to local needs. The various factions within the congregation were led to an acceptance of the principle of parish church–cathedral duality and helped towards reconciliation through compromise and a pleasing and appropriate design for the 'metropolitan church of Western Canada.'

'Enclosed and Fit for Service': The Construction of the Cathedral Church of St James, Toronto

Constructed from the 'white brick' that came into general use in Toronto in the 1840s and with dressings of buff Ohio stone, St James' is still a conspicuous landmark in the immediate neighbourhood, though today both more and less than the church that opened in June 1853 (Figure 2.8, p. 60). The tower, porches, and spire were added in several stages through the 1860s and 1870s; the galleries, however, were removed just fifteen years after the cathedral was completed.

In his original proposal, made in the summer of 1849, Cumberland had provided a choice between a two-towered façade and a front with a single central tower. Subsequently he enlarged the chancel and adopted the apsidal termination that George Smith had first offered, while shrinking the transepts to shallow projections (compare Figures 5.16 and 5.17 with 5.19). With financial constraints in mind, the Building Committee opted for the less costly alternative of a façade with a central tower.

Following his success in the competition for St James', Cumberland saw a great expansion in his architectural activity. Besides other major commissions in Toronto and elsewhere, he designed St James' Parochial School, immediately north of the cathedral on Church Street, and the Church of the Ascension (also for the Church of England) in Hamilton. The increased workload prompted him to invite Thomas Ridout, a civil engineer and the son of Thomas Gibbs Ridout, into partnership in 1850. For this reason the cathedral is always credited to Cumberland & Ridout, though Ridout's contribution is open to speculation.[81] Two years later Ridout was succeeded by William Storm, who had joined the office in 1848 or 1849, following an apprenticeship with William Thomas. Storm prepared the working drawings for the cathedral and designed many of its details (Frontispiece). His exceptional talent as a delineator was a particular asset to the partnership of Cumberland & Storm, which was active until about 1863.[82]

The plans for the Hamilton church were adopted in January 1850, well before a final plan was approved for St James'. The Church of the Ascension was an asymmetrical and picturesque composition in rough limestone that took striking advantage of the church's corner site by juxtaposing its chancel with a corner entrance through its tower. With the 'mountain' as a backdrop, it was located where residential blocks gave way to semi-rural settlement.[83] Although St James' was also located on a corner, it was in the heart of the commercial area of Toronto

5.18 'An Ideal old English Parish Church,' by A.W. Pugin, 1841.

and was besides a cathedral foundation. Hence Cumberland adopted a different governing aesthetic – the principle of 'regularity' or symmetry, which he regarded as appropriate for a great city church.

Both John Howard and Thomas Young had previously shown an awareness that a church in an urban setting deserved a particular type of treatment. In this they had followed ideas put forward by Sir John Soane. The *Church* echoed their concerns in its discussion of the St James' competition.

Henry-Russell Hitchcock has pointed out that the English architect A.W. Pugin led the way in establishing a distinction between rural and urban churches.[84] He published an image of an 'ideal old English parish church' in *True Principles* (1841) that was basically symmetrical in disposition and boasted a clerestory and an ornate western tower (Figure 5.18). This offered a model for town structures well before ecclesiologists realized the incongruity of transplanting rustic and picturesque types into urban situations.

As the 1840s proceeded, ecclesiologists took note of the problem and attempted to address it. But not until after St James' was begun did a clearer concept emerge in an article, 'On the Proper Characteristics of a Town Church,' by George Edmund Street.[85] Soon to become a leading architect of the High Victorian Movement, Street condemned the rudeness of 'rough walling stones' and argued that 'the sentiment they convey is one different from that which the polished and smooth surfaces of the neighbouring buildings demand.' He also suggested that a clerestory should be a 'ruled feature' because the 'completeness of effect that it gives is wonderful' and because it 'is the right place for the admission of light; in most cases the light from the lower windows being either partially or altogether obscured by surrounding buildings.' The steeple ought to be centrally positioned either at the crossing or at the west end; a spire was perhaps not essential, but if an element of the design it should be 'ornate and grand in its proportions.' There should be a 'regularity of parts,' since regularity distinguishes the works of man while irregularity typifies nature. If today this might seem to have implied approval for the classicizing 'pagan' churches of former times, it seems not to have embarrassed English ecclesiologists. Certainly Cumberland was aware of the classical symmetry of earlier English and Canadian churches. That he chose to depart from this principle at the edge of Hamilton while adhering to it in Toronto's core shows that he anticipated Street's argument.

Cumberland also shared Street's appreciation for the associative power of materials and forms, which is evident from an account of his visit to the Grand Trunk Railway works in 1855. Comparing stone and brick, he stated that stone built in a 'bold style' gives 'such complete assurance to the mind of permanent stability, and such satisfaction to the eye by the play of colour on its face that it tends to dissatisfy one with a material [i.e., brick] in itself unimpeachable but relatively inferior.'[86] Although his remarks may signify only that he considered stone more suitable for a railway viaduct in a picturesque location, they may also suggest that he would have preferred that quality of 'permanent stability' for a cathedral church. Certainly others held this view. In assessing the competitors' designs, the *Church* had regarded Cumberland's as probably the most suitable, given the 'meagreness of the material proposed' (brick with stone dressings). While additional funds from leasing the King Street frontage were still anticipated, he was even requested to make fresh plans with a view to using stone.[87] Ultimately, however, this alternative proved too costly.

St James' obviously accords with Street's call for a tall, clerestoried form in the city. Cumberland's spire, as designed, was indeed 'grand and ornate' (Frontispiece) and appears to derive from the Perpendicular Gothic form used by Pugin for his ideal church (Figure 5.18). It was a type widely imitated, particularly in the United States, where prominent architects had drawn on Pugin's precedent for large city churches.[88] By ecclesiological standards, St James' apsidal chancel is short in relation to the nave (although its relative length is twice that of its Georgian predecessors). Years later Cumberland's son said that his father had desired 'a choir of ample proportions' between the apse and the nave but that it had been omitted for 'motives' of economy.[89] The congregation's conservatism on matters of ceremonial form must have also been a factor: processions of choir and clergy were not introduced until 1889, and, since the singers originally were seated in the 'west' gallery near the organ, space was not required for them in the chancel.

Within Strachan's diocese, St James' apsidal termination had been anticipated at St Paul's Anglican Church in London, designed by William Thomas and completed in 1845.[90] There, however, it appeared tacked on to the boxy body of the church – a treatment that had earlier been deplored by the *Ecclesiologist* as a 'cheap and in some respects showy substitute for a full Chancel.'[91] Doubtless Cumberland was aware of the use of this feature by English architects, often for Roman Catholic churches.[92] Although the apse had been scorned by ecclesiologists as a foreign intrusion rather than an Anglican form, their prejudice subsided as it came to be employed by adventurous architects.[93] Cumberland used it with confidence at St James', and because it is a clerestoried church, the apse appears from the exterior as an extension of the nave, fully integrated into the complex of forms.

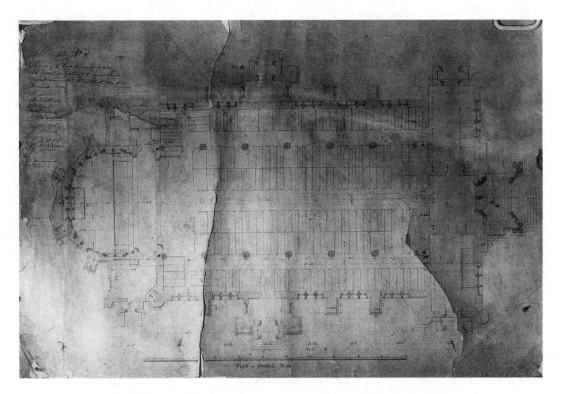

5.19 Ground-floor plan for second St James' Cathedral, by Cumberland and Ridout, 1850.

A comparison of the contract drawings of 1850 (Figures 5.19 and 5.20) with the church as completed in 1853 reveals an evolution in style towards a somewhat richer handling of detail and bolder treatment of form. The most striking departure is in the design of the trusses above the nave. The contract drawings show the roof exposed to the ridge (Figure 5.22). As the church was built, a ceiling was inserted at the level of the collar-beam, hiding the upper stage of the truss-work, which was doubtless simplified. The hammer-beams were bridged by a tie-beam that underlines the horizontal of the flat panelling above, and the central arch was elaborated with cusped divisions (Plate II.1). The result was a stronger, simpler, more 'muscular' composition – an interpretation rather than an imitation of English medieval precedents.[94]

Turning from the record of the drawings to the building itself, one is struck by the frontality and formality of the scheme. Viewed from an angle, the form of the cathedral is three-dimensional, even picturesque. The protruding forms of apse, transepts, and porches engender an emphatic external rhythm – an impressive sequence of solids and voids, had all porches been left open as originally intended. This effect is particularly striking at the main entrance, as one passes through the space carved out of the main porch – an arched opening deeply splayed and lined with colonettes. From there, as one moves through the enclosed space beneath the tower into the sudden expanse of the columned nave leading to the brilliant apse, the architecture has a markedly processional character. Victorians took pleasure in such a dramatic manipulation of architectural elements. The effect must have been even more arresting when the original keyhole doorframe and massive vestibule door were still in place (Figure 5.21).

5.20 Front elevation for second St James' Cathedral, by Cumberland and Ridout, 1850.

5.21 North elevation of chancel and vestries (l.) and vestibule door (r.),
by Cumberland and Ridout, 1850.

St James' advanced character is reflected not only in plan and form but also in vigorous and substantial details. Cumberland realized the possibilities of his building materials with spirit, superimposing a lighter rhythm of corbel tables and pilaster strips on projecting and receding forms. This diversity comes fully into play in the massive buttresses – square and octagonal – some with colonettes abutting, accented by pinnacles. He freely improvised on themes from the several phases of English Gothic – an eclectic approach that ecclesiologists had earlier deplored but which was now in vogue.[95] With mid-Victorian zest, he combined Early English lancet windows and Decorated windows with a Perpendicular spire (Frontispiece). Compared to the spare and tentative Gothicism of earlier Canadian churches, his design for St James' displayed a new robust decorative richness.

If the cathedral's exterior recalls Pugin's ideal church, the breadth and spaciousness of its interior are very different from the narrow volumes of many of Pugin's early churches. This became even more apparent with the removal of the side galleries (see below p. 209). The effect of expansiveness owes much to the wide intervals between the clustered piers that support the clerestory and to the balance of vertical with horizontal forces. Indeed, before the galleries were removed, the horizontality of their panelled fronts would have combined with the broad tie-beams of the roof and the deep cornices of the nave and aisles to challenge the accepted notion of Gothic verticality.

When St James' opened on 19 June 1853 it was, in accordance with Cumberland's limited commitment, a church that was 'enclosed and fit for service' – but with a stunted tower, and with porches and pinnacles yet to be added, it was an almost embarrassingly unfinished structure (Figure 2.8, p. 60), even when the total cost had climbed to the distressingly 'large sum' of almost £19,000.[96] On the interior the vault of the apse and the walls of the nave were plastered, scored, and coloured to represent stone. The wooden piers and arch of the chancel were painted to match the stone piers of the nave.[97] The roof timbers and pews were stained 'dark oak'. The *Church* reported that the sacred monogram 'IHS' was painted above the chancel arch in 'chaste antique characters' with a scroll carrying the text 'Glory to God in the Highest, on Earth, Peace, Good Will Towards Men'. It was hoped that a better place would be found for the pulpit and reading desk, which were temporarily placed in front of the communion table, with the officiating clergy 'elevated in the middle of the congregation' (Figure 6.4, p. 230). The *Church* concluded: 'We are all very much pleased to find the Church so admirably adapted for hearing.'[98]

The woodwork, including the organ case, and the furnishings were the work of Jacques & Hay, the leading Toronto firm of woodworkers and cabinet-makers.[99] Of the furnishings only the box pews remain, their sturdy shouldered forms outlined with deeply curved mouldings. The aisle pews, of an identical design, were removed in the 1970s. Cumberland (in later years a member of the vestry) was one of the donors of the clerestory windows that were installed in 1858 and 1859 and very likely was involved in the selection of their simple abstract design, favoured at mid-century.[100]

St James' was completed in stages. In 1865 William Storm raised the tower an additional thirty-four feet to house the main bell chamber, from which a peal of bells rang out that Christmas Eve (Figure 2.10, p. 62).[101] In 1873–4 the Toronto architect Henry Langley oversaw the completion of the tower and added the spire, transepts, and porches.[102] This later work agreed generally with the designs drafted by Cumberland & Storm in the early 1850s, while varying in detail. Storm provided three rather than two large openings on each side of the tower, producing a smoother transition from the narrow openings in the arcading below to the base of the spire above (compare Frontispiece and Plate I.1). Subsequently Langley took the spire to 314 feet, forty feet higher than originally intended. For the gabled and pinnacled porch to the west vestry he substituted a simple arched door, set off by colonettes, and he terminated the arched mouldings of the porches with carved heads.[103] The pinnacles that he added to the buttresses followed the original design. Those on the chancel, long since removed, gave it a spiky, restless silhouette.

Other improvements followed. In 1875 an illuminated clock with a prize-winning mechanism was installed in the tower, a gift from Toronto's citizens.[104] In the following year the cathedral grounds were enclosed by a brick and sandstone wall with cast-iron ornament, lamps, and entrance gates, the design furnished by Sir Casimir Gzowski, then a member of the vestry (Figures 5.23 and 5.24).[105] Regrettably, except for a short length of the wall that still stands on

5.22 Transverse sections for second St James' Cathedral, looking north (l.)
and south (r.), by Cumberland and Ridout, 1850. The design for the altar reredos (l.)
was never carried out; for the one actually installed, see Figure 3.3.

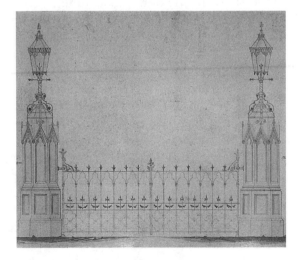

5.23 and 24 Elevations for St James' Cathedral wall, gates, and lanterns, as designed
by Sir Casimir Gzowski, 1876. Regrettably, the gates were given for scrap during
the Second World War and the fence was demolished in the 1960s.

Church Street in front of the Parish House, these embellishments were torn down in 1960 to encourage use of the grounds by the public.

With the additions of the 1870s the congregation could at last boast a structure worthy of being the 'mother church of the Diocese' – a remarkably workable fusion of parish church and cathedral. Relating as St James' does to ecclesiological ideals and theory, Pugin's concepts, and G.E. Street's more recent recommendations, it straddles chronologically and stylistically the decades of the 1840s and 1850s. Cumberland's interpretation of medieval precedents was freely eclectic and progressive, going well beyond the merely 'correct' Gothic. In St James' he created an architectural drama of exuberant rhythms and contrasting forms enhanced by the play of light and shadow (Plate I.1). It suggested a conscious response to John Ruskin, especially to the 'elements of sublimity' and the power of light and shade in architectural composition that Ruskin discussed in *The Seven Lamps of Architecture*. He had asserted there, 'I do not believe that ever any building was truly great, unless it had mighty masses, vigorous and deep, of shadow mingled with its surface. And among the first habits that a young architect should learn, is thinking in shadow, not looking at a design in its miserable liny skeleton; but conceiving it as it will be when the dawn lights it, and the dusk leaves it.'[106]

Since then ...

The internal modifications made to the cathedral over the years reflect developments in liturgical practice, changes in congregational needs and aspirations, and the ageing fabric of the building. Even before the spire and porches were added, the congregation had begun beautifying the chancel by refitting it in 1870 as a memorial to Bishop Strachan, who had died three years earlier.[107] Later, stained-glass windows imported from the studios of Franz Mayer & Co. in Munich were installed.[108] They reflected a European preference for rich colour and the compositional style of the Italian High Renaissance. The centre window, a replacement for an earlier one depicting 'the harvester Time,' was paid for by the congregation as a memorial to Dean Grasett following his death in 1882.[109] It replicates the grouping of figures from Leonardo da Vinci's Last Supper in the lower register, with a dynamic vision of the ascension above (Plate III.2).

The nave windows were put in place over a thirty-year period, the last installed in 1931.[110] As planned by Canon Edward Welch, they illustrate the rise of Christianity and its spread to the British Isles and eventually to Canada's shores. The first of these scenes, depicting the coming of the Holy Ghost to the apostles at Pentecost, was made in the New York studio of Calvert & Kimberly (Plate III.1). It contains opalescent and drapery glass (crumpled to simulate the three-dimensional folds of cloth) like that developed by Louis Comfort Tiffany.[111] The rest of the nave windows are more restrained in colour and pictorial style. Except for the one by N.T. Lyon Glass Co. of Toronto, illustrating episodes in the life of St Hilda, they are assumed to be of English manufacture – at least three came from Clayton & Bell of London.[112]

The series reaches a fitting conclusion with a window celebrating the works of John Strachan. In the upper half he holds a floor plan of the fourth St James' that shows a proposed extension to the chancel; angels display views of Trinity College, the institution he so diligently nurtured, and of the cathedral. In the lower section he presides over the historic meeting of the first synod of the diocese of Toronto, held at Holy Trinity Church in 1851.

5.25 Stuart Reid, designer of the window of the Call of St James in the
southwest vestibule, greeting HM the Queen, who had just dedicated it in memory of
members of the Governor-General's Horse Guards fallen in the wars, 29 June 1997.

Except for the baptistery window, the rest of the cathedral's large windows are of Canadian manufacture. In the animated scene encompassing the two lights of the west transept window, an angel proclaims Christ's resurrection; it was created by Robert McCausland Ltd of Toronto as a memorial to Henry Cawthra.[113] A new window in the vestibule, designed by Stuart Reid to honour the heritage of the Governor-General's Horse Guards and their members who died in the world wars, was unveiled by Queen Elizabeth II on 29 June 1997 (Figure 5.25).

Most significant of the structural modifications on the interior were the removal of the east and west galleries and the relocation of the choir and organ from the south gallery to the chancel in 1889–90 (Figures 6.6 and 6.7, pp. 233 and 237). These changes reflected the gradual adoption of cathedral-style worship.[114] Asked to report on this work when it was being contemplated, Frank Darling (of the architectural firm of Darling & Curry and a former student of G.E. Street) echoed the sentiments of Pugin and Ruskin.[115] He complained that the galleries 'ruin the vertical lines which in Gothic work are so essential' and pointed out that they blocked the light, thereby eliminating the 'charming accidental effects of light and shade' and the 'exquisite perspective made by intersecting lines of arches beyond arches, which one naturally expects to see in an arcaded building.'[116]

From the time of this renovation to about 1915, Darling took charge of improvements to the cathedral. In addition to minor assignments, he designed the gilded decoration of the ceiling of the apse.[117] With heads of cherubim emerging from a leafy background, it echoes happily the sculpted heads and foliated capitals of the clerestory shafts (Plate VI.2). Marble, and encaustic tiles imported from England, were laid in the chancel in 1914 further to enliven and enrich the space.[118] Darling also effectively transformed the little-used east transept-cum-porch into a baptistery (Plate II.2) by walling it off from the outer porch and inserting a raised stone floor and a still more elevated base for the font.[119] Samuel and Edith Nordheimer had it fitted up and enclosed with a decorative screen as a memorial to their two sons who had died in childhood. The window above, from the Franz Mayer studio, portrays Christ blessing the little children and was installed in memory of William Laidlaw's son. F. Hilton Wilkes designed the stone relief with canopy that was set against the rear wall in later years.[120]

In 1936, through the gift of William Herbert Cawthra and Alice Maude Beatty, the southeast vestibule was modified by Anthony Adamson (of Arthur & Adamson, architects) for use as a chapel dedicated to St George and in commemoration of the silver jubilee in 1935 of King George V.[121] The windows were designed by Peter Haworth from the architect's sketches: one celebrates the 'Christian amity existing between the nations of the British Empire,' (Plate IV.1) and the other shows a radiant 'Christ the King.' Suitable for small devotional services and private worship, the chapel now has a free-standing altar that allows the celebrant to face those gathered there.

In the 1940s the high altar, a memorial to Bishop Strachan, was moved to the end of the east aisle as the Lady Altar, to be used for occasional weekday and early Sunday services. About this time too Alan George designed a new high altar and other furnishings for the sanctuary.[122] In 1950 Sproatt & Rolph provided the triple sets of seats (sedilia) that were placed to either side of the altar to commemorate those who had died in the two world wars.[123] Five years later, when hope of enlarging the chancel by extending it northward had been abandoned, its floor was extended a few feet into the nave and enclosed on either side of the steps with a low stone wall (Figure 4.5, p. 121).[124] Also during this period the old vestry was converted to a sacristy, and a new vestry added at the northwest by George & Moorhouse, as a memorial to the Hon. Leighton Goldie McCarthy and his wife, Muriel Drummond Campbell, and in observance of the one-hundredth anniversary of the opening of the cathedral.[125] In a very real sense, all the many additions serve as memorials and, like the numerous fine marble and brass tablets on the cathedral walls, form part of an organic whole bearing witness to the cathedral's past while enhancing its present. Most recently the 'Bells of Old York,' a peal of twelve English change-ringing bells, were installed in the bell tower, fortuitously coinciding with the cathedral's bicentenary in 1996–7. They are named after the cathedral's two chapels and the ten churches within the deanery of St James, to symbolize the cathedral's special relationship with its surrounding parishes and recall its role in the early community.[126]

ASSOCIATED BUILDINGS

The Rectories

In 1836, aided by a government grant, St James' built its first rectory for Henry Grasett, who had arrived from Quebec the year before to serve as curate.[127] Located on the church grounds facing Adelaide Street, it was a two-storey brick house of dignified appearance, where he lived until

5.26 St James' Old Rectory, c. 1900.

5.27 St James' Rectory, built for Canon Welch in 1904 by Darling and Pearson, from the northwest. After the parish had gone deeply into debt to build the Parish House and this rectory, Canon Plumptre declined to live there, and it was let to the diocese for offices. This photo was taken in 1954.

his death in 1882 (Figure 5.26). The rectory was remodelled then for his successor, J.P. DuMoulin, who resided there only a few years. In 1886 it was leased to the Children's Aid Society.[128]

In 1902, rather than renovate the building, the vestry had it demolished and commissioned Darling & Pearson to design its replacement.129 Completed two years later on the same site but facing west towards the parochial school, the new rectory was a commodious brick house with a wide-hipped roof, a gabled main entrance, and an open porch at the south end (Figure 5.27). A form letter sent to parishioners requesting contributions towards the project said that it would be finished inside and out in a 'plain and simple character.' Containing a waiting room, three living rooms, eight bedrooms (three in the attic storey), and a basement kitchen, it provided ample space for family life as well as for the pastoral activities of the rector.130

In 1922 this rectory was leased to enable Canon Henry Plumptre to rent another house elsewhere, and in 1929 it was sold to the diocese for conversion to synod offices.131 When the diocesan centre was opened in 1959 (Figure 4.1, p. 110), Synod House, as the former rectory had come to be called, and the buildings immediately east of it, were demolished to enable the city to develop the area as a public park.132

St James' Parochial School

When John Strachan's first vocation as a teacher is recalled, it is not surprising that religious education has been a strong tradition at St James'. As early as 1820, when York had a population of only 1,240, Strachan described his Sunday school of thirty girls and fifty boys as a flourishing endeavour.133 In 1838 the *Church* noted that classes were then held at the (Upper Canada) Central School, with an average attendance of two hundred children.134 Probably the Sunday school continued there throughout the 1840s; as well, the vestry met in the school following the 1849 fire. Once the plans for the cathedral had been approved, the congregation decided to erect a two-storey parochial school on the church grounds facing Church Street.

Construction began in the spring of 1851; the school was opened the following December (Figure 5.28, and Figure 2.9, p. 61).135 Also designed by Cumberland & Ridout, it was symmetrical and built in white brick, with gabled porches and lancet windows that related it to the cathedral rising nearby. A tall gabled bellcote surmounted the façade. The layout provided separate entrances for girls and boys and classrooms on both floors. Rear doors led down to basement apartments and a large space set aside for a 'ragged school' (a term then used for schools for indigent children), though whether it was ever conducted there is unknown.136 Increased attendance and the various new uses for the school necessitated enlargements in the 1870s, until it could accommodate as many as thirteen hundred children and even the first classes of the forerunner of Wycliffe College (Figure 2.16, p. 73).137 But by the end of the century, with the area's residential population dwindling, Sunday-school attendance had greatly declined. Parochial activities, in contrast, had continued to expand, and the schoolhouse was used for these as well as for a diocesan centre. The building not only required repair but was considered inadequate to the needs of a 'modern parish.' Hence the vestry concluded that the only course open was to erect a parish house.

St James' Parish House

In the spring of 1908 the vestry invited the architects Darling & Pearson to prepare plans for a multi-functional building that was to 'touch all sides of life in the Parish – spiritual, intellectual,

5.28 St James Parochial School from southwest, perspective drawing c. 1858,
attributed to William Storm.

social and physical.'[138] The following year it approved a proposal for a three-storey structure, which was to occupy the same site as the Schoolhouse and to require about the same amount of land but which could be expanded eastward along Adelaide Street. Of 'white brick with stone trim in keeping with the cathedral, in the Tudor style and of ecclesiastical design,' the Parish House was opened in May 1910 (Figure 4.1, p. 110). As built, its long and rather sober façade on Church Street has much in common with Collegiate Gothic buildings of the period.

The scheme included offices, meeting rooms, and a gymnasium with a raised running track (Figure 3.13, p. 95). In planning the main hall, the architects borrowed from arrangements for Sunday schools developed in the last quarter of the nineteenth century.[139] Classrooms (with a gallery above) ranged along three walls opposite a platform and could be left open as part of the hall or shut off from it (and each other) by movable partitions. At the dedication of the building, Bishop Sweeny explained that St James' was 'entering a new experiment known in the United States as the Institutional Church' and that the Parish House was expected to set the standard for institutional work in the diocese and serve as a 'centre of life' for the parish.[140]

In the years since, there have been many changes to the building, with the most extensive undertaken in 1958 when it was renovated and the diocesan centre added at the east end, in preparation for the world-wide Anglican Congress of 1963.[141]

The Memorial Cross

Near the cathedral's southwest porch stands the memorial cross erected in 1924 to honour the forty-eight parishioners who died in the First World War (Figure 3.18, p. 107, and Plate I.3).

It was designed by the prominent Toronto firm of Sproatt & Rolph, by then much applauded for its Late Gothic Revival designs for Hart House and its adjoining Memorial Tower (the latter then under construction) at the University of Toronto.[142] The cross is reminiscent of the free-standing preaching and market crosses of the Middle Ages. Crisply carved from Indiana sandstone, it rises from four deeply buttressed piers set on a platform on which the names of the fallen are inscribed.[143] Its open base, slender height, and increasingly delicate detail contribute to an airy lightness that contrasts with the solid brick backdrop of the cathedral. The spire especially makes effective visual reference to St James' own soaring composition. On each Remembrance Sunday it is the site of an annual wreath-laying ceremony observed by the Royal Regiment of Canada.

St James' Cemetery and the Chapel of St James the Less

As early as 1833 the burying ground adjacent to St James' Church was regarded as a possible danger to public health. The *Canadian Freeman* strongly objected to its location in the centre of town, criticized it as a 'dangerous nuisance' overcrowded with graves, and condemned parts of it as a cholera swamp.[144] Eventually the vestry asked John Howard to report on its condition and was induced by his unfavourable comments to consider a new location.[145]

In 1844 Howard was retained to lay out a sixty-five-acre parcel of 'hill and dale' purchased from William Boulton that came to be known as St James' Cemetery.[146] It was entered at the southwest from Parliament Street just north of Wellesley Street at a point that overlooked the city; the land fell away towards the northeast – almost precipitately – into Rosedale Ravine (Figure 5.29). In laying out the cemetery with predominantly curvilinear drives, Howard was guided by the irregularities of the terrain and the principles of picturesque planning that had been adopted for 'rural' cemeteries elsewhere.[147] According to the *Church*, evergreens and groups of 'mournful looking hemlock, acacias, drooping willows, etc.' were to be planted.[148] These would have promoted a melancholy that early Victorians considered suitable in a cemetery. The first burials took place there in 1844, and the ground itself was consecrated the following year. Like many other nineteenth-century cemeteries, St James' was once enjoyed as a quasi-public park. Now open to all Christian denominations, it is still a pleasurable retreat, with scores of monuments and mausoleums of both historical and architectural interest.[149]

A gate lodge (replaced in 1905 by Darling & Pearson), with a room for an officiating clergyman and living quarters for the superintendent, and a separate receiving vault were first erected on the grounds.[150] In 1855, so that full funeral services could be conducted on the site, the vestry asked Frederic Cumberland to design a cemetery chapel, but the project was deferred until 1857.[151] By then the vestry probably foresaw that the building might serve also as a chapel of ease for those parishioners living some distance from the cathedral. Indeed, regular Sunday services began there in 1863, leading to the establishment of St Peter's, Carlton Street, and in 1883 St Simon the Apostle originated in the same way.[152]

Dedicated to St James the Less, the chapel stands on a slight rise just inside the southwestern entrance to the cemetery, admirably suited to its 'rural' site (Plate V.1). Except for the installation of a crematorium in the crypt and a columbarium in the base of the tower, it is still much the same as when it was completed late in 1861.[153] Its design is a congenial union of diverse parts that contrast with and yet complement one another. Diminutive details are set off against rough

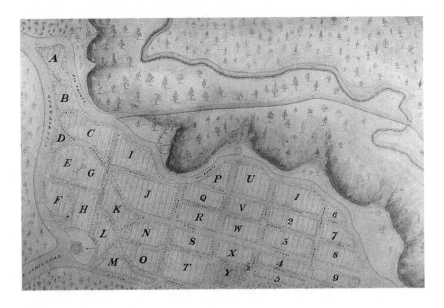

5.29 St James' Cemetery grounds as originally planned by John Howard, 1844.

stone walls and a slate roof. Its slender spire rises from a sturdy corner tower that is splayed at the base and clasped by a weighty corner buttress and stands as a striking foil for the open wooden porch next to it. A stepped walk leads up to the entrance, emphasizing the measured, processional aspect of the approach to the interior. Massive doors open to a wide centre aisle and deep chancel beyond. (The shallow transept on the south side was originally meant to seat a small choir.) Dramatizing the setting for the funeral rite, deep-set trefoil windows pierce low brick walls which carry the trusses of a sheltering wooden roof. In contrast with this simple treatment, the chancel arch rests on paired stone colonettes with foliate capitals (Plate V.2). St James the Less was begun while Cumberland & Storm were overseeing the completion of Toronto's University College and reflects that experience in its individuality and audacious handling of form and detail. Greatly admired when first built, the chapel still holds its place as one of Canada's most accomplished examples of Gothic Revival architecture. Even more than the cathedral perhaps, it exemplifies the enormous changes that took place in the character of religion and the design of churches in the short span of three decades.

6

Music and Worship

GILES BRYANT AND WILLIAM COOKE

MODEST BEGINNINGS, 1807–1839

ANY ATTEMPT AT PRESENTING a clear picture of either the music or the type of worship to be found at St James' in the first thirty-two years of its ministry proves frustrating. There is a sad lack of continuous factual records, and we have to proceed largely by deduction, by grasping at the snippets of mostly anecdotal reportage that have survived and by extrapolating from the known usual practices of Anglican worship at the time.

The Earliest Worship

On that basis, however, we can be fairly confident that the earliest worship in the church at York was a simple rendering of the services of the English Prayer Book of 1662. The clergyman would have read the priest's part, and the clerk, a lay officer who combined limited liturgical duties with those of a modern sexton, would have led the congregation in the prayers and responses that were allotted to them, as in any contemporary English parish church. The morning Sunday service would have consisted of Morning Prayer as far as the Collect for Grace, followed directly by the Litany and then, likely again with no break, by the first part of the Communion service. On most Sundays, however, there would have been no communion; in his return to Bishop Jacob Mountain's visitation articles of 9 July 1816, John Strachan reported that he celebrated it only quarterly.[1] On other Sundays the minister would have ended the service after the Prayer for the Church with one of the six collects still found at the end of the office in the 1962 Prayer Book and the final blessing. An evening service would have been straightforward Prayer Book Evensong, possibly with a sermon. The parish clerk might, in accordance with tradition, have been allowed to read the first lesson at Morning or Evening Prayer, but otherwise the service would have been taken exclusively by the single clergyman. Sermons, preached after the Nicene Creed in the morning and in the afternoon at the end of the office, were long by modern standards; Strachan's surviving ones run to ten to sixteen closely written pages.[2] With two creeds at the morning service, three recitals of the Lord's Prayer in the morning and two in the afternoon, and frequent prayers for the King and the royal family, the services would have struck most modern churchgoers as irritatingly repetitious.

The liturgical focus of these services would have been not the modest, nearly square communion table in the tiny sanctuary, but the towering three-decker pulpit (Figure 6.1), comprising

6.1 Top stage of the original three-decker pulpit of the first church at York, given by
Lieutenant-Governor Sir Charles Gore, as preserved at St Margaret's, Scarborough, at the end of
the nineteenth century; from a watercolour by Owen Staples. Besides being cut down,
the pulpit had been Gothicized by the time this picture was made.

the clerk's desk, the priest's, and the pulpit proper, one above the other, all surmounted by a
sounding board to help project the preacher's voice. From their desks in this structure the priest
and clerk would have read their parts at both Morning or Evening Prayer and the first half of
the Communion service. In the first church as originally built it stood right in front of the
sanctuary;[3] when the church was enlarged in 1818, it was placed halfway up the centre aisle on
the right side.[4] Both arrangements were common in Anglican churches built in the eighteenth

6.2 Georgian communion service given to St James' by John Henry Dunn in 1828, still in use.

century and indeed as late as the 1830s.[5] The first would have left the altar invisible from all the pews, and the second seems also to have partly obscured it. In practice, however, that would have created no difficulties; for on the rare 'Sacrament Sundays' the relatively few communicants were probably accustomed to 'draw near with faith' in a very literal sense, following the priest behind the three-decker and ranging themselves before the communion table in what was practically a separate room.[6]

There would have been little colour. An Anglican cleric in those days performed all his ministrations dressed in a simple surplice, worn with bands and a black tippet or 'preaching scarf' or else, if he had one, the hood of his university degree; before going up into the pulpit, he even changed the surplice for a black gown. According to John Langhorn, a missionary of the United Society for the Propagation of the Gospel, George Okill Stuart was not wearing a surplice at all in 1810,[7] but John Strachan was more punctilious. Whether the clerk ever boasted a surplice in the earliest days may be doubted; we should probably picture him in his best black Sunday suit, with a white stock and the bands that were also worn by lawyers, doctors, and professional men in general. The overall austerity seems to have been relieved only by crimson 'falls' on the pulpit and reading desks and a matching floor-length cloth over the communion table.[8]

Only at an actual communion would the table have been draped further in the required white linen. The priest probably performed the consecration standing at the (liturgical) north end. The clerk may have stood facing him at the south end; but not being in holy orders, he more likely remained sitting or kneeling with the congregation. Except at one point during the War of 1812, when the Revd Richard Pollard of Sandwich was a refugee at York, the first assisting ministers to be regularly admitted to the tiny sanctuary were probably the succession of divinity students and assistant curates that John Strachan began to employ in the following decade. In any case, there would have been little at the Communion for a second minister to do. A deacon or second priest might have been allowed to read a lesson. Any assisting clergy would certainly have helped to administer the elements, for the communion service presented by John Henry Dunn in 1828 includes two chalices and two small patens for administering the bread, as well as a flagon and a larger paten presumably used for the consecration (Figure 6.2).[9] Servers, however, were unknown and would have been completely superfluous. There was, of course, no processional cross, no incense, no portable tapers, and probably not even a pair of altar candles. The clerk most likely presented the alms. The bread and wine were almost certainly prepared beforehand, put on the table and veiled with a plain white corporal before the service began, and not uncovered until the offertory or perhaps the actual consecration. This was the immemorial practice of the medieval English church at low mass and remains common in rural churches in the Atlantic provinces to this day.

Nor again was there any of the seasonal variation that so characterizes Anglican worship nowadays. The pulpit and altar cloths did not change with the season in the fixed colour sequence with which we are now familiar. At Christmas some greenery evidently decorated the pews, in accordance with English tradition.[10] The only special feature of the liturgy at Easter was the anthems substituted for the Venite at Morning Prayer, and the one truly seasonal rite provided by the 1662 Prayer Book was 'A Commination, or Denouncing of God's Anger and Judgements against Sinners ... to be used on the First Day of Lent.'

As in later times, the Sunday morning service began at eleven o'clock.[11] Evening Prayer was probably at three, as it certainly was in later years; but in 1816 it was suspended for the winter, and after St John's, York Mills, was opened in 1817, Strachan would announce at the morning service at St James' on the fourth Sunday of every month that there would be no afternoon service, because he was taking that at York Mills.[12] According to Alexander Neil Bethune, who later succeeded Strachan as second bishop of Toronto, the afternoon services were poorly attended.[13]

Occasional offices provided some slight variety. Stuart often married people on Sundays; Strachan rarely did so but on the other hand preferred to hold baptisms as part of the normal Sunday services.[14] Strachan insisted that women must come to church for their churching but most likely had them do so on weekdays.[15] The Prayer Book provided special services for the anniversary of the reigning sovereign's accession and for three historical anniversaries: the martyrdom of King Charles I in 1649 (30 January), the restoration of the church and monarchy in 1660 (29 May), and the overthrow of the Gunpowder Plot in 1605 (5 November). From time to time, other special services were ordered by either royal or episcopal authority; during the long wars with France and then with the United States, every British victory was likely to elicit a service of praise and thanksgiving, and every reverse, one of humiliation and solemn prayer. Already in the 1820s St James' came to enjoy a kind of pro-cathedral status as the routine site for mass confirmations and visitations of the clergy by the bishop of Quebec on his visits to Upper Canada.[16] But to churchgoers, all those can have formed only rare breaks in an otherwise extremely uniform liturgical routine.

The Earliest Music

Where in this austere round of services was there a place for music? All lessons, prayers, and responses would certainly have been spoken, not chanted. English canon law and long-standing custom allowed, however, for hymns before and after services and sermons, and the rubrics of the Prayer Book prescribed an anthem after the third collect at Morning and Evening Prayer 'in quires and places where they sing.' Almost certainly, though, there was more; for outside the cathedrals and royal chapels it was at this time an almost universal custom in

Sunday worship to replace the Prayer Book psalms at morning and evening prayer with metrical versions, while in many churches the canticles were also sung in metre. The metrical paraphrase in general use was that of Tate and Brady, which dated from 1696 but was still called the 'New Version' to distinguish it from the 1562 version of Sternhold and Hopkins.

In earliest days, though, even the use of this version for congregational singing must have presented a great practical difficulty: only the more well-to-do worshippers would have had their own books, and many of the lower orders could not read. There were two solutions to this problem. In some places the clerk actually performed the metrical psalms and canticles as often excruciating solos; in others he 'lined them out,' or spoke each line before the congregation sang it.

When the light of history finally dawns on worship in what was still 'the church at York,' both methods are attested. We are told that 'In the year 1819, the attention of the clergy was directed to the improvement of the sacred music in the church; a Bass Viol, Bassoon, and Clarionet then supplied the place of an organ. It was resolved that an allowance of £20 shall be made to Mr Hetherington for instructing a school of singers.'[17] This is confirmed by a resolution of the vestry in that year 'that the annual stipend of £20 be paid to Mr. Harrington [sic], at present conducting a school for teaching [sacred] music, to commence from the time he began to sing in Church – and that the Church Wardens be authorized to repay out of the Church funds any sums hitherto advanced by Dr Strachan to singers.'[18] According to Henry Scadding, who had grown up worshipping at York before he became one of Strachan's earliest pupils and curates, Hetherington got his post after a competition: 'two rival choirs were heard on trial in the Church, one of them strong in instrumental resources, having the aid of a bass-viol, clarionet, and bassoon; the other more dependent on its vocal excellencies. The instrumental choir triumphantly prevailed, as we are assured.'[19]

Scadding characterized Hetherington as 'a functionary of the old-country village stamp. His habit was, after giving out a psalm, to play the air on a bassoon; and then to accompany with fantasias on the same instrument such vocalists as felt inclined to take part in the singing.'[20] We may legitimately imagine his mixed body of singers and instrumentalists as resembling those described by Thomas Hardy in *Under the Greenwood Tree* and *The Melstock Choir* or those depicted in Thomas Webster's well-known engraving 'The Village Choir.' Like the choir Hardy recalled from his youth, they may have found their place in the gallery. Hardy and Webster also give an accurate picture of the typical qualities of such choirs – musically dubious, highly autonomous, and often possessing only a tenuous loyalty to the church where they performed. One would like to think Hetherington's ensemble was a cut above that.

According to 'Notes on the Church,' Hetherington did not keep his post long, for 'in a few years his pupils had given place to a band of volunteer singers from the regiment of the garrison.'[21] This is again at least partly confirmed by the Vestry Minutes for 8 June 1825, which record a resolution 'that it is reasonable there should be a Collection for the Singers – and that Col Wells do arrange with Major Hillier in what way remuneration shall be made to [those of] the soldiers who attend.'[22] What this entry might rather suggest, however, is that the regimental band replaced Hetherington's amateur musicians, while his amateur singers kept singing. The instrumental music may well have been provided at this time by the band of the garrison, which paraded to the church most Sundays; Mrs Simcoe's diary attests to such performances at Quebec in the 1790s, and Larratt Smith was to hear them at St James' in the 1840s.[23]

Whatever the arrangement was, it collapsed when the obliging regiment was posted elsewhere; and according to 'Notes on the Church,' John Fenton, the parish clerk, then undertook to provide the musical parts of the service himself.[24] More likely though, Fenton's solos were born of necessity. Bethune remembered the singing in the first church as very indifferent and added that the younger members of the congregation neither took their part nor even knelt for prayers.[25] Scadding says that 'all expedients for doing what was, in reality, the work of the congregation itself were unreliable; and the clerk or choir-master too often found himself a solitary performer.'[26] As he tells it, 'Not infrequently, Mr. Fenton, after giving out the portion of Brady and Tate, which it pleased him to select, would execute the whole of it as a solo, to some accustomed air, with graceful variations of his own. All this would be done with great coolness and apparent self-satisfaction.' Others, though, were evidently not always so pleased; the author of 'Notes on the Church' characterized Fenton as 'a gentleman of taste, but of no remarkable compass of voice,'[27] and Scadding quotes William Lyon Mackenzie's *Colonial Advocate* as complaining that on one Sunday Fenton had chosen Psalm 12 as a deliberate swipe at the Reformers.[28]

A Toronto tradition affirms that at some time in the 1830s the garrison was a Highland Scottish regiment with at least one piper, but that bagpipes ever accompanied the psalm-singing at St James' is unlikely; for the story runs that, when ordered to march into St James' for their first church parade, the whole unit rebelled and continued up Church Street and west on to Adelaide Street to the then site of St Andrew's Presbyterian Church, with the piper playing 'This Is Nae My Own Hous.'[29]

The order of service for laying the cornerstone of the new church on 7 June 1832 called for three hymns: 'As purling from the mountain's side,' 'O Sovereign Lord, Almighty King,' and 'O Glory to the King on High.' The psalms, appropriately enough, were 84 and 122.[30] The surviving list of pews in the St James' Cathedral Archives shows that the six in front of the organ loft were at that time reserved for a choir. Anna Brownell Jameson wrote this account of the music in the spring of 1837: 'Owing to the exertions of an intelligent musician here, some voices have been so far drilled that the psalms and anthems at church are very tolerably performed; but this gentleman receives so little encouragement, that he is at the moment preparing to go over to the United States. The archdeacon is collecting subscriptions to pay for an organ which is to cost a thousand pounds; if the money were expended in aid of a singing-school, it would do more good.'[31]

It would be a mistake to read too much into Mrs Jameson's use of the word 'anthems,' which at this time could be applied to canticles or to any church music rendered by choir or soloist alone. With that qualification, though, the picture presented is a reasonably favourable one. The 'intelligent musician' must have been William Henry Warren, compiler of *A Selection of Psalms and Hymns for Every Sunday* (Toronto 1835), who described himself on its title page as 'organist of St James' Church, York, Upper Canada.' He had been appointed in 1834 and did indeed leave in 1838 but went to Christ Church Cathedral, Montreal. Warren's book included metrical psalms, chants, and hymn tunes, some of them his own compositions; these last were very likely the first used in Toronto, at least in Anglican worship, that did not come from English tune books. One is called 'York New Church'; it is rather funereal, as if inspired by the cholera epidemic. A more agreeable specimen of his style is his version of 'St Magnus'; some snappy rhythms appear, breaking the steady tread of half-note beats that we are used to, and there are some short ornamental flourishes. He set the Venite to a straitjacket of a chant that we would find awkward today but which is certainly reminiscent of English collections of the time. Only a later edition (1842) expanded into anthem-like music, but their absence from the first edition does not prove that anthems were never performed at St James' in Warren's time there; it may mean only that in 1835 he had not yet written them or judged that they had no commercial market. What does seem quite significant, however, is the settings of the Venite and the canticles. As late as 1832–3 a clerk, now William Andrews, was still lining out psalms at St James'; but if Warren's book fairly represents what he was used to performing there, then after his appointment at least certain parts of the service were being chanted in the Prayer Book versions, not sung by clerk or worshippers in metrical paraphrase.

Early Organs

This would have been virtually impossible without an organ. There is an obscure tradition that about this time a portable instrument, presumably a barrel organ, was occasionally carted from the Jarvis house over to the church. That, however, must at best have been a temporary expedient, and grander ideas seem to have figured in the plans for the new church from the outset. On 12 July 1830 John E. Goodson wrote to his sister Susanna Johns back in England: 'The New Church is going on rapidly, it is a large building and will require a good-sized organ: which I believe it is their determination to have: but having gone far beyond their means in the expenditure of the church, I question whether they will be able to get it till after the church is completed.'[32] On 28 September 1833 Strachan wrote to Mrs James Brown describing the new church and looking forward to acquiring both an organ and a 'Chime of Bells.'[33] And some time after Mrs Jameson's note in 1837, a notable organ was indeed bought and installed. It was built by Gray & Davidson of London, England, had two and a half manuals, and contained a great organ with eleven stops, a choir organ with eight, a swell organ with eight stops, an octave and a half of pedal pipes, four composition pedals, and two couplers – in all, twenty-seven stops and about 1,050 pipes. It cost 800 guineas sterling in London, and, with shipping and other charges, £1,200 Canadian on delivery.[34] Robertson notes that J.H. Dunn, generous to St James' as ever, had subscribed £800.[35]

In a letter of 26 September 1838 Strachan thanked Robert Gillespie for his help in securing the new instrument and choosing Dr Edward Hodges (1796–1867) as organist, saying that Hodges had 'electrified' the congregation by his playing.[36] But by November, to Strachan's considerable vexation, Hodges was on his way to New York. In replying to Hodges' letter of resignation, Strachan did not scruple to point out that he had been brought over from England at some expense, specifically to fill the position vacated by Warren and play the new organ.[37] As Hodges' son told it, though, 'The times were so bad, business so dull, everything is stagnant in the way of work, that Papa made up his mind not to stay any longer.'[38] In New York Hodges built himself a solid reputation at Trinity Church, Wall Street, and became well known for his advanced views on organ design.[39] His is the arrangement of the main theme from the last movement of Beethoven's Ninth Symphony that is found as 'Hymn to Joy' in our hymnals today. Scadding tells us that the organ he played on perished in the fire of 1839, and Robertson describes in detail the unsuccessful efforts to save it.[40]

A Victorian Parish and Cathedral Church, 1839–1897

Disaster and Recovery, 1839–1856

Just before the opening of the first cathedral in 1839, the mists begin to clear a little, largely thanks to the diaries of Larratt Smith, who sang in the choir himself. When the diaries begin in September 1839, the new building was still being finished and half the congregation was worshipping at Upper Canada College at the present corner of King and Simcoe streets. Two services every Sunday were now the rule. Mary Larratt Smith, in her edition of excerpts, states that the choir was then led by Mrs Draper, wife of the Conservative leader, William Henry Draper.[41] From the diary itself we learn that the bands of the garrison regiments provided a musical accompaniment to the singing and for some while in 1840 there were actually two different regimental bands playing in the cathedral – that of the 32nd Regiment and that of the 34th.[42] Often, though, no band turned up, and the singers had to perform with only the help of Colonel James Fitzgibbon's flute or with no accompaniment at all. Smith wrote under 6 October 1839: 'Singing abominable no one there in the evening but Cozens & Hepburne – Fitzgibbon trying to play failed – obliged to lead the treble without the flute.' He was better pleased with the effort on 15 December: 'Singing very well indeed present Hepburne Cozens – C. Fitzgibbon – McLeod myself – no flute – Ladies sung loud for first time.' On this occasion, at least, the choir consisted of five men and five women. In the summer of 1841 it seems to have been reorganized, for under 11 July Smith writes: 'Heard new choir under Crozier sing for first time.'

An entry in the manuscript Historical Register in the St James' Cathedral Archives, thought to have been compiled about 1905, gives 1841 as the beginning date for a subscription campaign for a new organ from Montreal that was to cost £225; according to Smith, the committee to raise this money was active in November.[43] By then a Mrs Gilkison was responsible for the choir.[44] Smith, who lodged in her house as well as singing under her at St James', reports that she suffered from chronic ill health and often had to stop playing because of coughing fits; on one Sunday 'Mrs Gilkison fainted after Te Deum & could not be restored till after 1st psalm when she was carried out.'[45] Smith also tells us much about the repertory, which included the anthems 'I will wash my hands in innocency' and 'Great is the Lord' and many selections from Handel's *Messiah*. Pieces were repeated with a frequency that would make a modern congregation revolt. People at the time, however, seem to have been pleased, for there are complimentary remarks about the choir's performance in the *Church* of 26 February 1842 (p. 135).

A small organ was in use again by the end of January 1842,[46] built by Mead of Montreal; according to a contemporary report, on its arrival, 'Many persons of the best taste, who were present, expressed great gratification and surprise at the mingled power and sweetness of its performance,'[47] but by the end of July it was 'much out of tune.'[48] The cathedral cash book records a payment to 'Messrs Mead on a/c organ £10.0.0' under 31 July 1842. This entry tends to bear out the persistent tradition that the organ now standing in the rear gallery of St Clement's Church, north Toronto, was originally used at St James' (Figure 6.3), for it is a small instrument of five stops made by Mead of Montreal. Evidently St James' bought this organ in 1842 and disposed of it three years later – not surprisingly, since it must have been distinctly undersized for a church that could hold in a pinch some two thousand people. This

6.3 Early organ from St James' Church, now at St Clement's, north Toronto.

little organ must be one of the most travelled in Canada: from Montreal to St James', to St Paul's, Bloor Street, to Trinity Church, Aurora, then to the Hilary house on Yonge Street and finally in 1965 to St Clement's.

William Andrews continued in office as clerk, but his duties as now outlined were more those of a senior sexton or verger, his only remaining liturgical function being to lead the responses. From Smith we can also glean a little about the trappings of worship at this time. He notes that a new set of cushions and cover for the 'sacrament table' were first used on 1 March 1840, ten weeks after the new church opened, and cost £90, and he remarks on 29 August 1841: 'Bishop's stall, curtained to day.' Vestments, however, were apparently still in short supply, because on Christmas day 1841 'service did not commence till past 12. surplice not arrived.'[49]

W.H. Warren's book *A Selection of Psalms and Hymns ... together with a Number of Chants* (Toronto 1835) was evidently used at St James', because a copy is extant inscribed 'St James Cathedral 1848.'[50] We also know that the new cathedral used *Psalms, Hymns and Anthems for the Dioceses of Quebec and Toronto* (1842) as its congregational hymn book, because there is a copy in the Cathedral Archives, inscribed 'Miller Pew 152 St James' Cathedral York U.C.' This book still contained metrical versions of all the psalms, though some were considerably shortened, but also a selection of hymns for many Sundays of the year and for the major church seasons. Some current favourites made their first known appearance at St James' here, such as 'Lo he comes! in clouds descending' and 'Hark, the herald angels sing.' The book also included the texts of forty-eight anthems. Handel, Mozart, and Haydn were represented, alongside lesser-known cathedral composers of the eighteenth century such as Arnold, Callcott, Attwood, Boyce, and Kent.

Minutes of vestry meetings over the next few years routinely contain votes of thanks to Mrs Gilkison and the volunteer choir. Two stoves were placed in the organ gallery at the south (i.e., rear) end of the church, confirming that the choir must have sat there. Mrs Gilkison was also paid for copying music, and several payments were made to J.P. Clarke for tuning the organ. Then in March of 1845 the vestry approved purchasing a new organ and disposing of the old one.

We should probably place under Mrs Gilkison's régime the earliest of F.W. Dixon's reminiscences of the cathedral choir.[51] He remembered being recruited from the Sunday school by members of the choir in the early 1840s: 'I was a boy soprano in the choir of the old church which was burned down on that memorable Good Friday morning in 1849' (actually Holy Saturday, 7 April). He mentioned a Mr Lang as principal tenor but unfortunately said little about what the choir sang, except for an anthem entitled 'Sound the loud timbrel,' which was a great favourite, being sung 'on an average at least once a month' but abruptly discontinued, the congregation 'having made the discovery that Tom Moore, its author, was either a Roman Catholic or was not quite so good a Christian as he ought to have been, I forget which.' In fact both charges could fairly have been laid against Thomas Moore, who is better remembered nowadays for 'Believe me, if all those endearing young charms' and 'The minstrel boy to the war is gone.' One cannot help but suspect that whoever revealed his faith or character was heartily sick of the anthem.

Mrs Gilkison has been seen as an early victim of discrimination: as Helmut Kallmann noted, her salary was reduced from £100 to £75 in 1846 and to £50 two years later.[52] In fairness, though, it should be noted that the cathedral was clearly in severe financial straits at the time. By June of 1848 she had resigned and James Paton Clarke was appointed organist; he was to be paid only the same £50 a year that Mrs Gilkison had been receiving at the end of her tenure, and out of that he was expected to continue to tune the organ and provide his own organ-blower – very likely a boy. This somewhat niggardly arrangement suggests that the church's treatment of Mrs Gilkison had indeed been born of necessity.

James Clarke had been born in Edinburgh and came to Canada in 1835, first settling as a farmer near Elora.[53] By 1842, however, as we have seen, he was being paid for organ and piano tuning at St James', and by 1845 he was definitely residing in Toronto. In that year he published *Canadian Church Psalmody*, with chants and tunes by himself. On his appointment to St James' this book may have come into use – at least for its music, for it is hard to believe that the straitened church would so quickly have replaced *Psalms, Hymns, and Anthems* with another book for use by the congregation. Clarke became an important figure in Toronto's developing musical scene, but his career at St James' was chequered, to say the least. The church burnt down again in 1849, and faced with the cost of rebuilding, the corporation stopped paying his salary. He nevertheless gallantly kept the choir together, and gave his own services free of charge, to lead the worship held at Holy Trinity Church during the rebuilding; according to Kallman, he managed to combine this effort with paying posts at the Toronto Normal School and the Toronto Academy, a boys' school.[54]

What Clarke played on at St James' is an interesting question. Samuel Thompson remembered that an organ had been installed in the first cathedral not long before the fire, at a cost of £1,200, supplied by May and Son of Adelphi Terrace, London, but it had perished completely in the blaze: 'I was a member of the choir, and with other members stood looking on in an agony of suspense, hoping against hope that our beloved instrument might yet be saved; but what the flames had spared, the intense heat effected. While we were gazing at the sea of fire visible through the wide front doorway, a dense shower of liquid silvery metal, white hot, suddenly descended from the organ loft. The pipes had all melted at once, and the noble organ was only an empty case, soon to be consumed with the whole interior of the building, leaving nothing but ghostly-looking charred limestone walls.'[55]

This is the only reference to the instrument bought to replace the Mead organ sold in 1845. Something of it may conceivably have survived the fire, since a cashbook entry for March 1850 charges £53.5.0 against the organ account as paid to P Hagr<..> and Vogt for 'repairs.'[56] More likely, though, the entry represents a late payment for repairs done before the fire. George Jardine, a New York organ-builder, had evidently heard that the organ was destroyed in the fire, for he wrote on 18 June 1849 offering to build a replacement.[57] The new organ, installed in the rear gallery, was in fact built by S.R. Warren of Montreal; the Cathedral Accounts record a payment to Warren of £1,569.1.05, and the Toronto *Patriot* reported that the new instrument was ready for trial on 2 June 1853 and played at the reopening of the church on the 19th.[58] In August the casework was paid for at a cost of £303.10.0; it was designed by the architect of the new cathedral, Frederic Cumberland, and executed by the Toronto firm of Jacques & Hay.[59]

In this organ Torontonians of the time considered that they had finally obtained a fit replacement for the one destroyed in 1839; it had three full manuals, thirty-seven stops, and 1,842 pipes. A writer in the *Daily Patriot* commented: 'as far as our own memory and judgment enable us to form an opinion, we have no hesitation in saying, that Mr. Warren had produced an instrument which may compare most favourably with any other ... We have looked over the specifications of the principal English organs, and remarked, that very few even in London contain greater power or variety.'[60] Much of the pipework of this organ survives in the instrument now in use.

Somewhat ungenerously, in the light of Clarke's unpaid service while the congregation was at Holy Trinity, the corporation did not rehire him but instead engaged R.G. Paige, who conducted the organ trials and played at the service for the opening of the new cathedral, 'assisted by members of his own family and a full choir of amateurs.'[61] The *Patriot* correspondent waxed quite lyrical about 'the delightful sweetness of the flute, dulciana, and viol de [sic] gamba, with the pleasing effect of the tremulet stop, of the swell organ; the fine tones of the cremona, violoncello, and kerotophon stops of the choir organ; the massive strength of the posaune and double diapason, in the great organ; and the impressive grandeur of the pedal stops, which constitute the chief feature of the organ, and are unusually powerful. With such an organ builder as Warren' he concluded, 'and such an organist and leader as Paige, St James' Church will be nobly provided; and our good City of Toronto may boast of cathedral music worthy of her position amongst the most flourishing cities of the world.'[62]

F.W. Dixon, too, remembered Paige as a fine choirmaster and organist but attributed much of his success to the good voices of his family; his wife and daughters all sang, and the oldest girl, Miss Georgie, was considered particularly good. The musical taste and organization of the time evidently allowed for solos at services, because hers came in for special mention. Paige, however, resigned in 1856, and apparently the choir left with him, and his successor, George F. Hayter, had to make do with a quartet. Hayter, too, soon left, as did the next organist, a Mr Fripp.

Stability and Achievement: John Carter and his Successors, 1856–1884

With the appointment of John Carter late in 1856, however, a new period of stability and achievement began. A musical committee was established by the vestry of 1859 and reported to the next meeting in 1860 that 'the success of the boy part of the choir, owing to the indefatigable exertions of the organist (Mr Carter), far exceeds their most sangwine [sic] expectations.' Thirty-five boys had been signed up, their parents agreeing to pay £5 should they default in their duties. Efforts to recruit adult male singers were less immediately successful, perhaps because the pay offered did not compensate for having to attend two Sunday services. Nevertheless, as Dixon recalled, the choir was able to render 'an anthem, "Bow down thine ear, Oh Lord"', arranged to music by Rossini for the visit of the Prince of Wales to the cathedral on 9 September 1860. By 1861 the choir consisted of twenty-eight treble boys, six alto boys, five ladies, eight tenors, and seven basses.[63]

The report to the vestry meeting of 1860 had expressed regret for the poor state of congregational singing, giving as the reason the lack of 'an authorized Hymn and Tune book.' This may have been part of the impetus that produced *A Selection of Chants and Tunes for the Diocese of Toronto* (Toronto 1861), co-edited by Carter, his predecessor Clarke, and G.W. Strathy. It included Carter's own tune 'Quebec.' Carter was one of four musical brothers, and at one time three of them were serving as organists in the cathedrals of Toronto, Quebec, and Montreal – a veritable musical Family Compact. George Carter compiled *A Selection of Anthems as Sung in the Cathedrals of Montreal, Toronto, and Quebec* (Montreal 1865), presumably intended as a companion to his brother's book. The congregation's hymn book at this time was evidently still *Psalms, Hymns, and Anthems*, though now in the fifth edition of 1855, of which the actual copy used by Prince Albert Edward in 1860, duly inscribed, remains in the Cathedral Archives. Within a few years, however, it seems to have been replaced by an English book, Kemble's *Selection of Psalms and Hymns*, of which specimens used at St James' also remain in the archives.

John Carter was popular and respected as both a choirmaster and an organist and played a key role in the cultural flowering of Toronto in the third quarter of the nineteenth century. Dixon recalled Carter's moving performance of 'the lovely andante from Beethoven's 5th Symphony, with a pathos and sublimity which could hardly be surpassed.' His presentation of Handel's *Messiah* at the new St Lawrence Hall on 17 December 1857 was the first known performance of a complete oratorio in what is now Ontario. He gave piano recitals and conducted Verdi's *Il Trovatore* at the Music Hall in 1866. He also directed a performance of his brother William's cantata *Placida, the Christian Martyr* at St James' Schoolhouse early in the 1870s.[64]

By then, though, his relations with the church were clearly becoming strained. The vestry meeting of 1860 had voted to spend £25 for a piece of plate, suitably inscribed, as a token of appreciation for his early efforts, but his request for a raise in 1862 was denied. To the authorities his salary of $450 a year must have seemed ample, to say the least, compared to what they had been paying Clarke and Mrs Gilkison. He left in 1878 amid a storm of angry letters back and forth, gleefully printed in full in the local press. From these it appears that neither side was living up to its undertakings, and the vitriolic letters only inflamed the situation. The choir, however, made it plain where its own sympathies lay by resigning with him en masse.[65]

It is some indication of the growth of musical talent and training in Toronto that Carter's successor, Edgar R. Doward, appointed the same year, had no trouble getting the choir back up to strength after this débâcle; by 1879 it numbered fifty-nine.[66] The next year St James' again adopted a new hymn book, Bickersteth's *Hymnal Companion* of 1870;[67] copies of this too are still preserved, bound or cased with prayer books used by worshippers at the time, in the Cathedral Archives. As might have been expected at a time when Dean Grasett and the leading lay pillars of St James' were engaged in a sharp controversy with Bishop Bethune and beginning to lay the plans for founding Wycliffe College as a rival to Strachan's Trinity, this was a pronouncedly evangelical book. The choice of hymns for services was delegated to a subcommittee of the musical committee, who were enjoined to pick only the 'well-known and deservedly popular.'[68] (Some things do not change!) A list of the sixteen anthems performed in 1882 mentions works by Handel Mozart, Spohr, Mendelsson, Stainer, Barnby, Smart, and Elvey, as well as the Rossini piece performed for the prince twenty-two years before. This was a fairly typical repertory for a church of St James' size and prominence at the time.

Doward left in 1884, and Walter A. Geddes served as interim organist from 1 July to 1 September, when Dr Charles Davies took up the post. The organ had received a fairly thorough overhaul in 1878. This cost $3,274.55 and included the conversion of the blowing system to hydraulic power.[69] On 16 September 1884 Davies played the first documented organ recital in the cathedral.

Worship under an Evangelical Dean, 1847–1882

While all this enrichment of the cathedral music was taking place, worship in its other aspects seems to have stood still. Henry James Grasett had succeeded Strachan as rector of St James' in 1847 and kept the post until his death in 1882. A stranger who had dropped into the first cathedral soon after Grasett took charge, and then returned forty years later, would have been impressed by the new Gothic church, very grand by Canadian standards, that had replaced the Georgian one and would have been equally struck by the advance in the scale and quality of the cathedral music, but in other respects he would have found very little change.

This is less surprising when it is realized that the ceremonial side of the Catholic Revival in the Church of England had little following anywhere in Canada at that time, even among those who considered themselves high-church. Although Strachan had been the first bishop in the Anglican Communion to welcome the teaching of the Oxford Movement as expressed in the *Tracts for the Times*, he was as uninterested as Newman and Keble themselves in reviving pre-Reformation vestments or ceremonial. Indeed he saw 'ritualism' as a dangerously divisive tendency in the church and was still warning against it in his charge to his clergy in 1865: 'While we concede the right, where it can be advantageously and satisfactorily exercised, to invest our

6.4 Interior of St James' Cathedral, c. 1875, from a photograph by William Notman,
showing the pulpit in the nave.

noble Ritual with all the attractions of which it is susceptible, none are justified in going beyond
its letter and spirit, none are warranted in making additions to what is laid down, in adopting
customs which the Church for centuries has ignored – in restoring vestments which have never,
or rarely, been introduced into our reformed Communion.'[70]

As for Grasett, he was a thoroughgoing low churchman, who had even refused to wear his
surplice to preach when ordered to do so by Strachan.[71] His opposition to rebuilding St James'
in the Gothic style in 1849 may have been largely a matter of taste but may also have been
grounded in foresight. He retained close family and other connections in England; and from
them he must have learnt early on that, wherever Gothic churches were built, there soon arose
demand for a kind of worship more suited to them than the plain, preaching-centred style that
his own party favoured.

With its shallow chancel and broad galleries all round the nave, St James' as rebuilt in 1849–53
may have looked like a Gothic church to untutored Canadian eyes, but it could be, and for forty
years was, used for exactly the same type of worship as its Georgian predecessor. One early
interior photograph shows the pulpit standing between the pews partway down the centre
aisle, where it would have blocked most worshippers' view of the altar (Figure 6.4). Another
shows the altar itself bare of all covering except the rubrical linen cloth, and the chancel
otherwise empty of furniture, presumably to accommodate those who would 'draw near' to take
the sacrament (Figure 6.5). A third shows the centre aisle filled with benches, presumably to
provide free seating for those who could not afford pews (Figure 6.6). Some half-dozen of

6.5 Interior of St James' Cathedral looking north, c. 1884, from a photograph by J.H. Noverre.
Note the bare altar in the empty chancel and the hardly visible rear gallery for the choir.

the pews themselves were of the double-box type, with half the seats facing backwards; but it
hardly mattered, because in St James' as run by Henry Grasett, there was nothing to see – no
processions, no ceremonial, and most certainly no vestments.

The oldest surviving register of preachers at St James' begins on 1 January 1845, when Grasett
was Strachan's curate and virtually his priest-vicar, as the bishop had become increasingly taken
up with his episcopal duties. It reveals a pattern of worship that endured scarcely unchanged

until after Grasett's death. When it opens there were two services on Sundays, morning and afternoon; but beginning on Trinity Sunday (30 May) 1858 an evening service was added. Only in 1883 does the register begin to specify that these were held at eleven, three, and seven o'clock, respectively, but it seems likely that those hours were established much earlier. The morning service was a communion on the first Sunday of most months throughout those years, except between November 1852 and Easter (27 March) 1853, when the congregation was unable to worship at the cathedral; it seems likely that the few other apparent exceptions merely represent a failure to record the number of communicants. On the remaining Sundays of each month the morning service presumably stopped, as the Prayer Book directed, after the Prayer for the Church, concluding with one of the final collects and the Blessing. There was also always a communion at the morning service on Christmas Day, Easter Sunday, and Whitsunday, and from 1860 onward on Ascension Day; otherwise the only regular morning celebration seems to have been for the diocesan synod.

Down to 1870 both the afternoon and evening services on Sundays seem to have been Evening Prayer. This was a widespread usage at the time both in Canada and in England, the earlier office being intended for the more leisured classes and the later one for their servants; it was explicitly provided for in the revised English lectionary of 1871, which allowed for different lessons at the two Sunday evensongs. But beginning on the Sunday after the Ascension (21 May) in 1871 the evening service at St James' on the third Sunday of every month is recorded as a communion. In the same year the afternoon Sunday service began to be discontinued for summer, which would suggest that the Sunday evening communions actually followed Evensong.

Services were also held on Easter Monday and Tuesday, Whitsun Monday and Tuesday, and all 'red-letter' feast days, though as the years went on these were increasingly entered as 'prayers only' (i.e., without a sermon), and after 1874 more and more such days are marked 'no service (no congregation).' The hour recorded for these services in J.P. DuMoulin's time was ten or eleven a.m., and it seems likely that that represents a much older tradition and those services in Grasett's time were Morning Prayer. During Lent, afternoon services were held on every Wednesday and Friday; down to 1849 the Friday services are entered as 'prayer and catechizing,' but in that year preachers' names begin to appear. Beginning on 9 January 1861, however, evening services were held on all Wednesdays in the Schoolhouse, and these were continued through Lent in place of the afternoon ones in the church; then beginning in 1870 the Friday Lenten services were also moved to that time and place. In Holy Week, however, morning services were held every day in the church, and there were always two church services on Good Friday.

Few other days were kept. The three historical anniversaries were abolished by royal warrant and act of Parliament in 1859, but Accession Day continued (22 June under Queen Victoria). The only 'black-letter' days ever observed were St Patrick (17 March) and St George (23 April), attended by the Irish and English national societies under their respective patronage, but after 1860 even these tended to be kept on the nearest Sunday – a tradition that the St George's Society still happily continues. In most years down to 1858, either 1 or 2 August was observed as the 'Anniversary of the Abolition of Slavery.' From 1863 onwards, a weekday in October or November was usually kept as Harvest Thanksgiving, latterly with a communion; in 1879 there were prayers on 9 October, the Thanksgiving Day appointed by the bishop, but the communion was on 6 November, the day appointed by the provincial government. Special

6.6 Interior of St James' Cathedral looking south, c. 1884. The nave galleries are still in place, but the present pulpit has been installed. The benches in the main aisle were presumably meant for worshippers who could not afford pews.

services were held for missions and with the attendance of such societies as the Orange Order, the Sons of England, and the Irish Protestant Benevolent Society, but usually as part of the regular evensong on Sunday afternoons.

Church parades to St James' by the British garrison ceased with the opening of St John's Church in Victoria Square in 1858, but the 10th Royal Grenadiers began an annual church parade to the cathedral from soon after its formation in 1862. This militia unit had a close connection with the church, in that the commanding officer was Dean Grasett's son Henry James and other prominent parishioners also held commissions, including the architect Frederic Cumberland.[72] The parade usually took place in May, which probably reflected the very old tradition of mustering and parading the militia on the sovereign's birthday. After the Great War it was naturally transferred to Armistice Day, and on the nearest Sunday it is still kept up by the Grenadiers' perpetuating unit, the Royal Regiment of Canada.

As a cathedral, St James' was also expected to hold special services for state occasions. At the memorial services for Prince Albert on Sunday 12 January 1862, for instance, the pulpit, reading desk, and chancel were draped in black, and a hatchment of the prince's arms was hung over the altar. John Carter and his choir performed suitable music by Handel and Mozart and a part at least of Beethoven's 'Grand Funeral March' in A flat.[73]

Throughout this period the Sunday morning communions normally attracted between one hundred and two hundred communicants, and the Sunday evening communions about half that number, except in very bad weather. Christmas and Easter always attracted many more communicants, but Whitsunday seldom drew more than fifty, unless it happened to be the first Sunday of the month, and Ascension Day was even less popular. W.S. Rainsford's mission in 1877 produced a remarkable increase: 429 at the evening communion on Lent 5 (18 March), 385 in the morning on Easter 2 (15 April), and 588 in the evening on Trinity 2 (10 June), all when he preached. Through to the end of 1879, the numbers remained at about double what they had been in 1876; but in 1880 they fell back to about what they had been before the mission.

The picture that emerges after Grasett's death in 1882 is one of a fairly typical evangelical church, except for the services on red-letter days and the comparative frequency of Holy Communion, which in many evangelical parish churches at this time would still have been celebrated only four or six times a year. This and the services on the red-letter days probably represent a survival from Strachan's later practice – the monthly communions on Sunday mornings, at least, are attested from 1840 onwards in Larratt Smith's diary – but may also represent what Grasett felt was expected of a cathedral. The Sunday evening communions, however, were a clear innovation in Grasett's time and were doubtless designed, like the evensongs with which they alternated, to reach domestic servants and others who could not conveniently attend at an earlier hour. In the Church of England evening communions seem to have been unknown until they were introduced by Walter Farquhar Hook as vicar of St Peter's, Leeds, in Yorkshire in 1852; Hook, however, held them only on weekdays that were eves of holy days, so that the factory workers who made up most of his congregation could communicate then.[74] When extended to Sundays, the practice was viewed as a mark of low churchmanship, because it discouraged fasting before communion.[75]

Ritualism Comes to St James', 1882–1897

Evening communions at St James' were probably not the only influence that St Peter's, Leeds, had on Anglican worship in Toronto in the third quarter of the nineteenth century. As rebuilt in 1841, that church had stalls in the chancel for a surpliced lay choir, which rendered the services in much the same way as they were traditionally done in the cathedrals and the royal chapels,[76] and in England its example was quickly imitated. But besides the reports from a steady stream of immigrants on these 'advanced' churches in the old country, there was soon an example nearer to hand.

At Holy Trinity, Toronto, completed in 1847 as a gift from a wealthy Englishwoman who wished to endow a church with free sittings for the poor, Henry Scadding had placed the choir in the chancel from the first. By 1859 it consisted of men and boys only and chanted the responses; by 1865 Scadding had put the choir into surplices, and the next year he introduced fully choral services, with the prayers being intoned.[77] Eastward celebration was the rule at Holy Trinity by October 1861.[78]

Continuously from 1848 there was also a congregation in Toronto of the Catholic Apostolic Church, more commonly but less accurately called the Irvingites;[79] and while its liturgy was largely adapted from the Book of Common Prayer, it was invested with all the trappings of the medieval English church – richly coloured mass vestments, hanging lamps perpetually burning in the sanctuary, and even revived Gregorian chant for the psalms, canticles, and suffrages. There the Litany was recited before the reserved sacrament, exposed on the altar, while clouds of incense rose, symbolizing, as in the Book of Revelation, the prayers of the saints.[80]

When St Matthias', Bellwoods Avenue, opened in 1874, some of these features could even be seen in an Anglican parish,[81] and the more 'advanced' students at old Trinity College on Queen Street West eagerly sought for excuses to desert the 'high and dry' services of their college chapel for the enchanting liturgical riches offered a mere two blocks away.[82] Sung Eucharists began at Holy Trinity in 1877; and in 1881, after a controversy that had led to the resignation of Frank Darling as rector, Darling's successor, John Pearson, placed lighted candles on the altar at the communion and introduced eucharistic vestments, changing with the liturgical season.[83]

The vast majority of Toronto Anglicans deplored these then-extreme usages, and the diocesan synod presented a petition against them to the provincial synod of Canada in 1868.[84] Scadding's example of dignified yet still clearly Protestant worship was more favourably received but still met with resistance; during the synod debate on the Toronto petition, Isaac Helmuth, then dean of London and later bishop of Huron, delivered an extraordinary tirade against surpliced choirs.[85] At St George the Martyr the choir had consisted only of men and boys from 1853 if not earlier and was moved to the front of the church in 1876. But the introduction of choir surplices there in 1881 proved more controversial, with Barlow Cumberland, son of the architect of St James', leading a vocal opposition.[86] This controversy, however, was checked by no less a person than Bishop Sweatman, who made a point of attending the surpliced choir's first service and gave an address there in which he warmly supported the innovation.[87]

From 1883 onwards, with the full cooperation of Canon DuMoulin as rector, the bishop also arranged for surpliced choirs to sing at the diocesan synod services at St James', with the singers being drawn from various parish churches where the custom was already established.[88] The bishop himself assumed the presidency of a Church Choir Association, and beginning in 1892 the member churches held notable combined services of choral Evensong every year at St James'.[89] These were much more ritually and musically 'advanced' than the usual Sunday services of the time: a fully surpliced choir processed in and out; the canticles were sung to settings of the English cathedral type; the psalms, Lesser Litany, and suffrages were chanted; and the rest of the service – even including the opening General Confession, Absolution, and Lord's Prayer – was monotoned. The processional hymn used in 1893 began: 'We come in the might of the Lord of Light In surplic'd train to meet Him.' If the conservative evangelicals who had so long dominated St James' came out to hear that, they must have felt that the bishop and rector were flinging down a gauntlet at their feet.[90]

Conversely, the combination of their endorsement with the examples of the synod services, the Choir Association service, and particularly the neighbour parish must have powerfully encouraged those at St James' who favoured a change. St George's was a fashionable 'West End' church, the very touchstone of respectability, and it is a measure of the Toronto Anglican élite's changing liturgical taste that by 1891 processional hymns, coloured stoles changing with the season, turning east for the Creed, and even eastward celebration were in regular use there. Another protest against those usages by Barlow Cumberland at the Easter vestry meeting that year only produced a unanimous vote of confidence in the rector.[91]

Such was the background to the changes in worship that began to take place at St James' very soon after Grasett's death in 1882, and it goes far to explain why the authorities acted slowly and with caution. At first the innovations touched only the times of the Sunday services: the afternoon service disappeared, and from Lent of 1884 the regular Sunday pattern was an early communion at nine a.m.; Morning Prayer at eleven, still followed by communion on the first Sunday of the month; and Evening Prayer at seven, followed on the third Sunday of the month by communion. The early communion was an alternative way of providing for the class of worshippers that could not get to church for the main service; it was preferred by high church-men because it facilitated taking the sacrament fasting. At St James', however, it attracted only small congregations, and the rule soon became to omit it on Sundays when there was another celebration and to suspend it altogether in summer. Since there was now a communion every Sunday, it would have been lawful under the canons of the Canadian provincial synod to omit the Ante-communion after Morning Prayer on the latter Sundays of the month; but whether the opportunity was taken, or how soon, does not appear from the service register.

In other particulars change was just as radical in the end but began rather more slowly and hesitantly. A newspaper account of 1885 still refers to 'the usual choir inspection of the people below during prayer' and describes the choir of twenty-five members as 'led by a choirmaster buried behind the clock and vigorously beating time with the only part of him visible, viz., a kid-gloved hand waving above his head';[92] but during that year the choir was being moved to the chancel regularly for Evensong and occasionally for the morning service, and a small organ, probably portable, was placed there to support their singing. There were evidently complaints, however, and for a time the choir returned to the organ gallery for all morning services. In 1889, however, when the galleries were removed, the choir moved definitively to the chancel. Warren supplied a new, or rather rebuilt, three-manual organ at a cost of $10,000; the contract, dated 10 November 1888, mentions reusing some of the old bellows and wind trunking, and the evidence of the pipes themselves suggests that much of the pipework of the old instrument was also merely transferred from the rear to the front of the church. The new instrument was divided on either side of the chancel; the keyboards were on the east side, and the new hydraulic blower was installed behind it, in what had hitherto been the bishop's vestry. Tenders for the casework went out in 1891, but it was not immediately executed; a Notman photograph of about this period shows the organ with the pipes at the heads of the aisles exposed (Figure 6.7), and the pipes in the chancel are still not cased in a choir photograph of 1905 (see below, Figure 6.10).

6.7 Interior of St James' looking north, c. 1891, from a photograph by William Notman.
The nave galleries are gone, and the eagle lectern has replaced the reading desk,
but the relocated organ pipes still lack their casing.

6.8 St James' choir c. 1895, on the front steps.

In 1889 the male members of the choir were ordered to wear surplices (but without cassocks) for both the morning and the evening service,[93] which may imply that they had already been in use for some while at Evensong. A contemporary picture shows about fifty men and boys in this garb accompanied by about a dozen ladies in more or less uniform hats and dresses, probably black (Figure 6.8). Cassocks were not to appear until 1897. But surplices were not the only innovation in 1889; at the same meeting of the Musical Committee where they were discussed, the rector proposed having the psalms and the amens chanted 'but had no desire to offend any member of the congregation.' In reply, 'M. Baldwin said that if there was no intention to sing the Prayers that he had no objections ... It being asked whether the Rector desired to have processional and recessional hymns, the rector replied that no change would be made except at the request of the Committee or Vestry. It was decided not to recommend any further change.'[94] Evidently, though, the choir did process up the main aisle from what is now St George's Chapel, which after the removal of the galleries became its vestry; for this was one of the changes complained of in a waspish contemporary tract entitled *The Progress of Ritualism in St James' Cathedral, Toronto*: '[Canon DuMoulin] has introduced processions, and occasionally, processional hymns. The choir and clergy assemble in the porch of the south entrance and give the signal of their approach by a loud Ah-men which may be heard on the south side of King St.; they then form in procession, enter the church, take their respective places in the chancel,

6.9   Stocks Hammond, organist and choirmaster 1896–7, 'a shadowy figure'
but very popular with his choir.

and canter through the service at railway speed, so that it is difficult to many, and impossible with some, to keep track much less join in the service – the primary object of assembling ourselves together in God's house on the Lord's day for public worship being entirely lost sight of, for the whole thing is monopolized by the clergy and choir.'[95]

The writer goes on to complain further that DuMoulin had taken to wearing his surplice to preach and had rearranged the furniture, moving the pulpit to its present position against the west side of the chancel arch, 'from which one-third of the congregation cannot see or hear' and substituting 'a gilded eagle lectern' for the reading desk. He claims these changes were made in bad faith and had more than half emptied the church and attributes a small fire that was started by an electrical fault in the organ mechanism to divine displeasure. 'Who,' he asks, 'would have thought that St James' Cathedral – a church and congregation which for over half a century remained faithful to the Protestant principles of the glorious Reformation – could have been, so soon after the lamented death of Dean Grasett, quietly converted into a Ritualistic theatre for the propagation of semi-popery?'[96]

Late Victorian Choirmasters and Organists

Amid all this upheaval the authorities had also grown dissatisfied with Charles Davies as organist and choirmaster, and when he resigned in 1886 they decided to split the two posts. This seems to have been an uncomfortable situation for both parties, since over the next few years both organists and choirmasters followed one another in unusually quick succession. W. Elliott Haslam served as choirmaster from 1886 to 1892, followed by E.W. Schuch. A.E. Carter became organist in July 1886 but was at some point replaced by George Bowles, who served until 1895. Charles Mockridge managed to work with Schuch for a year, but they then fell out so badly that the authorities decided to end the experiment and reunite the two posts.

The choirmasters of this period were efficient and hardworking men. Haslam was a distinguished teacher, specializing in the voice.[97] Under him an elaborate training system was put in place, which virtually indentured boys to the choir and, like the contract of John Carter's day, provided a stiff penalty for withdrawal. Haslam's own contract with the church required an anthem every Sunday, the same not to be repeated before three months had elapsed; one wonders how Mrs Gilkison would have reacted to that. Schuch was a highly respected musician, but little record remains of his work at St James', other than his inability to get along with successive organists, which led to his being asked to resign.

Dr Stocks Hammond (Figure 6.9) was appointed to the reunited post in 1896 but died in office the next year. He is a shadowy figure, and uncomplimentary comments have been made about his earlier work in England. That may help to explain why E.G. Strathy committed himself only to the significantly guarded remark that Stocks Hammond's brief tenure had made a great impression.[98] The vestry, however, expressed great regret at his passing, and with the choir he was evidently very popular; for when his interim replacement Humfrey Anger (1862–1913; served at St James' 1897–8), ventured to criticize him, many of the members, in the best St James' tradition, upped and left.[99] Anger rose above this, though, and went on to a distinguished teaching career at the Toronto (now Royal) Conservatory of Music from 1893 until 1913, when Healey Willan was hired as his successor.[100]

COMING OF AGE, 1897–1961

New Choirmaster, New Rector

It is a measure of the growing importance of Toronto both in the cultural world and in the Anglican Communion that the vacant post of organist and choirmaster elicited a hundred and fifty applications. Eventually it was offered to and accepted by Dr Albert Ham (1858–1940) from Taunton in England. When he took up his duties in November of 1897 the musical history of present-day St James' may be said to have begun. He had already distinguished himself in England in several church positions and brought with him the solid training (FRCO, Mus. Doc.) and experience of an organist in a large parish church. His presence quickly made itself felt at St James'; the report of the Musical Committee to the Easter vestry of 1898 reads as follows: 'It has long been felt desirable to abolish, if possible, the incongruous mixture of persons seen in the Chancel caused by having the surplice [sic] choir of men and boys, together with a number of ladies seated at the back. To overcome the difficulty, the training of the boys to a stage of efficiency that would enable them to lead the services without being reinforced by the ladies was decided upon and towards that end Dr Ham was requested to use his efforts. We are pleased to be able to state that about a month ago the change was effected and thus far with general satisfaction.'

6.10 St James' choir, 1905. Albert Ham, the choirmaster, appears under the organ pipes beside the rector, Canon Welch. In front of them are the two assistant curates: Derwyn Trevor Owen (l.), later bishop of Toronto and primate of all Canada, and L.W.B. Broughall (r.), later bishop of Niagara.

In fact an all-male choir seems to have been first proposed by Haslam eight years earlier.[101] The creation of this first legitimate choir of men and boys at St James' is said to have had the encouragement of the rector, Bishop Sullivan, who had succeeded DuMoulin in 1896. The reformed choir numbered thirty-six boys and twenty-five men; how they were accommodated in a space that was even smaller than it is now remains a mystery (Figure 6.10). Haslam had suggested only twenty men and 'a number of boys.'

In the same year the committee recommended introducing the revised edition of *Hymns Ancient and Modern*, in place of Bickersteth's *Hymnal Companion*. This change was one clear symptom of St James' conversion – musically, at least – from low to 'central' churchmanship. Another was the greater use of music in the rites themselves: Anglican chant quickly became the norm for the psalms, and the responses were also sung to the so-called Tallis Ferial and Festal harmonized chants, Ham expressing himself as dead against using any others. Ham himself also arranged Tallis's setting of the Litany and had the whole published as *Versicles, Responses and the Litany (Tallis)* (Oxford 1912). It was now possible to sing most of Mattins and Evensong from 'O Lord, open thou our lips' down to the anthem, and that probably became the established practice. Processional-style hymns also now came into regular use at the beginnings and ends of services.

Ham had not been in office long before he secured the support of a very congenial new rector. Edward Ashurst Welch, ex-provost of Trinity College, was the first rector of St James' since Strachan who was considered a high churchman and the first who could be called a product of the Oxford Movement. No revolution followed his appointment in 1899; he was well aware of the sharp cleavage between opposing schools in the Canadian church and had won great respect as provost of Trinity by his conciliatory stance, being the first head of Strachan's college to attend a Wycliffe convocation. On liturgical matters, as he wrote to his father in England, 'I'm quite willing to be shoved, but I shall not attempt to drag them.' Some shoving must have occurred, though, for about this time the Nordheimer family undertook to give a cross and two candles for the altar.[102] The cross was of brass, in a pattern particularly approved by the Ecclesiological Society, with the symbols of the four evangelists at the ends of the arms and the Lamb of God in the centre; with an altered base, it remains on the Lady Altar to this day (Figure 6.11). At the time and in a church that had been so closely involved in the founding of Wycliffe College, this was a bold move.

St James', however, quickly slid further down what the author of *The Progress of Ritualism* must have seen as a slippery slope. Gold, white, red, purple, and green frontals began to grace the altar, changing with the liturgical seasons, and the ministering clergy at the communion took to wearing matching coloured stoles in place of their hoods or scarfs. All these were embroidered by the Sisters of the Church, an Anglican order of nuns with a convent in west Toronto, and many remain in the Cathedral Archives, while the gold frontal continues in occasional use on the Lady Altar. They are elaborate and beautiful work, quite up to the best English standards of the time, the reds being the characteristic 'Sarum' shade. The inevitable story is told that a novice helping to do the white frontal (Figure 6.11) had the bad luck to prick her finger with her needle and stain the fabric. 'Never mind, my dear,' the mother superior is said to have comforted her;. 'just work another rose to cover the spot.'

A gradual but marked change also took place in the pattern of services. In Holy Week of 1900 Welch began 'lantern services' in the Schoolhouse daily at eight p.m., which continued every year at that season throughout his rectorship. These seem to have originated in England about 1870 and involved the use of magic-lantern slides;[103] but they were evidently something more liturgical and devotional than mere illustrated lectures on ancient Jerusalem, for the appendix to the subject index in the 1938 *Book of Common Praise* provides a list of recommended hymns for a 'Lantern Service on the Passion or Way of the Cross.' One imagines Welch's lantern services as anticipating in at least some respects the present Holy Week Stations of the Cross. After Easter 1901 a new pattern of Sunday services is discernible: Holy Communion every Sunday at eight a.m.; Mattins every Sunday at eleven, followed by a full Communion service on the first and third Sundays of every month; and Evensong at seven. The eleven-o'clock Communion on the first Sunday of the month is usually designated 'choral' in the register, which suggests that on the third Sunday the choir sang Mattins only and the following Communion was a said or at least a congregational one. Sunday-evening Communions ceased; Welch must have shared the view of another Edwardian high-churchman, Vernon Staley, who, when discussing evening communion in his Anglican instruction manual, quoted St Paul's words: 'We have no such

6.11 The old high altar of St James' with the cross and candles procured by Canon Welch and the fabled white frontal embroidered by the Sisters of the Church. When this photo was taken, c. 1950, the altar had been moved to its present position as the Lady Altar. For its original position, see Figure 3.3.

custom, neither the Churches of God.'[104] By 1901 communion on red-letter days was also usual, and there were two celebrations on both Ascension Day and Whitsunday, even though the latter was the fourth Sunday of the month. Thus the services of St James' began to approximate, for the first time, those of a contemporary English cathedral.

A tradition that had begun as far back as 1799, when there was public thanksgiving for Nelson's victory at the Battle of the Nile, but which took firm root under Welch, was that of having special services for national and imperial occasions, with appropriate special lessons and music. For the service at Queen Victoria's death, Welch also delivered a special sermon, 'A Mother in Israel,' which was afterwards printed up as a pamphlet. The regard in which the great queen was held is shown by the service register for 1901, in which 24 May (Friday) appears for the first time as Victoria Day. A more joyful special occasion was the coronation of King Edward VII and Queen Alexandra in 1902, which had had to be postponed when the king became seriously ill; some of the prayers and music of the actual coronation service were used, including Elgar's 'Imperial March.' In those days, before radio or television, services of this kind were the only means by which Torontonians could be drawn into a common observance of great occasions with their compatriots in other parts of Canada and the British Empire, in which most Canadian Anglicans then took at least as great a patriotic pride as in their own country. But the tradition was to outlast the coming of the new means of instant communication and continue to the present time.

St James' centenary was also celebrated under Welch, in 1904. The observances lasted for a week in June, and included special musical efforts. The anthems included works by Garrett, Darnton, Maker, and Cobb, while among the hymns were such favourites as 'O God, our help in ages past,' 'The God of Abraham praise,' and 'The Church's one foundation.' There was also a special centenary hymn, 'We thank thee for a hundred years,' written by Horace Moule, presumably for the occasion.

In 1906 the capacity of the organ was considerably enhanced by the installation of an echo organ in what remained of the rear gallery; it cost about $1,400 and was given by Mrs Gooderham in memory of her husband.[105] A contemporary photograph shows Ham seated at a four-manual console, still set into the base of the casework on the east side of the chancel (Figure 6.12). The fourth keyboard must have been added then, unless it had already been provided in 1888–9. In 1916 the chancel pipes of the main organ were at last enclosed in the present caseworks with their angels in relief.[106]

In the spring of 1908 Sir Frederick Bridge, organist and choirmaster of Westminster Abbey, visited Canada on a lecture tour. In his autobiography he relates that he had a few problems on his tour with rectors and the use of their churches, but at Toronto he fared much better: 'There, the Rector of St James' Cathedral, a man of liberal views, welcomed me, placing his church at my service, while the choir, under the direction of Dr. Ham – an admirable choirmaster and good all-round musician – rendered a selection of Cathedral music, from Dering to Wesley, in first-rate style.'[107]

Bridge went on to comment favourably on Ham's training of the boys, echoing the general verdict in Canadian musical circles that he was a fine trainer of voices of all ages. He was a strict disciplinarian, not above caning boys for misbehaviour, and a meticulous rehearser. He became a voice teacher at both the Toronto Conservatory of Music and the Canadian Academy and published a book entitled *A Manual on the Boy's Voice and its Culture* (London 1902) as well as articles on the subject in the Conservatory's *Quarterly Revue* and in the *Canadian Churchman* of May 1933. These last are a mine of common sense and reveal that he had a great love of plain-chant, favoured the old 'metred' style for Anglican chant and Merbecke for the Communion, and rejoiced to see 'sweet and effeminate' tunes disappearing while wishing to keep the best work of great Victorian composers such as Sullivan, Dykes, and Monk. His own setting for Tennyson's 'Crossing the Bar' appeared in the 1908 *Book of Common Praise*, the first official hymnal of the Church of England in Canada. For the centenary celebrations he supplied his own tune 'Cosgrave' for the processional hymn 'Age after age the Pilgrim Church hath trod,' with words specially written for the occasion by Charles Venn Pilcher, later an assistant at St James'. This is a fine, stirring melody, worthy of being revived. Ham had equal stature and reputation as an organist, helping to found the Canadian Guild (later Royal Canadian College) of Organists and serving as its first president.[108] He taught and examined for the University of Toronto and for two schools and also examined for Bishop's University in Lennoxville, Quebec.

6.12 Albert Ham, choirmaster, at the organ console, 1923.

St James' under Canon Plumptre, 1909–1935

Canon Welch returned to England in 1909, to be succeeded at St James' by Henry Pemberton Plumptre, sometime dean of Wycliffe College. Plumptre's liberal evangelical teaching is said to have distressed some of the younger members of the congregation who had learned their faith under the conservative 'Prayer Book catholic' Welch; but the new ornaments and stoles remained in use, and surviving records indicate little change in the pattern or character of the services. Indeed the frequency of communion actually increased: in 1913–14 there was an experiment with a morning communion at ten and later a quarter past on the second Sunday of every month, and a more successful innovation was a restored evening communion on the fourth Sunday, beginning in September 1913. Having, like Welch, grown up and received his education in England, Plumptre thoroughly appreciated the musical tradition and style of the English cathedrals and supported Ham's efforts to establish it at St James' just as warmly as had his predecessor. A conspicuous example is given by the entry in Plumptre's hand in the service register for Thursday 22 June 1911, under ten a.m., reading 'Coronation Service (official) His Majesty George V. Litany Sung by Rector & solemnities read. Full choir & orchestra of Drums etc.' Plumptre served on the committee that produced the first Canadian edition of the Prayer Book, which was authorized for trial use in 1915 and again with minor revisions in 1918 and became the only lawful book in 1922. This, however, made little change in the Sunday services.

Throughout Ham's tenure at St James' new choir repertoire continued steadily to appear. Although educated before the composers of the end of the nineteenth century had wrought their 'cleansing' effect on English church music, Ham was awake to the merits of the new school and brought in many of their works. At some point in his time St James' printed its own anthem book, containing 159 items; the book bears no date but must have come out after the coronation service for King George V, since it contains the words of a piece by Ham himself written for that occasion, as well as ten other pieces of his own. Other items are by Clarke-Whitfield, Elliott Button, A.W. Marchant, Frederick Bridge, John E. West, A.H. Brewer, Alfred Hollins, and Coleridge Taylor, all of which must have been introduced by Ham. There were a few works by such older composers as Tye, Purcell, and Farrant, who were only beginning to be rediscovered. Stanford's Te Deum in B flat was being sung as early as 1914, alongside works by Stainer, Gounod, Barnby, and Dykes. Holst's setting of 'Lullay myn lyking' was sung at Christmas in 1927 and 1928, and service leaflets of the period frequently list a Te Deum by 'Herbert Howell' – presumably Howells' unison setting in E flat, published in 1925, which must have been a daring innovation. About 1928 Novello published Ham's own *Six Hymns and Carols with Descants*, containing four traditional hymns with original descants and two new tunes of his own. The descant to 'Rockingham' and a bold chant for the Benedicite found their way into the revised *Book of Common Praise* of 1938. After the Great War of 1914–18 his piece variously titled *Armistice* or *Cease-fire* regularly featured in Remembrance Day services at St James', but in 1929 and 1930 it was replaced by music by Hamish MacCunn and a cantata by Stanford, *Last Post*.

A carol service had been instituted by 1929, given in both the morning and the evening on the Sunday after Christmas. On Good Friday it became a tradition to sing either Stainer's *Crucifixion* or Ham's own *Solitudes of the Passion*, with text chosen by Welch; and these services became so popular that people had to be turned away. In 1932 an extract from Elgar's cantata *The Banner of St George*, entitled 'It comes from the misty ages,' was sung as an anthem and a plainsong setting of 'I heard a voice from heaven' was used. If this all seems a trifle conservative compared to what was happening at some English cathedrals or even what Healey Willan was beginning to do in Toronto at St Mary Magdalene's, it represented a great advance at St James' and in local church music in general. Outside the church Ham did just as much to update choral music in Toronto through his secular choir the National Chorus, which gave the first local performances of works by Elgar, Parry, Bridge, Mackenzie, Coleridge Taylor, Holst, and Vaughan Williams. He also conducted the first local performance of Elgar's Symphony No. 1 in A flat.

Ham's own composing style, however, remained largely unaffected by this wealth of new music. A fair specimen is 'The desert shall rejoice,' in which a recitative for soprano is followed by a chorus that returns to close the piece after a second solo for tenor – a typical format of the late nineteenth century. His melodic turns and harmony were equally typical of that period, though avoiding the extreme chromaticism of Spohr or Gounod. His *Solitudes of the Passion* contains one overt quotation from Elgar's *Dream of Gerontius*.

In Ham's earliest years the musical committee had occasionally flexed its muscles by making minor criticisms of his work, but he soon came to be deeply valued and respected, and many testimonials remain to the excellence of his work at St James'. A special service was held in 1922 to honour his twenty-five years in office, at which he played 'Melodie' by Rachmaninoff and 'Introduction and Fugue' by Adolph Hesse, and the choir sang 'Blessed be the God and Father' by Samuel Sebastian Wesley. He also received from the church a piece of engraved plate and a cheque for $1,000 – a handsome sum at the time.[109] When in 1933 at the age of seventy-five he decided to resign, he was pressed to remain and had to insist that his health required him to leave. His final service included organ music by Bach, Brahms, and Rheinberger and anthems by Mendelssohn, Handel, Brewer, H.C. Stocks, and Ham himself – a representative sample of the music he had introduced and cultivated. Contemporary reports attest to the fine and careful singing on this occasion. The silver processional cross with ebony shaft now used at St James' was presented at this time as a memorial to his achievements. He retired to England, and there was some controversy afterwards over whether he did so by choice or from necessity; he was not granted a pension.

Ham's successor (1933–56) was William Wells Hewitt. He had been trained at Lincoln Cathedral by George Bennett and came to Toronto from Holy Trinity Church in Stratford-on-Avon. New repertoire was heard immediately: at Easter 1934 he was playing organ music by Karg-Elert, Vierne, and Parry, while the choir sang the more familiar works of Stanford and S.S. Wesley. Bach and Widor were heard the next year. At Easter 1936 there was a choral communion at half past nine with Harwood in A flat as the setting and a carol 'Love is come again'; Mattins at eleven featured both Stanford's Te Deum and his lengthy anthem 'Ye choirs of new Jerusalem,' while his B-flat Magnificat and Bairstow's 'Sing ye to the Lord' appeared at Evensong. In 1936, that was a day's music of which any church could be proud. In that same year St James' hosted 'the first Toronto massed festival of choirs,' held to mark the beginning of the work in Toronto of the School of English Church Music (later to become the Royal School of Church Music) 'with representations of 23 choirs, including several hundred boy choristers.'[110] It was perhaps in preparation for this event that some significant work was done on the organ by Casavant Frères – an overdue measure, it would seem, since Ham had been complaining about the action as long ago as 1921.[111] A new, freestanding console was supplied at the northwest corner of the choir stalls, and new pitman chests and a few ranks were added.[112]

Ham's retirement was followed within two years by Plumptre's. There had been a distinct liturgical falling off in his latter years as rector: by 1927 there was apparently only one communion service a month at eleven a.m., usually but not always on the first Sunday of the month, and the weekday services either had been given up or were not being recorded. Probably this was owing more to the depopulation of the neighbourhood than to any flagging energy on the part of the clergy; the congregation now came mainly from the wealthy neighbourhoods north of Bloor Street and seems to have had little interest in attending church on any days but Sundays and the great festivals. For a year and a half after Plumptre's retirement, St James' was in the charge of his former curate, Arthur Briarly Browne, who, as might have been expected, made no significant changes to the service pattern, though according to his own note in the register he was the first celebrant to sing the Proper Preface in the Communion.

A New Era, 1937 – 1961

However that may have been, a new liturgical era certainly began with the arrival of the next rector, Charles Edward Riley. Promptly from his arrival in August of 1937, daily Mattins and Evensong were resumed, now even on Saturdays, and regular weekday communions were also begun. From September of that year the main Sunday services assumed a new pattern that was to endure throughout Riley's tenure and indeed beyond: Holy Communion on the first and third Sundays of each month and Mattins on the others, with the Litany following on the last Sunday of the month. Beginning in September 1938, 'Intercessions' were added on weekdays at a quarter past twelve; on Monday 3 October these were styled, somewhat pathetically in retrospect, a 'Thanksgiving for Deliverance from War.' By 25 August of the next year they were being called a 'Service of Intercession re International Crisis,' and that title persisted until Great Britain went to war on 6 September, to be followed by Canada on the 10th.

Throughout Riley's long incumbency brief midday preaching services were held daily during Lent and attracted many people from the adjoining business district. While many distinguished visitors figured in these, the lion's share of the preaching fell to Riley himself. According to the Revd Gerald Moffatt, who served as his assistant during the war and became his son-in-law, 'His preaching was always firmly grounded in Scripture and Creeds, and was expressed with fervour and conviction. There was very little of Riley (except the fervour and some telling flashes of humour) and very much of the Church's Faith (as opposed to the chit chat and inconsequential autobiographical details heard from many pulpits today). A reasoned, objective apprehension of the Faith once delivered to the Saints was set forth, to be (it was hoped) received by the hearers.'[113] This style of preaching was to become characteristic of St James', notable later exponents being deans Gilling and Stiff and Canon Philip Hobson.

According to Moffatt, 'over the years of [Riley's] Rectorship, the Cathedral was transformed' and 'availability of all the Sacraments of grace was quietly but steadily promoted so that both inward and outward changes ... were effected.'[114] These, however, were gradual and cumulative, as might have been anticipated from the sensitive pastor who was largely responsible for the revisions in the second Canadian Prayer Book to the forms for ministry to the sick.[115] In its style of worship, St James' under Riley remained distinctly in the mainstream, as befitted a cathedral. At a time when Anglo-Catholic churches such as St Mary Magdalene's were using *The English Missal*, St James' possessed no more venturesome book than *The English Liturgy*, a beautifully printed altar book of the 1662 rite, minimally supplemented with a few sets of special collects, epistles, and gospels for saints' days, all of them authorized in one or more English dioceses. This was certainly used, for the pages containing the consecration prayer have been worn and crudely repaired, and parts of the service have been corrected in ink to agree with the first Canadian revision of the Prayer Book; but it was probably confined to 'low' celebrations. The main Sunday celebrations were almost certainly read from a pair of matching altar books of the first Canadian rite, in one of which the king's name in the Prayer for the Church Militant was neatly altered from 'George' to 'Edward' to 'George' again as the events of 1936 unfolded.

The musical repertory under Wells Hewitt settled down and changed little over his term of office; the Second World War seems to have made very little difference to the steady routine that he pursued once he had got things to his liking. Nor does he seem to have played as active a part in the larger Toronto musical scene as other choirmasters before and after. His one contribution to the revised *Book of Common Praise* of 1938 was his tune 'Stratford-on-Avon' for Charles Wesley's hymn 'O, for a thousand tongues to sing' – a good effort, but no competition for the traditional 'Richmond.' Tradition at St James' remembered him chiefly for his habit of singing along with the trebles in nearly everything. The latter years of his régime did see the return of the Royal School of Church Music in 1949, with a choral Evensong and recital on 7 March, combining the choirs of the cathedral, St Simon's, and Grace Church on the Hill, all conducted by G.H. Heath-Gracie, who later paid tribute to the fine singing of the choirs and the strength of Canadian hospitality. On Passion Sunday of 1955, Handel's *Passion of Christ* was sung.

Peace did bring a change in the appearance of the sanctuary, with the installation of the new English altar and the matching sedilia given as a memorial to the members of the parish fallen in the two great wars,[116] but these changes seem to have had little immediate effect on worship.

6.13 Clergy and choir c. 1960. The processional cross was still being carried by a choir man.
The four clergy in the front stalls are (l. to r.) Revd Kenneth Hill, assistant; Revd P.A. Rickard,
honorary assistant; Revd John Coombs, assistant; and Dean Riley.

A certain shift is discernible, however, with the arrival in 1951 of John Ames Coombs, who was
Riley's senior assistant in his last years as dean (Figures 4.3 and 6.13). Coombs was very much
a son of the parish; his father, F.J. Coombs, had been a boy chorister at St James' and served as
rector's warden from 1941 to 1943.[117] Daily Mattins and Evensong, which had been suspended
after the outbreak of the war owing to shortage of staff, were immediately resumed: On Advent
Sunday of 1951 (2 December) Coombs noted in the service register: 'Choir wore purple cassocks
today for the first time.' On the Wednesday in Holy Week of 1952 (9 April), Coombs led what
must have been the first true service at St James' of the Stations of the Cross; and on Advent III
of that year (14 December) he recorded in the register the first Corporate Communion of the
Cathedral Servers' Guild.

As in all Anglican churches of that time, the servers were all male and mostly adolescent boys.
From early on they wore not the Roman cottas usually seen in Anglo-Catholic churches but
servers' rochets: ankle-length gathered vestments without sleeves, eminently practical for altar

6.14 Choir Camp, Stewart Lake, Torrance, c. 1940.

serving and much favoured by Percy Dearmer and other English exponents of a style of worship that was dignified and ceremonious but in strict accordance with the Ornaments Rubric of the Prayer Book, which specifies that 'such Ornaments of the Church, and of the Ministers thereof at all times of their Ministration, shall be retained, and be in use, as were in this Church of England ... in the Second Year of the Reign of King Edward the Sixth.' Coombs used frequently to entertain the servers at the early Sunday communions to breakfast in his flat on the top floor of the Parish House or at a nearby restaurant, and he is still remembered fondly for his hospitality and good talk.

Little elaboration took place, however, in the ceremonial of the main Sunday services. The processional cross continued to be borne by a surpliced singing man (see Figure 6.13), and though two wooden portable candlesticks were at some point acquired, they seem to have been used only on the great festivals when there was a full procession. The practice of entering and leaving to hymns, which had so exercised the author of *The Progress of Ritualism*, was now discontinued, and the choir and clergy took to entering before the first hymn and leaving after the last, as in contemporary English cathedrals.[118] Although both Riley and Coombs owned eucharistic vestments and Coombs used his at St James' on weekdays, there seems to have been no attempt to introduce them on Sundays. At a time when even the bishop of Toronto never wore anything more elaborate than his rochet and a black chimere, and the bishop of Aberdeen and Orkney caused a minor sensation by appearing on a visit in a lace-trimmed rochet, cope, and mitre,[119] any more advanced usages at the Sunday services in the cathedral would probably have been impolitic, to say the least.

6.15 John Hooper, choirmaster 1956–65.

A milestone in the history of Anglican church music in Toronto was the foundation in 1954 of the Diocesan Choir School, with the strong encouragement of the then coadjutor bishop, Frederick Wilkinson, who in the next year succeeded as the diocesan. When Wells Hewitt retired in 1956, he was succeeded by the Choir School's music director, John D. Hooper (Figure 6.15). The appointment is said to have been suggested by Healey Willan, one of the chief founders of the school. Willan himself played a recital at St James' the next year, followed a week later by Godfrey Hewitt. On Passion Sunday 1956 the choir performed Wood's *Passion According to St Mark*. Ironically, under Hooper the choir's part in the normal Sunday services actually suffered some retrenchment: chants were used for the canticles at both Mattins and Evensong more often than choral settings, and Merbecke became the standard setting for the Communion. These changes suggest a wish to have the congregation join in more parts of the service, but that cannot have been the reason for singing the same anthem at both morning and evening services, as now began to happen from time to time. At two major diocesan services the choir's only 'solo' contribution was to sing Walford-Davies' 'God be in my head.'

MODERN TIMES, 1961–PRESENT

Worship in the English Cathedral Style, 1961–8

Riley retired after nearly a quarter-century as dean in 1961 and was succeeded by Walter Joseph Gilling. Gilling had spent part of the war attached to Chester Cathedral in England, serving under Dean G.W.O. Addleshaw, and shared Addleshaw's admiration for the Caroline divines, the high churchmen who had suffered for their loyalty to King Charles I and rebuilt the Church of England after the religious anarchy of the Commonwealth. His aim was to perform the services of the new Canadian revision of the Prayer Book, which received definitive approval in 1962, as they had performed the services of their own revision exactly three hundred years before – with fidelity, dignity, and decency, and in a style as much like that of English cathedrals as the size and wealth of St James' allowed.

The 1962 Prayer Book was a much more thorough revision than the 1922, particularly in the Communion rite, which represented a happy compromise between high-church and evangelical aspirations. It still required the Ten Commandments and the Litany at least once a month, and the latter regularly followed Mattins on the fourth Sunday but was occasionally shifted to follow Evensong instead. On Rogation Sunday and once in each of Advent and Lent it was sung in procession. At first Mattins remained the main Sunday-morning service except on the first and third Sundays of the month, when it was a choral Communion; but Communion soon appeared on the fifth Sunday as well. The nine-o'clock service was always Holy Communion, normally with one accompanied hymn at the offertory; on Christmas Day and Easter Day, however, a choral service was provided, less ambitious than the main one and sung by the men only of the cathedral choir. A brief experiment in the last years of Gilling's deanship with using the modern-language New Zealand liturgy at this service met with almost universal disfavour from the worshippers and was quickly dropped. Evensong continued at half past four, to which time it had been moved late in Riley's deanship from the nearly immemorial hour of seven. This change was a great convenience to the families of the choirboys, who now virtually all lived at a considerable distance from the church.

Gilling took his liturgical pattern neither from the Roman Tridentine rite nor from the English medieval rite of Sarum but from the English cathedrals as he knew them. For instance, when the chief morning service was Holy Communion, the epistle was read from the lectern and the gospel from the pulpit, with no escorting cross and lights, and incense remained unknown except perhaps at Epiphany. Vestments were still eschewed: for the worldwide Anglican Congress held largely at St James' in 1963 it was agreed that only Archbishop Ramsey of Canterbury would wear cope and mitre while all the other attending prelates adhered to rochet and chimere – much to the chagrin, it is said, of Bishop Wilkinson of Toronto, who had finally broken down and bought the other outfit for the occasion (Figure 6.16). In 1966 St James' did at last acquire a single precentor's cope, designed by Dorothy Shuter and given by St John's, York Mills, then celebrating its hundred-and-fiftieth anniversary (Figure 6.17).

The 1963 congress included services on a grand scale at Maple Leaf Gardens, for which the music was under the direction of John Sidgwick. The cathedral choir, however, continued to be responsible for the Sunday services at St James', and daily sung services were instituted for the duration, sung by a special choir of men and boys drawn from England, Canada, and the United States, with Gerald Knight, director of the RSCM, as choirmaster and John Dykes-Bower of St Paul's Cathedral in London, England, as the organist. The music sung was of the normal English cathedral standard, extending from Christopher Tye to John Joubert and including works by Willan and the American composer Leo Sowerby. The Toronto Diocesan Boys' Choir School took an active part in preparing the boys for this, under the direction of George Maybee. The Communion was celebrated according to the rites of all the chief provinces of the Anglican Communion, and significant numbers of Toronto Anglicans were thus exposed for the first time to the mainstream of twentieth-century Prayer Book revision as represented by the South African rite of 1923, the English and American revisions of 1928, and the Scottish revision of 1929.

6.16 Rt Revd Frederick Wilkinson, bishop of Toronto (l.), with the Most Revd Michael Ramsey, archbishop of Canterbury (r.), in St James' clergy vestry at the time of the 1963 world Anglican Congress. Behind them is Archbishop Ramsey's chaplain, Revd Ian Satterthwaite, later bishop of Gibraltar.

6.17 Dean Gilling in the cope presented by St John's, York Mills, St James' first daughter church, for its 150th anniversary in 1967. With the dean is Canon Lewis Garnsworthy, then rector of St John's, later bishop of Toronto and archbishop of Ontario.

Hooper had accepted the principalship of a high school, and, finding the combination of that work with his duties at St James' excessively burdensome, he resigned as organist and choirmaster in 1965. His successor (1965–9) was Norman Hurrle (1927–89; see Figure 6.18), who had had his training at the Royal School of Church Music in England and came to St James' from St Matthias', Westmount, where he had directed a choir of men and boys while teaching music for the Protestant Board of Education of Greater Montreal. Appreciating Hooper's predicament, the corporation decided to appoint Hurrle as St James' first full-time organist and choirmaster. Hurrle promised great things in return and set out wholeheartedly to deliver them; there was a rapid growth in the repertoire, which came under him to equal that of any cathedral choir in the world, except perhaps for the absence of the great Victorian composers, with whom he seems to have had little sympathy. He also oversaw a thorough refurbishment of the organ during 1965–7, which he had made one of his conditions for accepting the appointment and entered into with

6.18 Norman Hurrle, choirmaster 1965–9.

enthusiasm and dedication; the work was undertaken by Casavant Frères, under the direction of Alan T. Jackson.[120] Although little mechanical work was done, all the pipes were revoiced and eighteen new ranks installed. The set of three trumpets were removed to the rear gallery, where they speak much more freely, and the console was also refurbished. Hurrle's interest and good judgement are very largely responsible for making the organ the admired instrument it is today, eminently suited to both accompaniment and recital, with the best of its original character preserved and tonally completed in a sympathetic style.

Hurrle found a sympathetic ally in J. Warren Eling, who became Gilling's curate in 1964 and his precentor in 1968. Together they created the Advent Sunday service of lessons, carols, and anthems in that year, and also the festal First Evensong of Christmas. Both these services remain highlights of St James' liturgical year. For the centenary of Confederation in 1967 a Cathedral Centennial Choir was formed, consisting of men and boys recruited from throughout the diocese and rehearsed by Hurrle and his sub-organist Patrick Wedd. During the week of 20–7 August, while the International Congress of Organists was being held in Toronto, this ensemble sang a full round of daily services in the English cathedral style. The morning services of Mattins or Holy Communion included settings by Howells, Thalben-Ball, Wood, Palestrina, and Britten, while the Evensongs offered even richer fare with music by Byrd, Gibbons, Purcell, Stanford, and Rubbra, and the first Canadian performance of Walton's 'The Twelve.' Wedd's voluntaries and recitals were quite equal to the choral music, making the event a remarkable tour de force.

It was for this choir that a program of non-musical events to occupy the boys' spare time was first put in place and entrusted to Andrew Barlow, then a cathedral lay clerk and an

25

undergraduate at Trinity College. It proved so successful that it later became a feature of the regular choir schedule and continues to this day. Barlow went on to take a doctorate in educational psychology and become head of the Junior School at Royal St George's College, Toronto, where the experience gained with boys at St James' continues to stand him in very good stead.

Hurrle's repertoire required both boys and men to be first-class singers. A larger number of young men were recruited at this time, some being offered scholarships to help pay their university tuition. Boys were also actively recruited. Hurrle began first to dream of, and then to insist on, a permanent choir school at the cathedral on the English model. Unfortunately, his dogged adherence to his uncompromising standards and the mounting cost of his ambitious program began to attract criticism, to which he reacted with a certain want of tact. The Choir Advisory Committee, formed in 1967, began to find its work difficult, and Gilling and his churchwardens became concerned. As early as 1966 Hurrle had offered to resign if his requirements were not met, and a letter written in May of 1969, renewing the offer, was accepted. Wedd resigned along with him. They departed under a cloud, which should not be allowed to obscure the fact that they were responsible for establishing the standard of repertoire and performance that the choir and organist and choirmaster strive to maintain to this day.

Peter MacKinnon filled in as interim organist and choirmaster in the summer of 1969, and in September Aubrey Foy was appointed, with Gerald Webster as his assistant. Foy had a very similar background to Hurrle; born in Canada, the son of a clergyman in the diocese of Ottawa, he had trained at the RSCM and worked in London, England, for three years, assisted Gerald Wheeler at St Matthew's, Ottawa, and George Maybee at Kingston Cathedral, and come to St James', like Hurrle, from St Matthias', Westmount. He set out both to keep up Hurrle's standards for church music and to raise the profile of the cathedral in the musical life of Toronto, and he worked equally closely and congenially with Eling (Figure 6.19). Notable Anglican choirs and organists became more frequent visitors, including King's College, Cambridge, with Gerald Wheeler and Patrick Wedd returning for a recital. St James' also began to be used more for secular concerts, such as Ernst Haefliger's performance of Schubert's *Winterreise* for the Canadian Broadcasting Corporation in February 1971. The King's Singers made their Toronto début in the auditorium of St James' Parish House, just when, at least outside Britain, their talents were only beginning to be realized beyond the inner circle of conoisseurs of Tudor church music.

Ritualism Revived, 1968–1986

Eling was an avowed Anglo-Catholic, and during his precentorship ceremonial began to evolve rapidly. In the mid-1970s he and Foy introduced a spectacular music service for Ascension Day, in which the choir accompanied by an orchestra rendered a full Viennese mass setting in Latin. For this service the Gloria in Excelsis was removed to its older position near the beginning of the service, as the music demanded, and the vestments and ceremonial of the Tridentine Roman Rite were somewhat incongruously grafted on to the otherwise intact Prayer Book service. There was a full liturgical procession with banners at the start, a gospel procession to the middle of the centre aisle where the reading was intoned, and an offertory procession from the back of the nave in which the ciborium, containing wafers deposited by the individual worshippers as they

6.19 Choir and clergy in May 1973. On the left are Michael Bedford-Jones, assistant, and Dean Gilling, with Warren Eling, precentor, in front. At the right end of the second row are James Wrightson, organ scholar; Gerald Webster, sub-organist; and Aubrey Foy, choirmaster. In the middle of the choir, between the second and third rows, is Andrew Barlow, then in charge of the boys' recreation.

arrived, was borne up with the flagon by representatives of the congregation. Haydn's *Mass in Time of War* was performed this way in 1974, styled a solemn intercession for peace in the world, and Beethoven's *Mass in C* in 1975. Similar services, but without the orchestra and with somewhat less elaborate ceremonial, were performed at Christmas and Easter. For these, eucharistic vestments were required and now became usual for the celebrant at the Communion, but vestments for the other two sacred ministers were acquired only for red and white festal days. Carols in procession were now sung on the first Sunday after Epiphany, as well as on Christmas Eve. The custom of having special music on the evening of Passion Sunday also continued, and in 1972 anthems by Greene, Blow, King John of Portugal, and Bach were sung then in place of the sermon. Choral Evensongs were introduced on Wednesdays at half past five, serving musically as dress rehearsals for the following Sunday.

In 1973 Gilling retired, first dismissing both his curates, and Paul Walker functioned as priest in charge until Hugh Vernon Stiff stepped down as bishop of Keewatin to become dean of Toronto. Stiff's parents had come from the Tractarian parish of St Alban's, High Holborn, in London, England. Upon emigrating to Toronto they briefly sampled St James' under Plumptre but soon switched their allegiance to the flagship Anglo-Catholic parish of St Mary Magdalene; Daniel Stiff, Hugh's father, told Plumptre he had a fine church but it could do with a whiff of incense. The canon's rejoinder is not preserved.[121] At St Mary Magdalene, Hugh rose to be head server and master of ceremonies. He served his curacy at St Aidan's under the scholarly but eccentric ritualist Basil Redvers English and was briefly in charge there after English's retirement.[122] As might have been expected from this background, his installation on 9 May 1974 (Figure 6.20) was much the most spectacular service St James' had yet seen. The new bishop of Toronto, Lewis Garnsworthy, had already appeared in cope and mitre for his own enthronement, despite a warning from Chancellor Soward that by doing so he would divide the diocese. He conducted the installation in full ritual dress, and once inducted, Stiff was himself vested in a new golden cope, decorated with the cathedral's coat of arms, specially made by Dorothy Shuter for the occasion.

This proved but a foretaste of what was to come. In fairly short order Robert Pursel, who had become attached to St James' in 1972 under Gilling, while completing a doctorate in theology at Trinity College, was appointed priest-sacrist, and 'ritualism' began to blossom at St James' as never before. Altar servers now appeared in ample surplices like those of the clergy. Candlebearers appeared in albs with coloured apparels on the amices, which changed with the season. The crucifer, now drawn from the Servers' Guild rather than the choir, appeared in the same garb but with a tunicle over. A procession from the sanctuary for the reading of the gospel became a standard feature of the main Sunday Communion, eventually going to the middle of the nave. Sung Mattins became restricted to the second Sunday of the month and vanished altogether from any month in which that Sunday was a festival. Wednesday sung Evensongs disappeared in favour of evening choral Eucharists on red-letter feast days. Ian Storey, a doctoral student in classics at the University of Toronto who had succeeded Barlow as director of the choirboys' recreation, was now also appointed head server, and this happy combination induced a steady flow of boys with changed voices into the Servers' Guild, while young adult men also began to volunteer in greater numbers. On the great festivals six taperers took part in the opening procession and also escorted the gospel book, following a precedent that Pursel had discovered in the canons of one of the ancient ecumenical councils. The rest of the ceremonial on these occasions remained as elaborate as it had been under Eling's direction but was gradually purged of almost all distinctively Roman touches. The fiddleback chasubles that Eling had acquired gave place to Gothic ones, and worship at St James' became a pattern of a genuinely Anglican high-churchmanship.

Hand in hand with this change, however, went another development with which Anglican purists might have been less pleased. For the first time, apart from the brief and abortive experiment with the New Zealand liturgy, services at St James' now began to depart from a strict adherence to the Book of Common Prayer. Bishop Stiff rearranged the components of the communion in the order of the pre-Reformation services and the original English Prayer Book of 1549, with the Gloria in Excelsis placed before the Collect of the Day and the Lord's Prayer

6.20 Installation of Rt Revd Hugh Vernon Stiff as dean, 9 May 1974. Stiff, in rochet and chimere, kneels before Bishop Garnsworthy, who is wearing cope and mitre. On Stiff's left, wearing a cope, is Revd Paul Walker, priest in charge between deans Gilling and Stiff. The taperer in the rear on the right is Ian Storey, soon to be appointed head server.

directly after the Prayer of Consecration. On the great festivals the anthem was also moved from the communion of the people to the offertory, to accompany elaborate censing of the altar, the offered bread and wine, and the people; thus Daniel Stiff, still vigorous in his old age, saw his wish for incense at St James' fulfilled.

To make time for all this ceremonial, part of the Prayer Book rite introduced at the Reformation – notably the Comfortable Words after the Absolution – were omitted. At these 'solemn Eucharists' the formalized movements of the Sarum rite were followed, and these eventually became the normal Sunday routine at eleven o'clock. For the nine-o'clock Sunday Communion the 'Toronto Rite' was introduced, which was the Prayer Book service rearranged by Eugene Fairweather, professor of dogmatic theology at Trinity College, in the order regarded as primitive by the dominant school of liturgical scholarship. This rite was celebrated with the priest facing the congregation across a movable altar. A volunteer choir of men and women was formed to sing these services twice a month, originally under the direction of Foy's assistant organist, Gerald Webster, and has continued ever since.

Special rites for holy days also now began to appear. The Advent Carol Service, Candlemas, and Holy Saturday began with the church in darkness and featured choir processions from the rear of the nave, dramatic use of lights, and elaborate revived ceremonial from pre-Reformation England. On the first Holy Saturday when Stiff kindled the New Fire, this nearly had disastrous consequences, because the smoke sensors went off and triggered the fire alarm. The Toronto Fire Department arrived in force and would have hacked the main doors of the church to pieces had Foy not had the presence of mind to send out the cathedral verger, David Stewart, to wave them off in the nick of time. The rites of Maundy Thursday also appeared; after an evening Eucharist commemorating the Last Supper, the reserved host was borne in procession with cross and candles to St George's Chapel, where it was left 'in repose' amid a blaze of candles. The church was then darkened, and the choir sang Psalm 22 with fauxbourdons by Webster, while the servers stripped the sanctuary and the clergy washed the altar. Good Friday began with Mattins in a church bared of ornament and culminated with the bearing in of a large wooden crucifix and a simple act of veneration.

All this elaboration certainly attracted a considerable body of new worshippers and, at least initially, increased givings as well. Before long, however, the novelty began to wear off, and after 1981 the Ascension Day services were found not to pay their way and were scaled down. Nor was criticism wanting. Evangelical Anglicans in the diocese began to complain that they no longer felt comfortable in their cathedral. Bishop Stiff, a graduate of Trinity College, decreed that Theological Education Sunday should be observed as a service for the life and work of his own alma mater, to balance the traditional service for Wycliffe College that had been held at St James' for many years because of its involvement in the founding of that college. The first Trinity College service, a 'solemn eucharist' with all the traditional Sarum movements, provoked a tart comment from Howard Clark, chancellor of Trinity and former primate of all Canada. But Stiff shrugged this off and attracted such enthusiastic support that for several years the whole contingent of clergy and servers at this service could be drawn from Trinity graduates, Trinity students, or sons of Trinity teaching staff.

By the late 1970s, however, Stiff seems to have decided that liturgically he had now gone as far as his congregation would let him. No attempt was ever made to bring in communion from the reserved sacrament on Good Friday or to observe Corpus Christi. After a few years the observance of the Sunday next before Advent as the Feast of Christ the King was discontinued, because significant numbers of regular worshippers deserted the church for that Sunday and went where they could find a service in stricter accord with the Prayer Book. When the Book of Alternative Services (BAS) came out, only the trial Communion service in traditional liturgical language was introduced at the cathedral, and that only at the nine-o'clock Sunday communions, where the virtually identical Toronto Rite had already become established. Otherwise the experimental rites were represented only by a form used for baptisms, adapted not from the alternative Canadian book but from the closely related American Episcopal rite. Suggestions that the main Sunday service should be further assimilated to the BAS pattern met with a firm refusal, even when they came from the highest quarter. Although he had welcomed the experimental book when it came out, Stiff grew dissatisfied with it when he had used it week in, week out at the nine-o'clock Sunday services and came to the conclusion that it represented too radical a departure for his taste from the mainstream of Anglican liturgical tradition. Far from decreasing attendance, however, his conservative policy attracted many worshippers who had been upset by the changes introduced into the once familiar services of their parish churches.

Being for the most part staunch monarchists, these recruits were also pleased with the special service, commissioned by the government of Ontario, held to commemorate the silver jubilee of Queen Elizabeth II in 1977. The distinctive suffrages for the annual Accession Day service, which had appeared in the first Canadian Prayer Book but had been dropped from the revision of 1959–62, were reintroduced on this occasion and have been used at Evensong on the Sunday nearest Accession Day (6 February) in every year since.

Another drawing card of St James' under Stiff was the consistently high quality and varied character of the preaching. Though himself a very able preacher of the same school as Riley, he had no wish to monopolize his pulpit but instead gave full scope to his staff clergy and to a galaxy of able honorary assistants and distinguished visitors. Thus alongside the Riley tradition as continued by Stiff, Michael Bedford-Jones, and David Bousfield, worshippers at St James' could hear the more rhetorical and learned style of William McKeachie, Robert Pursel, and Fred Etherden; the resonant delivery of the ex-United-Churchmen Donald Henderson and Leonard Griffith, with their vivid painting of scenes from scripture; and also a more personal and anecdotal style that Gerald Moffatt might not have fully approved, but which appeared at its best from Glenn Pritchard. Guest preachers included such distinguished theologians of the Anglican Communion as Urban T. Holmes and Archbishop Donald Coggan of Canterbury. The junior members of the clerical staff were also expected to take their turn; and under the direction of a dean who required them to submit all their efforts for vetting beforehand, they made rapid strides.

A further attraction was the cathedral's adherence to traditional church music professionally rendered. After accepting a full-time teaching post at St Andrew's College, Aurora, in September 1977. Foy found it increasingly difficult to fulfil his duties at St James', and the authorities began to search for a successor. A year later he resigned, and the work devolved upon Mervyn Games, who had become assistant organist after Webster went to St Thomas's Church early in 1977. Games was an exceptionally young man to head the music program at a church of St James' stature, at least according to late-twentieth-century notions, and his undoubted gifts did not secure respect in all quarters for his very definite views on how pieces ought to be performed. He nevertheless led the music ably in a trying situation and was particularly successful in recruiting new boys for the choir. Disappointed in his hopes of making his new position permanent, he in turn left at the end of 1978 to become organist and choirmaster at St Paul's Cathedral in London, Ontario – a good beginning for what was to be a distinguished career.

In January 1979 Giles Bryant took up the duties, at first as an interim appointee; but he gave such satisfaction that the appointment was made permanent a few months later. Bryant was born in England in 1934 and first came to Canada in 1959. Besides singing professionally with the Festival Singers he had served in Toronto as an organist at Grace Church on the Hill, St Andrew's Presbyterian Church, and Trinity College and had succeeded Healey Willan at St Mary Magdalene's in 1968. He returned to England in 1975 to be music director at Cranborne Chase School but came back to Canada in 1978 to be conductor of the Festival Singers. Probably it was his work with them and at St Mary Magdalene's, where Bishop Stiff had grown up, that most commended him to the authorities at St James'. He has enjoyed the help of a succession of capable assistants – Norman McBeth from May 1979 until 1990, Ian Sadler briefly during 1990, and since then Christopher Dawes. All have continued the tradition of fine solo and accompanimental playing begun by Wedd and have shared the administrative load.

Bryant was also fortunate in that, shortly before his arrival, a Choir and Music Trust had been established. This enabled the cathedral to offer several choral scholarships tenable at Royal St George's College, an Anglican boys' school in Toronto established in the 1960s with a particular emphasis on cultivating traditional church music. In 1980 Bryant himself joined the school staff and so was able to train these scholars in both places. Private lessons were also made available to boys by some of the adult lay clerks, and the cumulative effect has been a noticeable improvement in the strength and quality of the boys' section, to the point where several boys have made solo recordings and sung solo engagements outside the cathedral. Like Hurrle before him, Bryant has also made full use of his connections with the larger musical world in Toronto to recruit young men of talent and promise for the choir.

He has also built on and extended the efforts begun by Foy and Eling to reach out to music-lovers beyond the regular worshippers. Beginning in the fall of 1979 the cathedral was made available for Tuesday lunchtime recitals by outside organists and chamber artists, and these came to attract a loyal audience, mostly of workers in the nearby financial district. A recording of Christmas music sold well and attracted favourable notice, and five other recordings have followed, reviving a practice begun under Hooper. Services also continue to be recorded occasionally for broadcast on radio or television. The choir has raised its profile in Toronto by performing in the Healey Willan centenary celebrations in 1980, at the opening of the new Roy Thomson concert hall on 25 September 1982, and regularly at the Toronto *Star*'s Christmas carol concerts since 1979. It has also given occasional performances elsewhere, as at Sudbury in 1982 and Belleville in 1988. The choral scholars and other boys enrolled at St George's have been able to make several visits to the British Isles and the European mainland under the auspices of the college. More touring could have been done; but Bryant has shown himself thoroughly in sympathy with the view, held by all his predecessors at least since Ham and most heartily endorsed by Bishop Stiff, that the choir exists first and foremost to render the services in the cathedral.

Conversely, however, the cathedral has played host to an increasing number and variety of visiting choirs and recitalists. Besides bringing in many Canadian and American choirs, Bryant's abiding connection with English church musicians has enabled him to attract the choirs of Winchester, Southwark, and Chichester cathedrals singing either concert programs or services. St James' also provided the setting of several concerts in the International Choral Festival of 1989. Choral Evensongs by both the boys' and girls' diocesan choir schools have become annual events and have given an important encouragement to talented young Canadian singers. Recitalists from at home and abroad have included Jane Parker-Smith, Melville Cook, John Tuttle, Harrison Oxley, Francis Jackson, Jean Guillou, David Liddle, Robert Noehren, and, most recently, Diane Bish. David Marcus-Roland has also acted as impresario for several concert series, each involving an assemblage of artists – by six different organists in 1981 and 1983, by six different choirs singing six Bach motets in 1985, and in 1989 'The Gifts of Music' featuring the cathedral choir, Bryant and McBeth as soloists, and visiting artists. Welcome encouragement has also been given from time to time to young Canadian instrumentalists by inviting them to accompany the services.

6.21 The cathedral choir and chorus, with Sinfonia Mississauga, performing Haydn's *Creation*,
31 January 1997.

All this high culture has been complemented by a series of 'hymn sings,' in which churchgoers and the public at large are invited to make a joyful noise unto the Lord. These have combined a good vocal workout with presentation of little-known background on the origin and history of favourites and an introduction to hymns that deserve to be known better, all wittily delivered. The format was conceived and first carried out by Marcus-Roland, but Bryant has increasingly found it a congenial outlet for his own interest in hymnography and his gifts as a raconteur. A similar format has been followed in the annual 'Celebration of Life for Seniors,' which has consistently attracted a large congregation, most of whom do not regularly worship at the cathedral. From the bicentenary commemorations in 1996–7 Bryant recruited an amateur St James' Cathedral Chorus, with the nine-o'clock choir as its core, which performed alongside the men and boys with Sinfonia Mississauga in Haydn's *Creation* in January 1997 and with the band of the Royal Regiment of Canada under Major Gino Falconi in a 'Last Night of the Proms' in May 1997, when the audience also joined with gusto in several pieces. Many who attended this concert expressed the hope that it would become an annual event, and it was repeated in 1998 to another full house.

The organ received a new solid-state console in 1979, made by J.W. Walker and Sons of England. Then in 1982, after a vigorous appeal launched by Bishop Stiff, the cathedral's interior was redecorated and repainted throughout, and as an adjunct the organ was completely cleaned. At the rededication service on 24 October 1982 the music included Liszt's monumental 'Fantasia and Fugue on *Ad nos ad salutarem undam'* – a major undertaking by McBeth – as well as works by Howells and Vaughan Williams. A celebratory concert followed on 17 November, devoted to English composers of the Restoration period. A minor coda to the restoration was the addition to the organ in 1984 of some wood pipes by Jerroll Adams of Michigan, effecting a slight tonal change.

The music for the restoration commemoration well exemplified two types of works that Bryant has particularly sought to add to the repertoire: pieces from the seventeenth century and the early part of the eighteenth and works by English composers of the first half of the twentieth. In tandem with this, however, the choir has also developed an impressive repertoire of modern French music by Duruflé, Langlais, Roger Ducasse, Vierne, and Dupré and has begun lately to undertake more recent Canadian compositions. As one might have expected from both Bryant's background and Stiff's, there has also been a marked increase in the use of plainsong, but not to the detriment of Anglican chant, which holds its own for the psalms at Morning and Evening Prayer.

Recent Liturgical Developments, 1986–Present

Hugh Stiff retired in 1986 and was followed by another Trinity graduate, Sheldon Duncan Abraham. The new dean's strengths lay in preaching, administration, and pastoral ministry rather than in liturgics, and he had no previous experience serving in a church where elaborate ceremonial was practised. With characteristic good sense, however, he undertook to maintain the type of worship that had made St James' a thriving church despite its lack of a local congregational base and recruited capable assistants with the required expertise. When Storey found he could no longer combine his work with the choristers and servers with his teaching responsibilities at Trent University, a successor was found from within the guild in William Sewers, who conscientiously maintained the standard of serving that Storey had established and continued to recruit able young men.

At the nine-o'clock Sunday Eucharist the modern-language rite from the BAS was introduced soon after Dean Abraham's arrival and met with general approval from the regular worshippers at that hour; it had already been in use for some years at a new service at half past seven on Christmas Eve. These services have proved particularly popular with the young families living in the many apartment buildings newly built in the neighbourhood and have helped the cathedral to attract a locally based body of worshippers for the first time since the 1920s. Deans Abraham and Stoute have enjoyed a cordial relationship with Bishop Finlay and readily fell in with his preference for BAS rites at most diocesan services, with the celebrant facing the people. At the same time, however, the full round of traditional services has been maintained for the many worshippers who seek them out from all over greater Toronto; indeed Abraham quickly won popularity by restoring to the services for the great festivals and midweek saints' days the parts of the Prayer Book rite that Bishop Stiff had been accustomed to omit and by returning the anthem to its rubrical place during the administration of the communion. As a cathedral, St James' continues to be a frequent host for state services and for interfaith services on other occasions of public importance.

About two weeks before Easter Sunday of 1989, right after the main morning service, Dean Abraham told the head server, William Sewers, that he wished women to be admitted to

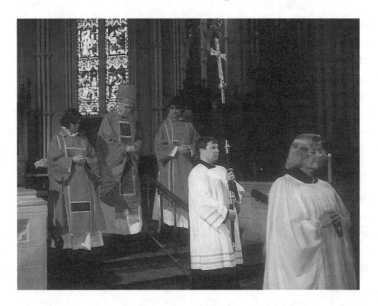

6.22 Most Revd Michael Peers, primate of all Canada, leaving the chancel after celebrating
the Eucharist, with the Revd Jane Watanabe as deacon and Jonathan Rudd as subdeacon, Whitsunday
1996. Preceding them are Paul Seddon, head server, and Leslie Derbecker, sacrist.

the Servers' Guild. This move was not strictly unprecedented, for Storey had on one occasion
recruited a server's sister to fill in for a missing taperer, and the only unfavourable comment
had come from one elderly worshipper who said: 'That boy's hair is much too long.' Sewers,
however, said he could not acquiesce in the innovation and immediately resigned. The servers
on duty got this news as they were changing out of their vestments in their vestry. The senior
members then asked the dean to meet with the guild, and this began three-way discussions also
involving those stewards, both men and women, who had been serving at the nine a.m. Sunday
Eucharists for some time. It soon appeared that everyone concerned wished to maintain the
standards and traditions of the guild, and six women were formally admitted in a service of
corporate worship in the following October. The Servers' Guild then resumed responsibility
for serving at the nine-o'clock services on Sunday morning.

Most servers welcomed all aspects of this change. The normal attrition that affected the guild
at this time, as young men went away to study or took on responsibilities that made continued
serving difficult, was misinterpreted by some parishioners as widespread disaffection among the
male servers with having women colleagues. In fact only three junior servers could be said to
have left directly because of the change, and they did so more out of loyalty to a very capable and
conscientious mentor than from any firm opinion on the question of admitting women. After
the main Easter Sunday Eucharist – the last service where he was master of ceremonies – Sewers
had received a round of hearty applause from his colleagues as a tribute to his years of distinguished leadership.

There had also, however, been some dissatisfaction with the way the news of the decision had
reached the guild; and to prevent similar problems in future, the senior servers asked the dean to
revive the office of priest-sacrist and bestow it on the Revd John Gibaut, an associate priest

attached to the cathedral while pursuing an advanced theological degree at Trinity College. The dean readily agreed, and Gibaut's liturgical knowledge, concern for high standards, and pastoral skills contributed greatly to the successful transition. Under his guidance the best traditions of the guild were ably maintained by the new head server, Paul Seddon (Figure 6.22).

A more serious loss occurred in 1991, after the Revd Carol Langley, the first woman cleric to serve on staff at St James', was ordained priest. This time three senior servers or sacrists submitted their resignations, because they could not in good conscience serve for a woman priest and felt they would be awkwardly placed if they made that a condition for continuing to serve. But one senior server who stepped down at this time felt able to return five years later, after the priesthood of women had ceased to be a contentious issue within the parish.

As a preacher Abraham was somewhat more inclined to strike a personal note than his three predecessors had been. Perhaps the most notable innovation in his sermons was an attempt to convey to the uninitiated the most generally accepted findings of Biblical criticism – something Stiff had always eschewed himself and interdicted to his curates, as likely to 'disturb the faithful.' In this matter Stiff proved a true prophet; for instance, Abraham's standard Easter Sunday sermon, which he intended to emphasize the spiritual reality of Christ's resurrection, regularly left some hearers in doubt whether he believed in the bodily resurrection at all. But his more pastoral sermons were universally esteemed, revealing as they did his deep human sympathy, and most regular worshippers grew to value his homely illustrations and understated wit.

Visits by distinguished guest preachers had already begun to taper off in Stiff's later years, probably because of the departure of McKeachie and Pursel with their extensive English and American connections, and a reduced number of honorary assistants also tended to lessen the variety, though not the quality, of the pulpit fare. An attempt to compensate by inviting the honorary canons to preach at evensong was not a uniform success. One senior canon, more distinguished for his pastoral ministry in his poor inner-city neighbourhood than for his pulpit skills, went on for over half an hour, managing to combine comment on his text with a panegyric of the Prince of Wales and a denunciation of the Book of Alternative Services, which he boasted was regularly used in his church on the fifth Sunday of every February.

In 1992 Philip Hobson arrived as priest-vicar and Jane Watanabe as associate priest. Both continued to serve after Dean Douglas Stoute was appointed in 1994. As preachers they formed a distinguished triad. Hobson, as was noted above, continued the tradition established by Riley but added a refined scholarship and culture reminiscent of Welch. Watanabe favoured the more personal and anecdotal style pioneered at St James', at least in living memory, by Pritchard. Stoute, as befitted a Cambridge man with an advanced degree in history, weaves historical and intellectual background into his sermons with a thoroughness that has probably not been seen at St James' since Plumptre's heyday.

In liturgical matters Stoute has displayed the same appreciation as Abraham for traditions of proven worth and like him has delegated a great measure of responsibility to his assistant clergy. He has been fortunate in having a pair of assistants who were expert in that field and made it a leading concern. In 1996, in recognition of his role in orchestrating the more elaborate services with the choirmaster under the dean's direction and in fostering the musical and liturgical tradition, Hobson was named a canon by Bishop Finlay – the first working assistant at St James' to have that title since Edmund Baldwin in Dean Grasett's time – and at the same time received the title of precentor from the dean. Then in June 1997, at the climax of the

6.23 HM Queen Elizabeth II and HRH the Duke of Edinburgh, with Bishop Finlay,
greeting the cathedral choir and staff after Morning Prayer, 29 June 1997

bicentenary celebrations (Figure 6.23), the bishop announced that both assistant clerics would be taking up incumbencies of parish churches in the autumn. As might have been anticipated, this announcement roused mixed feelings among those who serve in their several capacities in the chancel. It charged Bryant and Seddon with the somewhat unusual duty of 'running in' a new vicar and assistant both at the same time, to ensure that there is no sharp break in the liturgical tradition. They took up the challenge with the full force of their not inconsiderable talents and found the new members of the clerical staff – Judy Rois and Kevin Robertson – to be both quick and grateful learners.

The New Era

Within living memory, St James' ability to survive as a downtown church with no local worshippers was seriously questioned. In fact it has not merely survived but flourished, by meeting a very wide spectrum of demands and holding them all in a careful balance. Its dual status as both a cathedral and a parochial church has posed a particular challenge and one that is perhaps uniquely Canadian; for while many American Episcopal churches serve the same double function, relatively few of them have to exist in communities where the English cathedral tradition of music and worship is as well known and as keenly demanded as it continues to be in Toronto. There cannot be many churches in the English-speaking world that have to provide the full range of worship exemplified by a typical Sunday at St James': the devout simplicity of a traditional Prayer Book 'low' celebration at eight a.m.; an hour later, a parish communion according to a contemporary rite, celebrated at a nave altar by a priest facing the people, and with a setting and hymns designed to be sung by all; at a quarter after ten, Morning Prayer said quietly at a side altar; at eleven o'clock, a Prayer Book Eucharist celebrated with outward splendour to a high musical and liturgical standard, but still designed to engage the worshippers fully; and at half past four in the afternoon, an Evensong approaching most nearly to the English cathedral type, where the two hymns are all the singing expected from those in the pews, and they can otherwise make their offering through prayer and the contemplation of the Prayer Book office formally rendered to the glory of God.

It was a matter of some pride to those responsible for the services when Lionel Dakers, director of the Royal School of Church Music, wrote these kind words: 'We also need to take into account more fully the concept of worship as being fair shares for all. I have experienced this in widely varying circumstances. St James' Cathedral, Toronto, All Souls', Langham Place, London and the Church of St Thomas of Canterbury in Salisbury immediately spring to mind as particularly memorable instances where this has been carefully thought through, each in an entirely different way, so that all needs have been met. What resulted was an all-embracing comprehensiveness of worship, with no threat to the role of the choir.'[123]

The standards of music and liturgy at St James' are dictated by the interest, encouragement, and support of the clergy and the congregation. Both clergy and people seek the best in both endeavours and expect those responsible to rise to this demand. The traditions planted by Edward Welch and Albert Ham a century ago have been carefully fostered and jealously guarded by clergy and people, clerks and musicians, since that time. Those who tend them now are confident that they can prove valued and effective in God's service long after Christendom has entered its third millennium.

Bishops having jurisdiction over York (later Toronto) with their suffragans and assistants

SUFFRAGAN BISHOPS in the diocese of Toronto have never had titular sees. Until 1981 they and any assistant bishops acted throughout the diocese. In that year Archbishop Garnsworthy divided the diocese into areas, assigning the suburbs of Toronto and the outlying parts to area suffragans. Both the boundaries of the areas and the assignments of particular suffragans have since varied. For simplicity's sake and to save space, suffragans consecrated since 1981 are here designated 'area suffragan.'

The primate of Canada and the metropolitans of the eastern ecclesiastical provinces have no fixed sees. They are elected, originally by their fellow bishops and latterly by the appropriate synods. The metropolitans retain their current sees when chosen, and so until the 1960s did the primate. Hence several bishops of Toronto have served for parts of their episcopates as primates or metropolitans, taking the title 'archbishop of Toronto.' These are noted below.

Rt Revd Charles INGLIS, 1st bishop of Nova Scotia 1787–93
Rt Revd Jacob MOUNTAIN, 1st bishop of Quebec 1793–1825
Rt Revd Charles James STUART, 2nd bishop of Quebec 1825–36
Rt Revd George Jehoshaphat MOUNTAIN, Assistant bishop of Quebec 1836–7
       3rd bishop of Quebec 1837–9
Rt Revd John STRACHAN, 1st bishop of Toronto 1839–67
Rt Revd Alexander Neil BETHUNE, coadjutor bishop of Toronto 1866–7
       2nd bishop of Toronto 1867–79
Most Revd Arthur SWEATMAN, 3rd bishop of Toronto 1879–1909
       metropolitan of Ontario and primate of all Canada 1907–9
  Rt Revd William Day Reeve, assistant bishop of Toronto 1907–24
Most Revd James Fielding SWEENY, 4th bishop of Toronto 1909–32
       metropolitan of Ontario 1932
Most Revd Derwyn Trevor OWEN, 5th bishop of Toronto 1932–47
       primate of all Canada 1934–47
Rt Revd Alton Ray BEVERLEY, suffragan bishop of Toronto 1934–47
       6th bishop of Toronto 1947–55

Rt Revd Frederick Hugh WILKINSON, coadjutor bishop of Toronto 1953–5
    7th bishop of Toronto 1955–66
Rt Revd George Boyd SNELL, suffragan bishop of Toronto 1955–9
    coadjutor bishop of Toronto 1959–66, 8th bishop of Toronto 1966–72
Rt Revd Henry Robert Hunt, suffragan bishop of Toronto 1960–71
Most Revd Lewis Samuel GARNSWORTHY, suffragan bishop of Toronto 1968–72
    9th bishop of Toronto 1972–88, metropolitan of Ontario 1979–88
Rt Revd Allan Alexander Read, suffragan bishop of Toronto 1972–81
Rt Revd. Hugh Vernon Stiff, assistant bishop of Toronto 1977–86
Rt Revd Arthur Durrant Brown, area suffragan 1981–93
Rt Revd Desmond Charles Hunt, area suffragan 1981–6
Rt Revd Geoffrey Howard Parke-Taylor, area suffragan 1981–5
Rt Revd Basil Tonks, area suffragan 1981–6
Rt Revd Joachim Carl Fricker, area suffragan 1985–93
Rt Revd James Taylor Pryce, area suffragan 1985–present
Rt Revd Terence FINLAY, area suffragan 1986–7
    coadjutor bishop of Toronto 1987–8, 10th bishop of Toronto 1988–present
Rt Revd Douglas Charles Blackwell, area suffragan 1988–present
Rt Revd Michael Hugh Harold Bedford-Jones, area suffragan 1994–present
Rt Revd Victoria Matthews, area suffragan 1994–7
Rt Revd Anne Tottenham, area suffragan 1997–present

Staff Clergy of the Church at York, later St James' Church and Cathedral, Toronto with Deaconesses and Parish Workers

ASSISTANTS ARE LISTED BELOW the incumbent under whom they served and are repeated where necessary. Down to 1890 the list has been compiled chiefly from the registers; but since the registers mostly list only officiants, celebrants, and preachers, assistants who arrived as deacons may not be attested there for their first year or so of service. For John Strachan's incumbency we have listed all clergy who regularly ministered in the church, even if they were not on its payroll; for later times, honorary assistants have not been included. Strachan's absences in Cornwall in 1814 and in Great Britain in the 1820s also obliged him to leave various clerics in charge for prolonged periods while he remained the incumbent.

The incumbents who served before the formal creation of the rectory by Lieutenant-Governor Sir John Colborne in 1836 often used the title of 'rector' but are here styled 'parson.' While St Alban's was the de jure cathedral, the bishop was dean in his own right, but the rector of St James' was regularly subdean and president of the chapter.

(Revd Thomas RADDISH, missionary at York 1796–7)
Revd George Okill STEWART, parson of York 1800–12
Rt Revd John STRACHAN, parson of York 1812–36, rector of St James' 1836–47
   Revd Richard Pollard, parson of Sandwich, assistant c. 1812–13
   Revd Robert Addison, priest in charge 1814
   Revd William Macaulay, priest in charge 1820–1
   Revd George Archbold, priest in charge 1824
   Revd W.B. Brown, priest in charge 1824
   Revd John Wenham, priest in charge 1824
   Revd Joseph Hudson, assistant 1826–33
   Revd Thomas Phillips, assistant 1826–33, priest in charge 1826–7
   Revd Charles Dade, assistant c. 1827–30
   Revd Joseph Harris, assistant 1829–30
   Revd William Boulton, assistant 1830–33
   Revd Charles Matthews, assistant 1830–33
   Revd George J. Gwynne, assistant 1833–4
   Revd George Maynard, assistant 1837–8

Revd Henry Scadding, assistant 1839–47
Revd T.E. Welby, assistant 1840–1
Revd T.H.M. Bartlett, assistant 1842
Revd Alexander Sanson, assistant 1843–4
Revd W.H. Ripley, assistant 1844–6
Very Revd Henry James GRASETT, assistant 1835–47,
      rector of St James' 1847–82, dean of Toronto 1867–82
Revd George Bourn, assistant 1847–8
Revd Richard Mitchele, assistant 1848–9
Revd Canon Edmund Baldwin, assistant 1850–76
Revd A. Stewart, assistant 1856
Revd Samuel Johnson Boddy, assistant 1858–63
Revd Conway Edward Cartwright, assistant 1863–6
Revd J.S. Baker, assistant 1866–8
Revd. A.G.L. Trew, assistant 1868–9
Revd Arundel Charles Hill, assistant 1870–3
Revd Henry Harcourt Waters, assistant 1872–5
Revd Richard Waddilove Eustace Greene, assistant 1873–82
Revd Charles Raymond Matthew, assistant 1875–6
Revd Joseph Williams, assistant 1877
Revd William Stephen Rainsford, assistant 1878–82
Revd Canon John Philip DUMOULIN, rector of St James' 1882–96
      subdean of St Alban's 1889–96
Revd Richard Waddilove Eustace Greene, assistant 1882–5
Revd Dyson Hague, assistant 1882–5
Revd Hugh Pooley Hobson, assistant 1886–8
Revd William Grant, assistant 1886
Revd John Keal Powell, assistant 1888–9
Revd Henry Jackson Winterbourne, assistant 1889–92
Revd Walter John Creighton, assistant 1889–90
Revd James George Lewis, assistant 1890–2
Revd Arthur Herbert Manning, assistant 1892–4
Revd Charles John Boulden, assistant 1893–6
Revd Charles Henry Mockridge, priest in charge 1896
Rt Revd Edward SULLIVAN, rector of St James' and subdean of St Alban's 1896–9
Revd Charles Henry Mockridge, assistant 1896
Miss M.E. Dixon, deaconess 1896–9
Revd Richard Ashcroft, assistant 1897–9
Revd George Charles Wallis, assistant 1897–9
Revd Canon Edward Ashurst WELCH, rector of St James'
      and subdean of St Alban's 1899–1909
Revd Richard Ashcroft, assistant 1899–1900
Revd George Charles Wallis, assistant 1899–1901
Revd William Clark, assistant 1899–1901

Miss M.E. Dixon, deaconess 1899–1907
Revd Adam Urias de Pencier, assistant 1901–4
Revd Derwyn Trevor Owen, assistant 1902–7
Revd Lewis Wilmot Bovell Broughall, assistant 1905–7
Revd Gore Munbee Barrow, assistant 1907–9
Miss Boswell, deaconess 1907–9
Revd James Richard Hammond Warren, assistant 1908–9
Revd Canon Henry Pemberton PLUMPTRE, rector of St James'
        and subdean of St Alban's 1909–35
Revd Gore Munbee Barrow, assistant 1909–12
Revd James Richard Hammond Warren, assistant 1909–10
Miss Boswell, deaconess 1909–25
Revd Charles Venn Pilcher, assistant 1910–15
Miss Burpe, deaconess 1910–16
Revd Francis John Moore, assistant 1912–16, 1918–26
Revd Sidney Childs assistant, 1917–19
Revd Harold Douglass Caesar, assistant 1918–19
Miss G.H. Baldrey deaconess, 1918–19
Revd Arthur Briarly Browne, assistant 1926–35
Revd William John Minto Swan, assistant 1926–8
Revd William Alexander Brown, assistant 1928–31
Revd Arthur Briarly Browne, priest in charge 1935–7
Revd Kenneth Douglas Whatmough, assistant 1935–7
Very Revd Charles Edward RILEY, rector of St James' and dean of Toronto 1937–61
Revd Robert Lowder Seaborn, assistant 1937–41
Miss Elizabeth D. Gulliver, deaconess 1937–44
Revd Gerald Early Moffatt, assistant 1942–7
Miss Florence Lea (later Mrs Florence Lea Goddard), deaconess 1944–58
Revd William Michael Campbell Bothwell, assistant 1947–52
Revd John Ames Coombs, assistant 1951–61
Revd John Charles Bothwell, assistant 1951–3
Revd Ronald Edward Armstrong, assistant 1954–6
Revd Donald Whimbley Anderson, assistant 1957–9
Miss May Cameron, parish worker 1958–61
Revd Kenneth Hill, assistant 1958–61
Very Revd Walter Joseph GILLING, rector of St James' and dean of Toronto 1961–73
Revd Charles Albert Mitchell, assistant 1961–3
Revd William Ernest Moore, assistant 1961–4
Revd Keith William Gleed, assistant 1963–5
Revd James Allan Rix, assistant 1964–6
Revd John Warren Eling, assistant 1964–8, precentor 1968–73
Miss Gwendolyn Lodder, parish visitor 1964–73
Revd Victor Bruce Thorne Matthews, assistant 1966–9
Revd John Stafford Barton, vicar 1968–71

Revd Michael Hugh Harold Bedford-Jones, assistant 1968–73
Revd Douglas Charles Brown, assistant 1971–3
Revd Paul Garred Walker, assistant 1972–3
Revd William Noble McKeachie, associate 1972–3
Revd Robert Howard Pursel, associate 1972–3
Revd Paul Garred Walker, priest in charge 1973–4
Revd Douglas Charles Brown, assistant 1973–4
Revd William Noble McKeachie, associate 1973–4
Revd Robert Howard Pursel, associate 1973–4
Rt Revd Hugh Vernon STIFF, rector of St James' and dean of Toronto 1974–86
Revd Paul Garred Walker, assistant 1974–5
Revd Douglas Charles Brown, assistant 1974–5
Revd Michael Hugh Harold Bedford-Jones, assistant 1974–7
Revd William Noble McKeachie, associate 1974–8
Revd Robert Howard Pursel, associate 1974–5, priest-sacrist 1975–7
Revd Glenn Lawrence Pritchard, assistant 1976–7, vicar 1977–81
Revd Theo Ipema, assistant 1975–80
Revd James A. Bradley McCue, assistant 1979–83
Revd David Frederick Bousfield, vicar 1982–6
Revd Douglas N. Graydon, assistant 1984–5
Revd David Frederick Bousfield, vicar and priest in charge 1986–7
Very Revd Sheldon Duncan ABRAHAM, rector of St James'
        and dean of Toronto 1987–94
Revd David Frederick Bousfield, vicar 1987–8
Revd John Wilton, assistant 1987–90
Revd John Gibaut, associate priest-sacrist 1987–94
Revd Donald Dorrity, vicar 1989–92
Revd Donald Butler, priest on staff 1989–90
Revd Carol D. Langley, assistant 1990–92
Revd Philip Charles Hobson, vicar 1992–4
Revd M. Jane Watanable, associate 1992–4
Revd Philip Charles Hobson, vicar and priest in charge 1994
Very Revd Douglas Andrew STOUTE, rector of St James'
        and dean of Toronto 1994–present
Revd Philip Charles Hobson, vicar 1994–7, canon precentor 1996–7
Revd M. Jane Watanabe, associate 1994–7
Revd Judy Diane Rois, vicar 1997–present
Revd Kevin Thomas Robertson, assistant 1997–present

APPENDIX 3

Churchwardens and Deputy Wardens

EXCEPT DURING THE YEARS 1823–30 St James' has always had two churchwardens. By custom originally, and now by canon law, one is named by the incumbent and known as the rector's warden, while the other is elected by the vestry and known as the people's warden. In the following list the rector's warden always appears first. Down to 1939, the annual meeting of the vestry, at which the wardens are chosen, was held after Easter, and wardens served for 'split' years (for example, 1807–8, 1808–9). Since then it has been held in January or February and wardens are regarded as serving for calendar years (for example, 1981, 1982), and a double date implies service for two years or more.

1807–8	D'Arcy Boulton and William Allan	1868–9	George William Allan and George Duggan
1808–9	Thomas Ridout and William Allan		
1809–10	Samuel Jarvis and William Allan	1869–72	E.H. Rutherford and Clarke Gamble
1810–11	D. Cameron and William Allan		
1811–12	D. Cameron and John Denison	1872–81	J.K. Kerr and Clarke Gamble
1812–15	John Beverley Robinson and Henry J. Boulton	1881–3	Casimir Stanislas Gzowski and J.K. Kerr
1815–18	Alexander Wood and Thomas Ridout	1883–4	William Rees Brock and J.K. Kerr
1818–23	John Beverley Robinson and Henry J. Boulton	1884–90	William Rees Brock and O.A. Howland
1823–30	J.B. Macaulay	1890–2	Henry James Grasett, Jr and O.A. Howland
1830–2	S. Washburn and R. Stanton		
1832–41	R. Stanton and C.C. Small	1892–8	Henry James Grasett, Jr and R.N. Gooch
1841–9	Clarke Gamble and T.D. Harris		
1849–55	Lewis Moffatt and T.D. Harris	1898–1902	James Scott and A.S. Irving
1855–62	Joseph T. Ridout and T.D. Harris	1902–4	A.S. Irving and A.H. Campbell, Jr
1862–4	George Duggan and T.D. Harris	1904–8	J.H.G. Hagerty and A.H. Campbell, Jr.
1864–6	George Duggan and Thomas Galt		
1866–8	Clarke Gamble and George Duggan	1908–11	Frederick LeMesurier Grasett and A.H. Campbell, Jr

1911–12	Robert Inglis and Frederick LeMesurier Grasett
1912–16	Henry Brock and Frederick LeMesurier Grasett
1916–19	Henry Brock and D. Campbell Meyers
1919–20	Campbell Humphrey and D. Campbell Meyers
1920–2	Campbell Humphrey and W.B. Kingsmill
1922–3	Campbell Humphrey and H.D. Lockhart Gordon
1923–4	H.C. Scholfield and H.D. Lockhart Gordon
1924–9	H.C. Scholfield and C. Leslie Wilson
1929–31	W.B. Kingsmill and H.D. Lockhart Gordon
1931–5	G.R. Geary and H.W.A. Foster
1935–9	W.W. Denison and Elliot Grasett Strathy
1939–40	G. Lawton Ridout and Elliot Grasett Strathy
1940–1	G. Lawton Ridout and Ruggles George
1941–3	G. Lawton Ridout and F.J. Coombs
1944–5	F.J. Coombs and George Denison Kirkpatrick
1946–8	Clinton A. Neville and George Denison Kirkpatrick
1949–51	F. Hilton Wilkes and Colin M.A. Strathy
1952–3	Colin M.A. Strathy and W.B. Wellington
1954–5	W.B. Wellington and Robert B. Jackson
1956–60	Alexander M. Ramsey and Robert B. Jackson
1961–2	Alexander M. Ramsey and D. Martin Symons Robin E. Merry, assistant
1963–4	Robin E. Merry and D. Martin Symons

1964–7	Robin E. Merry and William J. Anderson
1967	James N. Harvie, deputy
1968–9	William J. Anderson and James N. Harvie
1968–9	Philip Wilson and R.H. Scrivener, deputies
1969–70	James N. Harvie and Godfrey Ridout
1969	R.H. Scrivener and William J. Anderson, deputies
1970	Philip Wilson, deputy
1971–2	James N. Harvie and W.L.G. James Philip Wilson and William N. Greer, deputies
1973–4	William J. Anderson and Sydney Wrightson
1975–6	John A. Seed and Sydney Wrightson Eric W. Nicholl, Kirk Merritt, and Kathleen R. Lewis, deputies
1976	John A. Seed and H. Murray James
1977	Sydney Wrightson (resigned) and H. Murray James William L.N. Somerville (replacement) Eric W. Nicholl, Stephen Clarke, and Jill Smith, deputies
1978	William L.N. Somerville and A. Leslie McDonald
1979	William L.N. Somerville and John A. Duff
1980–1	John A. Duff and J. Michael Esdaile Barry F.H. Graham and Murray H. McLachlan, deputies
1982	J. Michael Esdaile and Barry F.H. Graham James F. Lowe and Murray H. McLachlan, deputies
1983–4	Barry F.H. Graham and James F. Lowe Robert L. Falby and Roger Smith, deputies

1985   Robert L. Falby and James F. Lowe
        Paul F. Baston and
        Douglas Hunter, deputies
1986–7 Robert L. Falby and Paul F. Baston
1986   Douglas Hunter and
        James V. Emory, deputies
1987   James V. Emory and
        Barbara A. Hawkins, deputies
1988   James V. Emory and Paul F. Baston
        Barbara A. Hawkins and
        Edwin F. Hawken, deputies
1989   James V. Emory and
        Edwin F. Hawken
        Barbara A. Hawkins and
        Douglas Cook, deputies
1990–1 Barbara A. Hawkins and
        Edwin F. Hawken
1990   Douglas Cook and
        Philip Brown, deputies
1991   John B. Blain and
        Philip Brown, deputies

1992–3 John B. Blain and Philip Brown
        Edward Turner and
        Frederick S. Mallett, deputies
1994   Edward Turner and Philip Brown
        Pamela Stasiuk (later Guy) and
        Frederick S. Mallett, deputies
1995   Edward Turner and
        Frederick S. Mallett
        Pamela Guy and William Gow,
        deputies
1996–7 Frederick S. Mallett and Pamela Guy
1996   William Gow and
        Michael Scott, deputies
1997   Alfred Apps and Michael Scott,
        deputies
1998   Edwin F. Hawken and Jan Turner
        Barbara Ivey and
        Frank Walkingshaw, deputies

APPENDIX 4

Choirmasters, organists, and suborganists

Mr Hetherington, choirmaster 1819–c. 1825
William Henry Warren, organist 1834–8
Edward Hodges, organist 1838–9
Mrs W.H. Draper, choirmistress
    1839–c. 1840(?)
Mrs Gilkison, organist and choirmistress
    c. 1840–8
James Paton Clarke, organist and choirmaster
    1848–53
R.G. Paige, organist and choirmaster 1853–6
George F. Hayter, organist and choirmaster
    1856
Mr Fripp, interim organist and choirmaster(?)
    1856
John Carter, organist and choirmaster
    1856–78
Edgar R. Doward, organist and choirmaster
    1878–84
Walter A. Geddes, interim organist and
    choirmaster 1884
Charles Davies, organist and choirmaster
    1884–6
W. Elliott Haslam, choirmaster 1886–92
A.E. Carter, organist 1886–c. 1890
George Bowles, organist c. 1890–5
E.W. Schuch, choirmaster 1892–6
Charles Mockridge, organist 1895–6

Stocks Hammond, organist and
    choirmaster 1896–7
Humfrey Anger, interim organist and
    choirmaster 1897–8
Albert Ham, organist and choirmaster
    1898–1933
William Wells Hewitt, organist and
    choirmaster 1933–56
John Hooper, organist and choirmaster
    1956–65
Norman Hurrle, organist and choirmaster
    1965–9
Patrick Wedd, suborganist 1965(?)–9
Peter MacKinnon, interim organist and
    choirmaster 1969
Aubrey M. Foy, organist and choirmaster
    1969–77
Gerald Webster, suborganist 1969(?)–77
Mervyn Games, suborganist 1977
Mervyn Games, interim organist and
    choirmaster 1977–8
Giles Bryant, organist and choirmaster
    1978–present
Norman McBeth, suborganist 1979–90
Ian Sadler, suborganist 1990
Christopher Dawes, suborganist
    1990–present

APPENDIX 5

Presidents of the ACW
and its predecessors

A MISSIONARY SOCIETY seems to have been established at St James' in 1881. In 1888 it affiliated with the newly organized Woman's [sic] Auxiliary of the Board of Domestic and Foreign Missions of the Church of England in Canada and, in keeping with that body's constitution, began to elect a president as well as a secretary. By 1910 the parish group styled itself simply the Woman's Auxiliary. In 1968 a branch of the newly established Anglican Church Women was set up, but the old WA continued within this as the 'York Group.'

From 1900 onward the WA comprised both a Senior and a Junior Branch. In 1937 these were renamed the Afternoon and Evening Branches; but the Afternoon Branch was still considered the senior one, and its presidents were regarded as the leading women of the parish and are therefore are the ones listed here.

Before 1918 the president of the Senior Branch was often the rector's wife. From 1918 to 1935 the rector's wife was the honorary president of both branches. After that date the rector's wife continued to be honorary president of the Evening Branch, but the honorary president of the Afternoon Branch was the wife of the diocesan bishop. Until 1914 the officers of the WA served from March to February and their terms of office are accordingly expressed as 'split' years (e.g., 1888–9). After that date they run from January to December and are expressed as calendar years. Moira Esdaile, however, stepped down partway through her second year of office in 1980, and Jill Smith completed that year and then served for another.

Down to the reorganization of 1968, married women are listed by their husbands' names as was customary at the time.

PAROCHIAL MISSIONARY SOCIETY

| Miss Sybil Wilson | secretary | 1885 or earlier–1888 |
| Mrs W.R. Brock | president | 1888–9 |

WOMAN'S AUXILIARY

| Mrs. D.G. Hodgins | 1890–5 |
| Mrs J.P. DuMoulin | 1895–6 |

WOMAN'S AUXILIARY (CONT)

Mrs Edward Sullivan	1896–7
Mrs J.G. Hodgins	1897–9
Mrs E.A. Welch	1899–1908
Mrs H.P. Plumptre	1909–17
Mrs W. Assheton Smith	1918–20
Mrs F. LeM. Grasett	1921–4
Mrs A.H. Grasett	1925–31
Mrs W.E. Davidson	1932–7
Mrs H.W.A. Foster	1938–45
(Vacant 1946)	
Miss Adelaide F. Moss	1947–56
Mrs G.D. Kirkpatrick	1957–61
Mrs I.P. Cameron	1962–4
Miss Jean Masten	1965–7

ANGLICAN CHURCH WOMEN

Betsey Merry	1968–71
Mary Nesbitt	1972–5
Kathleen Lewis	1976–8
Moira Esdaile	1979–80 (1 1/2 years)
Jill Smith	1980–1 (1 1/2 years)
Jane Cook	1981–3
Barbara Hawkins	1984–5
Vivien Martin	1986
Barbara Falby	1987–8
Donna McLaren	1989–90
Marilyn Brown	1991–2
Jean Horsey	1993–4
Cecile Thompson	1995–6
Lorna Talbot	1997

Notes

ABBREVIATIONS

ACCA	Anglican Church of Canada Archives, Toronto
AO	Archives of Ontario, Toronto
AR	St James' Cathedral Annual Reports
BAS	The Book of Alternative Services (Toronto, 1985)
BCP	The Book of Common Prayer (editions cited as '1662', '1922 Canadian', '1962 Canadian', and so on)
CHR	*Canadian Historical Review*
CIHM	Canadian Inventory of Historical Microforms
CM	St James' Cathedral Corporation Minutes (cited by date), SJCA
C Russ	*The Correspondence of the Honourable Peter Russell*, ed. E.A. Cruikshank, 3 vols, Champlain Society, Toronto, 1932–6
C Sim	*The Correspondence of Lieut. Governor John Graves Simcoe*, ed. E.A. Cruikshank, 5 vols, Champlain Society, Toronto, 1923–31
DCB	*Dictionary of Canadian Biography* (cited by volume and date range)
DNB	*Dictionary of National Biography* (cited by entry)
DTA	(Anglican) Diocese of Toronto Archives
EC	*Evangelical Churchman*
EMC	*Encyclopedia of Music in Canada* (cited by page)
JCCHS	*Journal of the Canadian Church Historical Society*
LPSUC	Loyal and Patriotic Society of Upper Canada
NA	National Archives of Canada, Ottawa
RSCM	Royal School of Church Music
SJCA	St James' Cathedral Archives, Toronto
SJCM/N	*St James' Cathedral Magazine/Newsletter*
SLB	Strachan Letter Book, (MS.), Str P, AO
SPG	Society for the Propagation of the Gospel
SSAC Bulletin	*Bulletin of the Society for the Study of Architecture in Canada*
Str P	Strachan Papers (AO and TRL as specified)
Stu P	Stuart Papers, AO

TCA   Toronto City Archives
THB   Toronto Historical Board
TrCA   Trinity College Archives, Toronto
TRL   Toronto Reference Library
TRL, BR   Toronto Reference Library, Baldwin Room
TSJ   Toronto (Diocesan) Synod Journal, cited by year and page

I: A GEORGIAN PARISH, 1793–1839

1   The author would like to thank William Cooke for his advice in the preparation of this chapter.

2   Gt Britain, 31 Geo. III, c. xxxi 'Canada Act,' clauses 35–42; cf. Curtis Fahey, *The Anglican Experience in Upper Canada, 1791–1854* (Ottawa 1991), xv–xvi, 1–8, *et passim*. My contribution to this history of St James' owes a considerable debt to Dr Fahey's work in understanding Anglicanism in Upper Canada, which I have only been able to highlight here because of the constraints of space. For a critical assessment of Fahey's book, see Jud Purdy's review in the *JCCHS*, 36 (1994). Readers also may want to consult my other study of St James' in the Georgian era: 'The Church of England in York Upper Canada, 1793–1820,' MDiv thesis, Trinity College, Toronto, 1983, TrCA. For a general history of Upper Canada see Gerald M. Craig, *Upper Canada: The Formative Years, 1784–1841* (Toronto 1963). For a discussion of the clergy reserves, see Alan Wilson, *The Clergy Reserves of Upper Canada*, Canadian Historical Association Historical Booklet 23 (Ottawa 1969).

3   J. Mountain to Henry Dundas, SPG Report 1793, ACCA; cf. Mountain to Dundas, 15 Sept. 1794, in C. Sim, 3:91–4.

4   'Erastianism' is derived from the name of Swiss theologian Thomas Erastus (1524–83) and refers to the state's ascendancy and control over ecclesiastical affairs, particularly politically through a state church. An early proponent was the Anglican divine Richard Hooker, who defended the supremacy of the secular power in his *Laws of Ecclesiastical Polity* in the 1590s; F.L. Cross and E.A. Livingston, eds., *The Oxford Dictionary of the Christian Church*, 2nd ed. (Oxford 1978), 467–8.

5   E. Simcoe, 11 Aug. 1793, in Mary Quayle Innis, ed., *Mrs. Simcoe's Diary* (Toronto 1971), 103–4.

6   J.G. Simcoe to Dundas, 6 Nov. 1792, in *C Sim*, 1:251.

7   Carl Benn, *The Queen's Rangers: Three Eighteenth-Century Watercolours* (Toronto 1996), 5; Edith G. Firth, ed., *The Town of York, 1815–1834* (Toronto 1966), xxviii–xxix; and Craig, *Upper Canada*, 103–4, 161–4.

8   Benn, *Queen's Rangers*, 5; and Carl Benn, *Historic Fort York, 1793–1993* (Toronto 1993), 15–40.

9   Mountain, *A Charge Delivered to the Clergy of the Diocese of Quebec in the Year 1820* (Quebec 1820), 14–17; cf. Craig, *Upper Canada*, 165–81; and Strachan sermon, 'Now when they saw the boldness of Peter and John,' 21 Oct. 1832, Str P, AO.

10 Christopher Adamson, 'God's Continent Divided: Politics and Religion in Upper Canada and the Northern and Western United States, 1775 to 1841,' *Comparative Studies in Society and History* 36 (1994), 418; and W. Perkins Bull, *From Strachan to Owen* (Toronto 1937), 80.

11 SPG reports, *passim*, ACCA.

12 P. Russell to Mountain, 31 July 1797, in *C Russ* 1:234–5; Raddish Missionary Bond, 23 July 1796, and Memorandum, n.d., Fulham Papers, NA; and Thomas R. Millman, *Jacob Mountain: First Lord Bishop of Quebec* (Toronto 1947), 93–4.

13 Memorandum, n.d., D.W. Smith Papers, MTRL; Benn, 'Church of England,' 7–8; and Robert M. Black, 'Stablished in the Faith: The Church of England in Upper Canada, 1780–1867,' in Alan Hayes, ed., *By Grace Co-workers: Building the Anglican Diocese of Toronto, 1780–1989* (Toronto 1989), 25. For information about the Mississaugas, see Benn, *Fort York*, 34–9.

14 Russell to Simcoe, 9 Dec. 1797; and T.G. Ridout to George Ridout, 22 Dec. 1815, in Edith G. Firth, ed., *The Town of York, 1793–1815* (Toronto 1962), 46, 239–41; Firth, ed., *The Town of York, 1815–1834*, lxxi, xxxvii, 89 n22; Russell to the Duke of Portland, 20 Feb. 1797 and 18 July 1798, Russell to Mountain, 22 Feb. 1798; and John Stuart to the SPG, 7 Sept. 1799, all in A.R. Kelly, ed., *Jacob Mountain, First Lord Bishop of Quebec* (Quebec 1943), 239, 255; Mountain to Russell, 12 June 1799, and Russell to Mountain, 22 June 1799, in *C Russ*, 2:178–80, 3:249–50; respectively; *AR* (1833), 7–8; Millman, Mountain biography, *DCB*, 6:525–6; *Upper Canada Gazette*, 9 March 1799; Ernest Hawkins, *Annals of the Diocese of Toronto* (London 1848), 13; and A.H. Young, 'The Rev. Robert Addison and St. Mark's Church,' *Ontario History*, 19 (1922), 163.

15 J.P. Francis, 'Stuart, John' and 'Stuart, George Okill,' unpub. mss., n.d., ACCA; and A.J. Anderson, G. Stuart biography, *DCB*, 9:770–1.

16 See chap 5. The contractor may have been local builder John Smith; *History of Toronto and County of York*, 2 vols. (Toronto 1885), 2:148. On Berczy, see Mary Macaulay Allodi *et al.*, *Berczy* (Ottawa 1991). On the name, see *United Empire Loyalist*, 22 July 1826 ('Episcopal Church'); 2 June 1837 (St James'); and 21 Sept. 1828 (consecration).

17 St. James' Church Minute Book, 1807–30, *passim*, SJCA; various correspondence, Str P, AO, *passim*; and Millman, *The Life of Charles James Stewart* (London, Ont., 1953), 192, 208. See also Robert J. Burns, 'God's Chosen People: The Origins of Toronto Society, 1793–1818,' 1973, in J.M. Bumsted, ed., *Canadian History before Confederation*, 2nd ed. (Georgetown 1979), 263–76.

18 Minute Book, 1807–30, SJCA: List of Expenditures, 4 March 1807–4 March 1809, SJCA; *Upper Canada Gazette*, 28 Feb. 1807; Stuart to the SPG, 1809, in Firth, ed., *York, 1793–1815*, 209; Firth, ed., *York, 1815–1834*, 209 n 41; and 'Questions put by the Bishop, 9 July 1816,' in George W. Spragge, ed., *The John Strachan Letter Book, 1812–1834* (Toronto 1946), 118–23.

19 Mountain to the SPG, 16 Oct. 1801; and Stuart to the SPG, 1802, in Firth, ed., *York, 1793–1815*, 194–6; Firth, ed., *York, 1815–1834*, 141n66; G. Stuart to J. Stuart, 8 Nov. 1802, Stu P; *Upper Canada Gazette*, 14 Feb., 19 Sept., and 10 Oct. 1810; J.R. Robertson, 'The Old Blue School,' in George Dickson and Graeme Mercer Adam, eds., *A History of Upper Canada College* (Toronto 1893), 178–9; and A.H. Young, 'The Rev'd George Okill Stuart, M.A., LL.D.' *Ontario History*, 24 (1927), 513.

20 List of Expenditures, 4 March 1807–4, March 1809, SJCA; George Markland to John Strachan, 29 Nov. 1831, and Strachan to Markland, 30 Nov. 1831, SLB, 1827–39, 177–8, AO; Receipt, 7 July 1836, and Memorandum, 1 July 1838, Str P, AO; Strachan, 'A Report of the State of Religion in Upper Canada,' 1 March 1815, in Spragge, ed., *Strachan Letter Book*, 72–80; Elliot Grasett Strathy, *A Guide to the Cathedral Church of St. James* (Toronto 1932), 38; and *AR* (1883).

21 *Upper Canada Gazette*, 3 Oct. 1807.

22 Firth, ed., *York, 1793–1815*, lxx–lxxiii; Firth, ed., *York, 1815–1834*, lii, liv; and G. Stuart to the SPG, 8 Jan. 1802, in Firth, ed., *York, 1793–1815*, 195–6.

23 Benn, 'Church,' 99–102; and Paul Banfield, ed., 'A Bishop questions, a rector answers: Bishop Inglis' questionnaire of 1788,' *JCCHS*, 35 (1993), 34.

24 Minutes of the General Quarter Sessions of the Peace, 14 July 1802, in Firth, ed., *York, 1793–1815*, 100–1.

25 G. Stuart to the SPG, 17 Sept. 1804, in Firth, ed., *York, 1793–1815*, 198.

26 J. Stuart to James Stuart, 28 June 1804, Stu P.

27 Anderson, G. Stuart, biography, *DCB*, 9:771; Francis, 'Stuart, George,' 1; and G. Stuart to John Stuart, 17 July 1806, John Stuart to James Stuart, 8 Nov. 1802, and John Stuart to James Stuart, 28 June 1804, Stu P.

28 A.H. Young, 'A Quarrel in York,' unpub. MS. n.d., SJCA; and G. Stuart to John Stuart, 25 July 1803, Stu P.

29 G. Stuart Account Book, TRL; List of Expenditures, 4 March 1807–4 March 1809, SJCA; George Stephen Jarvis to Scadding, 5 Aug. 1869, and G. Stuart to the SPG, 8 Nov. 1802, in Firth, ed., *York, 1793–1815*, 203–5, 195–6, respectively; George Ridout to Mrs Thomas Ridout, 19 Oct. 1811, in Matilda Edgar, ed., *Ten Years in Upper Canada in Peace and War, 1805–1815*, (Toronto 1890), 64–5; and Henry Scadding, *Toronto of Old*, first pub. 1873 (Toronto 1966), 86–9.

30 G.M. Craig, Strachan biography, *DCB* 9:751–66; and Alexander Neil Bethune, *Memoir of the Right Reverend John Strachan* (Toronto and London 1870).

31 T.G. Ridout to Thomas Ridout, 16 June 1807, in Edgar, ed., *Ten Years in Upper Canada*, 25.

32 David Flint, *John Strachan: Pastor and Politician* (Toronto 1971), 34; Minute Book, 1807–30, Abstract of Pew Rent in Arrears, 4 June, 4 Dec. 1812, 4 March 1813, and various other entries for 1812, SJCA.

33 Firth, ed., *York, 1815–1834*, xlvi; Spragge, 'John Strachan's Contribution to Education,' *Canadian Historical Review*, 22 (1941), 147–58; and Strachan to Mountain, 10 Feb. 1818, in Firth, ed., *York, 1815–1834*, 145.

34 Strachan, *A Sermon Preached at York before the Legislative Council and House of Assembly* (York 1812). For another example of his loyalism, see *A Discourse on the Character of King George the Third* (Montreal 1810), which, among other things, compared the strengths of British liberties to the weaknesses of American ones. For a negative reaction to the Discourse, see 'A Friend of Peace,' letter, Kingston *Gazette*, 9 Oct. 1810.

35 Strachan to John Richardson, 30 Sept. 1812, in Spragge, ed., *Strachan Letter Book*, 15–17; and Sir George Prevost to Strachan, 16 Oct. 1813, J.B. Robinson Papers, AO.

36 Strachan to Prevost, Oct. 1812, in Spragge, ed., *Strachan Letter Book*, 12–13.

37 Kingston *Gazette*, 20 April, 13 Nov. 1813; Strachan, Speech on presenting a banner, n.d., in Spragge, ed., *Strachan Letter Book*, 10–12; Strachan to J.B. Robinson, 22 Nov. 1812, in Firth, ed., *York, 1793–1815*, 286–7; and Firth, ed., *York, 1815–1834*, 285 n 15, lxxvii.

38 LPSUC *Report* (Montreal 1817); LPSUC, *Explanation of Proceedings* (Toronto 1841); and Hamilton Craig, 'The Loyal and Patriotic Society of Upper Canada and Its Still-born Child – the "Upper Canada Preserved" Medal,' *Ontario History*, 52 (1960).

39 LPSUC, *Report* (1817), *passim*.

40 Adjutant-General, *General Regulations and Orders for the Army* (London 1816), 339; Strachan to John Owen, 1 Jan. 1814, in Firth, ed., *York, 1793–1815*, 324–5; Strachan to Alexander Thom, 9 Aug. 1813, DTA; Strachan to George Hillier, 17 Sept. 1820, in Spragge, ed., *Strachan Letter Book*, 204; and John Douglas, *Medical Topography of Upper Canada*, first pub. 1819, ed. Charles G. Roland, (Canton 1985), 27–35.

41 Strachan to Owen, 24 Feb. 1815, in Spragge, ed., *Strachan Letter Book*, 71–2.

42 Benn, *Fort York*, 48–58; Strachan to James Brown, 26 April/14 June 1813, in Firth, ed., *York, 1793–1815*, 294–6; and Articles of Capitulation, 27 April 1813, TRL.

43 Benn, *Fort York*, 58–66; Strachan to Brown, 26 April/14 June 1813, and Mrs Powell to W.D. Powell, 12 May 1813, in Firth, ed., *York, 1793–1815*, 294–6, 311, respectively; Firth, ed., *York, 1815–1834*, xcii;

Strachan to Owen, 15 April 1816, and List of the Persons confirmed, 21 Sept. 1813, in Spragge, ed., *Strachan Letter Book*, 115–16, 49.

44 Benn, *Fort York*, 66–8; and Strachan to unknown, 2 Aug. 1813, in Spragge, ed., *Strachan Letter Book*, 41–2.

45 Strachan to John Richardson, 30 Sept 1812, in Spragge, ed., *Strachan Letter Book*, 15–16; and Strachan to J.B. Robinson, 28 Sept. 1812, Robinson Papers, AO.

46 Strachan to Brown, May 1813, in Spragge, ed., *Strachan Letter Book*, 36–7. Unfortunately, it is difficult to judge Strachan's personal feelings completely because the 'most private' parts of his papers were destroyed about 1911, before the rest were donated to the provincial archives (C.W. Robinson to Miss Strachan, 21 Nov. 1911, Str P, AO).

47 Strachan to Mountain, 20 Sept. 1816, in Spragge, ed., *Strachan Letter Book*, 89–90; Strachan to Mountain, 20 Sept. 1815, TRL, Str P; Strachan to W.D. Powell, 18 Jan. 1814, TRL, Powell Family Papers; Bethune, *Memoir*, 54; Strachan poems, Str P, AO; J.L.H. Henderson, *John Strachan: Documents and Opinions* (Ottawa 1968), 283.

48 Henderson, *Documents*, 283; *Upper Canada Gazette*, 27 Feb. 1817; Memoranda, 1 Oct. 1813 and 1814, Strachan to Brown, May 1813, Strachan Memorial, 3 May 1814, Strachan to Mountain, n.d., 8 April 1816, and 15 Sept. 1816, Strachan to Owen, 15 April 1816, and Strachan to unknown, 16 June 1817, in Spragge, ed., *Strachan Letter Book*, 10, 66, 36–7, 63, 82, 106, 89–90, 111–16, 132–3, respectively; and 242 n202; W.W. Baldwin to Quetton St George, 29 July 1819, in Firth, ed., *York, 1815–1834*, 305–6; and Bethune, *Memoir*, 82.

49 [Strachan], 'History and Present State of Religion in Upper Canada,' *Christian Recorder*, 1 (1819), 12.

50 Strachan, *A Sermon, Preached at York, Upper Canada, on the Third of June, Being the Day Appointed for a General Thanksgiving* (Montreal 1814).

51 Craig, *Upper Canada*, 106–23.

52 Craig, Strachan biography, DCB; Fahey, *In His Name*, 62–8; and Wilson, *Clergy Reserves*, 11–12.

53 Firth, ed., *York, 1815–1834*, xlviii–xlix; Fahey, *In His Name*, 65–71, 76; Craig, *Upper Canada*, 176, 183–7; and Strachan to Samuel Smith et al., 18 July 1823, Str P, AO. For a study of education, see Susan E. Houston and Alison Prentice, *Schooling and Scholars in Nineteenth-Century Ontario* (Toronto 1988).

54 *AR* (1883); Bull, *Strachan to Owen*, 141; H.R.S. Ryan, 'The General Synod of the Anglican Church of Canada: Aspects of Constitutional History,' *JCCHS*, 34 (1992), 24; Craig, Strachan biography, DCB; Craig, *Upper Canada*, 171–3, 178–9, 235–40; and Wilson, *Clergy Reserves, passim*.

55 Ryan, 'General Synod,' 23, 57; John Webster Grant, *A Profusion of Spires: Religion in Nineteenth-Century Ontario,* (Toronto 1988), 81; and Patrick Brode, *Sir John Beverley Robinson* (Toronto 1984), 63–4.

56 C.A. Hagerman to John Macaulay, 17 Feb. 1821, in Firth, ed., *York, 1815–1834*, 185.

57 Paul Romney, 'From the Type Riots to the Rebellion: Elite Ideology, Anti-legal Sentiment, Political Violence, and the Rule of Law in Upper Canada,' *Ontario History*, 74 (1987), *passim*; and Chris Raible, *Muddy York Mud: Scandal and Scurrility in Upper Canada* (Creemore 1992), *passim*.

58 *Colonial Advocate*, 18 and 25 May 1826.

59 Raible, *Muddy York Mud*, 217; and Craig, *Upper Canada*, 113–14.

60 Quoted in Romney, 'Types Riot,' 130; cf. Christopher Moore, *The Law Society of Upper Canada and Ontario's Lawyers, 1797–1997* (Toronto 1997), 73–8.

61 Strachan, *A Sermon, Preached at York, Upper Canada, Third of July, 1825, on the Death of the Late Lord Bishop of Quebec* (Kingston 1826). For Mackenzie's critique of the sermon, see *Colonial Advocate*, 11 May 1826.

62 Fahey, *In His Name*, 75–6; and Craig, *Upper Canada*, 172–81.

63 Strachan, *Address to the Clergy of the Archdeaconry of York. By the Honorable and Venerable the Archdeacon of York. Delivered at Toronto on Wednesday the 13th September, 1837* (York? c. 1837).

64 Ibid., 128–9; Address of the Clergy Reserves Corp., 1824, and Strachan to John Henry Newman, 13 Aug. 1839, both in Str P, AO; cf. Fahey, *In His Name*, 99–103, 241–2.

65 Strachan, *Archdeacon Strachan's Letter to the Rev. Dr. Chalmers on the Life and Character of the Right Rev. Dr. Hobart, Bishop of the Protestant Episcopal Church in the State of New-York* (New York 1832). For another, more ecumenical and tolerant view by an Anglican priest in Toronto, see Joseph Harrington Harris, *A Letter to the Hon. & Ven. Archdeacon Strachan in Reply to Some Passages in His 'Letter to Dr. Chalmers on the Life and Character of Bishop Hobart'* (York 1833).

66 Adamson, 'God's Continent Divided,' 442; Fahey, *In His Name*, 91–5, 219–22; cf. Strachan sermons, 'We are confident and willing to be absent from the body, and to be present with the Lord,' 30 June 1822, 'Let your light so shine before men that they may see your good works' 22 Feb. 1829, and 'Another parable he spake unto them' 1 Feb 1835, all in Str P, AO

67 [Strachan], Kingston *Gazette*, 19 May 1812.

68 Fahey, *In His Name*, 150n.90; and Benn, *Fort York*, 93–107.

69 Strachan sermon, Hosea 6.5, 'And thy judgments are as the light that goeth forth,' 14 Dec. 1837, Str P, AO. Cf. the *Church* during this period for other Anglican views of the Rebellion and establishment.

70 *Colonial Advocate*, 9 March 1826.

71 SJCA, Historical Register. For Toronto history during this period, see Firth, ed., *York, 1815–1834*, introductory chapters.

72 Strachan to Mountain, 10 Nov. 1817, in Spragge, ed., *Strachan Letter Book*, 140–4. For more on St John's, see M. Audrey Graham, *150 Years at St. John's York Mills* (Toronto n.d.).

73 Quoted in Fahey, *In His Name*, 41.

74 Report of the proceedings of the meeting held at St James' Church, 10 Jan. 1831, and Appendix, 24 Apr. 1830, Str P, AO ; Strachan to Charles Stewart, 16 Oct. 1833, SLB, 1827–39; and Strachan, *A Form to be Used on Thursday, the 7th day of June, 1832, Being the Day Appointed to Lay the Foundation Stone of the Church of St. James, York, Upper Canada* (York 1832).

75 Strachan to the SPG, 1815, ACCA; Historical Register, SJCA; Arthur N. Thompson, Bethune biography, *DCB*, 10:53–7; *United Empire Loyalist*, 9 Oct. 1826; and Millman, *Life of Charles James Stewart*, 41–3. For more on Anglican itinerant missionaries, see Fahey, *In His Name*, 37–60.

76 Strachan to George Gwynne, 12 Oct. 1833, SLB, 1827–39, 234.

77 Service Registers: (Garrison) Baptisms (1826–57); Burials (1826–50); Missionary Baptisms (1832–8); Missionary Marriages (1836–7); and Service Register: Marriages (1824–32); Some Burials (1824), SJCA; and Strachan to the Bishop of Chester, 6 March 1831, and Strachan to Henry James Grasett, 5 Jan. 1836, SLB, 1827–39, 120, 252, respectively.

78 Registers: (Garrison) Baptisms (1826–57); Burials (1826–50); Missionary Baptisms (1832–8); Missionary Marriages (1836–7), SJCA; Chaplain-General to the Earl of Dalhousie, 6 April 1826, John Hothouse to Lord Aylmer, 21 Feb. 1832; Joseph Hudson to Col. Glegg, 12 May 1832; Hudson to Glegg, 4 June 1832; and Hudson to unknown, 7 April 1833, NA, RG 8, 66:184, 68:1–4, 17, 22, and 97, respectively. Millman, *Life of Charles James Stewart*, 192, 204; Strachan to the Archbishop of Dublin, 28 April 1834, and Strachan to Stewart, 16 Oct. 1833, SLB, 1827–39, 243, 235, respectively; and H.E. Turner, Grasett biography, *DCB*, 11:367–9.

79 Firth, ed., *York, 1815–1834*, 162–3; Strachan sermons, *passim*, AO, Str P; Strachan, *Syllabus of Lectures, to be Delivered at St. James's Church, Weekly during Lent. Divine Service to Commence Each Wednesday. At*

Eleven O'Clock, A.M. (Toronto 1836); and Strachan, *A Syllabus, or Heads of Lectures, on the History of the Christian Church, from our Lord's Ascension, to the Destruction of Jerusalem* (Toronto 1837). See also S.F. Wise, 'Sermon Literature and Canadian Intellectual History,' (original in 1965), in Bumsted, *Canadian History*, and for a gendered study see Cecilia Morgan, *Public Men and Virtuous Women: The Gendered Languages of Religion and Politics in Upper Canada, 1791–1850* (Toronto 1996).

80 Robert McGill to David Welsh, 6 April 1830, in Firth, ed., *York, 1815–1834*, 196.

81 For Strachan's view on the sacraments, see Strachan, *Church Fellowship. A Sermon, Preached on Wednesday, September 5, 1832. At the Visitation of the Honorable and Right Rev. Charles James, Lord Bishop of Quebec* (York 1832); and *A Letter, to the Congregation of St. James' Church, York, U. Canada, occasioned by the Hon. John Elmsley's Publication, of the Bishop of Strasbourg's Observations, on the 6th Chapter of St. John's Gospel* (York 1834).

82 Larratt Smith diary, 14 Nov. 1841, in Mary Larratt Smith, ed. *Young Mr Smith in Upper Canada* (Toronto 1980), 71.

83 Church, 8 July 1837; Fahey, *In His Name*, 244; and Grant, *Profusion of Spires*, 122–3.

84 Grant, *Profusion of Spires*, 29, 224; cf. Richard Cartwright to Isaac Todd, 14 Oct. 1793, and Cartwright to Todd, 1 Oct. 1794, *C Sim*, 2:88, 3:109, respectively.

85 *Patriot*, 21 Dec. 1841. The others were 2,401 Roman Catholics, 2,217 Presbyterians, 1,737 Methodists, 430 Baptists, 404 Congregationalists, 160 Catholic Apostolicals (Irvingites), 5 Quakers, 5 Unitarians, 3 Jews, and 132 people 'without religion.'

86 Registers: Marriages (1800–35); Baptisms (1807–36); Burials (1807–12) (No. 1); Marriages (1824–32); Some Burials (1824); Burials (1835–50); and (Garrison) Baptisms (1826–57); Burials (1826–50); Missionary Baptisms (1832–8); Missionary Marriages (1836–7), SJCA.

87 Ledger, 1832–8, SJCA; Ways and Means Committee minutes, 25 May 1831, Str P, AO; and *Upper Canada Gazette*, 17 July 1823.

88 Strachan to Anthony Hamilton, 5 Jan. 1820, in Spragge, ed., *Strachan Letter Book*, 197; and Katherine M.J. McKenna, *A Life of Propriety: Anne Murray Powell and Her Family, 1755–1849* (Montreal 1994), 235.

89 'Provisions Issued at the Expense of the Society for Relief of the Sick and Destitute at York,' 1–31 March 1829, 31 March 1829, Str P, AO; 'Society for the Relief of Poor Women in Childbirth, Constitution and Membership List,' 21 Oct. 1821, Jarvis-Powell Papers, TRL; McKenna, *Propriety*, 82–3; E. Colborne to Strachan, c. 1830, SLB, 1827–39.

90 'Subscribers for Relief of Widows & Orphan Children at York Episcopal Congregation,' 15 May 1833; and 'Amount Subscribed by the Different Christian Denominations for the Relief of the Widows and Orphan Children Caused by the Cholera at Toronto in the Years 1832 and 1834, 1834,' Str P, AO; and Geoffrey Bilson, *A Darkened House: Cholera in Nineteenth-Century Canada* (Toronto 1980), 53–61, 76–8, 85–9.

91 Quoted in Grant, *Profusion of Spires*, 104.

92 Address by his parishioners on John Strachan's work during the cholera epidemic, 9 May 1835; and Strachan sermon, 'Wherefore the Holy Ghost saith today if you will hear his voice harden not your hearts,' 8 July 1832, Str P, AO; [John Strachan], 'A Narrative of the Cholera,' 16 July 1847, in Henderson, ed., *Documents*, 130–1; and Bilson, *Darkened House*, 57.

93 Strachan to Todd, 1 Oct. 1812, in Spragge, *Letter Book*, 14–15; Strachan to Mountain, 10 Nov. 1817, in Firth, ed., *York, 1815–1834*, 178–9; Firth, ed., *York, 1793–1815*, 179 n 2; Account Book of the Bible and Prayer Book Societies, 1816–28, Allan Papers, TRL; [Strachan?], 'Bible Society of Upper Canada,' *Christian Recorder*, 2 (1820), 358.

94 Strachan to Mountain, 12 March 1819, Str P, TRL.
95 Strachan sermon, 'So the last shall be first and first last,' 23 Dec. 1804, Str P, AO; Robert McGill to David Welsh, 6 April 1830, in Firth, ed., *York, 1815–1834*, 196–7; Fahey, *In His Name*, 19, 89; and *First Annual Report of the Society for Converting & Civilizing the Indians, and Propagating the Gospel Among Destitute Settlers in Upper Canada, for the Year Ending October 1831* (York 1832).
96 Powell Family Papers, TRL, *passim*; cf. Edward Blewett to Strachan, 21 April 1822, in Firth, ed., *York, 1815–1834*, 268 and 268 n 14; and Strachan to unknown, 27 June 1831, SLB 1837–39, 143, Str P, AO; Mountain, *A Charge Delivered to the Clergy of the Diocese of Quebec in the Year 1820* (Quebec 1820); and Armine W. Mountain, *A Memoir of George Jehosphaphat Mountain* (London 1866), *passim*.
97 Strachan to Thomas Cartwright, 11 Sept. 1815, in Spragge, ed., *Strachan Letter Book*, 100–1.
98 Strachan to Mary Cartwright, 1815, in *ibid.*, 87–8.
99 McKenna, *Propriety*, 212–29.
100 Robert J. Burns, Markland biography, *DCB*, 9:534–6; and Robert Burns, '"Queer Doings": Attitudes towards Homosexuality in 19th-century Canada,' *Our Image: The Body Politic Review*, 6 (1976–7) *passim*. Whether the charges made against him in 1838 were accurate or mere innuendo will probably never be known with certainty.

2: THE MAKING OF AN EVANGELICAL CATHEDRAL, 1839–1883

1 Strachan to Ernest Hawkins, 21 April 1849, SLB, Societies 1839–1866, 108, AO.
2 Strachan to Archbishop of Canterbury, 6 Dec. 1840, *ibid.*, 126.
3 1847. John Strachan, *A Charge Delivered to the Clergy of the Diocese of Toronto at the Visitation in June MDCCCXLVII* (Toronto 1847), 67.
4 Strachan's sermons, No. 159 (26 Nov. 1841), AO.
5 Strachan to the Bishop of Nova Scotia, 15 May 1846, SLB, 1844–1849; quoted in SJCA, file 'John Strachan.'
6 Quoted in Bishop Frederick Wilkinson, 'Second John Strachan Memorial Address,' 1964, SJCA.
7 Grasett 'is in full charge of the parish,' SLB, Societies 1839–1866, 126 (Strachan to Archbishop of Canterbury, 6 Dec. 1840); 'Mr. Grasett was the principal clergyman,' examination of Henry Scadding, *In the Supreme Court of Canada*: ... [DuMoulin v. Langtry] *Case* (Toronto 1886), p. 43. See Grasett's obituary in *EC*, 6, 659–60 (23 March 1882) and (30 March 1882), 667–9; and H.E. Turner, 'Grasett biography,' *DCB* 11:367–9.
8 *AR*, Easter (1882), 11.
9 H.J. Grasett, ed., *Hymns for Use in Sunday Schools* (Toronto, 1876).
10 5 Jan. 1842, SLB, 1839–1843, 162.
11 4 Sept. 1845, SLB, 1844–1849, 119.
12 Donald Robert Beer, Henry Sherwood biography, *DCB* 8: 796–801.
13 Michael S. Cross and Robert Lochiel Fraser, Robert Baldwin biography, *DCB* 8:45–59.
14 *EC*, 2, (8 Nov. 1877), 408; George Metcalf, William Henry Draper biography, *DCB* 20:253–9.
15 'Table Shewing the State of the Diocese of Toronto,' in *A Charge, Delivered to the Clergy of the Diocese of Toronto, at the Triennial Visitation, 6 June 1844* (Cobourg 1844), CIHM 32804.
16 Carl Benn describes this development in chapter 1, above.
17 *In Chancery ... Attorney General v. Grasett* (Toronto 1854), CIHM 89380; *The Rectories of Upper Canada, Being a Return ...* (Toronto, 1852), CIHM 22304.

18 Chief Justice Robinson's judgment is published in the *Daily Colonist*, 13 April 1857 (clipping in SJA).

19 Vestry minutes, 18 July 1842, SJCA.

20 Churchwardens' circular of 1849, CIHM 44983.

21 In *Address and Report of the Venerable the Archdeacon of York, Together with the Proceedings of a Meeting of the Pew Holders and Persons Interested in St James' Church, held in the City Hall, January 9, 1839,* CIHM 63596. See also *Report of the Committee Appointed by the Congregation of St James' Church ... 9th January 1839,* CIHM 89486.

22 Vestry minutes, 26 Feb. 1844, SJCA.

23 *Globe*, 9 May and 12 May 1854; clippings in Vestry Minute Book, 1, SJCA.

24 A cemetery scrapbook and files are in SJCA. See also Vestry minutes, 27 April 1850.

25 Files in SJCA.

26 W.A. Langton, ed., *Early Days in Upper Canada: Letters of John Langton* (Toronto 1926), 277.

27 Address and Report of the Venerable the Archdeacon of York ... January 9, 1839, CIHM 89486; H.M. Carman and W.G. Upshall, eds., *The Story of the Church of St George the Martyr of Toronto Canada,* (Toronto 1945).

28 Minutes of a close vestry dealing with personnel and other confidential matters begin on 30 May 1881, but presumably such meetings were held at earlier dates without being minuted.

29 Charge at the Primary Visitation, 33.

30 *First General Report of the Church Society for the Year Ending 8 June 1843.*

31 *A Charge, Delivered to the Clergy of the Diocese of Toronto at the Triennial Visitation, 6 June 1844* (Cobourg 1844), CIHM 32804.

32 Church Society, General Report for the year ending 7 June 1843, DTA.

33 *Report of the Special General Meeting of the Church Society for the Diocese of Toronto Held on Wednesday 10th November 1852* (Toronto 1852), CIHM 89744, 24.

34 Strachan's pastoral letter of 2 April 1851, in TSJ 1851.

35 *A Charge Delivered to the Clergy of the Diocese of Toronto at the Visitation in May MDCCLI* (Toronto 1851), CIHM 53902, 13–14.

36 *Triennial Visitation of the Lord Bishop of Toronto and Proceedings of the Church Synod*, Toronto, 1853, CIHM 46297.

37 10 Feb. 1847, SLB, 1844–1849, 224.

38 25 Feb. 1847, SLB, 1844–1849, 228.

39 25 Feb. 1847, AO, Str P, Strachan Correspondence.

40 Obituary in EC 1, (8 June 1876), 10.

41 William Westfall, *Two Worlds: The Protestant Culture of Nineteenth-Century Ontario* (Montreal 1989).

42 Quoted in Lucy Booth Martyn, *Toronto: One Hundred Years of Grandeur* (Toronto 1978).

43 *Case of the Episcopal Churches* (1782).

44 This was the chief object of the lay committee of the Church Society. Church Society Minute Book 1842–1850 (I-2a Ch.), 28 April 1842, DTA.

45 John Paterson-Smyth, 'Toronto Cathedral Question,' typescript, DTA and SJCA. *The Third Annual Report of the Church Society, for the Year Ending 31 March 1845* (Cobourg 1844) CIHM 32804, 470, indicates that Strachan had given the Society 500 acres of land at some point after 28 April 1842.

46 *Third Annual Report of the Church Society.*

47 In the letter concerning preaching in the surplice.

48 Strachan to Hawkins, SLB, Societies 1839–1866, 78.

49 17 Sept. 1846, SLB, Societies 1844–1849, 198.

50 Strachan to SPCK, 14 April 1849, SLB, Societies 1839–1866, at back of book, 27.

51 Primary sources include Vestry minutes, Minutes of the Building Committee, occasional documents (many microfilmed in the CIHM collection), and letters to newspapers (some clippings in SJCA).

52 Strachan, *Thoughts on the Rebuilding of the Cathedral Church of St James* (Toronto 1850), CIHM 62487.

53 Vestry minutes, 1 Feb. 1854, SJCA.

54 'The project remains in abeyance in the hope of future unanimity.' Strachan to St John's, Prescott, 27 July 1859, SLB, 1852–1866, 8.

55 Westfall, *Two Worlds*, 131.

56 See, for instance, Vestry minutes, 28 March, 11 April 1853, 2 May 1854, SJCA.

57 *Globe*, 25 June 1855, and *Colonist*, 28 June 1855 (clippings in SJCA).

58 Church Society Annual Reports for 1848–9, 1849–50, 1850–1, and 1851–2 include parochial reports from St James', DTA.

59 Alan L. Hayes, *Holding Forth the Word of Life* (Toronto: Little Trinity, 1992).

60 [Strachan,] *Circular, Addressed to the Poorer Families of the United Church of England and Ireland Residing in Toronto* (Toronto, 1847), CIHM 43174.

61 Anne Storey, *The St. George's Society of Toronto* (Toronto: St George's Society, 1987).

62 Grasett to Strachan, 25 Feb. 1847, Str. P, Strachan Correspondence, AO.

63 Bethune seems to have thought so; *ibid*, 11 Jan. 1867.

64 *Globe*, 2 Nov. 1867.

65 J.D. Livermore, 'The Personal Agonies of Edward Blake,' *Canadian Historical Review* 56 (1975), 45–58.

66 Vestry minutes, 1 Oct. 1867, SJCA.

67 SJCA, List of pledges, among miscellaneous documents on building of present church.

68 Vestry minutes, 17 April 1876, SJCA.

69 *A Profusion of Spires* (Toronto 1988), 170.

70 Reports of activities are in *AR*, first available for the year ending Easter 1879. See also Mrs F. le M. Grasett, comp., 'History of St. James Women's Auxiliary,' typewritten, in SJCA; reports in *EC*, 2, (27 Dec. 1877); 513; 3 (17 May 1877), 2, and 530 (3 Jan. 1878), 530; 4 (4 Sept. 1879), 262, and (19 June 1879), 82, etc.

71 *EC*, (1879), 660.

72 *AR*, Easter 1879, 7.

73 Alan Hayes, ed., *By Grace Co-workers*. For discussion and bibliography, see 45–57.

74 T.A. Reed, *A History of the University of Trinity College* (Toronto 1852), 59–69.

75 Vestry Minutes, 29 March 1875, SJCA.

76 Sydney Anne Woolcombe, *Grace Church-on-the-Hill 1874–1964* (Toronto 1964).

77 *Church Herald*, 2 Feb. 1871 and 23 March 1871; Vestry minutes 10 April 1871; TSJ, esp (1884), 79–101; *In the Supreme Court of Canada. Appeal ... [DuMoulin v. Langtry] Case* (Toronto 1888).

78 W.S. Rainsford, *A Preacher's Story of his Work* (Toronto: Morang, 1904); Rainsford, *The Story of a Varied Life: An Autobiography* (Garden City, N.J., 1924); *EC*, 1, (1 March 1877) pp. 658–9, (8 March), 674–5, (15 March), 690, (15 March), 698–9, (10 May 1877), 818, 2. (17 May 1877), 2, (14 June 1877), 66; essay by Darren Marks for a course at Wycliffe College.

79 Rainsford file, SJCA.

80 Vestry minutes, 2 April 1877, SJCA.

81 See Alan L. Hayes, Sheraton biography, *DCB* 13: 948–9.

82 Vestry minutes, 10 April 1882, SJCA.

83 *Mail and Empire*, 19 March 1932 (clipping in SJCA).

84 Vestry minutes, 12 June 1882, SJCA; *EC*, 7, (15 June 1882), 71–2, (29 June), 98–9; (20 July), 136; (27 July), 151.

85 Since 1954 York Township has been part of Metropolitan Toronto.

86 Hayes, ed., *By Grace Co-workers* 67–9, 84–5; E.M. Chadwick, *Monograph of the Cathedral of St. Alban the Martyr* ([1921]); William Cooke, manuscript 'Notes,' SJCA.

87 Letter from Bishop Sweatman (signed) 'Arthur Toronto', 21 Jan. 1885, SJCA.

3: SUCCESS AND DISTRESS, 1883–1935

1 The anonymously written, self-published *History and Directory: St. James' Cathedral* (Toronto 1899), 35, SJCA, had many other claims of confidence!

2 *Ibid.*, 7.

3 *(Might's) Toronto City Directory 1899* (Toronto 1899); J.M.S. Careless, *Toronto to 1918* (Toronto 1984), 149.

4 Geoffrey J. Matthews, cartographer/designer, 'The Emergence of Corporate Toronto,' *Historical Atlas of Canada: Addressing the Twentieth Century 1891–1961*, vol. 3 (Toronto 1990), Plate 15, 170–1.

5 Austin Seton Thompson uses the phrase in *Jarvis Street: A Story of Triumph and Tragedy* (Toronto 1980), 132.

6 Grant, *A Profusion of Spires*. The last unnumbered plate in the book gives the view up Bond Street.

7 Henry Scadding, *Toronto of Old*, ed. F.H. Armstrong (Toronto 1966), 99. He penned these words in his edition of 1873.

8 Careless, *Toronto to 1918*, 201–2.

9 The list is spread out between advertisements in *History and Directory*, 39–47.

10 'The printed, six-page 'Draft Report of the Finance Committee to the Vestry' of 1888 that preceded and described the project in detail is simply entitled *St. James' Cathedral* (SJCA) and originally called for $14,000. The financing is described in a group of documents printed 25 May 1889 under the heading 'Special Appeal,' SJCA. The list of wardens, 1807–1931, can be found in Elliot Grasett Strathy, *A Guide to the Cathedral of St. James* (Toronto 1932), 48; see also Appendix 3.

11 The cost for that substantial building had been $21,000; Dyson Hague, 'The History of Wycliffe College,' in *The Jubilee Volume of Wycliffe College* (Toronto 1927), 39. A photograph can be found in the preceding plate.

12 The list is spread out between advertisements, *History and Directory*, 39-47.

13 See Henry James Morgan, ed. *The Canadian Men and Women of the Time*, (Toronto 1898 and 1912) and C.G.D. Roberts and A.L. Tunnell, eds. *The Canadian Who's Who 1936–1937*, (Toronto 1936).

14 'Draft Report of the Finance Committee,' SJCA.

15 Service Registers, 1890s–1940s, SJCA.

16 See the registers entitled Baptisms: St. James' Cathedral Toronto, SJCA.

17 This information is found in 'St. James' Marriages' 1807–1908, transcripts of registers by Ontario Genealogical Society, SJCA. Unfortunately the information provided is not as consistently helpful as what is found in the baptismal records.

18 See the statistical tables in Careless, *Toronto to 1918*, 201, and James T. Lemon, *Toronto since 1918* (Toronto 1985), 196.

19 James Scott to O.A. Howland, 20 Feb. 1899, Churchwardens' File: Selection of Rector, 1899, SJCA.

20 'Desire to Co-operate,' *Star Weekly*, 13 June 1913.

21 'Rector's Report,' *AR* (1914), 8.

22 *Ibid.* (1908), 25.

23 In 1910, at the height of the fervour for the new parish house and sympathy for the 'social gospel,' the park lots and the nearby, though small, Wellesley properties yielded almost $9,000 – about 20 per cent of St James' revenues from all sources for that year. *AR* (1911), 14–18.

24 See, for instance *AR* (1899), 7.

25 'Churchwardens' Report' (1929), 8. In 1910, the Finance Committee had consented to accepting $20,000 from the city as payment for the expropriation of six lots for a playground (for the poor local children). 'Churchwardens' Report,' *AR* (1911), 12.

26 Nicole Graham sums up the cathedral's predicament in 'Mission Impossible: The Social Gospel without a Bowling Alley. St. James', Its Ownership of Local Slums and Community Outreach,' undergraduate essay, University of Toronto, 1995, 21–9.

27 *Hush*, 22 Dec. 1934, 2; 29 Dec. 1934, 2.

28 *Church of England Tracts for the Times, Nos. 9–10,* (Toronto 1890/91?). Each tract is four pages in length.

29 Philip Carrington, *The Anglican Church in Canada* (Toronto 1963), 118.

30 Service Register, 24 July 1898–18 March 1912, SJCA. For a description of Cody's evangelical reputation in this period, see D.C. Masters, *Henry John Cody: An Outstanding Life* (Toronto 1995), 32–49.

31 Master, *Henry John Cody*, 129–30.

32 Scadding notes that it had been installed as an integral part of the $7,500 beautification project of that year; Scadding, *Toronto of Old*, 99.

33 William Cooke, 'The Diocese of Toronto and its Two Cathedrals,' *JCCHS*, 37 (1985), 101. Much of the reconstruction that follows is based on this careful piece of research.

34 This is found in a leaflet entitled 'The Second Congress of the Church of England in Canada,' dated 14 October 1884, SJCA.

35 'Rector's Report,' *AR* (1909), 6.

36 'Annual Vestry Meeting, 1910,' *AR* (1910), 5.

37 *Ibid.*, 6.

38 *Ibid.*, 4.

39 In a helpful paper on Rainsford, Darren Marks suggests that the issue was Rainsford's opposition to Trinity College, 'William S. Rainsford: Forgotten Founder of Toronto's Evangelical Anglicans 1877–1882' graduate paper, Wycliffe College, 1996, 15–16. But Sweatman was not a Trinity man, and the wrangling over all candidates proposed for the appointment of 1882 suggests that the real issue was the same one that arose in 1899, and later: 'turf war' between the vestry of St James' (the pewholders gathered for legal ends) and successive bishops of Toronto.

40 E.H. Gifford to the Churchwardens, 20 Feb. 1899, Churchwardens' File: Selection of Rector 1899, SJCA.

41 'The undersigned Members ... ,' 10 Oct. 1899, *ibid.*

42 Alan Hayes, 'Managing the Household of Faith: Administration and Finance 1967–1939,' in *By Grace Co-Workers*, 237–8.

43 This exchange of April 1918 is found in *AR* (1919), 8–9.

44 The proceedings and outcome are nicely summed up in Cooke's 'The Diocese of Toronto and Its Two Cathedrals,' 110.

45 *AR* (1934), 6.

46 Vestry minutes, St. James' Cathedral, 28 Jan. 1935, reel 7, SJCA.

47 *AR* (1935), 7; emphasis added.

48 The full story can be found in the 'Churchwardens' Report,' *AR* (1888), 7–8.

49 'Report of the Churchwardens,' *AR* (1892), 12.

50 See the 'Churchwardens' Report,' *AR* (1893), 12; (1894), 12; (1895), 12; (1896), 5; (1897), 6; (1898), 6.

51 'Parish House Committee,' *AR* (1909), 20–22.

52 'The Churchwardens' Report,' *AR* (1922), 6.

53 'The Churchwardens' Report,' *AR* (1930), 7; (1931), 6–7.

54 'The Churchwardens' Report,' *AR* (1935), 5–6.

55 See the figures in *AR* (1918), 16–20.

56 For the former two see CM, 4 April and 6 May, 1919, SJCA.

57 'The Churchwardens' Report,' *AR* (1923), 7.

58 See CM, 21 Dec. 1925. The churchwardens gently cautioned them to use the rectory only as a clubhouse but took no other action!

59 'The Rector's Report,' *AR* (1918), 8. St. James' probably gave its rectors $5,000 per year out of the York Rectory Fund, the maximum allowable after the settlement of the endowment war with the diocese. See Hayes, 'Managing the Household of Faith,' in *By Grace Co-workers*, 237–8.

60 Richard E. Ruggle gives this as Cody's salary, though he acknowledges that Cody shared part of the amount with poorer clergymen, who were often paid well under $1,000, or less than a typist: 'The Saints in the Land, 1867–1939,' in Hayes, ed., *By Grace Co-workers*, 196.

61 *AR* (1905), 4–5.

62 *AR* (1910), 3.

63 'Churchwardens' Report' and 'Report of the Musical Committee,' *AR* (1898), 6–7, 14.

64 'Music Committee,' *AR* (1931), 12.

65 'Rector's Report,' *AR* (1903), 6–7. This is the first of many annual rector's reports.

66 'Rector's Report,' *AR* (1912), 8–9.

67 *SJCM* Jan. 1906, 1–4. The publication was launched in December 1898 and seems to have wound down some time in 1909, after which no issues appear to be extant. Most of the issues in this period can be found in SJCA.

68 'Sunday School,' *AR* (1907), 22.

69 'Report of the Boys' Guild,' *AR* (1890), 33.

70 *SJCM* Dec. 1903, 3; (Feb. 1904), 3–4.

71 *SJCM* Dec. 1904, 2.

72 *AR* (1900), 28–43.

73 *AR* (1891), 38; (1892), 32.

74 *AR* (1915), 9, 56–58.

75 *AR* (1936), 17–29.

76 'History of St. James' Cathedral W.A., 1889–1939,' SJCA, 15.

77 *AR* (1892), 36; (1891), 37.

78 *AR* (1890), 33–4. It contains a full description of the Brotherhood.

79 'Rector's Report,' *AR* (1914), 8.

80 *SJCM* March 1906, 3.

81 'Report of St. James' Cathedral Morning Sunday School,' *AR* (1890), 19.

82 'St. James' Cathedral Sunday School,' *AR* (1918), 34–5; 'Sunday School,' *AR* (1923), 26–7.

83 'Deaconess Work,' *AR* (1901), 16.

84 *AR* (1910), 8.

85 'Rector's Report,' *AR* (1914), 8.

86 See Shields' sermon, 'The Christian Attitude toward Amusements,' in Leslie K. Tarr, *Shields of Canada* (Grand Rapids, Mich., 1967), 208–18. It was preached on 13 February 1921 but was on an issue that had been coming up for some time. Shields, of course, sounded much more sectarian and bellicose than Plumptre.

87 See the 'Saint James' Cathedral Parish House Annual Reports' in *AR*, 1912–15.

88 Interview with Harry Wright, 5 May 1997. Mr Wright, born in 1912, was involved in the boys' clubs in the early 1920s.

89 'Brotherhood of St. Andrew,' *AR* (1927), 31.

90 'District Visitors' Society,' *AR* (1890), 24; (1892), 23.

91 'Report of the Deaconess,' *AR* (1897), 20–1; (1911), 4.

92 'Rector's Report,' *AR* (1914), 11.

93 See the chart in *AR* (1934), 10.

94 See S. Gould, 'Personality and Service,' *Jubilee Volume of Wycliffe College*, 63ff., and the parish expenditures in *AR* (1893), 6. In the budget year 1892–93, $247.50 was collected for divinity students at Wycliffe College, and $45.00 for those at Trinity. Philip Carrington called St James' one of the headquarters for evangelicals in this period, *The Anglican Church in Canada*, 199.

95 'Brotherhood of St. Andrew,' *AR* (1896), 31.

96 'Librarians' Report,' *AR* (1890), 21; 'Brotherhood of St. Andrew,' *AR* (1892), 35.

97 This comment was found in *Parish and Home*, 6, the periodical bound with early issues of the parish magazine: *SJCM*, Dec. 1898.

98 R.J. Renison, 'Edward Sullivan,' in W.B. Heeney, ed., *Leaders of the Canadian Church. First Series* (Toronto 1918), 228.

99 See F.C. Macdonald, *Edward Ashurst Welch: A Memoir* (Cambridge 1936), 34, and Archdeacon Davison, 'J. Philip Dumoulin,' in Heeney, ed., *Leaders of the Canadian Church. First Series* (Toronto 1918), 268–9.

100 'Churchwardens' Report,' *AR* (1886), 6; 'Report of Churchwardens,' *AR* (1898), 6.

101 'Churchwardens' Report,' *AR* (1888), 6–8.

102 'Report of the Deaconess,' and 'Soup Kitchen Report,' *AR* (1897), 20–22; 'Deaconess' Report,' *AR* (1898), 19.

103 Macdonald, *Welch*, 1, 5, 12–16, 23–34.

104 Charles E. Riley, *Derwyn Trevor Owen: Primate of All Canada* (Toronto 1966), 16, 29, 39–40.

105 Notes by the Rector,' *SJCM* (March 1905), 3.

106 E.A. Welch, *Stretching Forward: A Sermon Preached in the Chapel of Trinity College* (Toronto 1895). Yet one of his sermons from his St James' years speaks of 'the shedding of His blood ... for the putting away of sin,' in Macdonald, *Welch*, 44.

107 'Notes by the Rector,' *SJCM*, Feb. 1904, 2.

108 'Notes by the Rector,' *SJCM*, (April 1904), 2.

109 Richard Allen, *The Social Passion: Religion and the Social Reform in Canada 1914–1928* (Toronto 1971), 15; Ramsay Cook, *The Regenerators: Social Criticism in Late Victorian Canada* (Toronto 1985), 267 n.2. The most notable Anglican exponent was the indefatigable Canon Vernon; see Nancy Christie and

Michael Gauvreau, *A Fully Orbed Christianity: The Protestant Churches and Social Welfare in Canada 1900–1940* (Montreal 1996), 216–18.

110 *AR* (1904), 3.

111 'Notes by the Rector,' *SJCM*, March 1904, 3.

112 Among others, David Marshall argues that 'a clear distinction must be drawn between religion and other phenomena, such as political ideologies' *Secularizing the Faith: Canadian Protestant Clergy and the Crisis of Belief* (Toronto 1992), 6. Such theories as his see the 'social gospel' as a sign of secularization, of religious bodies leaving their proper sphere for the sake of 'relevance.' But for many nineteenth- and early-twentieth-century Christians, including those at St James', the opposite was true. Social action was a sign of resistance to secularization, which they saw as dividing religion and society, once completely united, into separate spheres.

113 'Rector's Report, *AR* (1907), 7.

114 'The Rector's Message,' in *St. James' Cathedral: Description and Plans of Parish House* (Nov. 1909), 4, SJCA.

115 Not only had *SJCM* ceased publication in 1909 or thereabouts, but the 'Rector's Reports' to vestry ceased to be included in *AR* in 1918.

116 Masters, *John Henry Cody*, 49–50.

117 'Desire to Co-operate,' *Star Weekly*, 13 June 1913.

118 'The Rector's Report,' *AR* (1913), 10; (1914), 10.

119 See 'Bishop Urged to Action on Theological Views of Rev. Canon Plumtre,' *Globe*, 18 Feb. 1928, and 'Bishop Satisfied with Explanation by Canon Plumtre,' *Star Weekly*, 18 Feb. 1928. The controversy had started because of Plumptre's comment in the 19 January 1928 issue of the *Canadian Churchman*.

120 *AR* (1924), 3, 29.

121 See *AR*, beginning with 1924.

122 See 'Establishment Work,' *AR* (1928), 35.

4: THE BEAUTIFUL DOWNTOWN CATHEDRAL, 1935–1997

1 Churchwardens to Bishop of Toronto, 8 April 1918, CM 'Report of the Sub-Committee re the proposed use of St. James' Cathedral as either the Pro-Cathedral or the Diocesan Cathedral,' General Cathedral Committee of the Synod of Toronto, 1935, SJCA.

2 TSJ, (1936), 52–3. See T.A. Reed, 'The Story of the Cathedral,' in *The Order of Services at the Consecration of St. James' Cathedral*, 17 Oct. 1939.

3 TSJ (1934), 82–6; 'Report of the Sub-Committee re the Proposed Use of St. James' Cathedral as Either the Pro-Cathedral or the Diocesan Cathedral,' 1935, SJCA; TSJ (1935), 78–82.

4 *Statutes Affecting the Diocese of Toronto*, 1940, 64–6.

5 Dean Gilling and the churchwardens raised the question in January 1963, *AR* (1962), 6 and 19. Dean Stiff raised it again in the 1970s.

6 Memorandum of Agreement, original text, TSJ, 16 May 1935, 80–1, and final text, 15 March 1940, SJCA; *AR* (1938), 7.

7 'Memorandum of Agreement', 15 March 1940, SJCA; see also the text of the memorandum as approved by synod in 1935, in TSJ (1935), 80–1. The two versions differed. That of 1935 provided for the agreement to be reviewed only when there was a new bishop or new rector, whereas the one of 1940 permitted either party to terminate the relationship at any time, on one year's notice in writing.

8 Succeeding editions of *Crockford's Clerical Directory* list the canons until the edition of 1980–2, which is the last to include Canadian clergy.

9 Hayes, ed., *By Grace Co-Workers*, 83–4, 97–100.

10 *AR* (1936), 7–8.

11 BCP (1918), 21.

12 *AR*, (1943), 16.

13 Interview with Stephen Bemrose-Fetter, Metropolitan United Church, Toronto, 1997.

14 *AR* (1936).

15 CM, 28 Aug. 1936; *AR* (1936), 5–10.

16 Elliot Grasett Strathy, 'Addenda' (Oct. 1938) to *A Guide to the Cathedral Church of St. James Toronto* (1932); CM, 2 Feb. 1937; *AR* (1936), 9.

17 *AR* (1934), 7; the revenue side of the annual budget in the 1930s included the entry 'City of Toronto, Care of Grounds.'

18 'The St James area, Insurance Plan,' Underwriters' Survey Bureau, July 1954, SJCA; a photograph with the caption, 'No, It's Not Old Quebec,' was printed in the Toronto *Telegram*, 1937 (clipping in SJCA) and was published on the cover of the 1953 and 1958 editions of the guide to the cathedral.

19 Gerald E. Moffatt, comp, *All the Blessings of This Life: the Memoirs of Charles Edward Riley* (Toronto 1986).

20 CM, 15 April 1954.

21 CM, various dates, 1937–9; *AR* (1939), 10.

22 Centenary leaflet, 1939; Order of Service, 17 Oct. 1939; Service Register, 1939.

23 CM, 1939; *AR* (1939), 12.

24 *AR* (1939), 5.

25 *AR* (1940), 10.

26 *Ibid.*; W.G. Cooke, memorandum, 'Colours Deposited in the Cathedral Church of St. James,' listing colours and the standard presented between 1813 and 1943 and deposited between 1898 and 1971, [1973], SJCA; interview with Captain Bruce Barbeau, 1995.

27 *AR* (1940), (1941), and (1943); CM, 28 May 1943.

28 CM, 1946 and 1947; *AR* (1946) and (1947); Cooke, 'The Altar Hangings of Saint James' Cathedral,' July 1981, SJCA.

29 CM, 20 Feb. 1953.

30 *AR* (1954), 7–8; (1955), 18–19.

31 *AR* (1959) and (1960); notes by William Cooke, 1997; CM, 23 Feb. 1971.

32 Service Registers for 1935 and 1936, SJCA.

33 TSJ, 1920–45.

34 Service leaflet, 24 March 1940; Service Registers, 1940.

35 Interview with Joyce Sowby, 1995.

36 *AR* (1939), 14; (1940), 10.

37 *A Pilgrim's Guide to St James' Cathedral* (1953), 11–12.

38 Service Registers, 1950 and 1955; Lenten Services leaflet, 1950, 1952, and 1957; Service leaflets for Christmas 1952, Easter 1953, and 8 Sept. 1957; *AR* (1955), 19 (1958), 17.

39 Interview with John Bothwell, 1996.

40 *A Pilgrim's Guide to the Cathedral Church of St James, Toronto, Canada*, revised edition 1958; 'Lent, 1952,' SJCA.

41 Riley, 'The Cathedral,' c. 1957, SJCA; AR, for 1955, 7–8.

42 Riley, 'The Cathedral,' c. 1957, SJCA; CM, 1 April 1960; Moffatt, *All the Blessings*, 42.

43 Photograph in *AR* (1964), 4; *Pilgrim's Guide*, 1968 edition.

44 *AR* (1959) and (1960).

45 CM, 11 March 1969; *AR* (1970); Interim report of the churchwardens, 21 May 1971, SJCA.

46 *AR* (1970) and (1971); CM during 1962 and 1963; *AR* (1964), 11; '$25 Million Arts Centre Drafted,' Toronto *Star*, 25 Sept. 1962; 'A "Great White Way" Downtown,' *Telegram*, 25 Sept. 1962.

47 Gilling's report, *SJCN*, Dec. 1973.

48 Development Feasibility Study, St James Cathedral/York Rectory Lands, Anglican Church of Canada, presented by Canderal Limited, 25 March 1991, SJCA.

49 Drawings of the St James' area for 1968, 1974, 1981, made by Terrell Bond, from aerial photographs in the Map Library, University of Toronto, in SJCA; *SJCN*, May–June 1972; Restoration Appeal brochure, Oct. 1979; 'To the Glory of God,' a photo album, July 1982; *SJCN*, Advent 1982; *SJCN*, May 1983; interview with Joyce Sowby, 1995; interview with Captain Bruce Barbeau, 1995.

50 CM, 11 Aug. 1970 and 23 Feb. 1971.

51 CM, 12 July and 30 Aug. 1961, and 6 March 1964.

52 *AR* (1961), 44.

53 Zita Barbara May, *Pilgrim's Guide to the Cathedral Church of St James'*, c. 1961, with later editions about 1963 and 1968, SJCA.

54 CM, 9 and 16 Feb. 1967.

55 Service leaflet, 7 Jan. 1973.

56 Interview with Joyce Sowby, 1995; CM, various dates, 1961.

57 *AR* (1966); *SJCN*, 1966.

58 Gilling, 'Functions of a Dean and Cathedral in the Inner City,' 1964, SJCA.

59 *Ibid.*, 14; 'Foreword,' *AR* (1964), 6–7.

60 Service leaflets, 10 Dec. and 17 Dec. 1967; 'Liturgical Experiment,' in *AR* (1968), 23–5; CM, 9 June 1970; 'Rector's Report,' Jan. 1971, in *AR* (1970); Gilling, *SJCN*, Dec. 1973; notes by William Cooke, 1997.

61 St James' welcome leaflet for the Anglican Congress, 1963, SJCA; CM, 12 Sept. 1963; George M. Snell, 'The Anglican Congress of 1963,' in Hayes, ed., *By Grace Co-workers*, 287–92; Memoir by George Snell, Dec. 1995, SJCA; E.R. Fairweather, ed., *Anglican Congress: Report of Proceedings, 1963* (Toronto 1963).

62 Snell, Memoir, SJCA.

63 *SJCN*, Feb. 1971; 'An Explanation of the Signs and Symbols,' 1972.

64 CM, 10 Aug. and 17 Aug. 1965, and 5 Jan., 23 Feb., and 11 May 1966; *ibid.*, 23 Jan. 1968.

65 *SJCN* (Feb. 1971); Aubrey M. Foy, 'Music Report,' 25 Jan. 1971, in *AR* (1970).

66 'Advisory Board,' 11 Sept. 1974, in *SJCN* (Lent 1975); 'Wardens' Report,' in *AR* (1974), 3–4.

67 *SJCN*, summer 1974.

68 *AR* (1976); CM, 23 Aug. 1977; conversations with Glenn Pritchard, 1996, and David Bousfield, 1997; interview with Giles Bryant, 1995.

69 CM, 10 Oct. 1974; service leaflet for the dedication of the chapel, 16 March 1975, SJCA.

70 'The Rector's Annual Report for 1980,' in *AR* (1980); Hayes, ed., *By Grace Co-workers*, 131–2.

71 *SJCN*, Lent 1981.

72 See 'The Rector's Annual Report 1984,' in *AR* (1984), 3–4.

73 Pritchard, 'The Cathedral as a Place of Worship,' *SJCN*, Lent 1981.

74 Pritchard, 'The Role of a Cathedral To-Day,' *SJCN*, Advent, 1980.

75 'Music and Choir Report 1981,' in *AR* (1981).

76 'Rector's Report,' *AR* (1980), 2; *SJCN*, Ascension 1980.

77 *SJCN*, Lent 1980.

78 *SJCN*, Lent 1981.

79 *AR* (1984), 3–4; BAS, 229–55; notes by William Cooke, 1997.

80 William Cooke is the source of this point about the rectors' birthplaces.

81 Interviews with Duncan Abraham, 1995 and 1997.

82 Abraham, 'A Vision,' *SJCN*, Easter 1988.

83 Interview with Douglas Stoute, 1995; note by Douglas Stoute, 1997; 'Rector's Report,' Feb. 1996, in *AR* (1995); interview with Moira Esdaile and Helen Watson, 1995; notes by William Cooke, 1997.

84 Vestry minutes, 11 Feb. 1996, item 5; interview with Moira Esdaile and Helen Watson, 1995; notes by William Cooke, 1997.

85 Interview with Douglas Stoute, 1995; interviews with Philip Hobson, 1995 and 1997; various service leaflets, 1987, 1995–7.

86 Interview with Joyce Sowby, 1995; interview with Moira Esdaile and Helen Watson, 1995.

87 Interviews with Philip Hobson, 1995 and 1997.

88 Interview with Jane Watanabe, 1995.

89 Interview with Giles Bryant, 1995; Lunch Hours at St. James', Free Concerts in the Cathedral, 1994–5 and 1995–6; 'The King of Instruments at the Cathedral Church of Saint James, Toronto,' Bicentennial International Organ Recital Series, 1996–7.

90 Interview with Bernard von Bieberstein, 1995.

91 Conversation with Bishop Terence Finlay, 1997; interviews with Douglas Stoute and Philip Hobson, 1995.

92 Interview with Moira Esdaile and Helen Watson, 1995; interview with Giles Bryant, 1995.

93 Liturgical Arts Festival: A Contemporary and Historical Church Art Exhibition, curated by Helen Bradfield, St. James' Cathedral, 14 Sept. to Oct. 15, 1989.

94 For example, *AR* (1985), with figures for 1983–5.

95 *SJCN*, Easter 1988; service leaflet, 27 Oct. 1991; *Anglican* (Jan. 1995), 1; and (June 1995), 5; service leaflet, 29 June 1997.

96 Margaret Best, 'Plus ça change ... ,' *SJCN*, Lent 1975; 'Ringing in the Next Century, the Bells of St. James,' 1995, SJCA; 'The Bermondsey Bells Coming to Toronto in 1997,' *SJCN*, Advent 1996; 'Welcome Reception Greets Bells at Pier 51,' *SJCN*, Easter 1997.

97 'St. James' Cathedral 200 Year Anniversary[sic],' 1996, 3.

98 'Report of the Sub-Committee re the Proposed Use of St. James' Cathedral as Either the Pro-Cathedral or the Diocesan Cathedral,' 1935, SJCA; *AR*(1931), 7; C.E. Woollcombe, *Grace Church on-the-Hill, 1874–1964* (Toronto 1964).

99 Parish Boundaries, Parish of St James, 17 May 1918, Property File, DTA; Hayes, ed., *By Grace Co-Workers*, 87–8; *Parish of St. Andrew-by-the-Lake, Toronto Island, 1875–1975* (Toronto: n.d.); W. Arthur Hand to W.J. Gilling, 17 Feb. 1965, Parochial Boundaries Commission, (Anglican), DTA; Boundaries for the Parish of St James' Cathedral, St James Deanery, 8 May 1984, Parochial Boundaries Commission, DTA.

100 Maps of land use, 1885 and 1941, by Nadine A.H. Deacon, and 'Metropolitan Toronto Average Family Income 1971,' in Richard P. Baine and A. Lynn McMurray, *Toronto: An Urban Study*, rev. ed. (Toronto 1977), 31, 34, 70; Seton Austin Thompson, *Jarvis Street*; CM, 30 July 1978 and 4 Nov. 1979.

101 Elliot G. Strathy, 8 Feb. 1935, in CM, 1935, SJCA; 'Sketch Showing the Various Properties Owned by the Corporation at Present,' with letter of F. Hilton Wilkes to the Vestry Clerk, 30 Jan. 1935, SJCA; Park Lot Properties (Part), 1936, SJCA.

102 *Mail and Empire*, 29 Jan. 1935, SJCA; *Hush*, 22 Dec. and 29 Dec. 1934, SJCA; Strathy, 8 Feb. 1935, *Canadian Churchman*, 1935, SJCA; AR (1935), 8; notices from the Office of the Housing Inspectors between 1936 and 1938, SJCA; Elmes Henderson and Son to L.V. Wright, 4 June 1937, SJCA; AR (1937), 5, 8; clipping from AR (1938), 6; 'General Maintenance Account,' in AR (1943); CM, various dates, 1935–45.

103 Baines and McMurray, *Toronto: An Urban Story*, 73–4.

104 Churchwardens to the Mayor of Toronto, 18 May and 13 Nov. 1944, SJCA; CM, 16 Nov. 1945 and 11 Jan. 1947.

105 AR (1962), 5–6; Gilling, 'Functions of a Dean and Cathedral in the Inner City,' 1964, SJCA, 2; AR (1965), 5.

106 AR (1947), 39; Gilling, 'Inner City,' 2; AR (1988), 1; *SJCN* (Lent 1976).

107 *Toronto 150: Portrait of a Changing City* (Ottawa 1985), 15, 20.

108 *SJCN*, Feb. 1971; A. Myrlene Boken, 'Report for the Diocesan Planning Study, Sept. 1993, St James portion,' Table 1; 'St James' Cathedral 200 Year Anniversary[sic],' 1996, 4; 'New Deputy Warden Welcomed at Annual Vestry,' *SJCN*, Easter 1997.

109 Interviews with Duncan Abraham, Douglas Stoute, Philip Hobson, and Jane Watanabe, 1995.

110 Statistical returns for the years indicated, TSJ.

111 Statistical returns, 1935–60, *ibid.*

112 These names are ubiquitous in brass plates, stone markers, stained glass, and wooden plaques throughout the cathedral; the list of churchwardens is permanently mounted in the southwest vestibule; 'Memorials and Bequests (from 1935 to 1962),' AR (1962), 15–16; for the social connections of these and other St James' names, see Edward Marion Chadwick, *Ontarian Families: Genealogies of United Empire Loyalists and Other Pioneer Families of Upper Canada* (Belleville 1972).

113 AR (1950), 5.

114 Baptismal registers for 1935 and 1936; service leaflets for Easter 1935, 1936, and 1937, SJCA; 'The Easter Offering,' April 1935, SJCA.

115 CM, 1943–62, *passim*; *ibid.*, 8 Aug. 1962, and 11 June 1968; AR (1983); CM, 14 May, 9 June, 17 Sept. 1987; brass plaques tell the family history of many pews; interview with Philip Hobson, 1997.

116 AR (1936), 10; (1948), 17; (1956), 7; (1962), 19; (1967), 12.

117 Interview with Joyce Sowby, 1995.

118 'Report on the Inventory of Parish Resources,' 1970, SJCA; Baptismal Registers for 1965, 1970, and 1981.

119 *SJCN*, Nov. 1971.

120 Reginald W. Bibby, *Anglitrends: A Profile and Prognosis. A Study Carried Out for the Anglican Diocese of Toronto* (April 1986), 10–11.

121 Report on the Inventory of Parish Resources, 1970, SJCA; Statistical Returns, for 1940, 1950, 1955, 1960, and 1975, TSJ; AR (1952), 45–6; AR (1964); Parish list for the financial campaign of 1979, SJCA; Bibby, *Anglitrends*, 117.

122 AR (1962), 19.

123 'Report on the Inventory of Parish Resources,' 1970, SJCA.

124 CM, 14 Jan. 1969.

125 Interview with Jane Watanabe, 1995; interview with Douglas Stoute, 1995.

126 Interview with Moira Esdaile and Helen Watson, 1995; interview with Barbara Hawkins, 1995.

127 Statistical Returns, TSJ, 1955–96.

128 *AR* (1985), with figures for 1983–5; Rector's Annual Report for 1971, in *SJCN*, Feb. 1972.

129 All the financial figures that follow, unless otherwise stated, are based on the annual reports to vestry, *AR* (1929–96). The numbers for Tables 4.2, 4.3, and 4.4 are derived from these reports, but for purposes of analysis I have reconfigured them. It was common practice much of the time to place certain kinds of revenue under expenditures and reduce the expenditure totals and also to place some expenditures under revenue in some years. I have added such revenue and expenditures to the appropriate sides and increased the totals accordingly. Hence these figures frequently differ from the totals published in the annual reports. Because I have rounded the percentages to the nearest whole number, the total may be more or less than 100 per cent.

130 The items in Table 4.3 represent my attempt to find categories that fit the figures as given in the annual reports to vestry while also permitting comparisons over time. The actual categories varied year by year, but I have regrouped the figures according to the items shown.

131 *AR* (various years, 1935–96); CM, 12 Jan. 1982; interview with Giles Bryant, 1995; interview with Philip Hobson, 1997.

132 CM, various dates, 5 Jan. 1966–8 July 1969; *AR* (1967), 19–22.

133 CM, 5 July 1976–23 Aug. 1977; Syndey Wrightson to Hugh Stiff, 2 June 1977, SJCA.

134 For comparison: the 1995 budget of the Church of the Redeemer, Toronto, designated 9 per cent for music (Church of the Redeemer, Annual Report for 1995); St Peter's Church, Toronto, paid about 3 per cent (interview with Gordon Finney, 1997); 'Cathedral Music as Christian Outreach,' *SJCN* (Lent 1975).

135 CM, 17 Nov. 1975; 'Restoration, 1979–1982,' *AR* (1982), 6.

136 *AR* (1961), 14; 'B.F.H. Graham, Property Report,' *AR* (1987); 'Graham, Property Report–Tower Restoration,' *AR* (1991).

137 CM, 10 July 1934.

138 CM, variously, 1957–97.

139 CM, 19 Dec. 1990, 12 Dec. 1991, 10 Dec. 1992, and 3 Feb. 1994; 1991 Diocesan Apportionment Calculation, *ibid.*, 17 Oct. 1990; 1997 Diocesan Apportionment Calculation, TSJ.

140 As in Table 4.3, I have attempted to fit the figures from the annual reports to vestry into categories that allow for comparison over the whole span of years. I use 1938 instead of 1937, since it represents a recovery from the Depression.

141 CM, 12 Jan. 1982, 24 Jan., and 11 April 1983.

142 *AR* (1931), (1945), (1948), (1951), (1981), (1996); interview with Robert F. Hollands, 1997.

143 CM, 9 Feb. and 8 March 1938; *SJCN*, 1967; *AR* (1970) and 1971.

144 'Report of the Inventory of Parish Resources,' by Trevor Morrison, 1970, SJCA; 'Report by the Churchwardens to the Corporation and Ad Hoc Advisory Members of the Congregation,' 26 March 1971, and 'Report by the Rector and Churchwardens to the Special Committee of the Board of Administration and Finance, Diocese of Toronto,' 13 April 1971, with accompanying forecasts of operations, 1971–80, SJCA.

145 Figures were published in 'Give Your Church an Anniversary Gift' (1972); 'The Stewardship Campaign,' 1976; Dean Abraham to Members of St James' Cathedral, July 1990; and 'Response '92,' SJCA.

146 CM, various dates, Sept. 1987–1990s; 'Development Feasibility Study, St James Cathedral/York Rectory Lands, Anglican Church of Canada,' presented by Canderal Limited, 25 March 1991, SJCA; churchwardens' report to vestry, Feb. 1997, in *AR* (1996).

147 *AR* (1964), 15.

148 'Churchwardens' report,' *AR* (1975), 3; Minutes of special vestry meeting, 1976.

149 Financial Statements for 1990, and for 1996; Churchwardens Report, *AR* (1996).

150 CM, various dates, 1935–45.

151 Financial Statements for 1976, 16.

152 CM, 14 July 1970.

153 Minutes of the Investment Committee, 19 Nov. 1937 and 20 Oct. 1939, SJCA; CM, 8 Dec. 1937 and 27 Oct. 1939.

154 The lists of holdings for these years are in Financial Statements for 1976; *AR* (1984); *AR* (1989); RBC Dominion Securities, Canadian Dollar Account Statement, Cathedral Portfolio of St James Cathedral, 31 Dec. 1996.

155 *AR* (1984); see 'Tops in Their Fields, 1988' and 'Largest Canadian Financial Institutions, 1988' (source: *The Financial Post* 500), in 1990 *Canadian World Almanac and Book of Facts* (Toronto 1989), 343 and 345.

156 'Rector's Report,' *AR* (1987), 32.

157 *SJCN*, Ascension 1977; 'Investment Committee, The Cathedral Church of St. James,' CM, 12 Jan. 1982, 466.

158 CM, 15 Oct. 1987; *ibid.*, 11 Sept. 1990, 8 Nov. 1990, 20 Feb. 1991, 30 May 1991.

159 Statistical returns, 1920s–95, TSJ; Service Register/Vestry Book, various dates, 1935–95.

160 BCP (1918), 265, 275–6; Order of Services, 24 March 1940; Order of Services, 9 May 1943.

161 Lenten Services leaflet, 1950; Service Registers/Vestry Books, various years, 1935–95; BCP (1918), 291; BCP (1962), 88–9; Easter Day service leaflet, 1953; service leaflet, 6 Jan. 1963; 'Service Statistics, 1981–1983,' in *AR* (1983).

162 See service leaflet, 15 Dec. 1957; service leaflet, 26 March 1967.

163 Most of what follows about parish groups is drawn from the Annual Report to Vestry, 1935–65.

164 Leaflet, 'The Way of Renewal,' 7 Oct.–25 Nov. 1934, SJCA.

165 *AR* (1958) and (1960).

166 *AR* (1939), (1945), (1947); T.G. Wallace, *The Duties of Churchwardens and Sidesmen* (Toronto 1930), 14–15; Canon 16 of *Constitution and Canons, Diocese of Toronto*, 1961 edition.

167 J.S. Grasett, 'History of the W.A., St. James Cathedral' (1935), SJCA; Beatrice H. Kilpatrick, '1939–1964, Reminiscences of 25 Years, Afternoon Branch of the Women's Auxiliary of the Cathedral Church of St. James, Toronto' (1964), SJCA.

168 Full reports of the WA were published in the annual reports to vestry.

169 *AR* (1935–64); Acts 9:36–42.

170 See *AR* (1935–60s, particularly 1944, 1952); *AR* (1965); CM, 19 Oct. 1937, 26 Jan. and 2 June 1939.

171 See *AR* (1935–60); TSJ, 1955 and 1960; *AR* (1964), 18.

172 Service leaflet, 24 March 1940; *AR* (1943), 15, and for 1946, 18; CM, 2 Feb. 1940 and 2 Oct. 1941; annual Christmas cards, SJCA; interview with Margaret Peel, 1995.

173 *SJCN*, Easter 1992; 'Parish Profile,' Diocese of Toronto, 2 Nov. 1994, 2; interview with Jane Watanabe, 1995.

174 *AR* (1966), 5.

175 Canon 17 of *Constitution and Canons*, 1961 edition, Diocese of Toronto; *AR* (1962), 6; (1964), 9; (1965), 9; (1967), 9–10.

176 *AR* (1967), 9–11; (1968), 9; CM, 8 July 1969, and 12 Jan. 1970; *SJCN*, Pentecost 1994, 2; *AR* (1975).

177 *AR* (1976); *SJCN*, spring 1975; *SJCN*, summer 1975; *SJCN*, autumn 1975.

178 *AR* (1966), 5; Tour Guides' Association, *AR* (1968), 35; for most of the 1970s the Sunday leaflet listed the Coffee Hour Committee as a separate parish society chaired by a man, but there was also a women's Coffee Hour Group; *SJCN*, 1967; *AR* (1952), 19; *SJCN*, Ascension 1977; *AR* (1977) and (1979); interview with Margaret Peel, 1995; interview with Moira Esdaile and Helen Watson, 1995.

179 CM, 20 Oct. and 6 Dec. 1965.

180 *SJCN*, Ascentiontide 1976.

181 CM, 22 Sept. 1970.

182 'Christian Education Report,' *AR* (1968), 27–8; CM, 11 Nov. 1969; Michael Bedford-Jones, *SJCN*, Feb. 1971 and Michaelmas 1976.

183 Minutes of the Church School Working Group, 1969; *SJCN*, Jan. 1972; *ibid*., Ascensiontide, 1976; 'The Church School, a New Direction,' *ibid*. Thanksgiving 1995; 'Parish Profile,' 2 Nov. 1994, SJCA; interview with Br. Michael Stonebraker, 1995.

184 Service leaflet for 16 Nov. 1986.

185 The cathedral's newsletter (*SJCN*) and the Sunday leaflets told parishioners about these educational opportunities in numerous articles over the years.

186 William Cooke, 'Regaining the Past: the Archives of St. James,' *SJCN*, spring 1975; *AR* (1975), 3.

187 'Anglican Church Women,' *AR* (1968), 28–30; *SJCN*, March 1973; *AR* (1981); *SJCN*, spring 1975.

188 'Final Report of the Renewal '69 Committee,' Sept. 1969, and 1970 Annual Report of the Renewal '70 Committee,' 7 Dec. 1970, SJCA; *SJCN* (Nov. 1971); *AR* (1979); Steering Committee for the Restoration Appeal, 25 July 1979, SJCA.

189 Interview with Barbara Hawkins, 1995; biographical article on Barbara Hawkins, *SJCN* (Easter 1990); interview with Abraham, 1995; Wallace, *Churchwardens and Sidesmen*, 3.

190 'Meet Our New Deputy Warden,' *SJCN* (Pentecost 1994); Vestry Minutes, 11 Feb. 1996.

191 Interview with Margaret Peel, 1995; articles on the ACW and the York Group, *SJCN*, spring 1975; *AR* (1989); 'York Group,' *SJCN*, Epiphany 1993; 'York Group,' *SJCN*, Epiphany 1994.

192 *SJCN*, 1967; *AR* (1989).

193 CM, 5 July and 19 Aug. 1976.

194 *AR* (1976).

195 CM, 28 Aug. 1984–22 May 1985; 'Report of the Outreach Committee,' 3–4, in *AR* (1987); memorandum on the dispute between the diocese and the corporation on the auditorium lease, by Barry Graham to Duncan Abraham, 29 Sept. 1989, SJCA; interview with Duncan Abraham, 1995; interview with Barbara Hawkins, 1995.

196 *SJCN*, Sept. 1983 and Sept. 1987; *AR* (1987); *SJCN*, Easter 1988; Local Outreach Committee Report, 1989, in *AR* (1989); Barbara Hawkins, 'Christmas: A Special Time for Thinking of Others,' *SJCN*, Christmas 1990; CM, 30 May 1991; 'Victoria–Shuter Non-Profit Housing Corporation,' *SJCN*, Advent 1995; interview with Barbara Hawkins, 1995.

197 *AR* (1967), (1968); CM, 12 March 1968; *AR* (1970); CM, 14 Dec. 1971; *AR* (1975); CM, 14 Feb., 14 March, and 25 April 1989; *SJCN*, summer 1989; *AR* (1990); CM, 27 April 1992; *SJCN*, Thanksgiving 1995, 5; *AR* (1995).

198 *AR* (1992–5); *SJCN*, Pentecost 1995, 7.

199 Rector's Report, *AR (1974)*, 2; 'Dean's Report,' ibid. 1975, 2; notes by William Cooke, 1997, SJCA.

200 Wendy Fletcher-Marsh, *Beyond the Walled Garden: Anglican Women and the Priesthood* (Toronto 1996), 77, 121–2, 261.

201 *SJCN* (March 1973); 'Rector's Report,' *AR (1972)*, 8; CM, 11 Aug. 1970.

202 Service leaflets, 1976 onward; 'Readers 11 a.m.,' 1995, SJCA.

203 Actually, the remark by Stiff that people circulated around the cathedral and the diocese was: 'There'll be no tits in the chancel.' Interview with Joyce Sowby, 1995; interviews with Elizabeth Kilbourn, 1997; interview with John Gibaut, 1996; see also Giles Bryant, 'Bishop Stiff (1916–1995), a Personal Appreciation,' *SJCN*, Advent 1995, 1, where Bryant suggests that Stiff 'might have been called a misogynist' while also noting that many men and women held a 'deep and lasting affection' for him.

204 *SJCN*, Lent 1978; 'Report of the Sacristans' Guild for 1987,' in *AR (1987)*; 'Report of the Servers' Guild,' in *AR (1987)*; *SJCN*, Christmas 1987; CM, 14 March 1989, and 12 Feb. 1990; interviews with Duncan Abraham, 1995 and 1997, John Gibaut, 1996, Barbara Hawkins, 1995, and Mary Jane Tuthill, 1997; *SJCN*, Christmas 1989; Server's Guild, Service Availability List and Servers Needed for Services, 1993, SJCA; notes by William Cooke, 1997.

205 CM, 30 May and 2 July 1991; SJCN (fall 1991).

206 CM, 29 June 1967; 'Report of the Choir Advisory Committee,' *AR (1968)*, 19–22.

207 Interviews with Giles Bryant, 1995 and Bernard Von Bieberstein, 1995; CM, 19 Aug. 1976–23 Aug. 1977; The Final Report of the Dean's Task Force, June 1989, SJCA; 'Parish Workshop–Saturday May 7, 1994,' SJCA. Newsletter features over the years included: 'Cathedral Music as Christian Outreach,' *SJCN*, Lent 1975; see also issues for spring 1979, summer 1988, Thanksgiving 1988, and Christmas 1988; and 'Young Choristers,' Pentecost 1993.

208 *SJCN*, Easter 1997, 5; Bicentennial Homecoming Weekend Celebrations, May 30–June 1, 1997, SJCA.

209 Interviews with Elizabeth Kilbourn, 1997, Ansley Tucker, 1997, David Bousfield, 1997, and Duncan Abraham, 1995; 'The Rev. Elizabeth Kilbourn,' *SJCN*, Christmas 1989.

210 Michael Esdaile, 'A Conference Report,' *SJCN*, Easter 1988.

211 'Final Report of the Dean's Task Force,' June 1989, SJCA; Duncan Abraham to the Members of St James' Cathedral, July 1989, SJCA; *SJCN*, summer 1989; CM, 23 Nov. 1989 and 16 Jan. 1990.

212 Interview with Donald Butler, 1997; article on Butler, *SJCN*, Thanksgiving 1989; notes by William Cooke, 1997.

213 Minutes of the Vestry meeting, 4 Feb. 1990, 2; interview with Duncan Abraham, 1995; CM, 12 Feb. 1997.

214 Interview with Carol D. Langley, 1997; 'Welcome to our Assistant Curate,' *SJCN*, Christmas 1990; interview with John Gibaut, 1996; notes by William Cooke, 1997; notes by Duncan Abraham, 1997; interview with Donald Butler, 1997; *SJCN*, fall 1991; BCP (1962), 77–8.

215 Interview with Jane Watanabe, 1995; notes by William Cooke, 1997; 'Parish Profile,' 2 Nov. 1994, SJCA.

216 Service leaflet for the Ordination of Deacons, 4 May 1997, SJCA.

217 Interviews with John Gibaut, 1996, Duncan Abraham, 1995 and 1997, Giles Bryant, 1995, Joyce Sowby, 1995, and Elizabeth Kilbourn, 1997; *AR (1992)*; 'Homosexuality–Challenged and Challenging,' three study sessions, May 1993.

218 'Parish Workshop–Saturday May 7, 1994,' SJCA.

219 'Draft Confidential: Towards a Vision for St. James' Cathedral,' presented to vestry, Feb. 1997, 3.

220 J.H. Churchill and Alan Webster, 'From Close to Open: A Future for the Past,' in David Marcombe

and C.S. Knighton, eds., *Close Encounters: English Cathedral and Society since 1540* (Nottingham 1991), 161–84. See also T.R. Beeson, *Mission and Management in the Cathedral* (Great Britain, 1991).

5: ARCHITECTURE

1 Carl Benn wrote on the first church (1807–33), and Shirley Morriss is responsible for the rest of the chapter. Carl Benn would like to thank the Revd Douglas Graydon for his architectural renderings of the 1807 structure and express his appreciation to William Cooke for editorial advice. Shirley Morriss would like to acknowledge her indebtedness to Douglas Richardson for suggesting the architectural history of St James' Cathedral as a subject for study, for his encouragement in the writing of a thesis and an article on F.W. Cumberland's church architecture, and for his helpful assistance in the preparation of this work; and to Stephen Otto for a thoughtful reading of the text and his editorial suggestions.

2 'Report of the proceedings of the meeting held at St James' Church,' 10 Jan. 1831, Str P, AO.

3 Anne Powell to George Murray, 31 Mar. 1807, in Firth, ed., *York. 1793–1815*, 201.

4 George Okill Stuart to SPG, 1 July 1805, copy, SJCA; General Account of Expenditures, 4 March 1810, March 1812, Minute Book, 1807–30; SJCA, and engraving: 'First Church Built at Toronto,' in Ernest Hawkins, *Annals of the Diocese of Toronto* (London 1848), reproduced as Figure 1.4 (p. 9).

5 Stuart to the SPG, 18 Sept. 1807, copy, SJCA; A.N. Bethune, *Memoir of the Right Reverend John Strachan* (Toronto 1870), 83. The interior description is somewhat conjectural, based on period documentation, supplemented by what was typical for Anglican churches constructed during the period, along with what is known about York's church from the 1818 renovations. See James Strachan (pseud.; actually by John Strachan), *A Visit to the Province of Upper Canada in 1819*, first published 1820 (New York 1968), 141; John Stuart to the SPG, 15 March 1794, in Richard A. Preston, ed., *Kingston before the War of 1812* (Toronto 1959), 289–90; Hélène Bergevin, *Églises protestantes* (Louisville, PQ: 1981), 182–3; G.W.O. Addleshaw and Frederick Etchells, *The Architectural Setting of Anglican Worship* (London 1948), 162–5; Marion MacRae and Anthony Adamson, *Hallowed Walls: Church Architecture of Upper Canada* (Toronto 1975), 11–15, 34–42; and Henry Scadding, *Toronto of Old: Collections and Recollections* (Toronto 1873), 120–2, 148.

6 List of expenditures for 1821, Minute Book, 1807–30, SJCA; and Addleshaw and Etchells, *Architectural Setting*, 165–8.

7 M.J. Hatchett, *The Making of the First American Book of Common Prayer, 1776–1789* (New York 1982), 1.

8 G. Stuart to the SPG, 8 Feb. 1807, in Firth, ed., *York, 1793–1815*, 201; William Boulton to Mrs Boulton, 30 Nov. 1833, in Firth, ed., *York, 1815–1834*, 220–1; Scadding, *Toronto of Old*, 120–1; and General Accompt of Expenditures, 4 March 1810, March 1812, Minute Book, 1807–30, SJCA.

9 John Strachan to Patrick Hartney, 30 Nov. 1814, and memorandum, n.d., in Spragge, ed., *Strachan Letter Book*, 66, 104.

10 John Douglas, *Medical Topography of Upper Canada* (1819) quoted in Firth, ed., *York, 1793–1815*, 334–5; Memorandum, 11 July 1818, War Loss Claim, 1 March 1824, NA, RG 8, British Military Records, 65:304; and John Duncan, *Travels through Part of the United States and Canada* (1818); Firth, ed., *York, 1815–1834*, 178, 304.

11 Strachan to Anthony Hamilton, 5 Jan. 1820, in Spragge, ed., *Strachan Letter Book*, 197.

12 C.A Hagerman to John Macaulay, 17 Feb. 1821, in Firth, ed., *York, 1815–1834*, 185; MacRae and Adamson, *Hallowed Walls*, 51; Scadding, *Toronto of Old*, 120–2; and list of expenditures, 1821, Minute Book, 1807–30, SJCA.

13 'Sketch Shewing the Church Ground and Site of the New Church,' 24 Oct. 1831, SJCA; MacRae and Adamson, *Hallowed Walls*, 50–2; and Scadding, *Toronto of Old*, 122.

14 N.d., quoted in MacRae and Adamson, *Hallowed Walls*, 51.

15 Scadding, *Toronto of Old*, 121.

16 Meeting of parishioners, 9 Aug. 1819, Minute Book, 1807–30, SJCA; and Firth, ed., *York, 1815–1834*, iii.

17 'Report of the proceedings of the meeting held at St James' Church,' 10 Jan. 1831, with an appendix of 24 April 1830, AO, Str P, 49.

18 Petition of St James' Anglican Church to Lieut. Gov. Sir John Colborne, 26 April 1830, in Firth, ed., *York, 1815–1834*, 197–8.

19 G. Murray (Colonial Office, London) to Sir John Colborne, 15 Sept. 1830, SJCA.

20 'The State of the Church ...,' n.d., AO, Str P, M535, package 7; see also William Boulton to Mrs. William Boulton, 30 Nov. 1833, in Firth, ed., *York, 1815–1834*, 220–1.

21 Robert Stanton, churchwarden, to John Macauley, 23 March and 15 April 1831, Macauley Papers, MS 78 and MU 5836, AO (courtesy of Stephen Otto). J. Douglas Stewart speculates that Macauley, a prominent Kingston merchant and former pupil of Strachan, recommended Rogers as architect; see Thomas Rogers biography, *DCB*, 8:760.

22 *Colonial Advocate*, 2 June 1831, 1.

23 See the agreement and specifications in John Ross Robertson, *Landmarks of Toronto*, 6 vols. (Toronto, 1896–1914), 2:1025–34; see also MacRae and Adamson, *Hallowed Walls*, 206–7. For Chewett and Ritchey, see Eric Arthur, *Toronto, No Mean City*, 3rd ed., rev. Stephen A. Otto (Toronto 1986), 243 and 269.

24 'A form ... Church of St. James, York, Upper Canada,' SJCA.

25 See Addleshaw and Etchells, *Architectural Setting*, 52–8 and 247–50, for references to the auditory type.

26 Undated contract with John Lacey, SJCA, and Strachan to Mrs James Brown, 28 Sept. 1833, in Firth, ed., *York, 1815–1834*, 219.

27 Anna Brownell Jameson, *Winter Studies and Summer Rambles in Canada*, 3 vols. (London 1838), 1:274.

28 Strachan to Brown, and 'The State of the Church ... Ways and Means', n.d., Str P, AO, M535, package 7.

29 Reprinted in the *Brockville Recorder*, 11 Oct. 1833, 2 (courtesy of Stephen Otto).

30 'Address and Report of the Venerable Archdeacon of York January 9, 1839,' TRL, BR, 283.713.S76.3; see also the *Church*, 12 Jan. 1839, 119.

31 See 'Report of the Committee appointed by the Congregation of St James' Church. 9th January 1839,' TRL, BR, 283.713.T59. Howard's and Young's recommendations are appended. For Howard's solution to the division of the windows see TRL, BR, L26, 332. Young specifically referred to Soane's church in the 'New Road,' Holy Trinity, erected in 1826 on what is now known as Marylebone Road.

32 Building Committee Minutes 1839–40, 25 Feb., 12 and 21 March 1839, SJCA.

33 Shirley Morriss, Thomas Young biography, *DCB*, 8:959–61; see also Montreal *Gazette*, 30 Aug. 1836, 1, and the Home District Quarter Sessions Minutes, Jan.–May 1837, AO, RG 22 (both references, courtesy of Stephen Otto). For Young's treatment of King's College see Douglas Richardson with J.M.S. Careless, G.M. Craig, and Peter Heyworth, *A Not Unsightly Building: University College and its History* (Oakville, Ont., 1990), 33–40.

34 *Commercial Herald*, 2 Nov. 1839, 3 (courtesy of Stephen Otto).

35 Thomas Young to Thomas Hector, 3 Aug. and 29 Oct. 1839; see also Building Committee Minutes, 26 Aug. 1839, SJCA.

36 'Report of the Committee,' 5.

37 *Church*, 28 Dec. 1839, 102.

38 *Ibid.*, 26 Feb. 1842, 135.

39 Historical Register, c. 1890 (1905), 17 and 19, SJCA; see also Vestry minutes, 1842–1907, 21 Dec. 1849, SJCA.

40 [A.W.H. Rose], *The Emigrant Churchman in Canada by a Pioneer of the Wilderness*, edited by the Rev. Henry Christmas, 2 vols. in 1 (London 1849), 1:84.

41 Frederick H. Armstrong, *A City in the Making* (Toronto 1988), 'Map of 1849 fire area,' 256 and 271–2; see also *Examiner*, 11 April 1849, 2–3.

42 'Report of the Committee Appointed by the Vestry of St. James's Church to Report on the Rebuilding of the Church,' 5 May 1849, 1–2; see also 'Conditions etc. of Competition Designs of St James' Church, Toronto,' 4 June 1849, SJCA.

43 Strachan to the Rev. Ernest Hawkins, 21 April 1849, SLB, 1839–1866.

44 'Report of the Committee,' 5 May, 1849, 2, and 'Conditions.'

45 With the possible exception of St Paul's, Yorkville, where the visual records conflict, the Anglican churches erected in the Toronto area in the 1840s – St John's, York Mills, 'Little' Trinity, and St George the Martyr – were all in some sort of Gothic. Holy Trinity was required to be Gothic by the terms of the donor; see MacRae and Adamson, *Hallowed Walls*, 99–100 and 105–6.

46 'Report of the Committee,' 5 May 1849, 2.

47 The standard account of the Ecclesiological Society and its work is James F. White, *The Cambridge Movement: The Ecclesiologists and the Gothic Revival* (Cambridge 1962). For a summary of its influence in Canada see Harold Kalman, *A History of Canadian Architecture*, 2 vols. (Toronto 1994), 1:279–96.

48 'Church Architecture,' *Church*, 10 Sept. 1847, 34.

49 On the changing relationship between church and state, see William Westfall, *Two Worlds: The Protestant Culture of Nineteenth-Century Ontario* (Montreal 1989), especially chapters 4 and 5.

50 *Church*, 7 June 1849, 179.

51 *Ibid.*, 13 Sept. 1849, 2, and 20 Sept. 1849, 30.

52 Frederick Armstrong and Peter Baskerville, Frederic William Cumberland biography, *DCB*, 11:225–9; see also Richardson, *A Not Unsightly Building*, 53–4, and for the most recent account of Cumberland's early years and a discussion of his church architecture, Geoffrey Simmins, *Fred Cumberland: Building the Victorian Dream* (Toronto 1997), chapters 1, 2, and 12.

53 *Church*, 8 Jan. 1842, 106.

54 Historical Register, 21, SJCA.

55 *Ecclesiologist*, 5 (Feb. 1846), 81.

56 *Ibid.*, 8 (April 1848), 276–7.

57 *Church*, 13 Sept. 1849, 26.

58 George H. Smith to Churchwardens Thomas D. Harris and Lewis Moffat, 10 Aug. 1849, SJCA; St Andrew's was designed by [J.W.?] Tate in partnership with George Smith; see Sandra Coley, 'The Church of St. Andrew and St. Paul: Architecture and Patronage,' *SSAC Bulletin*, 16 no. 1 (March 1991), 4–6.

59 'Second Report of the Committee Appointed by the Vestry of St. James's Church, to Report on the Rebuilding of the Church,' 4 Dec. 1849, 2, SJCA.

60 'Bramhall' to the 'Vestry-Men of the Parish of St. James,' 17 Dec. 1849, TRL, BR, Broadside Collection (1849).

61 F.R.S. to the Editor, *Globe*, 4 Dec. 1849, 467; see also 'Second Report of the Committee,' 4 Dec. 1849,

1, and Building Committee Minutes, 27 Oct. 1849, SJCA.

62 *Ecclesiologist*, 2 (April 1843), 120.

63 F.R.S. to the Editor, *Globe*.

64 'An Act to Enable the Rector and Church Wardens of the Protestant Episcopal Church of St. James, Toronto, to Lease Part of the Land heretofore Occupied by Them as the Site of a Church and Burying Ground, 30 May 1849,' Canada (Province), Laws, Statutes, etc., *The Provincial Statutes of Canada, 1848–1849*, 645; see also *Patriot*, 6 Feb. 1850, 3.

65 Thomas to W. Wakefield (an anti-leasing member of the building committee), 8 Nov. 1849, included in 'Resolutions and Amendments, to be Submitted to the Vestry of St. James's Church,' 14 Dec. 1849, SJCA; see also drawing showing an outline of Thomas' plan superimposed on the old walls; C-11-49-0-2-(55)7. Horwood Collection, AO.

66 Kivas Tully, 'Memorandum for the Congregation of St. James' Church,' 12 Dec. 1849, Broadside Collection, 1849, TRL, BR.

67 'Report of the Committee,' 5 May 1849, 5, and 'Second Report of the Committee,' 4 Dec. 1849, 3; see also 'Resolutions and Amendments,' 5–8, SJCA.

68 *Patriot*, 6 March 1850, 3; 9 March 1850, 2; 23 March 1850, 2; and 27 March 1850, 2.

69 Building Committee Minutes, 9 April 1850, SJCA.

70 Ibid., 26 July and 1 Aug. 1850. The contract drawings, dated 18 November 1850 (SJCA), indicate that the church was to be built on the foundations of the old side walls; in fact, it was centred between Church Street and the eastern limit of what was thought of as the church site – 'an open space 260 feet square' (see 'Conditions,'); see also 'Report of the Building Committee,' included in Vestry minutes, July 1850.

71 For Metcalfe, Wilson & Forbes, see Arthur, *Toronto* (rev. Otto), 268.

72 *Church*, 13 Sept. 1849, 2.

73 Thomas to Wakefield, 8 Nov. 1849, SJCA.

74 For Wills's design for Fredericton Cathedral see Douglas Richardson, Frank Wills biography, *DCB*, 8:942, and Kalman, *Canadian Architecture*, 1:282–3.

75 *Church*, 13 Sept 1849, 26.

76 *Ibid*., 11 Oct. 1849, 42.

77 *Ibid*., 24 Jan. 1850, 102 (courtesy of Robert Hill).

78 *Ecclesiologist*, 18 (Dec. 1857) 357–9; see also Richardson, 'Frank Wills,' 944.

79 White, *The Cambridge Movement*, 106–9.

80 Included in Vestry minutes, 11 April 1853.

81 For more on Thomas Ridout see Arthur, *Toronto* (rev. Otto), 257.

82 Douglas Richardson discusses the individual abilities of both Cumberland and Storm as well as the nature of their partnership in *A Not Unsightly Building*, 52–5, 77, and 83–6; see also Shirley Morriss, William George Storm biography, *DCB*, 12:991–4.

83 Shirley G. Morriss, 'The Nine-Year Odyssey of a High Victorian Goth: Three Churches by Fred Cumberland,' *Journal of Canadian Art History*, 2 (summer 1975), 43–6.

84 Henry Russell Hitchcock, *Early Victorian Architecture in Britain*, 2 vols., first published London 1954 (New York 1972), 1:75–8.

85 See, for example, *Ecclesiologist*, 6 (Dec. 1846), 206 and 9 (April 1849), 331, leading up to Street's article in 11 (Dec. 1850), 227–33.

86 Frederic Cumberland, 'Some Notes of a Visit to the Works of the Grand Trunk Railway, west of

Toronto, February, 1855,' *Canadian Journal*, 3 (May 1855), 225–6.

87 Building Committee Minutes, 17 and 19 Jan. and 4 Feb. 1850, SJCA.

88 Perhaps the most notable example is Richard Upjohn's Trinity Church, New York City, 1840–6; see Phoebe Stanton, *The Gothic Revival and American Church Architecture* (Baltimore 1968), Fig. 11–15.

89 [Frederic] Barlow Cumberland, 'The Story of a University Building,' *Canadian Magazine*, 17 (July 1901), 236.

90 For an early view of St Paul's from the east, see Archie Bremner, *City of London, Ontario, Canada; The Pioneer Period and the London of Today* (London, Ont. 1897), 22; on enlargements to the east end see Frederick H. Armstrong and Daniel J. Brock, *Reflections on London's Past* (London, Ont. 1975), 26–7.

91 *Ecclesiologist*, 2 (April 1843), 120.

92 Phoebe Stanton gives examples of Pugin's apsidal chancels in *Pugin* (New York 1971), Figs. 18, 19, 27 and 32.

93 For George Street's encouragement of the form see *Ecclesiologist*, 13 (Aug. 1852), 257.

94 Cumberland and Storm owned studies of medieval architecture such as Raphael and J. Arthur Brandon, *An Analysis of Gothick Architecture*, 2 vols. (London 1847) and *Open Timber Roofs of the Middle Ages*, 2 vols. (London, 1849), both in Thomas Fisher Rare Book Library, University of Toronto, and see below n. 95.

95 Malcolm Thurlby sees St James' apse as a reduced version of Lichfield Cathedral's Lady Chapel and the exterior elevation of its nave as inspired by Salisbury Cathedral; see 'Medieval Toronto,' *Rotunda*, 24 (spring 1992), 28–31. See also William Dendy and William Kilbourn, *Toronto Observed, Its Architecture, Patrons, and History* (Toronto 1986), 56–9. Cumberland owned a copy of John Britton's *History and Antiquities of the Cathedral Church of Salisbury* (London 1814) now in Thomas Fisher Rare Book Library, University of Toronto.

96 Following the failure of the contractors Metcalfe, Wilson & Forbes early in 1852, the Building Committee neglected to meet for a lengthy period, during which time a 'variety of extras unauthorized by the Committee were introduced on the Building' to form a large part of the increased cost; see 'Report of the Building Committee,' in Vestry minutes, 1 Feb. 1854, SJCA; there is no extant document that details the 'extras' or who was responsible for including them.

97 William Cooke, 'The Diocese of Toronto and Its Two Cathedrals,' *JCCHS* 37 (1985), 113, n 21.

98 *Church*, 23 June 1853, 2.

99 'Specifications ... Jacques & Hay, Contractor,' n.d., AO, Horwood Collection; see also *United Empire*, 16 June 1853, 3 (courtesy of Stephen Otto). Ruth Cathcart includes a history of the firm in *Jacques & Hay, 19th Century Toronto Furniture Makers* (Erin, Ont., 1986), 11–29.

100 Vestry minutes, 18 April 1858 and 9 May 1859.

101 The plans and contract are in the SJCA; for the tender call see the daily *Globe*, 29 Sept. 1864, 3, and see 29 Dec. 1865, 2, for the ringing of the bells.

102 The *Mail*, 22 June 1872, 2, details the anticipated work (courtesy of Stephen Otto); Langley's elevations for the transepts and porches and articles of agreement are at SJCA; his plans for the completion of the tower and addition of the spire are at AO, Horwood Collection. For Langley's body of work, see Douglas Richardson and Angela K. Carr, Henry Langley biography, *DCB*, 13: 572–5.

103 The heads are probably the work of Thomas Mowbray; see William Cochrane, ed., *The Canadian Album: Men of Canada*, 2 vols. (Brantford, Ont., 1891), 1:259.

104 Commemorative letter to the Dean of Toronto, 24 Dec. 1875 (typescript), SJCA; see also Graham Jones, *The Tower Clock of the Cathedral Church of St. James, Toronto* (Toronto 1997), 11–21.

105 *EC*, 5 Oct. 1876, 322.

106 John Ruskin, *The Seven Lamps of Architecture*, vols. 7–9, *The Complete Works of John Ruskin*, 39 vols. ed. E.T. Cook and Alexander Weddeburn, first published 1849. (London 1903), 8:116; for Ruskin's influence on Cumberland see Richardson, *A Not Unsightly Building*, 73–6.

107 Scadding, *Toronto of Old*, 99.

108 *AR* (1893), 12, SJCA; Shirley Ann Brown generously gave me access to her preliminary book text on Toronto's stained-glass windows.

109 *Globe*, 6 Nov. 1867, 3 (courtesy of Brian Gilchrist), and *AR* (1882), 7, and (1884), 12.

110 *AR* (1931), 6–7.

111 A memorial to William Jarvis, this window has been attributed to Tiffany Glass and Decorating Company of New York City; (see E.G. Strathy, *Guide*), 17; but a brochure of Calvert & Kimberly Co. (photocopy, SJCA) lists the window among that firm's commissions. Thomas Calvert apprenticed with Tiffany before leaving in 1899 to form Calvert & Kimberly; see *Stained Glass (Stained Glass Association of America Bulletin)*, (winter 1934–5), 114–15.

112 *SJCM*, Nov. 1903, 3, and Sept. 1905, 2; see also 'St. James' Cathedral, the Windows,' Aug. 1907 (loose page), and 'Order of Service ... Easter 1912,' SJCA. In Strathy, *Guide*, Frontispiece and 17–35 reproduce the chancel and nave windows.

113 'St. James' Cathedral, the Windows' and Strathy, *Guide*, 35.

114 Draft Report of the Finance Committee to the Vestry of St. James Cathedral upon the subject of Repairing and Adorning the Church,' n.d., SJCA: see also *AR* (1889), 14.

115 For Darling see Arthur, *Toronto* (rev. Otto), 244, and William Dendy, 'Darling & Pearson,' *Dictionary of Art* (New York, 1996), 8:528.

116 Frank Darling, 'Architect's Report ... ', n.d., appended to 'Draft Report.'

117 *AR* (1898), 6.

118 *AR* (1914), 19; see also Katharine A. Lochnan, 'Victorian Tiles in Toronto,' *Canadian Collector*, 16 no. 5 (Sept.–Oct. 1981), 55–6 (courtesy of Douglas Richardson).

119 Darling, 'Architect's Report,' 5, and *AR* for 1893, 12.

120 *AR* (1935), 6.

121 *AR* (1936), 8; see also *Evening Telegram*, 11 Dec. 1936, 15, and 5 Jan. 1937, 11.

122 *AR*, for 1941, 10; (1946), 15.

123 *AR* (1950), 16; see also plans, AO, Horwood Collection.

124 *AR* (1955), 18–19.

125 *AR* (1953), 29–30.

126 *SJCN*, Easter 1997, 1, and order of service: 'The Dedication of the Bells of Old York, June 27, 1997,' SJCA; see also Jones, *The Tower Clock*, 22.

127 Strachan to John Joseph, Private Secretary to the Lieutenant Governor, 24 March 1836, mentions that a house had been leased; *Appendix to the Journal of the House of Assembly of Upper Canada*, no. 1.1. no. 68, (1836). See also *AR* (1883), 8. Strachan had built his own residence in 1818 (later known as 'the Palace') on a large property west of Yonge Street – see pp. 16–17 and 40 above – and he conjectured that this might have caused the government to delay full funding of a rectory.

128 Strathy, *Guide*, 38.

129 *AR* (1902), 58–9, and (1904), 28.

130 'Re St. James' Cathedral Rectory,' 20 March 1903, SJCA.

131 *AR* (1929), 7.

132 Corporation of the City of Toronto, Council Minutes 1959, Appendix A, 2402 and 2783–4, TCA.

133 Strachan to Anthony Hamilton, 5 Jan. 1820, in Spragge, ed., *Strachan Letter Book*, 197; for population totals see Firth, ed., *York, 1815–1834*, lxxxii.

134 *Church*, 20 Oct.1838, 70.

135 Vestry minutes, 9 April 1849, SJCA. Though Robertson in his 'Plan of Cathedral Fire, 1849' (*Landmarks of Toronto*, 2: 620), shows a school at the northwest corner of the church grounds, untouched by the fire, its location there cannot be otherwise documented.

136 Apart from the plans in AO, Horwood Collection, there is very little documentation of this commission; see brief reports in the *Church*, 5 June 1851, 353, and 8 Jan. 1852, 180. See also Simmins, *Fred Cumberland*, pp. 84, 89–90.

137. *AR* (1882), 21, and Henry Langley's undated plans for an enlargement, SJCA.

138 Vestry minutes, Easter 1908, SJCA; see also 'The Rector's Message,' St. James' Cathedral Parish House, Final Plans, November 1909, SJCA.

139 For this type of plan see Angela Carr, *Toronto Architect Edmund Burke* (Montreal 1995), 22–4.

140 Bishop Sweeny's address (carbon copy) in 'Minutes. Parish House Building Committee 20.x.1908–28.iii.1911,' SJCA.

141 Diocese of Toronto, Minutes of the Executive Committee, 20 Dec. 1928 and 15 Jan. 1929, DTA.

142 See Andrea Kristof, 'Sproatt and Rolph,' *Canadian Encyclopaedia*, 3 vols., 2nd ed. (Edmonton, 1988), 3:2064, and also Dendy and Kilbourn, *Toronto Observed*, 194–8.

143 *Memorial Cross, St. James' Cathedral*, a pamphlet printed for the dedication of the cross on 24 June 1924, with an essay by the Revd Henry Plumptre.

144 *Canadian Freeman*, 2 May 1833, in Firth, ed., *York, 1815–1834*, 258; see also *Church*, 6 Sept. 1844, 36.

145 Vestry minutes, 18 July 1842, SJCA; for Howard see Arthur, *Toronto*, (ed. Otto), 251, and Edith G. Firth, John George Howard biography, *DCB*, 11:426–8.

146 Vestry minutes, 8 April 1844 and 27 April 1850, SJCA.

147 Howard had the use of a guidebook to Mount Auburn Cemetery, near Cambridge, Mass., that he borrowed from Churchwarden Thomas Harris. Founded in 1831, it was the first North American cemetery to be planned according to these principles; see Shirley G. Morriss, ed., *The Journal of John George Howard 1839–49*, 7 vols. in 3 (Toronto 1987), 4:164.

148 *Church*, 6 Sept. 1844, 36.

149 See A[manda] Sebris, '19th Century Toronto Marble Workers as Producers of Funerary Monuments,' 5 vols. in 3, research paper, University of Toronto, 1992, SJCA; see also Dendy and Kilbourn, *Toronto Observed*, 81–3.

150 *City of Toronto and County of York Directory for 1850–1* (Toronto 1850), lxxxiv.

151 Vestry minutes, 23 April 1855, 27 April, 11 and 19 May 1857, SJCA.

152 Vestry minutes, 6 April 1863, SJCA and *AR* (1884), 20; see also *Globe*, 27 Jan. 1863, 2 (courtesy of Stephen Otto), and Robertson, *Landmarks*, 4:35–7 and 96.

153 The progress of the project can be followed in the *Globe*: tender call for the construction of the foundations and vaults (16 Sept. 1858, 3) and a report stating that the work 'is now being proceeded with' (28 July 1859, 2). After an interval during which the plans were considerably modified, construction was resumed: tender call for the 'erection of a chapel ... ' (4 Jan. 1861, 3) and a description of the 'recently erected' chapel (26 Feb. 1862, 1). The drawings, plans, and specifications are in AO, Horwood Collection.

6: MUSIC AND WORSHIP

1 SLB 1, (1812–1834), 153.
2 Carl Benn, 'The Church of England in York, Upper Canada: 1793–1820,' honours thesis for Faculty of Divinity, Trinity College, Toronto, April 1983, 104 (TrCA). Benn prints two of Strachan's sermons from this period as appendixes, pp. 141–60.
3 'Notes on the Church in Toronto,' *Canadian Ecclesiastical Gazette*, 2 Jan. 1862, 4; Alexander Neil Bethune, *Memoir of the Right Reverend John Strachan* (Toronto 1870), 83.
4 Henry Scadding, *Toronto of Old* (Toronto 1873), 121.
5 Nigel Yates, *Buildings, Faith, and Worship* (Oxford 1991), 87–9 and 93–103.
6 G.W.O. Addleshaw and Frederick Etchells, *The Architectural Setting of Anglican Worship* (London 1948), 28, 175–9.
7 John Langhorn to Dr Morice of the Society for the Propagation of the Gospel, 8 May 1810; printed in A.H. Young, 'More Langhorn Letters,' *Ontario History*, 29 (1933), 65.
8 John Ross Robertson, *Landmarks of Toronto*, 6 vols. (Toronto 1894–1906), 1:504.
9 Notice in Toronto *Loyalist*, 1 March 1828.
10 Scadding, *Toronto of Old*, 122.
11 Letter of John S. Brock to Daniel DeL. Brock, 23–5 Aug. 1817, Tupper Papers, AO.
12 SLB 1812–1834, 153; Henry Scadding and J. George Hodgins, ed., *Jubilee of the Diocese of Toronto: 1839 to 1889* (Toronto, 1890), 40.
13 Bethune, *Memoir of John Strachan*, 84.
14 Register 1, 1800–36, SJCA. For Strachan's own account of a Sunday baptism that he conducted at what became St John's, York Mills, see James Strachan (pseud.), *A Visit to the Province of Upper Canada in 1819* (Aberdeen 1820), 141–3.
15 SLB 1812–1834, 154.
16 For contemporary accounts see *Christian Recorder* (July 1820), 167–72; Toronto *Loyalist*, 26 Aug. and 2, 9, and 16 Sept. 1826; and Kingston *Chronicle*, 3 Sept. 1826.
17 'Notes on the Church,' 6.
18 Church Record and Account Book, 1807–30, SJCA.
19 Scadding, *Toronto of Old*, 143.
20 *Ibid*., 143.
21 'Notes on the Church,' 6.
22 Minute Book 1, SJCA.
23 *The Diary of Mrs John Graves Simcoe*, ed. John Ross Robertson (Toronto 1911) 55, Larratt Smith's diaries, 31 May 1840, etc., TRL, BR.
24 'Notes on the Church,' 6.
25 Bethune, *Memoir of John Strachan*, 84.
26 Scadding, *Toronto of Old*, 146.
27 'Notes on the Church,' 6.
28 Scadding, *Toronto of Old*, 145–6.
29 Oral tradition current at St Andrew's Presbyterian Church, Toronto. The 79th Regiment of Highlanders was certainly attending St Andrew's in 1831; see Edith Firth, *York, 1815–1834*, 201 and 203.
30 *A Form to be Used on Thursday, the 7th day of June, 1832*, Str P, AO.
31 Anna Brownell Jameson, *Winter Studies and Summer Rambles in Canada* (London 1838), vol. 1, 274.

32 Letter in the possession of Christopher Johns, England.

33 Firth, *York, 1815–1834*, 219.

34 *United Empire*, 16 June 1853, giving 1837 as the date of installation. We owe this reference to Stephen Otto.

35 Robertson, *Landmarks*, 1:506; see also Scadding, *Toronto of Old*, 146.

36 SLB 3, 1827–41, 46.37 Strachan to Hodges, 1 Nov. 1838, *ibid.*, 53.

38 Letter from George Frederic Handel Hodges, dated 10 Nov. 1838, in F.H. Hodges, *Edward Hodges, Doctor in Music of Sidney Sussex College* (New York 1896), III.

39 Roseann Penner Kaufman, 'The Historical Context of Organ Consulting, Part II,' *American Organist*, Nov. 1994, 43–4; see also John Ogaspian, *English Cathedral Music in New York – Edward Hodges of Trinity Church* (Richmond, Va, 1996).

40 Scadding, *Toronto of Old*, 147; Robertson, *Landmarks*, 1:506, citing *Palladium*, 4 Jan. 1839.

41 Mary Larratt Smith, *Young Mr Smith in Upper Canada* (Toronto 1980), 20.

42 Larratt Smith Diary, 14 June 1840, TRL, BR.

43 'I Call at Mrs Gilkison's & found Committee of ways & means for the Toronto organ': Larratt Smith Diary, 18 Nov. 1841, BR. In *Young Mr Smith* Mary Larratt Smith seems to have misread 'Toronto' in this entry as 'Monte' (p. 71). See also the entry for 16 November.

44 Larratt Smith Diary, 8 Nov. 1841, TRL, BR.

45 *Ibid.*, 17 April 1842. Here 'Te Deum' seems to be an error for 'Venite'.

46 *Ibid.*, 31 Jan. 1842.

47 *Toronto Herald*, 10 Feb. 1842. (We owe this reference to Stephen Otto.)

48 Larratt Smith Diary, 31 July 1842, TRL, BR.

49 *Ibid.*, 25 Dec. 1841.

50 TRL, BR 783.9 S25.

51 F.W. Dixon, 'Music in Toronto,' *Mail and Empire*, 7 Nov. 1896. For the reminiscences of another chorister at this time see William Henry Pearson, *Recollections and Records of Toronto of Old* (Toronto 1914), 149 and 267–70.

52 *EMC*, 528; Vestry Minute Book, 1842–1908, SJCA.

53 *EMC*, 273.

54 *Ibid.*

55 *Reminiscences of a Canadian Pioneer* (Toronto 1884), 241–2.

56 Cashbook beginning 1850, SJCA. This was probably George Vogt, father of Augustus, an organ-builder who came to Canada to escape the European revolutions of 1848.

57 Autograph letter, SJCA. In this Jardine refers to a visit to Toronto two years earlier to discuss the provision of an organ.

58 Toronto *Patriot*, 3, 6, and 21 June 1853, as cited by Reed in 'Church Music in Canada,' II.

59 Cathedral Accounts, SJCA; *United Empire*, 16 June 1853.

60 *Daily Patriot*, 16 June 1853, as reprinted in *United Empire* of same date. (We owe this reference to Stephen Otto.)

61 *Daily Patriot*, 21 June 1853, as cited by Reed.

62 *Daily Patriot*, 16 June 1853, as reprinted in *United Empire*. Here 'tremulet' and 'kerotophon' appear to be printer's errors for 'tremulant' and 'keraulophon.'

63 Music Committee Minutes, 1 April 1861, SJCA.

64 *EMC*, 224.

65 Letters transcribed in Music Committee Minute Book under 1878 and pasted to front endpaper and flyleaf of Vestry Minute Book, 1842–1908, SJCA; report of Music Committee to Vestry, 14 April 1879, in *ibid*.

66 Report of Music Committee to Vestry, 14 April 1879, SJCA.

67 Music Committee minutes, 21 Sept. 1880 and 22 Jan. 1881, SJCA.

68 Report of subcommittee of Musical Committee to Vestry, 14 April 1879, in Vestry Minute Book, 1842–1908, SJCA.

69 Report of Musical Committee to Vestry, 14 April 1879, SJCA.

70 J.L.H. Henderson, *John Strachan: Documents and Opinions* (Toronto [1969]), 275.

71 Strachan to Grasett, 6 Sept. 1845, SLB 1844–1849, 119; see also p. 44 above.

72 D.J. Goodspeed, *Battle Royal*, 2nd edn. (Brampton, Ont., 1979), 8–10 and 24.

73 Report in Toronto *Leader*, reprinted in *Canadian Ecclesiastical Gazette*, 15 Jan. 1862.

74 C.J. Stranks, *Dean Hook* (London 1954), 63 n.

75 *The Oxford Dictionary of the Christian Church*, 2nd ed., rev. F.L. Cross and E.A. Livingstone (Oxford 1983), 488.

76 Addleshaw and Etchells, *Architectural Setting*, 211–13.

77 Scadding, *On a Sung Service and its Appurtenances* (Toronto, 1874), 1–3; T.A. Reed, 'A History of the Church of the Holy Trinity 1847–1910', 117–18, TRL, BR.

78 *Ritualism in Toronto* (Toronto 1861), anonymous pamphlet reprinted from a letter to the *Leader* and signed 'A Prayer Book Churchman.'

79 P.E. Shaw, *The Catholic Apostolic Church, Sometimes Called Irvingite: A Historical Study* (Morningside Heights, NY, 1946), 115.

80 Columba Graham Flegg, *'Gathered under Apostles': A Study of the Catholic Apostolic Church* (Oxford 1992), 227–9 and 265–7. For accounts of Catholic Apostolic worship in Toronto see Robertson, *Landmarks*, 4:544–9, and Dorothy Darlington, 'Recollections of the Catholic Apostolic Church,' M 94–01, Box 2, series 3–6, No. 5, ACCA.

81 Robertson, *Landmarks*, 4:65–6.

82 Oral tradition at Trinity College, Toronto. For the character of the chapel services see 'The Reminiscences of Canon Arthur Jarvis, UE,' *Trinity College Historical Society*, 1:2 (1992), 29.

83 Reed, 'Church of the Holy Trinity,' 66 and 71–2.

84 *The Debates on Ritualism in the Provincial Synod of the Church of England and Ireland* (Montreal 1868), 5ff.

85 *Ibid*., 60.

86 H.M. Harman and W.G. Upshall, *The Story of the Church of St George the Martyr* (Toronto 1945), 25.

87 *Parish Church Work* (St George's parish magazine) (Dec. 1881).

88 *St Matthias' Parish Magazine* (May 1883), 3: *St George's Parish Magazine* (July 1883), 2.

89 S. Frances Harrison, 'Choirs and Choir Signing in Toronto,' *Dominion Illustrated Monthly*, Jan. 1893, 750.

90 Order of Service, Toronto Church Choir Association: Second Annual Festival, 1893, SJCA.

91 Harman and Upshall, *Story of the Church of St George the Martyr*, 42

92 Reprinted in Robertson, *Landmarks*, 4:369–70.

93 Music Committee Minutes, 2 Dec. 1889, as amended 8 March 1890, SJCA.

94 *Ibid*.

95 MM 53 C 3655, No. 9, ACCA. The tracts are undated, but the author quotes as from 'the 27th of March last' an article that appeared in the *EC* of 27 March 1890.

96 *The Progress of Ritualism*, as above.

97 For his career see EMC, 590.

98 Strathy, *Guide*, 43.

99 Report of Music Committee to Vestry, 11 April 1898, in Vestry Minute Book 1842–1908, SJCA.

100 *EMC*, 24.

101 Music Committee Minutes, 15 Nov. 1889, SJCA.

102 F.C. Macdonald, *Edward Ashurst Welch ... : A Memoir* (Cambridge 1936), 33–4 and 38. Though dated 1912, the cross was fairly certainly ordered while Welch was still rector.

103 *Oxford English Dictionary* under Lantern *sb* 9, citing the *Church Times*, 20 Aug. 1897.

104 Vernon Staley, *The Catholic Religion* (London 1893) 282, quoting I Corinthians 11:16.

105 Letter of C.W.F. Talbot, vestry clerk, to Albert Nordheimer, 21 Dec. 1926, SJCA. According to this document, the work had been under consideration for about eight years.

106 Cathedral Account Book, December 1914–July 1919, 72, SJCA. E.G. Strathy in his *Guide*, 2nd ed. (1949) seems to have been slightly confused about the organ cases; for he states that they were installed in 1896 in memory of William Henry Beatty, who did not die until 1912 (p. 15). Probably the cases at the heads of the aisles date from 1896, while those in the chancel were made in Beatty's memory and paid for in 1916. The chancel cases are distinctly coarser work, as one might expect if they were made in wartime.

107 *A Westminster Pilgrim* (London 1919), 218. The Westminster choir, together with that of St George's Chapel, Windsor, paid another visit in the spring of 1927. Again there were compliments from the visitors to the choir of St James'. 'Rector's Monthly Letter,' May 1927, SJCA.

108 The same post was held by one of Ham's successors, Giles Bryant, 1990–92.

109 Printed circular from Albert Nordheimer, chairman of the Musical Committee, Nov. 1922, SJCA.

110 John Cozens, 'Choir Music across Canada,' *Anglican*, June 1978.

111 Letter of Ham to Albert Nordheimer, 23 Feb. 1921, SJCA, complaining of trouble with the echo organ at the rear and with the pedal stops on the west side of the chancel.

112 Contract dated 10 June 1936, giving a cost of $13,850, SJCA.

113 Gerald E. Moffatt, *All the Blessings of This Life* (n.p., 1986) 42.

114 *Ibid.*, 42–3.

115 *Ibid.*, 42.

116 The new altar was mostly financed by a bequest from 'a very unassuming retired public school teacher named Edith Langton'; *ibid.*, 43.

117 *Ibid.*, 43; list of wardens in southwest vestibule of the cathedral. See also Appendix 3.

118 C.E. Riley, 'The Cathedral', (n.p.; n.d.), SJCA.

119 Reminiscence of the Revd Keith Gleed, then a boy chorister at St James', communicated to W.G. Cooke.

120 J.W. Walker and Sons of England submitted a quotation, which remains in SJCA.

121 Reminiscences communicated to W.G. Cooke by Bishop Stiff.

122 Reminiscences communicated to W.G. Cooke by his own family.

123 Lionel Dakers, *Church Music in a Changing World* (London 1984), 106.

Contributors

CARL BENN is a curator with Heritage Toronto and a part-time instructor in the Department of History at the University of Toronto. His most recent books are *Historic Fort York, 1793–1993* (Toronto: Natural Heritage, 1993), and *The Iroquois in the War of 1812* (Toronto: University of Toronto Press, 1998).

ALAN HAYES has taught at Wycliffe College, Toronto, since 1975 and now holds the Bishops Frederick and Heber Wilkinson Chair in Church History there. He is also a serving Anglican priest in the diocese of Toronto and a member of the diocesan Archives Committee. He was both the general editor and a contributor to *By Grace Co-Workers*, a history of the Anglican diocese of Toronto (1989). He has also written a parish history of Little Trinity Church, Toronto, entitled Holding Forth the Word of Life (1992), entries for the *Dictionary of Canadian Biography*, and articles for the *Journal of the Canadian Church Historical Society*.

PAUL H. FRIESEN is Professor of History and Chair of the Humanities and Social Sciences at Tyndale College, Toronto, and an associate priest at the Church of St Mary Magdalene, Toronto. He is president of the Canadian Society for Church History for 1997–8. He wrote a chapter for *By Grace Co-Workers* and has contributed to the *Journal of the Canadian Church Historical Society, Church History*, and the *Canadian Historical Review*.

C. THOMAS McINTIRE is Professor of the History of Christianity at Trinity College, Toronto, and a member of both the Department of History and the Centre for the Study of Religion in the University of Toronto. He has many publications in his field.

SHIRLEY MORRISS obtained her MA from the University of Toronto in 1976 with a thesis entitled 'The Church Architecture of Frederic William Cumberland.' She has since extended her studies to the work of other nineteenth-century Toronto architects, contributing to *The Dictionary of Canadian Biography* and editing *The Journal of John George Howard*, 1833–1849 (Torono, 1987).

GILES BRYANT has been actively engaged in choral music ever since 1941, when he began to sing as a treble in his school chapel choir. He has been organist and master of the choristers at St James' Cathedral since 1979 and is concurrently head of choral music at Royal St George's College, Toronto. He became national president of the Royal Canadian College of Organists in 1990. He has conducted ensembles, lectured, and adjudicated in Canada, Great Britain, and the United States, and contributed to the new *Grove's Dictionary of Music* and the *Encyclopedia of Music in Canada*.

WILLIAM COOKE is an independent scholar, editor, and author living in Toronto. He has contributed to the *Journal of the Canadian Church Historical Society* and to other scholarly journals and has also written tracts on various aspects of Anglican worship published by the Toronto Branch of the Prayer Book Society of Canada. He has worked for many years at organizing and maintaining the archives of St James' Cathedral, where he now has the title of honorary archivist, and he is a long-standing member of the cathedral Servers' Guild.

Picture Credits

St James' Cathedral gratefully acknowledges the assistance of the persons and institutions listed below for the pictures specified, which they have procured, taken specially for this book, or allowed to be reproduced from their respective collections. Pictures not listed come from the collection of the St James' Cathedral Archives.

Archives of Ontario, Toronto: Frontispiece (C11–49–0–5, [750] 1); Figures 2.13 (Sir Casimir Gzowski fonds, F 1044–3–0–0–S4317), 5.14 (C11–682–0–1, [640] 1), 5.15 (C11–682–0–1, [640] 2), 5.16 (C11–49–0–22, [55] 5), 5.17 (C11–49–0–1, [55] 19), 5.28 (C11–64–0–2, [749] 1), and 6.4 (Benson Family fonds, F 507–1–3–17)

Baldwin Room, Toronto Reference Library: Figures 1.3, 1.4, 1.5, 1.7, 1.10, 1.12, 1.13, 2.3, 2.7, 2.10, 2.11, 2.12, 2.15, 3.18, 5.13, 5.29, 6.1, 6.5, 6.6, and 6.7

Carl Benn: Figure 1.8

Harry Cantlon: Book Jacket; Plates I.1, I.3, I.4, II.1, II.2, II.3, III.1, III.3, III.4, VI.1, VI.2, VII, and VIII

Diocese of Niagara Archives, Anglican Church of Canada, Cathedral Place, Hamilton, Ontario: Figure 3.10

Diocese of Toronto Archives, Anglican Church of Canada, Toronto: Figures 3.6, 3.7, and 3.12

Agnes Etherington Art Centre, Queen's University, Kingston, Ontario: Figure 5.11 (Acc. 30–91)

Thomas Fisher Rare Book Library, University of Toronto: Figure 2.5

General Synod Archives, Anglican Church of Canada, Toronto: Figures 4.7 and 6.17

Revd Douglas Graydon: Figures 5.1, 5.2, 5.3, 5.4, and 5.5

Pamela Guy: Figure 6.22

Thomas W. Hanlon: Figure 4.3

Michael Hudson: Figures 2.2, 4.10, 4.11, 4.12, 4.13, 4.14, 4.16, 4.18, 4.20, 5.25, 6.21, and 6.23; Plates I.2, III.2, and VI.2

Revd Theo Ipema: Figure 4.9

Shirley Morriss: Figures 5.12 (from Thomas H. Shephard and James Elmes, *Metropolitan Improvements: or, London in the Nineteenth Century* (London 1827), pl. 7) and 5.18 (from Augustus Welby Pugin, *The True Principles of Pointed or Christian Architecture* [London 1841], p. 50)

National Archives of Canada, Ottawa: Figures 1.1 (C 100660), 1.2 (C 40137), 1.6 (NMC 22819), and 2.6 (C 2790)

Royal Ontario Museum, Toronto: Figure 2.1

Mark Russell Collection: Figure 2.8

Toronto City Archives: Figures 2.4, 3.2, 3.4, 3.5, 3.14, and 3.17

Toronto Historical Board, Fort York, Toronto: Figure 1.14

Trinity College Archives, Toronto: Figure 1.9 (P 1098/0074)

Mary-Jane Tuthill: Figure 4.19

Pamela Watson: Figure 4.15

Wycliffe College, Toronto: Figure 2.16

Index